HISTORY OF ASCETICISM IN THE SYRIAN ORIENT

I

THE ORIGIN OF ASCETICISM
EARLY MONASTICISM IN PERSIA

CORPUS
SCRIPTORUM CHRISTIANORUM ORIENTALIUM
EDITUM CONSILIO
UNIVERSITATIS CATHOLICAE AMERICAE
ET UNIVERSITATIS CATHOLICAE LOVANIENSIS

Vol. 184

SUBSIDIA

TOMUS 14

HISTORY OF ASCETICISM IN THE SYRIAN ORIENT

A Contribution to the History of Culture in the Near East

I

THE ORIGIN OF ASCETICISM
EARLY MONASTICISM IN PERSIA

BY

ARTHUR VÖÖBUS

Dr. theol. (Tartu)
Professor at the Chicago Lutheran Theological Seminary
Formerly Assoc. Professor at the University of Tartu

LOVANII
IN AEDIBUS PEETERS
1958

PREFACE

This is another work which I have carried in my refugee's bag. Fortunately, it already had been given shape in manuscript form and existed no longer only in collected materials. Otherwise it would not have been salvaged, and the work in this comprehensive form would not have been completed. Nor would I have started over again — too much of my life and energy had been put into it.

The present work is an investment of labor of more than a quarter of a century. I started it in June 1932. After some studies in the history and expansion of Christianity in the Syrian Orient, and after having listened to the voice of the original sources, the importance of the present subject increasingly impressed itself upon me. I still remember — so vividly — that early morning hour, so full of excitement and illumination, when the perspectives for research in this *terra incognita* opened themselves to my eyes. I then devoted myself to the pursuit of this project.

Long years of intense study, of growing penetration into the sources, accompanied with the joys of discovery, of the widening of horizons, of study periods abroad in the manuscript-collections, followed. Hand in hand with the research, I was building up a special library of Oriental sources designed to serve me in this endeavor.

The determination to continue this research has been put to very hard tests. Twice have I lost my home — in 1940 and 1944 — my special library, much of the collected materials, and all of the resources which had enabled me to carry out my work. The fruits of my labors I had to carry through fire and water on the ways of fleeings from the inferno. There were times when I had lost the hope that I would be allowed to complete my undertaking, and also times of such hardship and difficulty that it required the greatest of mental and physical effort to continue my research.

Now I have kept it in the process of work under all sorts of conditions long enough, and I send it forth from my hands.

In looking back I wish to testify that I have been continually filled with awe at the wonder of God in my life. My heart trembles at His gift of grace to me while my colleagues, of cherished and unforgettable memory, at my Alma Mater with the same hopes and aspirations, the same devotion to their research, have experienced the utter destruction of everything.

It remains for me to express my deep sense of gratitude to persons and institutions to whom I owe so much.

I think with deep gratitude of my teachers and colleagues, of all the deep and rich spiritual atmosphere at the University of Tartu, which I was privileged to inhale. This atmosphere instilled in me the courage to lay plans for a long-range work like this and the will to bring them to realization. The inspiration of my Alma Mater has had a lasting impact on my life. It has instilled something in me that has remained with me on all the roads which I have had to wander.

For generous privileges courteously granted me, I desire to acknowledge a debt of gratitude which I owe to the officials of many manuscript-collections whose treasures I was permitted to use in Europe and the Near East, as well as to many libraries in Europe, the Orient and America. Their courtesy, kindness and patience in meeting all my manysided and endless wishes has been immeasurably generous.

To Rev. Walter Freitag, S.T.M., I owe my hearty thanks for the diligence and care with which he read the manuscript and improved its English.

To Prof. Dr. R. Draguet, at the Catholic University of Louvain, I express my most cordial gratitude for the great privilege of having the edition of my five volumes work included in the *Corpus Scriptorum Christianorum Orientalium*. I feel myself deeply honored by the acceptance of my work in this series of the highest scholarly reputation and fame. I am also grateful to him for his kindness in sharing with me the burden of proofreading.

I am under deep obligation, gratefully acknowledged, to the John Simon Guggenheim Memorial Foundation in New York. I am profoundly grateful for its interest in the history of the culture of the Syrian Orient as expressed in the form of a Fellowship granted to me. This magnanimous assistance made it possible to accomplish the last phase in the manuscript studies, thus enabling me to finish this volume and prepare it for publication. What this generosity really means to my endeavors in the service of research, by making possible the completion of this part of my work after labors of a quarter of a century, so that finally the edition of my work can be started — can never be adequately expressed.

*
**

I dedicate this work to my parents, Karl Eduard Vööbus and Linda Helene, in gratitude for all their love and trouble.

I am thankful that my mother is still with me. My father was separated from us in the catastrophe that befell Estonia, was lost to our sight and not seen again — as in innumerable cases. As I learned much later, he died in 1955. Humbly do I now lay down this dedication *in memoriam,* a wreath upon his grave in a country which I am permitted to visit only in my thoughts and dreams.

Requiem aeternam dona ei, Domine, et lux perpetua luceat ei!

Christmas 1957. A. Vööbus.

INTRODUCTION

In Syrian asceticism and monasticism we have to do with an unusual phenomenon. Not only was it an important and powerful factor in the Syrian realm in the East. It was also instrumental in other cultures of the Orient. The significance of this needs amplification and a closer look.

First of all the impact of primitive Syrian asceticism upon the development of Christianity in the lands of the Euphrates and Tigris was both incisive and deep. In fact, its role was predominant from the beginning of Christianity in this area, able to produce a form of Christianity notably different from that known in the West. To be sure, the later historical development — when the forces of Hellenism were groping slowly eastward — could not leave this unchanged. But even after the ascetic movement lost its sovereign place in the structure of the Syrian congregations, its influence was expressed in new ways and it thus remained a constitutive element of Syrian Christianity.

The later form of Syrian asceticism, monasticism, is a phenomenon that deserves the interest and attention of the historian for its own sake. There is more than one reason for this. As an autochthonous form of monasticism, it antedates the origin of monasticism in Egypt. Nor does the originality and genius that shaped its physiognomy deserve any less attention. The same passionate psyche which had formerly been devoted to pre-Christian deities, now determined the ascetic ideals. As against Coptic and Greek monasticism in Egypt and Greek monasticism in Palestine and Asia Minor, Syrian monasticism is conspicuous as a definitely independent phenomenon, engendered by its own spiritual genius, whose exotic features, engrafted deep into its face, stand out in relief.

Further the significance of Syrian monasticism, which makes itself manifest in several facets of the spiritual development of the Syrian Orient such as the religious, social and cultural areas is something which excites every historian interested in the formation of the spiritual face of the East.

The endeavors and achievements of ascetics have exercised influence upon society in every era. The secret of their charm is their austere and rigorous life. In this respect, the grotesque and bizarre manners of Syrian monasticism exercised an immense fascination upon the Syrians. Indeed, the guidance of the religious and moral life of the religious masses slipped into their hands. They secured an authority of such dimension that no less than the worldly authorities of the Byzantine rule joined the adoring masses rather than to risk conflict with these powerful men. The immense authority of the monks also secured them an entrance into ecclesiastical affairs, the direction of which they gradually assumed. And if we do not overlook the significance of Syrian monasticism in its missionary activities in transforming the semi-pagan and pagan communities in the orbit of the Syrian Orient, nor their missionary work beyond the boundaries of Syria, Mesopotamia and Persia, we get an idea of the magnitude of the influence Syrian monasticism exercised in the domain of the religious life of the Syrians.

Syrian monasticism was also instrumental in the social domain. It is a paradox that a monasticism so grotesque and bizarre also had room not only for social concern but also for initiative for social action. In the disorderly conditions of the Orient, which was leading even toward the growing impoverishment of the masses, the responsible part of Syrian monasticism acted as a rescue squad. In the ocean of human need and suffering it prepared its huts, cells and monasteries as islands within which the afflicted could find understanding, care and help. Nor did it shrink back from using its prestige to challenge the civil powers in the interest of the suppressed and rightless ones.

The role of Syrian monasticism in the area of culture requires special mention. For in this respect, its profile bears another of its noblest features. In various ways, it made a real contribution to the treasury of spiritual and intellectual culture. Particularly important are the activities in book-production, in the creation of literature, in the pedagogical field by their establisment of schools, and in the field of learning and scholarship — many monasteries were the centers of learning, craft and art. There is no area of spiritual culture that has escaped the influence of Syrian monasticism, not even the history of the New Testament text[1]. Such a contribution became an inestimable asset for the history of Syrian culture.

Nor is this all that must be said concerning the significance of Syrian monasticism. Research into its impact elsewhere unfolds before us not only its very momentous role in the history of Christianity as viewed against the spectrum of the whole of Christendom, but also its pervasiveness throughout the other areas and cultures of the Orient. Its dynamic would not be restrained to the Syrian orbit alone. In fact, Syrian monasticism was a powerful spiritual force contributing to the history of civilization not only on its home ground but also in the Semitic and non-Semitic cultures of the Near East, Central and Eastern Asia and Africa. This much alone excites one's interest in the phenomenon of Syrian monasticism. Its surprising potency and spiritual power in this latter respect, requires us to consider this contribution as far-reaching and momentous.

For a bird's-eye view let us start with the activities of Syrian monasticism in Armenia. Immediately after Taron became an important center of missionary activity of the Syrians, a process of dissemination began which was to establish in Armenia the same pattern of doctrine and practice as was current in its spiritual mother, the Syrian church. Their influence reveals itself everywhere we turn. It can be seen in the activity of the missionaries, in the Syrian schools, in the liturgy, Christian terminology and ancient Christian art, in architecture and in the textual history of the New Testament[2]. In the Armenian language, these beginnings left many deep vestiges of Syriac terminology. And this was mainly the work of monks who dared to continue in competition with the Greeks for the soul of the Armenians. Moreover, Syrian monasticism did not only constitute a troop of workers, but supplied the men who held the highest administrative posts in the growing church. Even the little and limited information which the tradition has preserved in the Armenian sources — partly discolored by the Graeco-phile authors — speaks clearly enough and testifies to how deeply Chris-

[1] See the chapter « The Role of Monasticism in the History of the Gospel Text » in Vööbus, *Studies in the History of the Gospel Text in Syriac*, p. 127 ff.

[2] Vööbus, *La première traduction arménienne des Évangiles*, p. 581 ff.

tianity in this area became the operation-field for Syrian monasticism in the ancient church.

The lively activity of Syrian monasticism in Armenia did not shrink back from spreading its influence into Georgia. This is quite understandable because, until the middle of the fourth century, Kharthli located in Eastern Georgia, belonged to Armenia. There is something else to be said in connection with this. The inscriptions which recent findings have brought to light, show that the official language of the country was not Georgian at that time, but an Aramaic dialect [3]. This situation must have been attractive to Syrian monasticism, and thus its efforts to expand its influence to this area. The influence of Syrian monasticism in this rough mountainous district between the Black and Caspian Seas, known in the ancient world as Iberia, has been immortalized by the stream of hagiographical sources in Georgian reflecting the type of spirit the Syrian monks imported here from Mesopotamia. The legendary accretions of the traditions do not hinder us from observing something which had left its vestiges even in this corner of the Orient.

Another domain which constantly received impulses from Syrian monasticism, was in the neighboring areas southward — where the Arabic speaking kinsmen lived, whether in tents or in settlements. The beginnings of the Christian mission to the Arabs already had a history before the separation took place between the Monophysites and Diophysites. This, however, did not bring an end to their work for both factions competed in their missionary efforts to win the soul of the Arabs. The tribes in their tents along the boundaries between Mesopotamia and Persia fell completely under their influence. In the area starting with the province Arabia and including the territory north of the Persian Gulf, there were places in which Syrian monasticism gained considerable strength. Its feelers early reached out to the vast region between the Red Sea and the Persian Gulf though here with success in but a few places.

With regard to the influence of Syrian monasticism among the Arabs, another important process took place after the Islamic conquest of Syria, Mesopotamia and Persia and the arabization of

3 NYBERG, *Quelques inscriptions antiques découvertes récemment en Géorgie*, p. 233 f.; ALTHEIM, STIEHL, JUNKER, *Inschriften aus Gruzinien*, p. 1 ff.

these areas. It must be said that one cannot understand the sudden rise of the Islamic culture without the factor of all the accomplishments of the Syrian culture in the formation of which Syrian monasticism played the most important role.

The influence of Syrian monasticism also embraced Abyssinia. Here too it effected a vitalization of religion. The start of christianization had been established earlier, but this, according to all indications had remained dormant and the work of Frumentius had ended in stagnation. The Ethiopic tradition admits that the country owes the new impulses that helped bolster the strength of the Christian religion to Syrian monasticism. The arrival of a group of Syrian monks occurred in the second part of the 5th century, possibly towards the end of the century. In the Ethiopic sources, these men are celebrated as those who reshaped the spiritual face of the country. They introduced Christian discipline, reformed customs, and fostered religious, monastic and ecclesiastical institutions. They also gave the church its liturgy, and introduced a version of the biblical text. As the evidence laid down in the Ethiopic biblical text shows, it clearly bears the mark of the Syrian biblical traditions and the signature of the Syriac idiom [4]. Thus, as the information stands, the impact made by Syrian monasticism upon Christendom in the land of the Negus, covered the entire field of spiritual life.

This picture which reveals the amazing amplitude of the influence of Syrian monasticism, is still not yet fully described. This expansion even went beyond the Eastern boundaries of the Syrian Orient. Our look should scan the most important areas in this vast scene.

That Syrian monasticism had found its way to the peoples in Central-Asia, is certain, although the information we can gather from the sources leaves much to be desired.

The influence of Syrian monasticism can be traced in the Christianity of India. This seems to be mainly the merit of monasticism's missionary zeal that Christianity in India was brought into closer contact with the Syrian church in Persia and received fruitful stimuli from it for its growth. The route from Persia to India

[4] Vööbus, *Die Spuren eines älteren äthiopischen Evangelientextes im Lichte der literarischen Monumente,* p. 18 ff.

was covered with monasteries that created new communication lines and enlivened the interchange in the spiritual life between these areas.

Finally, an illustration of the dynamic force of Syrian monasticism is its penetration even to China. The Christian faith was established here in the 7th century — centuries before the Franciscans arrived. Chinese documents and archaeological remains, above all the monument of Si-ngan-fu, speak of the agile activity of the Syrian monks and their courage for competing with the Buddhist monasteries. For a while the movement even attracted the sympathy of the authorities of the country. And when these promising overtures were replaced by an hardened attitude in the proclamation of King Wu-Tsung in 845 A.D. prohibiting the activities of the immigrant monks they found new fields of operation in Central Asia.

It is a strange circumstance, that the important area of research with which the present study deals, has remained a *terra incognita* in Oriental studies. For the first time, the phenomenon of asceticism in the Syrian Orient unfolds itself on the pages of the present work. This has remained so despite the fact that, from time to time, voices have arisen which called this research an important desideratum in the field of Oriental, historical, Christian-Oriental and cultural historical studies. Among the large chorus of voices who have repeated the demand for the urgent study, the great authority of the field of Syrology, Prof. I. B. Chabot may be chosen as spokesman. In the year 1900, he stated this old truth again, this time with the encouraging remark, namely the hope that the time was not far off when we would have all the necessary sources in edited form. This would finally permit the writing of an adequate study about the origins and the development of monasticism in the Syrian Orient [5]. A scholar of his calibre was fully aware of this deplorable situation.

The period that followed proved that this hope was too optimistic. Some steps were made but not in the sense that Prof. Chabot had in mind. In the years 1910 and 1911, Anatolios published a work on Syrian monasticism in the Proceedings of the Clerical Academy

5 '... le moment n'est pas éloigné où l'on aura enfin sous la main tous les documents qui permettront d'écrire une étude consciencieuse sur les origines et le développement du monachisme en Orient', *Histoire du Youssef Bousnaya*, p. VII.

in Kiev [6], but this was based on very limited footing, since only the Greek sources of Theodoret, Sozomenus, a.o. were used. No attempt was made to employ the Oriental sources. S. Schiwietz's study, published in 1938 [7], rests on the same bulk of sources, plus material in Ephrem the Syrian, Jūlianā Sabā and Abraham Qīdūnaiā, sources of Syriac provenance, which had been edited and translated, which he utilized. The study of J. van der Ploeg [8] is an introduction of a general kind to some of these questions and discusses the monasticism of the Nestorians in the light of the work of Thomas of Marga.

Now it is 58 years since the above-mentioned words of Prof. Chabot were written, and the issue has remained on its dead point. In the year 1942 van der Ploeg had to declare with resignation that the time had not yet come to write the history of Syrian monasticism.

That this situation is not due to neglect, is needless to say. It is obvious that there were other reasons. In fact, there were several reasons which would account for this situation.

In the first place — naturally — the status of the sources must be mentioned. The sources necessary for a study in the history of the Syrian asceticism and monasticism are inedited in the manuscripts, and are scattered throughout the manuscript collections in Europe and the Orient [9]. A situation like this makes research which must, at the same time, be a pioneer-work and a systematic utilization of the documents, difficult and slow. It also demands a particular patience.

With this hangs together another difficulty. Since so much material has not been edited, and this requires much time, how much less can we speak of a critical examination and evaluation of these sources before we can use them for historical purposes. This critical work, however, is inevitable before the synthetic work can begin, no matter how much this spade-work is a time-consuming affair. Indeed, a student might easily spend the whole of his life

6 Ieromonach ANATOLIJ, *Istoričeskij očerk sirijskago monašestva do poloviny VI věka*, Kiev, 1911.

7 *Das morgenländische Mönchtum* III : *Das Mönchtum in Syrien und Mesopotamien und das Aszetentum in Persien.*

8 *Oud-syrisch monniksleven*, Leiden 1942.

9 See also DRAGUET, *Pères du désert*, p. VIII.

in reading and evaluating these sources and find at the end that he had scarcely begun to write a line of synthesis.

Further, the status of the sources and the literary-critical assessment of their value, involves something else which does not attract students to tackle these issues. This is the fact that research in the history of Syrian asceticism and monasticism must have the boldness to create the premises of investigation also in the related areas which are necessary as a background for the ascetic phenomenon. When ordinarily for a special question the information in regard to the background material is at the student's disposal, this is not so in the realm of the Syrian Orient. These very same reasons have kept students from carrying out research in the historical, ecclesiastical, economic and cultural domains. Up to now, there is no church history of Syrian Christendom, no history of the culture, whether spiritual or intellectual.

These are the main factors which have made the task of research formidable and have exercised such an influence that research into the origins, development and the history of Syrian asceticism and monasticism have had to be content with an orphan's share.

Since, in the preceding pages, we have touched upon the condition of the sources, it would also be appropriate to add to this propaedeutic, a few introductory words concerning the sources upon which one must depend and on the use that is made of them in undertaking the task of writing the history of Syrian asceticism and monasticism.

Naturally, there is no substitute for the Syriac sources themselves. In these, we see the appearance, life and activities of Syrian monasticism through the eyes of the indigenous people as told by them in their own tongue. The Syrian literary heritage offers us a huge and colorful material some of which is published in text editions, but most of which is hidden in the manuscripts. Certain kinds of source-material deserve to be especially delineated.

In the first place, the documents of a legislative character as first rate sources should be mentioned : the rules and canons given for monks and monasteries by abbots, bishops and synods. Naturally material like this, due to its objective character and value, deserves an especial estimation by a historian. Its particular value necessitated a systematic search for these in the manuscripts. As a result, new, unknown texts, as well as an enlargement of the bulk of manuscript evidence for texts which were known earlier has emerged [10]. Each of these texts is a deposit of highly prized information.

The material which leads us to the heart of monasticism and provides us with the data for its history is manifold. Rich is the genre of literature dedicated to the memory of the heroes of the ascetic life. To cast into the mould of the tale the life-story of ascetic virtuosi became the favorite art of the Syrians. There are many texts whose credentials are in order, others are works of many hands of many ages, and must have floated about anonymously in the broad stream of traditions. The annual commemoration of monastic masters which was made the tradition in the monastic communities also became an important source for literary production. The form of biography, encomium and panegyric, and less useful poetical *mēmrā* has been widely cultivated by Syrian monks in immortalizing their masters and teachers. Much of this material has not survived directly but in the works of authors who have used it. Through the centuries these texts accumulated and were collected in the libraries of the monasteries. These codices in turn provided the stimuli for writing works dealing with the development of monastic life in a particular monastery, place or area. That which Theodoret of Cyrrhos accomplished in his *Historia religiosa* found imitators, particularly among the Eastern Syrians.

This genre contains many disparate texts. The river of hagiography is a mighty river into which the streams of all kinds of tributaries have poured and which was discolored, speaking historically, by the media through which it passed. Much in this genre of literature originated and was manipulated without the discipline and control of historical facts. In moving through this terrain, one must always remember that circumspection and caution are the allies of criticism. But even from these sources, something of valuable can occasionally be extracted by a delicate use of the historical method, so that a historian can move along not just on the highways but on the byways as well.

10 *Syriac and Arabic Documents : Legislative Sources of Syrian Monasticism, edited, translated and furnished with literary historical data by* Vööbus.

Further, an invaluable branch in our sources, not covered by the observations just made, lies in the literary heritage created by monks themselves. Most of the Syriac literature was produced by monasticism, embracing exegetical and hermeneutic works, homilies, tracts, correspondence, hymns, prayers, poetry, etc. All this material offers the best guidance to the thought-world of the monastic movement. Of particular value for our purpose are works which deal directly with the ideals and practice of asceticism.

This material lands us in difficulties, too. Owing to its particular value, the last genre of literature also raises critical problems. Before many texts can be employed, source-criticism is absolutely necessary. It frees the texts from the dust and accretions they have accumulated through the centuries, and makes them shine out afresh in all their pristine clarity. Only such a methodical treatment of the sources gives us safe ground on which to build. This work has been carried out. Some of these preparatory studies in the form of literary-critical investigations, like on Aphrahaṭ[11] and Ephrem[12], have been separately published. Others will follow and the results of still other literary-critical and source-critical studies will be included in this work.

Finally, for an undertaking like this it was necessary to delve into all the sources that Syriac literature provides in order to gather all the relevant information piece by piece. And indeed, as the research has shown, all of these — the one more, another less — add to our study in Syrian asceticism and monasticism : annalistic literature, homilies, theological tracts, commentaries, stories, letters, official acts, reports, formulas, liturgical books, poetry etc., etc. In addition to the materials in the Syriac sources, Syrian monasticism's deep imprint on the pages of Greek, Latin, Armenian, Ethiopic, Arabic and Persian literatures has been taken into account.

11 See the chapter « The Internal Problem in Aphrahaṭ's Seventh Homily » in Vööbus, *Celibacy, A Requirement For Admission to Baptism in the Early Syrian Church*, p. 59 ff.

12 Vööbus, *A Letter of Ephrem to the Mountaineers; Untersuchungen über die Authentizität einiger asketischer Texte, überliefert unter dem Namen « Ephraem Syrus »; Beiträge zur kritischen Sichtung der asketischen Schriften, die unter dem Namen Ephraem des Syrers überliefert sind; Ein neuer Text von Ephraem über das Mönchtum; Literary-Critical and Historical Studies in Ephrem and His Role in Syrian Monasticism.*

In addition to the literary sources, a wealth of information appears in the inscriptions, Christian art and archeological finds and this, too, is included.

In short — no source of knowledge, in fact, pertaining to literature whether edited or inedited, art and archeology is out of place in such an undertaking which purposes to get out of the shallow backwater to the open sea of enquiry — towards new horizons in knowledge.

The whole work consists of five volumes. Of these each treats a segment whose boundaries are more or less sharply delineated by the impingement of incisive historical events within certain geographical areas.

The present volume deals with the background : pre-history, early asceticism and origin of monasticism, tracing the development of monasticism under the rule of the Sassanides to the period of dogmatic controversies in the last part of the 5th century.

The second volume treats the development and growth of monasticism under the Byzantine rule and carries the treatment to the last part of the 5th century, as in volume I.

The third volume is devoted to monasticism among the Monophysites and deals with its period of blossoming, its fate through the events of the Islamic conquest and its history under the rule of the Umajjads and Abbasids. This treatment covers the period to the end of the Arabic Empire in the 10th century.

The fourth volume traces monasticism among the Nestorians under the same aspects and within the same period as the preceding volume.

The fifth volume is devoted to the aftermath of Syrian monasticism in which we will treat the Monophysite and Diophysite movements together. It traces the fate of monasticism since the break-down of the Islamic Empire, the renaissance attempts and the catastrophe that befell Syrian Christianity under the Mongolian invasion of Timur Lenk.

The publication of the work is started with the hope that the edition of the complete work will not be extended to a long period.

Besides the index of names and places attached to each volume, there will be a general subject index for the whole work in the fifth volume.

LIST OF ABBREVIATIONS

AASS = *Acta sanctorum.* Bruxelles.

AB = *Analecta Bollandiana.* Bruxelles.

AbhGWG = *Abhandlungen der k. Gesellschaft der Wissenschaften zu Göttingen.* Göttingen.

AbhKM = *Abhandlungen für die Kunde des Morgenlandes.* Leipzig.

AbhPAW = *Abhandlungen der preussischen Akademie der Wissenschaften.* Berlin.

Acta apostolorum = *Acta apostolorum apocrypha,* ed. R. A. Lipsius et M. Bonnet, I-II. Lipsiae, 1898-1903.

Acta Guriae et Shamonae = *Acta S. Guriae et Shamonae exarata syriace a Theophilo Edesseno a Chr. 297,* ed. I. E. Rahmani. Romae, 1899.

Acta Maris = *Acta S. Maris, Assyriae, Babyloniae ac Persidis seculo I apostoli,* ed. J. B. Abbeloos AB IV (1885), 43 ff.

Acta martyrum = *Acta martyrum et sanctorum,* ed. P. Bedjan I-VII. Parisiis, 1890-97.

Acta martyrum orientalium = *Acta sanctorum martyrum orientalium,* ed. St. Ev. Assemani, I-II. Romae, 1748.

ActCUT = *Acta et Commentationes Universitatis Tartuensis.* Tartu.

Abdīšōʿ, *Catalogus* = Ebedjesus, *Catalogus librorum syrorum,* ed. J. S. Assemani BO III, 1. Romae, 1725.

Abū'l-Maʿāli, *Bayān* = Abū'l-Maʿāli, *Il Bayān al Adyān,* ed. F. Gabrieli, RRANL. Roma, 1932.

Adam, *Grundbegriffe* = Adam, A., *Grundbegriffe des Mönchtums in sprachlicher Sicht* ZfKg LXV (1954), 209 ff.

Aithalla, *Epistula* = *Aithallae episcopi Edesseni epistula ad christianos in persarum regione de fide,* ed. J. Thorossian. Venetik, 1942.

Alexander of Lycopolis, *Contra Manich. opiniones* = *Alexandri Lycopolitani Contra Manichaei opiniones disputatio,* ed. A. Brinkmann. Lipsiae, 1895.

Altheim, Stiehl und Junker, *Inschriften aus Gruzinien* = Altheim, F., Stiehl, R., und Junker, H., *Inschriften aus Gruzinien,* AnnIPHOS IX (1949), 1 ff.

Ammianus, *Rerum gestarum libri* = Ammianus Marcellinus, *Rerum gestarum libri qui supersunt,* ed. C. U. Clark, I-II. Berolini, 1910-15.

Amr, *De patriarchis* = Amr, *De patriarchis nestorianorum commentaria,* ed. H. Gismondi. Romae, 1896.

Analecta sacra = *Analecta sacra et classica Spicilegio Solesmensi parata*, ed. J. B. PITRA, V. Parisiis-Romae, 1888.

ANATOLIJ, *Istoričeskij očerk sirijskago monašestva do poloviny VI věka*, Kiev, 1911.

Ancient Syriac Documents = *Ancient Syriac Documents relative to the Earliest Establishment of Christianity in Edessa*, ed. W. CURETON. London, 1864.

Anecdota syriaca = *Anecdota syriaca*, ed. I. P. N. LAND, I-IV. Lugduni Batavorum, 1862-75.

ANIS = *Alt- und Neu-Indische Studien*. Hamburg.

AnnIPHOS = *Annuaire de l'Institut de philologie et d'histoire orientales et slaves*. Bruxelles.

Annus ecclesiasticus = *Annus ecclesiasticus*, ed. J. MARTINOV. Bruxellis, 1863.

ANTIOCHUS, *Pandectes* = *Antiochus Laurae S. Sabae monachus Pandectes scripturae sacrae*, PG LXXXIX.

APHRAHAṬ, *Demonstrationes* = APHRAATES, *Demonstrationes*, ed. I. PARISOT, PS I, 1-2. Parisiis, 1894-1907.

Apocryphal Acts = *Apocryphal Acts of the Gospels*, ed. W. WRIGHT. London, 1871.

AnSS = *Ānandāśrama Sanscrit Series*. Poona.

Anugītā = *The Anugītā*, tr. by K. T. TELANG, SBE VIII. Oxford, 1882.

AUGUSTINUS, *Contra Faustum* = AUGUSTINUS, *Contra Faustum*, ed. I. ZYCHA, CSEL XXV. Vindobonae, 1891.

AUGUSTINUS, *De civitate Dei* = AUGUSTINUS, *De civitate Dei*, ed. E. HOFFMANN, CSEL XXXX. Vindobonae, 1900.

AUGUSTINUS, *De haeresibus* = AUGUSTINUS, *De haeresibus*, ed. J. P. MIGNE, PL XLII.

AUGUSTINUS, *De moribus Manich.* = AUGUSTINUS, *De moribus Manichaeorum*, ed. J. P. MIGNE, PL XXXII.

AUGUSTINUS, *De utilitate credendi* = AUGUSTINUS, *De utilitate credendi*, ed. J. P. MIGNE, PL XLII.

AUGUSTINUS, *Epistulae* = AUGUSTINUS, *Epistulae*, ed. J. P. MIGNE, PL XXXIII.

BANG, *Der manich. Erzähler* = BANG, W., *Der manichäische Erzähler*, *Le Muséon* XXXIV (1921), 1 ff.

BAR BAHLUL, *Lexicon syriacum* = BAR BAHLUL, *Lexicon syriacum*, ed. R. DUVAL, I-III. Paris, 1901.

BARDENHEWER, *Geschichte altk. Literatur* = BARDENHEWER, *O.*, *Geschichte der altkirchlichen Literatur*, I-V. Freiburg, 1913-32.

BARDY, *L'Indiculus* = BARDY, G., *L'Indiculus de haeresibus du Pseudo-Jérome*, RchSR (1929), 403 ff.

BARḤADBEŠABBĀ, *Fondation des écoles* = BARḤADBEŠABBĀ, *Cause de la fondation des écoles.* ed. A. SCHER, PO IV, 4. Paris, 1908.

BARḤADBEŠABBĀ, *Histoire* = BARḤADBEŠABBĀ, 'ARBAÏA, *La seconde partie de l'histoire ecclésiastique,* ed. F. NAU, PO IX, 5. Paris, 1913.

BAR 'EBRAIĀ, *Chronicon ecclesiasticum* = *Gregorii Barhebraei chronicon ecclesiasticum,* ed. J. B. ABBELOOS et T. J. LAMY, I-III. Parisiis-Lovanii, 1872-77.

BAR 'EBRAIĀ, *Lettre au Denḥa* = *Une lettre de Bar Hébréus au catholicos Denḥa I,* ed. J. B. CHABOT, JA Neuvième ser. XI (1898), 75 ff.

BAUMSTARK, *Geschichte syr. Literatur* = BAUMSTARK, A., *Geschichte der syrischen Literatur,* Bonn, 1922.

BEHE = *Bibliothèque de l'École des Hautes Études, sc. philologique et historique.* Paris.

BeO = *Biblica et orientalia.* Roma.

BERNARD, *Odes of Solomon* = BERNARD, J. H., *The Odes of Solomon.* JThS, XII (1911), 1 ff.

BERT, *Aphrahats Homilien* = BERT, G., *Aphrahat's des persischen Weisen Homilien,* TuU III. Leipzig, 1888.

Bet- und Beichtbuch = *Ein manichäisches Bet- und Beichtbuch,* ed. W. HENNING, AbhPAW. London-Berlin, 1937.

BibAHG = *Bibliothek arabischer Historiker und Geographen,* ed. H. VON MŽIK. Leipzig, 1926-30.

BibGA = *Bibliotheca geographorum arabicorum.* Lugduni Batavorum.

BibVK = *Bibliotheca veterum patrum antiquorumque scriptorum ecclesiasticorum,* ed. A. GALLANDI, I-XIV. Venetiis, 1677-1731.

Bibl. orientalis = *Bibliotheca orientalis,* ed. J. S. ASSEMANI, I-III. Romae, 1719-1728.

BibZ = *Biblische Zeitschrift.* Freiburg i. B.

Biographie de Bardesane = *Une biographie inédite de Bardesane l'Astrologue,* ed. F. NAU. Paris, 1897.

AL-BIRUNI, *Chronologie orient. Völker,* = AL-BIRUNI, *Chronologie orientalischer Völker,* ed. E. SACHAU. Leipzig 1878.

BONWETSCH, *Unter Hippolyts Namen überl. Schrift* = BONWETSCH, G. N., *Die unter Hippolyts Namen überlieferte Schrift Über den Glauben,* TuU XXXI, 2. Leipzig, 1907.

Book of Himyarites = *The Book of Himyarites. Fragments of a hitherto unknown Syriac work,* ed. A. MOBERG. Leipzig, 1924.

BOUSSET, *Religion des Judentums* = BOUSSET, W., *Die Religion des Judentums.* Berlin, 1926.

BRAUN, *Ausgewählte Akten* = BRAUN, O., *Ausgewählte Akten persischer Märtyrer.* Kempten-München, 1915.

BRAUN, *De Nicaena synodo* = BRAUN, O., *De sancta Nicaena synodo,* KSt IV, 3. Münster, 1898.

BRAUN, *Buch der Synhados* = BRAUN, O., *Das Buch der Synhados.* Stuttgart und Wien, 1900.

Breviarium chaldaicum = *Breviarium chaldaicum,* ed. P. BEDJAN, I-III. Parisiis, 1886-97.

BROCKELMANN, *Lexicon syriacum* = BROCKELMANN, C., *Lexicon syriacum.* Halis Saxonum, 1928.

Buddha-Karita = *The Buddha-Karita of Asvaghosha,* tr. by E. B. COWELL, SBE XLIX. Oxford, 1894.

BullIFAO = *Bulletin de l'Institut Français d'Archéologie orientale.* Le Caire.

BullJRL = *Bulletin of the John Rylands Library.* Manchester.

BURKITT, *Early Christianity* = BURKITT, F. C., *Early Christianity outside the Roman Empire.* Cambridge, 1902.

BURKITT, *Eastern Christianity* = BURKITT, F. C., *Early Eastern Christianity.* London, 1904.

BURKITT, *Evangelion da-Mepharreshe* = BURKITT, F. C., *Evangelion da-Mepharreshe* I-II. Cambridge, 1904.

BURKITT, *Ephraim's Quotations* = BURKITT, F. C., *Ephraim's Quotations from the Gospel,* TaS VII, 2. Cambridge, 1901.

BURKITT, *Religion of the Manichees* = BURKITT, F. C., *The Religion of the Manichees.* Cambridge, 1925.

BURKITT, *Syriac Speaking Christ.* = BURKITT, F. C., *Syriac Speaking Christianity, The Cambridge Ancient History* XII. Cambridge, 1939.

Canones apostolorum aethiopice = *Canones apostolorum aethiopice,* ed. W. FELL. Lipsiae, 1871.

CASPARI, *Alte und neue Quellen* = CASPARI, C. P., *Alte und neue Quellen zur Geschichte des Taufsymbols und der Glaubensregel.* Christiania, 1879.

CBU = *Contributions of the Baltic University.* Hamburg-Pinneberg.

CH = *Church History.* Chicago.

CHAVANNES, *Cinq cents contes* = CHAVANNES, E., *Cinq cents contes.* Paris, 1911.

CHRISTENSEN, *L'Iran* = CHRISTENSEN, A., *L'Iran sous les Sassanides.* Copenhague, 1944.

Chronica minora = *Chronica minora,* ed. I. GUIDI, CSCO Scr. Syr. III, 4. Parisiis, 1903.

Chronicon Edessenum = *Chronicon Edessenum,* ed. I. GUIDI, in *Chronica minora,* 1 ff.

Chronicon maroniticum = *Chronicon maroniticum,* ed. E. W. BROOKS, in *Chronica minora* II, CSCO Scr. syr. III, 4. Parisiis, 1904.

Chuastuanift = *Chuastuanift, das Beichtgebet der Manichäer,* ed. W. RADLOFF. St. Petersburg, 1909.

CLEMENS, *Excerpta ex Theodoto* = CLEMENS, *Excerpta ex Theodoto,* ed. O. STAEHLIN, GCS XVII, Leipzig, 1909.

CLEMENS, *Stromata* = CLEMENS, *Stromata,* ed. O. STAEHLIN, GCS XV, XVII. Leipzig, 1906-09.

Codex Theodosianus = *Codex Theodosianus,* ed. T. MOMMSEN et P. M. MEYER, I-II. Berolini, 1905.

Codices Avestici = *Codices Avestici et Pahlevici Bibliothecae Universitatis Hafniensis.* Copenhague, 1935.

Commonitorium = *Commonitorium,* ed. J. P. MIGNE, PL XLXI.

CONNOLLY, *Aphraates* = CONNOLLY, R. H., *Aphraates and Monasticism,* JThS VI (1905), 522 f.

CONNOLLY, *Original Language* = CONNOLLY, R. H., *Greek the Original Language of the Odes of Solomon,* JThS XIV (1913), 530 ff.

Constitutiones apostol. = *Didascalia et constitutiones apostolorum,* ed. F. X. FUNK I. Padebornae, 1905.

Coptic Gnostic Papyri = *Coptic Gnostic Papyri,* ed. P. LABIB, I. Cairo, 1956.

Corpus haereseologicum = *Corpus haereseologicum,* ed. F. OEHLER, I-III. Berolini, 1851-61.

CSCO = *Corpus scriptorum christianorum orientalium.* Parisiis-Lovanii.

CSEL = *Corpus scriptorum ecclesiasticorum latinorum.* Vindobonae.

CUASCAnt = *The Catholic University of America Studies in Christian Antiquity.* Washington.

CUMONT, *Recherches* = CUMONT, F., *Recherches sur le manichéisme,* I-III. Bruxelles, 1908-1912.

CYRIL OF JERUSALEM, *Catecheses mystagogicae* = CYRIL OF JERUSALEM, *Catecheses mystagogicae,* ed. J. P. MIGNE, PG XXXIII.

CYRIL OF SCYTHOPOLIS, *Vita Euthymii* = *Kyrillos von Skythopolis,* ed. E. SCHWARTZ, TuU XLIX, 2. Leipzig, 1939.

Damaskusschrift = *Die Damaskusschrift,* ed. L. ROST, KlT CLXVII. Berlin, 1933.

Dhammapada = *The Dhammapada,* tr. by F. M. MÜLLER, SBE X, Oxford, 1881.

Diatess. italiano = *Il Diatessaron in volgare italiano, Testi inediti dei secoli XIII-XIV,* ed. V. TODESCO, A. VACCARI, M. VATTASSO, SeT LXXXI. Città del Vaticano, 1938.

Diatess. persiano = *Diatessaron persiano,* ed. G. MESSINA, BeO XIV. Roma, 1951.

Dīnkard = *The Dīnkard, The Original Pahlavi Text,* ed PESHOTAN SANJANA I-XIX. Bombay, 1874-1928.

DIONYSIOS TELL MAḤRĒ, *Chronique* = *Chronique de Denys de Tell-Mahré, quatrième partie,* éd. par I. B. CHABOT, BEHE CXII. Paris 1895.

Doctrina Addaei = *The Doctrine of Addai the Apostle,* ed. G. PHILLIPS. London, 1876.

DRAGUET, *Pères du désert* = DRAGUET, R., *Les pères du désert. Textes choisis et présentés.* Paris, 1949.

DUNCAN, *Baptism* = DUNCAN, E. J., *Baptism in the Demonstrations of Aphraates the Persian Sage,* CUASCAnt VIII. Washington, 1945.

DUSSAUD, *Découvertes de Ras Shamra* = DUSSAUD, R., *Les découvertes de Ras Shamra et l'Ancien Testament,* Paris, 1937.

DUVAL, *Littérature syriaque* = DUVAL, R., *La littérature syriaque.* Paris, 1907.

AL-DŽĀHIZ, *Kitāb al-ḥajawān* = AL-DŽĀHIZ, *Kitāb al-ḥajawān,* I-IV. Cairo, 1323-24.

AL-DŽĀHIZ, *Risāla* = AL-DŽĀHIZ, *Risāla fi redd en-naṣāra,* ed. J. FINKEL. Cairo, 1926.

Early Judaeo-Christian Documents = *Some Early Judaeo-Christian Documents in the John Rylands Library,* ed. A. MINGANA. London, 1917.

EETS = *Early English Text Society.* London.

ELĪIā, *Opus chronologicum* = ELIAS NISIBENUS, *Opus chronologicum,* ed. E. W. BROOKS et I. B. CHABOT, CSCO Scr. syr. III, 7, 8. Parisiis, 1909-10.

Ełišē, *Patmowtʿiwn wardananç* = Ełišē, *Patmowtʿiwn wardananç.* Constantinople, 1871.

EPHREM, *Carmina Nisibena* = EPHRAEM, *Carmina Nisibena,* ed. G. BICKELL. Lipsiae, 1866.

EPHREM, *Contra haereses* = *Des hl. Ephraem des Syrers Hymnen Contra haereses,* hrsg. von E. BECK, CSCO Scr. syr. LXXVII. Louvain, 1957.

EPHREM, *Contra Julianum* = *Des hl. Ephraem des Syrers Hymnen De Paradiso und Contra Julianum,* hrsg. von E. BECK, CSCO Scr. syr. LXXVIII. Louvain, 1957.

EPHREM, *De fide* = *Des hl. Ephraem des Syrers Hymnen De fide,* hrsg. von E. BECK, CSCO Scr. syr. LXXIII. Louvain, 1955.

EPHREM, *De Paradiso* = *Des heiligen Ephraem des Syrers Hymnen De Paradiso und Contra Julianum,* hrsg. von E. BECK, CSCO Scr. syr. LXXVIII. Louvain, 1957.

EPHREM, *Hymni de virginitate* = EPHRAEM, *Hymni de virginitate,* ed. I. E. RAHMANI I-II. Scharfensi, 1906-1908.

EPHREM, *Hymni et sermones* = EPHRAEM, *Hymni et sermones,* ed. T. J. LAMY, I-IV. Mechliniae, 1882-1902.

EPHREM, *Opera omnia* = EPHRAEM, *Opera omnia quae extant syriace,* ed. P. MOBARREK, I-III. Romae, 1737-43.

EPHREM, *Opera omnia gr.* = EPHRAEM, *Opera omnia quae extant graece,* ed. J. S. ASSEMANI, I-III. Romae, 1732-46.

EPHREM, *Prose Refutations* = *S. Ephraim's Prose Refutations of Mani, Marcion and Bardaisan,* ed. C. W. MITCHELL, I-II. London, 1912-21.

EPHREM, *Sermones duo* = *Ephraemi Syri Sermones duo,* ed. P. ZINGERLE. Brixen, 1868.

EPHREM, *Srboyn* = *Srboyn Ep'remi matenagrowt'iwnk'* I-IV. Venetik, 1836.

EPHREM, *Srboyn meknowt'iwn* = *Srboyn Ep'remi meknowt'iwn gorcoy aṙak'eloy,* ed. N. AKINIAN. Vienna, 1921.

EPHREM, *Testament* = *Le Testament de S. Éphrem,* ed. R. DUVAL, JA Ser. IX, XVII (1901), 243 ff.

EPIPHANIUS, *Panarion* = EPIPHANIUS, *Panarion,* ed. K. HOLL, GCS XXV, XXXI, XXXVII, Leipzig, 1915-33.

Er = *Eranos.* Uppsala.

Euphemia = *Euphemia and the Goth,* ed. F. C. BURKITT. London, 1913.

EUSEBIUS, *Chronographia* = EUSEBIUS, *Chronographia,* ed. A. SCHOENE, I-II. Berolini, 1866-75.

EUSEBIUS, *Commentaria in Psalmos* = EUSEBIUS, *Commentaria in Psalmos,* ed. J. P. MIGNE, PG XXIII.

EUSEBIUS, *De martyribus Palaestinae* = EUSEBIUS, *De martyribus Palaestinae,* ed. E. SCHWARTZ, in *Historia ecclesiastica,* Paralipomena, p. 907 ff., Leipzig, 1908.

EUSEBIUS, *Hist. eccl.* = EUSEBIUS, *Historia ecclesiastica,* ed. E. SCHWARTZ, GCS IX. Leipzig, 1903.

EUSEBIUS, *Syriac History of the Martyrs* = *History of the Martyrs in Palestine by Eusebius,* ed. W. CURETON. London, 1861.

EUSEBIUS, *Vita Constantini* = EUSEBIUS, *Vita Constantini,* ed. I. H. HEIKEL, GCS VIII. Leipzig, 1902.

Evagriana syriaca = *Evagriana syriaca,* ed. J. MUYLDERMANS. Louvain, 1952.

Evangelium veritatis = *Evangelium veritatis,* ed. M. MALININE, H. C. PUECH et G. QUISPEL. Zürich, 1956.

EVODIUS, *De fide* = EVODIUS, *De fide contra manichaeos,* ed. J. P. MIGNE, PL XLII.

EZNIK, *Ełc ałandoç* = EZNIK, *Ełc ałandoç.* Venetik, 1875.

FAUSTUS, *Patmowt'iwn Hayoç* = FAUSTUS, *Patmowt'iwn Hayoç.* St. Peterburg, 1883.

FGNK = *Forschungen zur Geschichte des neutestamentlichen Kanons.* Leipzig.

FIRDAUSĪ, *Šāhnamā* = FIRDAUSĪ, *Šāhnamā, Le livre des rois,* éd. J MOHL, I-VII. Paris, 1838-78.

Formula antiqua = *Formula antiqua receptionis manichaeorum,* ed. A. GALLANDI, BibVP XIV. Venetiis, 1731.

Fo-sho-hing-tsan-king = *The Fo-sho-hing-tsan-king,* tr. by S. BEAL, SBE XIX. Oxford, 1883.

FOUCHER, *L'art gréco-bouddhique* = FOUCHER, A., *L'art gréco-bouddhique de Gandhâra,* I-II. Paris, 1905-18.

FRANKENBERG, *Verständnis der Oden* = FRANKENBERG, W., *Das Verständnis der Oden Salomos.* Giessen, 1911.

FUNK, *Haggadische Elemente* = FUNK, S., *Die haggadischen Elemente in den Homilien des Aphrates des persischen Weisen.* Wien, 1892.

GCS = *Die griechischen christlichen Schriftsteller der ersten drei Jahrhunderte.* Leipzig.

Ginza = *Ginza; der Schatz oder das grosse Buch der Mandäer, übersetzt von* M. LIDZBARSKI, QRlg XIII, 4. Göttingen-Leipzig, 1925.

GĪWARGĪS, *Poemi siriaci* = *Poemi siriaci di Giorgio vescovo degli arabi,* ed. V. RYSSEL, RAL CCLXXXVIII. Roma, 1892.

GRANT, *Date of Tatian's Oratio* = GRANT, R. M., *Date of Tatian's Oratio,* HTR XLVI (1953), 99 ff.

Greek and Latin Papyri = *Catalogue of the Greek and Latin Papyri in the John Rylands Library Manchester,* ed. by C. H. ROBERTS, III. Manchester, 1938.

GREGORIUS THEOLOGUS, *Poemata historica* = GREGORIUS THEOLOGUS, *Poemata historica,* ed. J. P. MIGNE, PG XXXVII.

GREGORIUS TURONENSIS, *Miracula* = GREGORIUS, *Miracula et opera minora,* ed. W. ARNDT et B. KRUSCH, SRerM II.

GWYNN, *Syriac Version* = GWYNN, J., *The Older Syriac Version of the Four Minor Catholic Epistles,* Hermathema VII (1890), 281 ff.

Habakkuk Commentary = *Habakkuk Commentary,* ed. W. H. BROWNLEE, in *The Dead Sea Scrolls of St. Mark's Monastery* I. New Haven, 1950.

Handschriftenreste = *Handschriftenreste in Estrangelo-Schrift aus Turfan,* ed. F. W. K. MÜLLER, AbhPAW II. Berlin, 1904.

HARNACK, *Chronologie* = HARNACK, A. VON, *Chronologie des altchristlichen Literatur* I. Leipzig, 1897.

HARNACK, *Überlieferung* = HARNACK, A. VON, *Die Überlieferung der griechischen Apologeten des zweiten Jahrhunderts,* TuU I. Leipzig, 1882.

HARNACK, *Marcion* = HARNACK, A. VON, *Marcion : das Evangelium vom fremden Gott,* TuU XLV, Leipzig, 1921.

HARNACK, *Mission und Ausbreitung* = HARNACK, A. VON, *Die Mission und Ausbreitung des Christentums in den ersten drei Jahrhunderten,* I-II. Leipzig, 1924.

HARNACK, *Tatians Diatessaron* = HARNACK, A. VON, *Tatians Diatessaron und Marcions Commentar zum Evangelium bei Ephraem Syrus,* ZfKg IV (1881), 471 ff.

HARRIS, *Tatian* = HARRIS, R., *Tatian : Perfection According to the Saviour,* BullJRL VIII. (1924).

HAUSHERR, *L'erreur du Messalianisme* = HAUSHERR, I., *L'erreur fondamentale et la logique du Messalianisme,* OCP I (1935), 328 ff.

HAUSHERR, *Messalianisme* = HAUSHERR, I., *Le Messalianisme, Atti del XIX Congresso Internazionale degli Orientalisti.* Roma, 1938.

HAUSHERR, *Quanam aetate prodierit Liber Graduum* = HAUSHERR, I., *Quanam aetate prodierit Liber Graduum,* OCP I (1935).

HEGEMONIUS, *Acta Archelai* = HEGEMONIUS, *Acta Archelai,* ed. C. H. BEESON, GCS XVI. Leipzig, 1906.

ḤENANĀ, *Statutes* = *Statutes of the School of Nisibis,* ed. A. VÖÖBUS, PapETSE XII. Stockholm, 1958.

HENNING, *Neue Materialien* = HENNING, *Neue Materalien zur Geschichte des Manichäismus,* ZDMG XC (1936).

HIERONYMUS, *Adv. Jovinianum* = HIERONYMUS, *Adversus Jovinianum,* ed. J. P. MIGNE, PL XXIII.

HIERONYMUS, *Commentaria in Amos* = HIERONYMUS, *Commentaria in Amos,* ed. J. P. MIGNE, PL XXV.

HIERONYMUS, *Commentaria in ep. ad Galatas* = HIERONYMUS, *Commentaria in epistulam ad Galatas,* ed. J. P. MIGNE, PL XXVI.

HIERONYMUS, *De viris inlustribus* = HIERONYMUS, *De viris inlustribus,* ed. E. C. RICHARDSON, TuU XIV. Leipzig, 1896.

HIERONYMUS, *Vita Hilarionis* = HIERONYMUS, *Vita Hilarionis,* ed. J. P. MIGNE, PL XXIII.

HIERONYMUS, *Vita Malchi* = HIERONYMUS, *Vita Malchi,* ed. J. P. MIGNE, PL XXII.

HIPPOLYTUS, *Kommentar zum Daniel* = *Hippolyt's Kommentar zum Buche Daniel und die Fragmente des Kommentars zum Hohenliede,* ed. G. N. BONWETSCH, *Hippolytus Werke,* I, 1, GCS I. Leipzig, 1897.

HIPPOLYTUS, *Philosophumena* = HIPPOLYTUS, *Philosophumena sive omnium haeresium refutatio,* ed. J. P. MIGNE, PG XVI, 3.

Histoire de Jabalaha = *Histoire de Mar Jabalaha, de trois autres patriarches, d'une prêtre et de deux laïques, nestoriens,* éd. P. BEDJAN. Paris, 1895.

Histoire de Youssef Bousnaya = *Histoire du moine Rabban Youssef Bousnaya par son disciple Jean bar Kaldun, traduite du syriaque par* J. B. CHABOT, Paris, 1900.

Histoire nestorienne = *Histoire nestorienne,* éd. A. SCHER, J. PERIER, P. DIB et R. GRIVEAU, PO IV, 3; V, 2; VII, 2; XIII, 4. Paris, 1907-19.

Historia Mar Pethion = *Historia S. Mar Pethion martyris*, ed. J. Corluy, AB VII (1888), 8 ff.

Hoffmann, *Auszüge* = Hoffmann, G., *Auszüge aus syrischen Akten persischer Märtyrer*, AbhKM VII, 3. Leipzig, 1880.

Honigmann, *Ostgrenze* = Honigmann, E., *Die Ostgrenze des byzantinischen Reiches*. Bruxelles, 1935.

HS = *Horae semiticae*. Cambridge.

HTR = *Harvard Theological Review*. Cambridge, Mass.

Ibn Hazm, *al-fisal* = Ibn Hazm, *al-fisal fi'l-milal wa'l-Ahwāl' wa'n-nihal*, I-V. Cairo, 1928-29.

Ibn Rosteh, *Kitāb al-a'lāk an-nafīsa* = Ibn Rosteh, *Kitāb al-a'lāk an-nafīsa*, ed. M. J. Goeje, BibGA VII, Lugduni Batavorum, 1892.

IFAB = *Institut Français d'archéologie de Beyrouth.*

Irenaeus, *Adv. haereses* = Irenaeus, *Contra omnes haereses libri quinque*, ed. A. Stieren I-II. Lipsiae, 1853.

Isḥaq of Antioch, *Homiliae* = *Homiliae S. Isaaci Syri Antiocheni*, ed. P. Bedjan. Paris, 1903.

Išō'dad, *Commentaries* = *The Commentaries of Išō'dad of Merv*, ed. M. D. Gibson, HS V-VII, X, XII. Cambridge, 1911-16.

Išō'denaḥ. *Chasteté* = *Le livre de la chasteté composé par Jésusdenah évêque de Baçrah*, éd. I. B. Chabot, MAH XVI. Paris, 1896.

JA = *Journal asiatique*. Paris.

Jābāla Upaniṣad = *Jābāla Upaniṣad*, AnSS XIX. Poona, 1878.

Jacobi ep. Nisibeni sermones = *Jacobi episcopi Nisibeni sermones*, ed. N. Antonelli. Romae, 1756.

Ja'qōb of Edessa, *Two Epistles* = *Two Epistles of Mār Jacob*, ed. W. Wright, JSLit X (1867), 434 ff.

Jargy, *Fils et filles du pacte* = Jargy, S., *Les « fils et filles du pacte » dans la littérature monastique syriaque*, OCP XVII (1951), 304 ff.

Jātaka = *Jātaka*, ed. V. Fausböll, I-IV. London, 1877-1908.

Joannes Chrysostomus, *De virginitate* = Joannes Chrysostomus, *De virginitate*, ed. J. P. Migne, PG XLVIII.

Joannes Chrysostomus, *In ep. ad Galates commentaria* = Joannes Chrysostomus, *In epistolam ad Galatas commentaria*, ed. J. P. Migne, PG LXI.

Johannesbuch = *Das Johannesbuch, herausgegeben und übersetzt von* M. Lidzbarski. Giessen, 1905-1915.

Josephus, *Antiquitates* = *Flavii Josephi opera*, ed. B. Niese, I-IV. Berolini, 1887-90.

Josephus, *De bello judaico* = *Flavii Josephi opera*, ed. B. Niese, VI. Berolini, 1885-95.

JOSEPHUS, *Vita* = *Flavii Josephi opera,* ed. B. NIESE IV. Berolini, 1890.

JOSEPHUS, *Slavonic Bell. jud.* = FLAVIUS JOSEPHUS, *Vom jüdischen Krieg, Buch I-IV. Nach der slavischen Übersetzung deutsch herausgegeben* von A. BERENDTS und K. GRASS, ActCUT. Tartu, 1924.

JRAS = *Journal of the Royal Asiatic Society.* London.

JSLit = *Journal of Sacred Literature.* London.

JThS = *Journal of Theological Studies.* Oxford.

JULIANUS, *Opera* = *Juliani Imperatori quae supersunt praeter reliquias apud Cyrillum omnia,* ed. F. C. HERTLEIN, I-II. Lipsiae, 1875-76.

Julianos der Abtrünnige = *Julianos der Abtrünnige: Syrische Erzählungen,* ed. J. G. E. HOFFMANN. Leiden, 1880.

JUSTINUS MARTYR, *Apologia I* = JUSTINUS MARTYR, *Apologia I pro christianis,* ed. J. P. MIGNE, PG VI.

JUSTINUS MARTYR, *Dialogus* = JUSTINUS MARTYR, *Dialogus* in *Die ältesten Apologeten,* herausgegeben von E. J. GOODSPEED. Göttingen, 1914.

KAHLE, *Cairo Geniza* = KAHLE, P., *The Cairo Geniza.* London, 1947.

Kephalaia = *Kephalaia,* ed. C. SCHMIDT. Stuttgart, 1935.

KHAYYATH, *Syri orientales* = KHAYYATH, G. E., *Syri orientales,* Romae, 1870.

KlT = *Kleine Texte,* Berlin.

KITTEL, *Eine synagogale Parallele* = KITTEL, G., *Eine synagogale Parallele zu den Benai Qejama,* ZntW XVI (1915), 235 f.

KOCH, *Taufe und Askese* = KOCH, H., *Taufe und Askese in der alten ostsyrischen Kirche,* ZntW XII (1911), 37 ff.

KODĀMA, *Kitāb al-Kharādj* = KODĀMA IBN DJA'FAR, *Kitāb al-Kharādj,* ed. M. J. GOEJE, BiblGA VI. Lugduni Batavorum, 1889.

KRÜGER, *Geschichte altchr. Literatur* = KRÜGER, G., *Geschichte der altchristlichen Literatur in den ersten drei Jahrhunderten.* Freiburg und Leipzig, 1895.

KSt = *Kirchengeschichtliche Studien.* Münster.

KUGENER-CUMONT, *Recherches sur le manichéisme* = KUGENER, M. A., et CUMONT, F., *Recherches sur le manichéisme,* I-II. Bruxelles, 1912.

KUKULA, *Tatians sog. Apologie* = KUKULA, R. C., *Tatians sogenannte Apologie.* Leipzig, 1900.

Kullavagga = *Vinaya Texts,* tr. by T. W. R. DAVIDS and H. OLDENBERG, SBE XX. Oxford, 1885.

LABOURT, *Christianisme* = LABOURT, J., *Le christianisme dans l'Empire perse sous la dynastie Sassanide 224-632.* Paris, 1904.

Laien-Beichtspiegel = *Laien-Beichtspiegel,* übersetzt von W. BANG, *Le Muséon* XXXVI.

LASSUS, *Sanctuaires chrétiens* = LASSUS, J., *Sanctuaires chrétiens de Syrie;*

essai sur la genèse, la forme et l'usage liturgique des édifices du culte chrétien en Syrie, du IIIe siècle à la conquête musulmane, IFAB, Bibliothèque archéologique et historique XLIII, Paris, 1947.

Laws of Manu = *The Laws of Manu,* tr. by G. BÜHLER, SBE XXV. Oxford, 1886.

LAZAR, *Patmowt'iwn Hayoç* = LAZAR, *Patmowt'iwn Hayoç,* ed. G. TER-MKRTČEAN and S. MALXASEAN. Tiflis, 1904.

LE COQ, *Buddhistische Spätantike* = LE COQ, A. VON, *Die buddhistische Spätantike in Mittelasien.* Berlin, 1922-33.

LEFORT, *Une citation copte* = LEFORT, L. TH., *Une citation copte de la pseudo-clémentine 'De virginitate',* BullIFAO XXX, (1931).

Légende d'Aaron = *La légende d'Aaron de Saroug,* éd. F. NAU, PO V, 5. Paris, 1910.

Légende de Mar Bassus = *La légende de Mar Bassus martyr persan,* ed. J. B. CHABOT. Paris, 1893.

Legenden des Nā-ro-pa = *Die Legenden des Nā-ro-pa. Nach einer alten tibetischen Handschrift übersetzt* von A. GRÜNWEDEL. Leipzig, 1933.

Legends of Eastern Saints = *Legends of Eastern Saints,* ed. A. J. WENSINCK, I-II. Leyden, 1911.

LEWY, *Calendrier perse* = LEWY, H., *Le calendrier perse, Orientalia* X (1941).

Liber graduum = *Liber graduum,* ed. M. KMOSKO, PS I, 3. Parisiis, 1926.

Liber pontificalis = *Liber pontificalis,* ed. L. DUCHESNE, I-II. Paris, 1886.

Liège Diatessaron = *The Liège Diatessaron,* ed. D. PLOOIJ and C. A. PHILLIPS, VKAiW Letterk NR XXIX, 1, 6; XXXI. Amsterdam, 1929-38.

Life of John the Baptist = *Life of John the Baptist,* ed. A. MINGANA, in *Christian Documents in Syriac, Arabic and Garshuni,* WS I. Cambridge, 1927.

LIDZBARSKI, *Manichäische Schrift* = LIDZBARSKI, M., *Die Herkunft der manichäischen Schrift,* SbPAW. Berlin, 1916.

LIDZBARSKI, *Nazoraios* = LIDZBARSKI, M., *Nazoraios,* in ZfS I (1922), 230 ff.

LOHMEYER, *Galiläa und Jerusalem* = LOHMEYER, E., *Galiläa und Jerusalem.* Göttingen, 1936.

MAH = *Mélanges d'archéologie et d'histoire.* Paris-Rome.

Mahāvagga = *Vinaya Texts,* tr. by T. W. R. DAVIDS and H. OLDENBERG, SBE XVII. Oxford, 1882.

Mahrnāmag = *Ein Doppelblatt aus einem manichäischen Hymnenbuch,* übersetzt von F. W. K. MÜLLER, AbhPAW. Berlin, 1912.

Mandäische Liturgien = *Mandäische Liturgien,* ed. M. LIDZBARSKI, AbhGWG NF XVII. Göttingen, 1920.

Manichaean Psalm-Book = *A Manichaean Psalm-Book,* ed. G. R. C. Allberry. Stuttgart, 1938.

Manichaica = *Manichaica,* ed. C. Saleman. St. Petersbourg, 1912.

Manichäische Homilien = *Manichäische Homilien,* ed. H. J. Polotsky. Stuttgart, 1934.

Manichäische Hymnen = *Manichäische Hymnen,* ed. W. Bang, *Le Muséon* XXXVIII (1925), 30 ff.

Manich. kosmogon. Hymnus = *Ein Manichäischer kosmogonischer Hymnus,* ed. W. Henning, NachGWG. Göttingen, 1932.

Manual of Discipline = *The Manual of Discipline,* ed. M. Burrows, *The Dead Sea Scrolls of St. Mark's Monastery* II, 2. New Haven, 1951.

Manuscrit manichéen = *Un manuscrit manichéen,* ed. P. Alfaric, RHLR VI (1920), 66 ff.

Mari, *De patriarchis* = Mari, *De patriarchis nestorianorum commentaria,* ed. H. Gismondi. Romae, 1899.

Marmorstein, *Nachahmung Gottes in der Agada* = Marmorstein, A., *Die Nachahmung Gottes in der Agada,* in *Jüdischen Studien, J. Wohlgemut zum 60. Geburtstag.* Frankfurt a. M., 1928.

Marquart, *Eranšahr* = Marquart, J., *Eranšahr,* AbhGWG. Göttingen, 1901.

Martyrium Simeonis = *Martyrium beati Simeonis Bar Sabba'e,* ed. M. Kmosko, PS I, 2. Parisiis, 1907.

Martyrologes et ménologes = *Martyrologes et ménologes orientaux,* éd. F. Nau, PO X, L. Paris, 1915.

Mātīkān = *Mâtîkân ê hazâr dâtastân. The Laws of the Ancient Persians,* ed. S. J. Bulsara, I-II. Bombay, 1937.

Maude, *B'nai Q'yama* = Maude, M., *Who were the B'nai Q'yama?,* JThS XXXVI (1935), 13 ff.

Megilloth genuzoth = *Megilloth genuzoth,* ed. E. L. Sukenik, I-II. Jerusalem, 1948.

Μηναῖον, II = Μηναῖον, II. Venice, 1612.

Michael Syrus, *Chronique* = *Chronique de Michel le Syrien,* éd. I. B. Chabot, I-III, Paris, 1899-1924.

Mingana, *Early Spread* = Mingana, A., *The Early Spread of Christianity in Central Asia and the Far East.* Manchester, 1925.

Miscell. Coptic Texts = *Miscellaneous Coptic Texts,* ed. E. A. W. Budge. London, 1915.

Mitteliranische Manichaica = *Mitteliranische Manichaica aus chinesisch Turkestan von F. C. Andreas,* ed. W. Henning, SbPAW. Berlin, 1932-34.

Monumenta syriaca = *Monumenta syriaca* I, ed. P. Zingerle. Oeniponti, 1869.

Morceaux choisis = *Morceaux choisis de littérature araméenne*, éd. J. E. MANNA, I-II. Mossoul, 1901-02.

MÜLLER, *Ehelosigkeit* = MÜLLER, K., *Ehelosigkeit aller Getauften in der alten Kirche*, SGV CXXVI. Tübingen, 1927.

MÜLLER, *Kirchengeschichte* I. Tübingen, 1941.

NAbh = *Neutestamentliche Abhandlungen*. Münster.

NachGWG = *Nachrichten der Gesellschaft des Wissenschaften in Göttingen*. Göttingen.

EN-NADIM, *Kitāb al-Fihrist* = EN-NADIM, *Kitāb al-Fihrist*, ed. G. FLÜGEL, R. ROEDIGER et A. MÜLLER, I-II. Leipzig, 1871-72.

Nārāyana = *Nārāyana*, AnSS XIX. Poona, 1878.

Narratio de Simeone = *Narratio de S. Simeone Bar Sabbaʿe*, ed. M. KMOSKO, PS I, 2. Parisiis, 1907.

NARSAI, *Homiliae et carmina* = NARSAI, *Homiliae et carmina*, ed. A. MINGANA, I-II. Mausilii, 1905.

NARSAI, *Statutes* = *Statutes of the School of Nisibis*, ed. A. VÖÖBUS, PapETSE XII, Stockholm, 1958.

NEMBN = *Notices et extraits des manuscrits de la Bibliothèque Nationale*, Paris.

Neṣḥānā = *Neṣḥānā*, ed. P. BEDJAN, in *Acta martyrum et sanctorum*, IV, 507 ff. Parisiis, 1894.

Nouveaux fragments de la ps.-clémentine = *Nouveaux fragments de la pseudo-clémentine*, ed. L. TH. LEFORT, *Le Muséon* XLII (1929), 265 ff.

Nouvelle réc. de la vie d'Abercius = *Une nouvelle récension de la vie d'Abercius*, éd. E. BATAREIKH, OC IV (1904), 278 ff.

NSzGT = *Neue Studien zur Geschichte der Theologie und der Kirche*. Berlin.

NYBERG, *Quelques inscriptions antiques* = NYBERG, H. S., *Quelques inscriptions antiques découvertes récemment en Géorgie*, Er XLIV (1946), 228 ff.

OC = *Oriens Christianus*. Rome-Leipzig-Wiesbaden.

OCP = *Orientalia christiana periodica*. Roma.

Odes of Solomon = *The odes and Psalms of Solomon*, ed. J. R. HARRIS and A. MINGANA, I-II. Manchester, 1916.

OLZ = *Orientalistische Literaturzeitung*. Leipzig.

O'LEARY, *Syriac Church* = O'LEARY, DE LACY EVANS, *The Syriac Church and Fathers, a Brief Review of the Subject*. London, 1909.

Opera selecta = *Ephraemi Syri, Rabulae, Balaei aliorumque opera selecta*, ed. J. J. OVERBECK. Oxonii, 1865.

ORIGENES, *Commentaria in Matth.* = ORIGENES, *Commentaria in Matthaeum*, ed. E. KLOSTERMANN, GCS XL. Leipzig, 1935.

ORIGENES, *Fragmenta* = *Die Homilien zu Lukas in der Übersetzung des Hieronymus und die griechischen Reste der Homilien und des Lukas-Kommentars,* ed. M. RAUER, GCS XXXV. Leipzig, 1930

ORTIZ DE URBINA, *Intorno al valore* = ORTIZ DE URBINA, I., *Intorno al valore storico della Cronaca di Arbela,* OCP II (1936), 5 ff.

Oxyrhynchus Papyri = *The Oxyrhynchus Papyri,* ed. B. P. GRENFELL and A. S. HUNT, I-VI. London, 1898-1908.

Pahlavi Texts = *Pahlavi Texts,* translated by E. W. WEST, I-V. *Sacred Books of the East* V, XVIII, XXIV, XXXVII, XLVII.

PapETSE = *Papers of the Estonian Theological Society in Exile.* Stockholm.

Passion arabe de ʿAbd al-Masiḥ = *La Passion arabe de S. ʿAbd al-Masich,* ed. P. PEETERS, AB XLIV (1926), 294 ff.

Pātimokkha = *Pātimokkha,* translated by T. W. R. DAVIDS and H. OLDENBERG, SBE XIII. Oxford, 1881.

Patmowtʿiwn žołovoç = *Patmowtʿiwn žołovoç hayastaneayç ekełeçwoy,* Vałaršapat, 1874.

Patrum Nicaenorum nomina = *Patrum Nicaenorum nomina,* ed. H. GELZER, H. HILGENFELD et O. CUNTZ. Lipsiae, 1898.

PAYNE SMITH, *Thesaurus syriacus* = *Thesaurus syriacus,* ed. R. PAYNE SMITH, G. H. BERNSTEIN, G. W. LORSBACH aliique, I-II. Oxonii, 1879-1901.

PEETERS, *Date du martyre de Syméon* = PEETERS P., *La date du martyre de S. Syméon, archevêque de Séleucie-Ctésiphon,* AB LVI (1938), 118 ff.

PEETERS, *Légende de Jacques* = PEETERS, P., *La légende de S. Jacques de Nisibe,* AB XXXVIII (1920), 285 ff.

Pepysian Harmony = *The Pepysian Gospel Harmony,* ed. M. GOATES, EETS Orig. Ser. CLVII, London, 1922.

PETRUS SICULUS, *Historia Manichaeorum* = PETRUS SICULUS, *Historia Manichaeorum,* ed. J. P. MIGNE, PG CIV.

PG = *Patrologia graeca,* ed. J. P. MIGNE. Parisiis.

PHILO, *Opera* = *Philonis Alexandrini opera quae supersunt,* ed. L. COHN et P. WENDLAND, I-V. Berolini, 1886-1906.

PHILOSTORGIUS, *Hist. eccl.* = PHILOSTORGIUS, *Historia ecclesiastica,* ed. J. BIDEZ, GCS XXI. Leipzig, 1913.

PHILOXENOS, *Hérésies christologiques* = PHILOXENOS, *Les hérésies christologiques,* in *Documents pour servir à l'histoire de l'église nestorienne,* éd. F. NAU, PO XIII, 2. Paris, 1919.

PHOTIUS, *Bibliotheca* = PHOTIUS, *Myriobiblon sive Bibliotheca,* ed. J. P. MIGNE, PG CIII, CIV.

PHOTIUS, *Contra Manichaeos* = PHOTIUS, *Contra Manichaeos,* ed. J. P. MIGNE, PG CII.

Pistis sophia = *Pistis sophia,* ed. C. SCHMIDT. Kopenhagen, 1925.

PL = *Patrologia latina,* ed. J. P. MIGNE. Parisiis.

PLINIUS, *Historia naturalis* = *C. Plinii Secundi Naturalis historiae libri XXXVII,* ed. C. MAYHOFF, I-V. Lipsiae, 1892-1909.

PLOOIJ, *Enkratitische Glosse* = PLOOIJ, D., *Eine enkratitische Glosse im Diatessaron,* ZntW XXII (1923), 1 ff.

PO = *Patrologia orientalis.* Paris.

PONSCHAB, *Tatians Rede* = PONSCHAB, B., *Tatians Rede an die Griechen.* Metten, 1895.

PS = *Patrologia syriaca.* Parisiis.

Ps. Cl. de virginitate = *Clementis Romani epistolae binae de virginitate syriace,* ed. J. T. BEELEN. Lovanii, 1856.

Ps. Cl. de virginitate coptice = *De virginitate de S. Clément ou de S. Athanase?,* éd. L. TH. LEFORT, *Le Muséon* XL (1927).

PS. DIONYSIUS, *Chronicon* = *Chronicon anonymum Pseudo-Dionysianum vulgo dictum,* ed. I. B. CHABOT, CSCO Scr. syr. III, 1, Parisiis, 1927.

Ps.-Klement. Homilien = *Die Pseudoklementinen I, Homilien,* ed. B. REHM, GCS XLII. Berlin, 1953.

PS. HIERONYMUS, *Indiculus de haeresibus* = HIERONYMUS, *Indiculus de haeresibus,* in *Corpus haereseologicum,* ed. F. OEHLER, I-III. Berolini, 1851-61.

PREUSSER, *Baudenkmäler* = PREUSSER, L., *Nordmesopotamische Baudenkmäler altchristlicher und islamischer Zeit.* Leipzig, 1911.

PUECH, *Recherches* = PUECH, A., *Recherches sur le discours aux Grecs de Tatien.* Paris, 1903.

QRlg = *Quellen der Religionsgeschichte.* Göttingen und Leipzig.

QUASTEN, *Patrology* = QUASTEN, J., *Patrology,* I-II. Westminster, 1950-53.

Qumran Cave = *Qumran Cave I, Discoveries in the Judaean Desert,* by D. BARTHÉLEMY and J. T. MILIK. Oxford, 1955.

RAL = *Rendiconti della Reale Accademia nazionale dei Lincei.* Rome.

RAM = *Revue d'Ascétique et de Mystique.* Toulouse.

AR-Rāzī, *Livre de la conduite* = ABû BAKR MUHAMMAD B. ZAKARIYYÂ AR-Râzî, *Le livre de la conduite du philosophe,* éd. par P. KRAUS, *Orientalia* NS IV (1935), 329 ff.

RBén = *Revue bénédictine.* Maredsous.

RchSR = *Recherches de science religieuse.* Paris.

Recognitiones = *S. Clementis recognitiones,* ed. J. P. MIGNE, PG I.

Relations entre Abgar et Jésus = *Les relations entre Abgar et Jésus,* éd. S. GRÉBAUT, ROC XXI (1918-19), 75 ff.; 190 ff.; 253 ff.

Reliquiae sacrae = *Reliquiae sacrae,* ed. M. J. ROUTH, I-V. Oxonii, 1846-48.

RHLR = *Revue d'histoire et de littérature religieuses.* Paris.

RHR = *Revue de l'histoire des religions.* Paris.

Richter, *Auseinandersetzung der syr. Christen* = Richter, A., *Über die älteste Auseinandersetzung der syrischen Christen,* ZntW XXXV (1936), 101 ff.

ROC = *Revue de l'Orient chrétien.* Paris.

Rücker, *Zitate aus dem Matthäusevangelium* = Rücker, A., *Die Zitate aus dem Matthäusevangelium im syrischen «Buche der Stufen»,* BibZ XX (1932).

Rufinus, *Hist. eccl.* = Rufinus, *Historia ecclesiastica,* ed. T. Mommsen, in *Eusebius Werke* GCS IX. Leipzig, 1903-08.

Sachau, *Chronik von Arbela* = Sachau, E., *Die Chronik von Arbela. Ein Beitrag zur Kenntnis des ältesten Christentums im Orient,* AbhPAW. Berlin, 1915.

Sacr. conciliorum collectio = *Sacrorum conciliorum nova et amplissima collectio,* ed. J. D. Mansi, V-VI. Florentiae, 1761.

Šahrastānī, *Kitāb al-milal wa al-niḥal* = Šahrastānī, *Kitāb al-milal wa al-niḥal,* ed. W. Cureton, I-II. Leipzig, 1923.

Šāyast-nē-šāyast = *Šāyast-nē-šāyast. A Pahlavi Text on Religious Customs,* ed. J. C. Tavadia, ANIS III. Hamburg, 1930.

SBE = *Sacred Books of the East.* Oxford.

SbPAW = *Sitzungsberichte der Preussischen Akademie der Wissenschaften.* Berlin.

Schäfers, *Altsyrische antimark. Erklärung* = Schäfers, F., *Eine Altsyrische antimarkionitische Erklärung von Parabeln des Herrn und zwei andere altsyrische Abhandlungen zu Texten des Evangeliums,* NAbh VI, 1-2. Münster, 1917.

Schatzhöhle = *Schatzhöhle,* ed. C. Bezold. Leipzig, 1883.

Scher, *Étude supplémentaire* = Scher, A., *Étude supplémentaire sur les écrivains syriens orientaux,* ROC XI (1906), 1 ff.

Schiwietz, *Das morgenländische Mönchtum* = Schiwietz, S., *Das morgenländische Mönchtum,* III : *Das Mönchtum in Syrien und Mesopotamien und das Aszetentum in Persien.* Mödling, 1938.

Schmidt-Polotsky, *Mani-Fund* = Schmidt, C., und Polotsky, H. J., *Ein Mani-Fund in Agypten,* SbPAW. Berlin, 1933.

Schürer, *Geschichte des jüd. Volkes* = Schürer, E., *Geschichte des jüdischen Volkes im Zeitalter Jesu Christi,* I-III. Leipzig, 1901-11.

Schwen, *Afrahat* = Schwen, P., *Afrahat : seine Person und sein Verständnis des Christentums,* NSzGT II. Berlin, 1907.

Ṣelība, *Martyrologe* = *Le martyrologe de Rabban Sliba,* ed. P. Peeters, AB XXVII (1908), 139 ff.

Šem'on of Bet Aršam, *Epistula* = *Simeonis epistula de Barsauma episcopo*

Nisibeno, deque haeresi nestorianorum, ed. J. S. ASSEMANI, BO, I, 346 ff. Romae, 1719.

ŠEM'ON OF BET ARŠAM, *Sopra i martiri omeriti* = *La lettera di Simeone vescovo di Beth Aršam sopra i martiri omeriti,* ed. I. GUIDI, RAL. Roma, 1881.

SERAPION OF THMUIS, *Against the Manichees* = SERAPION OF THMUIS, *Against the Manichees,* ed. R. P. CASEY. Cambridge, 1931.

SeT = *Studi e Testi.* Città del Vaticano.

SEVERUS, *Homilia* CXXIII = SEVERUS, *Homilia* CXXIII, ed. M. A. KUGENER, in *Recherches sur le Manichéisme* II, Bruxelles, 1912.

SGV = *Sammlung gemeinverständlicher Vorträge und Schriften aus dem Gebiet der Theologie und Religionsgeschichte.* Tübingen.

Škand-gumānīk vičār, = *Škand-gumānīk vičār,* éd. et traduit par P. J. MANASCE, Fribourg, 1945.

SOCIN, *Zur Geographie* = SOCIN, A., *Zur Geographie des Ṭur 'Abdīn,* ZDMG XXXV (1881), 237 ff.

SOCRATES, *Hist. eccl.* = SOCRATES, *Historia ecclesiastica,* ed. J. P. MIGNE, PG LXVII.

Soghdische Texte = *Sogdische Texte II von F. W. K. Müller,* ed. W. LENTZ, SbPAW. Berlin, 1934.

Sources syriaques = *Sources syriaques,* ed. A. MINGANA. Leipzig, 1908.

SOZOMENUS, *Hist. eccl.* = SOZOMENUS, *Historia ecclesiastica,* ed. J. P. MIGNE, PG LXVII.

Spicilegium syriacum = *Spicilegium syriacum Containing Remains of Bardesan, Meliton, Ambrose and Mara Bar Serapion,* ed. W. CURETON. London, 1855.

SRerM = *Scriptores rerum Merovingicarum.*

SSin = *Studia sinaitica.* London.

STAEHLIN, *Altchristliche griech. Literatur* = STAEHLIN, O., *Die altchristliche griechische Literatur,* in W. VON CHRIST, *Geschichte der griechischen Literatur* II, 2. München, 1924.

STRZYGOWSKI, *L'ancien art chrétien* = STRZYGOWSKI, J., *L'ancien art chrétien de Syrie.* Paris, 1936.

Studia syriaca = *Studia syriaca,* ed. I. E. RAHMANI, I-IV. Scharfensi, 1904-09.

SUHRĀB, *Kitāb 'ağā'ib al-aqālīm* = SUHRĀB IBN SERĀFYŪN, *Kitāb 'ağā'ib al-aqālīm as-sab'a,* ed. H. VON MŽIK, BibAHG V. Leipzig, 1930.

Synaxaire arménien = *Le synaxaire arménien,* éd. G. BAYAN et MAX DE SAXE, PO V, 3; VI, 2; XV, 3; XVI, 1; XVIII, 1; XIX, 1; XXI, 1-6. Paris, 1910-1930.

Synaxarium Constantinop. = *Synaxarium Constantinopolitanum,* ed. H. DELEHAYE, Propylaeum ad AASS Nov. Bruxellis, 1902.

Synodicon orientale = *Synodicon orientale,* éd. I. B. Chabot, NEMBN XXXVII. Paris, 1902.

Syriac and Arabic Documents = *Syriac and Arabic Documents : Legislative Sources of Syrian Monasticism, edited, translated and furnished with literary historical data* by A. Vööbus, PapETSE XI. (under the press).

Tabari, *Ta'rikh ar-rusul* = Tabari, *Ta'rikh ar-rusul wa'l-mulūk,* ed. J. Barth, Th. Nöldeke, P. de Jong, I. Guidi, S. Guyard, M. J. Goeje, M. Th. Houtsma etc., I-XV. Lugduni Batavorum, 1879-1901.

Ṭaksā dekahnē = ܛܟܣܐ ܕܟܗܢܐ, Mossoul 1928.

Talmud = *Der babylonische Talmud,* ed. L. Goldschmidt. Leipzig, 1899-1935.

Tatian, *Oratio* = Tatianus, *Oratio adversus graecos,* ed. J.P. Migne, PG VI.

Tatiani evang. harmoniae arabice = *Tatiani evangeliorum harmoniae arabice,* ed. A. Ciasca. Romae, 1888.

Tertullianus, *Adv. Marcionem* = Tertullianus, *Adversus Marcionem,* ed. A. Kroyman, CSEL XLVII. Vindobonae, 1906.

Tertullianus, *Adv. Valentinianos* = Tertullianus, *Adversus Valentinianos,* ed. A. Kroyman, CSEL XLVII. Vindobonae, 1906.

Tertullianus, *De ieiunio* = Tertullianus, *De ieiunio adversus psychicos,* in *Tertulliani opera,* ed. A. Raifferscheid et G. Wissowa, CSEL XX. Vindobonae, 1890.

Tha'ālibī, *Histoire* = Tha'ālibī, *Histoire des rois des perses,* éd. H. Zotenberg. Paris, 1900.

Theodor Abu Qurra, *Traité inédit* = *Traité inédit de Théodore Abou-Qūrra,* ed. P. L. Cheikho. Beyrouth, 1912.

Theodor of Mopsvestia, *In ep. Pauli Commentarii* = Theodor of Mopsvestia, *In epistulas B. Pauli Commentarii,* ed. H. B. Swete, I-II. Cambridge, 1882.

Theodor of Mopsvestia, *On Baptism* = Theodor of Mopsvestia, *On Baptism,* ed. A. Mingana, WS VI. Cambridge, 1933.

Theodoretus, *Haeret. fab. compendium* = Theodoretus, *Haereticarum fabularum compendium,* ed. J. P. Migne, PG LXXXIII.

Theodoretus, *Hist. eccl.* = Theodoretus, *Historia ecclesiastica,* ed. L. Parmentier, GCS XIX. Berlin, 1954.

Theodoretus, *Hist. religiosa* = Theodoretus, *Historia religiosa,* ed. J. P. Migne, PG LXXXII.

Theodoros bar Koni, *Liber scholiorum* = Theodoros bar Koni, *Liber scholiorum,* ed. A. Scher, I-II, CSCO Scr. syr. II, 66. Parisiis, 1912.

Thesaurus armeniacus = *Nor bargirkh haykazean lèzowi,* ed. G. Awetikhean, H. Siwrmelean, J. B. Awgerean, I-II. Venetik, 1836-37.

Thomas of Marga, *Book of Governors* = Thomas of Marga, *The Book of*

Governors : the Historia monastica, ed. E. A. W. BUDGE, I-II. London, 1893.

TIMOTHEUS CONSTANTINOP., *De receptione haeretic.* = TIMOTHEUS CONSTANTINOPOLITANUS, *De iis qui ad ecclesiam accedunt, sive de receptione haereticorum*, ed. J. P. MIGNE, PG LXXXVI.

TITUS OF BOSTRA, *Contra manichaeos* = *Titi Bostreni contra manichaeos libri quatuor syriace*, ed. P. A. DE LAGARDE. Berolini, 1859.

TR = *Theologische Rundschau.* Tübingen.

Traité manichéen = *Traité manichéen retrouvé en Chine*, trad. par E. CHAVANNES et P. PELLIOT, JA X, XVIII (1911-12).

TaS = *Texts and Studies.* Cambridge.

Türkische Manichaica = *Türkische Manichaica aus Chotscho*, ed. A. VON LE COQ, AbhPAW. Berlin, 1911, 1919, 1922.

TuU = *Texte und Untersuchungen.* Leipzig.

TLZ = *Theologische Literaturzeitung.* Leipzig.

UAj = *Usuteaduslik Ajakiri.* Tartu.

Une curieuse homélie grecque = *Une curieuse homélie grecque inédite, sur la virginité adressée aux pères de famille*, ed. D. AMAND et M. C. MOONS, RBén LXVIII (1953), 35 ff.

VAN DER PLOEG, *Oud-syrisch monniksleven* = VAN DER PLOEG, J., *Oud-syrisch monniksleven.* Leiden, 1942.

Vark' ew vkayabanowt'iwnk' = *Vark' ew vkayabanowt'iwnk'* I-II. Venetik, 1874.

Vāsishtha = *Vâsishtha, The Sacred Laws of the Aryas*, translated by G. BÜHLER, SBE XIV. Oxford, 1892.

Versions grecques des actes = *Les versions grecques des actes des martyrs persanes*, éd. H. DELEHAYE, PO II, Paris, 1905.

Veterum mathem. opera = *Veterum mathematicorum opera*, ed. M. THEVENOT. Parisiis, 1693.

Videvdat = *Avesta*, übersetzt von F. WOLFF. Berlin-Leipzig, 1924.

Vie de Mar Benjamin = *La vie de Mar Benjamin*, ed. P. SCHEIL, ZfA XII (1897), 62 ff.

Vie géorgienne de Porphyre = *La vie géorgienne de S. Porphyre de Gaza*, éd. P. PEETERS, AB LXI (1941), 101 ff.

Vie des martyrs d'Orient = *Vie des saints martyrs d'Orient*, éd. A. SCHER, I-II. Mossoul, 1906.

VILLECOURT, *Date et l'origine des 'Homélies spirituelles'* = VILLECOURT, L., *La date et l'origine des 'Homélies spirituelles' attribuées a Macaire, Comptes rendus des séances a l'Académie des Inscriptions et Belles-Lettres*, 1920.

Vita Abercii = *Vita et conversatio S. P. N. Abercii episcopi Hierapolitani*, AASS Oct. IX, Parisiis et Romae, 1869.

Vita Theodori = Βίος καὶ πολιτεία, ed. J. Pomjalovsky. St. Petersburg, 1892.

Vita of Nino = *Vita of Nino*, ed. E. S. Thaqaishvili. Tiflis, 1891.

Vitae virorum celeb. = *Vitae virorum apud monophysitas celeberrimorum*, ed. E. W. Brooks, CSCO Ser. syr. III, 25. Parisiis, 1907.

VKAvW = *Verhandelingen der koninklijke Akademie van Wetenschappen*. Amsterdam.

Vööbus, *Askees* = Vööbus, A., *Askees juudakristlaste juures* (*Asceticism among the Jewish Christians*), UAj XIV (1939).

Vööbus, *Beiträge zur krit. Sichtung* = Vööbus, A., *Beiträge zur kritischen Sichtung der asketischen Schriften die unter dem Namen Ephraem der Syrers überliefert sind*, OC XXXIX (1955), 48 ff.

Vööbus, *Celibacy* = Vööbus, A., *Celibacy, A Requirement for Admission to Baptism in the Early Syrian Church*, PapETSE I. Stockholm, 1951.

Vööbus, *Early Versions* = Vööbus, A., *Early Versions of the New Testament. Manuscript Studies*. PapETSE VI. Stockholm, 1954.

Vööbus, *Einfluss des altpal. Targums* = Vööbus, A., *Der Einfluss des altpalästinischen Targums in der Textgeschichte der Peschitta des Alten Testaments*, *Le Muséon* (LXVII), 215 ff.

Vööbus, *Ein neuer Text von Ephraem* = Vööbus, A., *Ein neuer Text von Ephraem über das Mönchtum*, OC XL (1958).

Vööbus, *Evangelienzitate der Märtyrerakten*, = Vööbus, A., *Die Evangelienzitate der persischen Märtyrerakten*, *Biblica* XXXI (1951), 222 ff.

Vööbus, *Karitative Tätigkeit* = Vööbus, A., *Einiges über die karitative Tätigkeit des syrischen Mönchtums. Ein Beitrag zur Geschichte der Liebestätigkeit im Orient*, CBU LI. Pinneberg, 1947.

Vööbus, *Letter of Ephrem* = Vööbus, A., *A Letter of Ephrem to the Mountaineers*, CBU XXV. Pinneberg, 1947.

Vööbus, *Liber graduum* = Vööbus, A., *Liber graduum : Some Aspects of its Significance for the History of Early Syrian Asceticism*, in *Charisteria Johanni Köpp*, PapETSE VII. Holmiae, 1954.

Vööbus, *Literary Critical Studies* = Vööbus, A., *Literary Critical and Historical Studies in Ephrem of Edessa*, PapETSE X, Stockholm, 1958.

Vööbus, *Manichaeism and Christ. in Persia* = Vööbus, A., *Manichaeism and Christianity in Persia under the Sassanids : Some notes on Manichaean Eccelesiology and its Background*, YELSA I. New York, 1953.

Vööbus, *Merkwürdige Pentateuchzitate* = Vööbus, A., *Merkwürdige Pentateuchzitate in der Ps. Klementinischen Schrift De virginitate*, will be published in OC XLIII.

Vööbus, *Messaliens et les réformes de Barçauma* = Vööbus, A., *Les messaliens et les réformes de Barçauma de Nisibe dans l'église perse*, CBU XXXIV. Pinneberg, 1947.

VÖÖBUS, *Monachisme primitif réfléchi dans les écrits de Éphrem* = VÖÖBUS, A., *Monachisme primitif réfléchi dans les écrits de Éphrem le Syrien*, about to be published in *L'Orient syrien*. Paris.

VÖÖBUS, *Neue Angaben* = VÖÖBUS, A., *Neue Angaben über die textgeschichtlichen Zustände in Edessa in den Jahren ca 326-340*, PapETSE III. Stockholm, 1951

VÖÖBUS, *Origin of Monasticism* = VÖÖBUS, A., *Origin of Monasticism in Mesopotamia*, CH XX (1951), 27 ff.

VÖÖBUS, *Peschitta und Targumim* = VÖÖBUS, A., *Peschitta und Targumim des Pentateuchs. Neues Licht zur Frage der Herkunft der Peschitta aus den altpalästinischen Targumim. Handschriftenstudien*, PapETSE IX. Stockholm, 1957.

VÖÖBUS, *La première trad. arménienne* = VÖÖBUS, A., *La première traduction arménienne des Évangiles*, RchSR XXXVII (1950), 581 ff.

VÖÖBUS, *Researches* = VÖÖBUS, A., *Researches on the Circulation of the Peshitta in the Middle of the Fifth Century*, CBU LXIV. Pinneberg, 1948.

VÖÖBUS, *Significance of the Scrolls* = VÖÖBUS, A., *The Significance of the Dead Sea Scrolls for the History of Early Christianity*, YELSA II. New York, 1958.

VÖÖBUS, *Spuren eines ält. äthiop. Ev.-Textes* = VÖÖBUS, A., *Die Spuren eines älteren äthiopischen Evangelientextes im Lichte der literarischen Monumente*, PapETSE II. Stockholm, 1951.

VÖÖBUS, *Statutes* = VÖÖBUS, A., *Statutes of the School of Nisibis*, PapETSE XII. Stockholm, 1958.

VÖÖBUS, *Studien zu den persischen Ev.-Texten* = VÖÖBUS, A., *Studien zu den persischen Evangelientexten.* In manuscript. Will be published later.

VÖÖBUS, *Studies* = VÖÖBUS, A., *Studies in the History of the Gospel Text in Syriac*, CSCO CXXVIII. Louvain, 1951.

VÖÖBUS, *Syriac and Arabic Documents* = *Syriac and Arabic Documents : Legislative Sources of Syrian Monasticism, edited, translated and furnished with literary historical data, by* A. VÖÖBUS, PapETSE XI. (under the press).

VÖÖBUS, *Syrische Herkunft* = VÖÖBUS, A., *Syrische Herkunft der Pseudo-Basilianischen Homilie über die Jungfräulichkeit* OC XL (1956), 69 ff.

VÖÖBUS, *Untersuchungen* = VÖÖBUS, A., *Untersuchungen über die Authentizität einiger asketischer Texte, überliefert unter dem Namen 'Ephraem Syrus'*, CBU LXII. Pinneberg, 1947.

VÖÖBUS, *La vie syriaque de S. Aḥa* = VÖÖBUS, A., *Quelques observations sur la vie syriaque inédite de S. Aḥa*, PapETSE VIII. Stockholm, 1956.

VÖÖBUS, *Zur Geschichte altgeorg. Evangelientextes* = VÖÖBUS, A., *Zur Geschichte des altgeorgischen Evangelientextes,* PapETSE IV. Stockholm, 1953.

WADDINGTON, *Inscriptions* = WADDINGTON, W. H., *Inscriptions grecques et latines de la Syrie.* Paris, 1870.

WALDSCHMIDT-LENTZ, *Manichäische Dogmatik* = WALDSCHMIDT, E. und LENTZ, W., *Manichäische Dogmatik aus chinesischen und iranischen Texten.* SbPAW. Berlin, 1933.

WALDSCHMIDT-LENTZ, *Stellung Jesu im Manich.* = WALDSCHMIDT, E. und LENTZ, W., *Die Stellung Jesu im Manichäismus,* AbhPAW. Berlin, 1926.

WENSINCK, *Qejama* = WENSINCK, A. J., *Qejama und Benai Qejama,* ZDMG LXIII (1909), 561 ff.

WENSINCK, *Weiteres zu Qejama* = WENSINCK, A. J., *Weiteres zu Qejama und Benai Qejama,* ZDMG LXIV (1910), 812 ff.

WILMART, *Fausse lettre latine de Macaire* = WILMART, A., *La fausse lettre latine de Macaire,* RAM III (1922), 411 ff.

WILMART, *L'origine véritable des 'homélies pneumatiques'* = WILMART, A., *L'origine véritable des 'homélies pneumatiques',* RAM I (1920), 361 ff.

WRIGHT, *Syriac Literature* = WRIGHT, W., *Short History of Syriac Literature.* London, 1894.

WS = *Woodbrooke Studies,* Cambridge.

YAQUT, *Muʿjam al-buldān* = YAQUT, *Muʿjam al-buldān,* ed. F. WÜSTENFELD, I-XI. Leipzig, 1866-73.

YASNA = *Pahlavi Texts,* tr. by E. W. WEST, SBE V. Oxford, 1881.

YELSA = *Yearbook of the Estonian Learned Society in America.* New York.

YOVHAN, *Patmowtʿiwn* = *Patmowtʿiwn Yovhannow katʿołikosi.* Jerusalem, 1867.

YOVHAN MANDAKOWNI, *Čarkʿ* = YOVHAN MANDAKOWNI, *Čarkʿ.* Venetik, 1860.

ZAHN, *Tatians Diatessaron* = ZAHN, T., *Tatians Diatessaron,* FzGNK I. Erlangen, 1881.

ZDMG = *Zeitschrift für die Deutsche Morgenländische Gesellschaft.* Halle.

ZfA = *Zeitschrift für Assyrologie.* Weimar.

ZfKg = *Zeitschrift für Kirchengeschichte.* Stuttgart.

ZfS = *Zeitschrift für Semitistik und verwandte Gebiete.* Leipzig.

ZntW = *Zeitschrift für die neutestamentliche Wissenschaft.* Giessen-Berlin.

DE ZWAAN, *Edessene Origins* = ZWAAN, J. DE, *The Edessene Origins of the Odes of Solomon,* in *Quantulacunque, Studies Presented to K. Lake.* London, 1937.

PART I

THE EARLIEST ASCETICISM AND MONASTICISM

CHAPTER I

THE GENESIS OF ASCETICISM AMONG THE SYRIANS

1. THE ORIGIN OF SYRIAN CHRISTENDOM

The sources have been reluctant in lifting the veil that covers the beginnings of Christianity in the lands of the Euphrates and Tigris. Only very slowly have they allowed us a glimpse of this expression of Christianity. Much of these beginnings is left in impenetrable darkness. Regrettably little information about the earliest period has survived, and even among this information not all is reliable.

First we have to discard traditions which give an entirely wrong impression of the beginnings of Christianity in Mesopotamia, because these indicate that the process of the early expansion of Christendom developed in the general framework of Hellenistic Christendom. We are told that Palūṭ was consecrated as bishop of Edessa by Bishop Serapion of Antioch (189-209) [1]. The information that Antioch became a part of the scene so early is a free fabrication. Obviously this information was invented to add more importance to this shadowy figure, who in his struggle for the orthodox group needed support desperately.

Other similarly misleading information which places the development in Mesopotamia in the context of the life-situation in Hellenistic Christianity, appears in Eusebius. In connection with the Passover controversy at the time of Bishop Victor (189-99), Eusebius refers to the ecclesiastically organized synods in several countries which included those held in Osrhoene and in the towns there [2]. But this account is also a fiction since mention of this does not

[1] *Doctrina Addaei*, p. 52.

[2] *Hist. eccl.*, V, 23, 4, p. 490.

appear in Rufinus' Latin translation [3]. The text used by Rufinus for his translation did not yet include this accretion.

Valuable information which places the whole picture in a realistic light comes from the end of the second century in Edessa. According to this report the orthodox group of Christians at that time could finally order their rows so far as appointing a bishop was concerned [4]. This one appeared in the person of Palūṭ [5]. But our critical judgment of this situation must be influenced by the report of Ephrem who describes the situation in Edessa without any embellishment. The way he curses the heretics clearly reveals the humiliating situation that was current. The heterodox groups had usurped such power that they even took the name 'Christians', so that the orthodox believers had to be contented with being called 'Palutians' [6]. This situation means that there already was a Christianity of older traditions in Edessa, as certainly was true elsewhere, that drew upon sources other than those which were drawn upon by those who rallied around Palūṭ.

But what was this earliest form of Christianity in Mesopotamia? Can we penetrate farther back?

Fortunately we have some chronological and historical data which help us to work our way to a still earlier phase. The first data come from the district beyond the Tigris, and are preserved in the Chronicle of Arbēl, a document which claims that the earliest part of the tradition it contains rests upon the testimony of a certain teacher Abel who was well informed about the earliest history of Ḥadiab.

In the critical estimation of this source every extravagant claim regarding its value would have surprised the author himself, who has not used some sources which we know today [7]. Nevertheless its

3 *Hist. eccl.*, p. 491.

4 The claim that the organized church under an orthodox bishop existed in Edessa already in the third quarter of the second century, *Biographie inédite de Bardẹsane*, p. 6, is simply a fabrication.

5 *Doctrina Addaei*, p. 52.

6 *Contra haereses*, XXII, 6, p. 80.

7 It is surprising that even such documents as the Acts of ʿAqebšmā, which belonged to the early collection of these sources, see pag. 211, have not been used. This is the more strange since these acts were a product of the tradition of Arbēl and its province.

major assumptions in their gist may root in historical tradition. If this document merits our trust then the beginnings of Christianity unfold themselves in the following way. This document speaks of Mār Addai who converted Mār Peqīdā. Although his parents opposed his conversion violently, Peqīdā followed Addai[8]. Later the same Mār Peqīdā became the first bishop of Ḥadiab.

If the chronology of our document can be trusted at all, the years of his episcopacy can be approximately determined. It is said that Peqīdā's successor Šemšōn became the first martyr of the church in Ḥadiab. This crowned his missionary harvest in the villages in Arbēl's surroundings. We may believe that this important event in the life of the new church was indelibly impressed upon its memory. It happened seven years after the victory of Trajan over Khosrov[9]. This event took place in the year 116 A.D. Consequently, in the year 123 the church in Ḥadiab lost its leader.

It is therefore easy to go further back. The chronicle says that Šemšōn could rule no longer than two years. Thus in the year 121 the bishop of Bēt Zabdai, Māzrā, came with a caravan of merchants to Ḥadiab and heard of the presence of a Christian community there. We are told that he so won their confidence that they permitted him to enter their assembly. They told him that they had been six years without a leader and asked him to consecrate Deacon Šemšōn, a co-worker of the late Peqīdā, as bishop. Thus, we reach the end of Peqīdā's episcopacy in ca 115 A.D. The chronicle says that he ruled for ten years; therefore, he must have started his rule in ca 105.

Thus in the light of this document the Christian faith, appearing in Ḥadiab around the year 100, must have proved to have been successful. In the same report we read that the Christian faith spread not only in Arbēl, but also in the villages on the mountains[10].

The above information in the Chronicle of Arbēl helps us to fill the gap in our information concerning the oldest period in Edessa, too. If, by the beginning of the second century the Christian faith had already won converts among the inhabitants of the mountain

8 *Sources syriaques*, p. 3.
9 *Ibid.*, p. 5.
10 *Ibid.*, p. 3.

villages in Ḥadiab, then there can be no doubt that the Christian faith had been established before the end of the first century in Edessa and also in Osrhoene, which were on the highway connecting Arbēl with Palestine and Syria.

We cannot travel beyond the point we have reached within the limits of the evidence available. But besides this information that we have about the chronological side of the problem, other data permit us to recognize that the origin of the Christian message in Mesopotamia must have been related to Aramaean Christianity in Palestine.

This appears quite natural, when we consider the fact that in other Eastern countries the Jewish community appears to be the channel through which the first seed of the Christian Kerygma was transplanted, even in countries where the Jewish community was not particularly strong. For instance, some hints have been preserved in the Georgian tradition, regarding the coming of Christendom [11]. These hints can be interpreted to mean that the Jewish synagogue could have been the medium for the earliest appearance of the Christian message. This is all the more natural in the Aramaean Orient where there were far stronger Jewish communities than in Georgia.

But we are not left with mere guesses. Concerning the beginnings of the Christian communities in Edessa we can learn something from a document known as the *Doctrina Addaei*. In using this expansion of the legend of Abgar, the greatest caution is necessary. But some elements may still be considered as recollections that survived in certain data which may constitute the historical core of the document. It is narrated here that when Addai came to Edessa he contacted a certain Tobia and stayed in his home. This Tobia, regarding whom the narrative in Eusebius leaves us to guess his origin [12], appears in this tradition as a member of a Jewish family which was of Palestine. Thus, Addai contacted the Jewish community in Edessa and established the first Christian nucleus there [13]. This indicates the first contact of the Christian message

11 *Vita of Nino,* p. 14 ff.

12 *Hist. eccl.,* I, 13, 11.13, p. 90.

13 *Doctrina Addaei,* p. 5 f.

with the Edessene population. Thus, a Palestinian emissary starts the work in Edessa and connects the new movement with the traditions of Palestinian Aramaean Christianity.

Nothing prohibits us from assuming that what happened in Edessa occurred elsewhere. Moreover, it would be strange if the development in Edessa would have been an isolated phenomenon. In fact, some hints are preserved which indicate a similar procedure in Ḥadiab. Concerning the beginnings of Christianity there similar conditions are spoken of by Abel, the teacher, in his information about the earliest days of the church in this territory. Mār Addai, as we have already seen, laid the foundation also in Ḥadiab. The chronicle says about Noah, who became bishop of Ḥadiab ca 150, that his parents were Jews of Babylonia and lived in Jerusalem. Noah was converted to the Christian faith and after returning, the family settled in Arbēl, 'because there were many Jews there' [14]. It is also remarkable that the earliest bishops of Arbēl bear Jewish names : Isḥaq, Abraham, Noah, Abel. Only later do we find Syrian names [15]. All this is said only *inter alia*. Abel does not tell us anything directly about the possible role of the Jewish synagogue in the Diaspora.

Even if we do not entirely trust this source [16], nevertheless only hypercriticism would overthrow these traditions which leave the impression that the earliest phase in the growth and development of the Christian mission here was of Jewish Christian provenance. The earliest figures of primitive Christianity in this mountainous area, however dimly they appear, were Christian Jews who held close to the areas where there were Jewish communities. This is what the tradition embedded in this chronicle says in its simple and unmistakable manner and this we do not dare reject.

This is not all that can be said on the question of Christian origins in the Syrian Orient. Besides these scanty direct references of historical nature preserved in the literary tradition, there is enough, if we pay it the attention it deserves, to lead us to the same conclusion by other paths namely, that the origins of Chris-

14 *Sources syriaques*, p. 13.

15 *Ibid*, p. 6 f., 13.

16 See also criticism raised by ORTIZ DE URBINA, *Intorno al valore*, p. 5 ff.

tianity in the lands of the Euphrates and Tigris must have been of Palestinian Aramaic provenance.

Certain interesting facts speak loudly enough. For they open several avenues leading us behind this phase of the development of Christianity which is beginning to show itself in the light of history. Particularly telling are the observations made possible by an investigation into the genesis of the Old Testament in Syrian Christianity. For neither the Greek Old Testament, which became the scriptural authority for Hellenistic Christianity, nor the Hebrew original text was translated into Syriac. But the Scriptures of the Palestinian synagogue, no longer understood in the Hebrew idiom, were adopted according to the Aramaic version of the sacred books. These were the ancient Palestinian Targumim which were furnished with exegetical and homiletical accretions. Now the astonishing fact is this, that just these books cast in the Western Aramaic tongue were rephrased and transliterated into the East Aramaic idiom, i.e. into Syriac [17]. The very fact that this is the foundation of the Scriptures in the primitive Syrian church is sententious. New finds regarding this ancient stratum in the text, which was erased by the successive revision of later centuries [18], throw additional important light upon the questions under study.

Further it is hardly less rewarding to investigate the exegetical traditions of early Syrian Christianity. In this respect the Syriac literature provides us with valuable material. From these we learn that the traditions of interpretation reflected in the earliest authors bear an outspoken Jewish mark [19]. This is another clue which points to the close relation between the synagogical traditions and the ancient church in the Syrian Orient.

Finally also another domain should not be overlooked, that of the discoveries in the area of ancient Christian art, its design and motifs as this manifests itself in the residuum which has survived the vicissitudes of centuries. Here one observes something of the contours which seem to be of a Jewish impress [20]. This seems to point

17 Vööbus, *Einfluss des altpaläst. Targums*, p. 215 ff.

18 Vööbus, *Peschitta und Targumim*, p. 30 ff.

19 Funk, *Haggadische Elemente*, p. 24 ff.

20 Needless to say in this area we cannot expect more than dim outlines.

to the part which the artistic heritage of the synagogue once had played in the origin af the archaic Syrian-Christian art.

Thus far, a review of the significant facts has unfolded a number of coordinates in the ancient development, which were so decisive before that time when the Syrians took this development into their own hands and ably continued to re-mould the traditions. However successful the Syrians were in this an ancient under-layer shines through betraying the real nature of the Christian beginnings in the lands of the Euphrates and Tigris.

Thus, in the twilight of Christian history in the lands of the Euphrates and Tigris, we perceive something peculiar to the genesis of the Christian movement. The historical eye can see little, but that which we can see commends itself as trustworthy by its naturalness. It is natural that the pioneer work in the expansion of the Christian faith in these Semitic areas was carried out not by Greek-speaking Hellenistic Christianity but by Aramaic-speaking Christians who possessed the *lingua franca* of the contemporary Orient. It is, indeed, also natural that the Aramaean Christian traditions spread along the ancient high-way which connected Palestine over Edessa with Ḥadiab in the Empire of the Arsacides. Finally that which we see in this twilight about the transition of the Christian message from the Aramaean Jewish community to the native Syrian communities is also quite natural. The more so since this process seems to have appeared in countries with unimportant Jewish settlements. Conversely, the far more important Jewish communities in Mesopotamia must have performed a far more significant function in the process of initiating the Christian faith into the Syrian Orient. It is a corollary that, in Mesopotamia, the circles of the God-fearers, analogous to those in the sister-synagogues in the Hellenistic world must have played a considerable role in transmitting the primitive Kerygma to the indigenous Syrian scene. The expansion of the Christian movement westward, which early established its headquarters at Antioch on the Orontes, the near Eastern metropolis of Hellenistic culture, and which started a vigorous missionary campaign in the Hellenistic world throughout Asia Minor, Macedonia and Greece — insofar as its main trends and views are concerned — stands revealed in the light of history. Indeed its victorious spread and large scale success has left unmistakable vestiges in the earliest Christian literature. But the story of this grandiose campaign within the orbit of the Greek tongue has obscured another movement which emanated from the Palestinian Aramaean Christian communities in the opposite direction. For emissaries from the small Aramaic-speaking communities quietly carried the message of the good news towards the Orient where their kinsmen in the Jewish communities, and their Semitic relatives in the Syrian Orient, lived. But this phase of the expansion was not as glamorous and did not leave behind such telling vestiges.

2. THE CHARACTER OF THE PRIMITIVE SYRIAN CHRISTIANITY

Now we have to move on to the next question. This is the question regarding the character of the primitive Christianity in the Syrian Orient.

When we look into our sources in search of possible clues, we must be contented only with some hints. When we keep in mind the extreme scarcity of sources, we hardly dare to expect more. But it is of interest to observe that these clues unexpectedly come from more than one area of tradition. It is time to listen to them.

There is only one document which claims to know anything about the character of the most primitive Christianity in Edessa, namely the *Doctrina Addaei*. We are told here that when Addai came to Edessa, he started successful missionary work among the Jews and then among the Gentiles. That Jews were also a part of this enterprise is mentioned in several places. This document leaves no doubt that this Christianity was ascetically oriented. Repeatedly it is said that poverty was observed. When Addai rejects the gifts from Abgar, he says that in his life he has not received anything from him. Addai acts strictly according to the demand of Jesus that the Christian should possess nothing in this world [21].

Particularly interesting is the remark about virginity which was introduced into the new congregation. This practice is described in the following words : 'but all the *qeiāmā* of men and women was abstinent and glorious, and they were holy and pure and dwelt

21 *Doctrina Addaei*, p. 8; see also p. 48, 50.

singly and abstinently without defilement, in watchfulness of the service gloriously' [22].

Is there something here which in substance can go back to the recollections of the actual situation? Or is this picture taken from the conditions in the Mesopotamian church in later times and projected back into the earliest period? Who has the courage to decide this? The odds are not greater for the second possibility than for the first one. The legendary fabrication could well have used some earlier sources and in this way it may have preserved a historical kernel regarding the ascetic character of the most primitive form of Syrian Christianity.

This, however, is not the only consideration. Another consideration awaits mention. This is in connection with the conversion of Tatian, a Syrian, and his important work on the gospel harmony he produced.

Tatian was converted to Christianity when he was in the West. Then gradually he adopted a rigorous form of Christian life that was radically ascetic [23]. It may be that this was the type of Christianity that existed already among Syrians. When one reads his bitter and exaggerated arguments against anything in the Hellenistic world, and his candid statements about his penchant for everything 'barbarian' or Oriental [24], one might reasonably ask whether as to Christian convictions, Tatian himself looked towards the Orient as a more reliable source of tradition. This would be a very natural thing to expect. In this case the nature of Christianity among his country-men provided the context in which Tatian interpreted the meaning of the Christian faith.

An even further indication comes from the way Tatian arranged

22 ܥܡܐ ܕܝܢ ܟܠܗ ܕܓܒܪ̈ܐ ܘܢܫ̈ܐ. ܢܟܦܝܢ ܗܘܘ ܘܩܕܝܫܝܢ. ܘܡܬܢܟܦܝܢ ܗܘܘ ܘܕܟܝܢ ܘܡܚܣܢܐܝܬ ܘܢܟܦܐܝܬ ܚܝܝܢ ܗܘܘ ܕܠܐ ܛܘܠܫܐ. ܒܫܗܪܘܬܐ ܕܬܫܡܫܬܐ ܫܘܒܚܐܝܬ, *ibid.*, p. 50. In the letter of Abgar the substance of the Christian message is summarized in a remarkable way : ተደንገሉ ፡ ዘማውያን ፡ በትምህርቱ ፡ ... ጻድቃን ፡ ኮኑ ፡ ኃጥኣን ። ቅዱሳን ፡ ኮኑ ፡ ርኩሳን ። 'through his teaching the licentious began to live as a virgin... the sinners became righteous ones and the impure became saints', *Relations entre Abgar et Jésus*, p. 75.

23 See pag. 34 ff.

24 *Oratio*, col. 868.

his harmonistic work, written probably in Syriac [25]. In this case the purpose was practical in order to furnish the Syrian communities with the sacred text. As we shall see, Tatian wove ascetic elements into the text. Could he have done this if the Christian development among the Syrians had taken a different course? Rather, would it not be probable that he kept his eye on the needs of Syrian Christians? The extracanonical traditions, borrowed from the Aramaic Gospel according to the Hebrews, which Tatian wove into his gospel harmony [26] seem to speak in favor of this suggestion. Thus, these considerations seem to give certain plausibility to the assumption that ascetically colored Christianity appeared in Syria and Mesopotamia as early as the mission which entered these territories through Palestinian Aramaean Christian channels. There are still some other ways which must be employed in our attempts to penetrate to the character of the primitive Christianity. These ways, to be sure, do not lead us directly to the earliest layer in the tradition, but in any case closer to the neighborhood of it. We have to work with the premise which is safe, namely that the traditions which we have in ancient sources, like the Odes of Solomon [27] and the treatises of Aphrahaṭ [28], are older than the age of these documents which have preserved them. In the picture which these documents manifest loom the contours of more primitive Christianity. Therefore it is necessary to anticipate here very briefly some of the results of studies which will be presented later.

These contours that loom disclose very peculiar features. We are first impressed with the covenant-consciousness in the primitive Syrian Christianity [29]. The Christian faith is perceived as a new covenant, and this is the decisive factor determining all others in the understanding of the new religion, even to the shaping of its implications. The covenant (*qeiāmā*) assumes the structural position of moulding all its theology, ethics and organization. This *qeiāmā*, which also means 'oath', 'a solemn promise', characterizes the believers even insofar as their name is concerned. These Christans are

25 Vööbus, *Early Versions*, p. 5 f.

26 *Ibid.*, p. 20 f. against Baumstark's theory.

27 Pag. 62 ff.

28 Pag. 173 ff.

29 Pag. 97 ff.

benai qeiāmā and *benat qeiāmā,* translated 'the sons of the covenant' and 'daughters of the covenant', actually in the Semitic simply 'covenanters'. Further, men and women in this new relationship into which the *qeiāmā* has placed them, are called to struggle not only against evil but also against the physical-natural conditions of the world [30]. Thus the covenant-consciousness expresses its content with a negative estimate of this world, and practically, by correlation, it results in asceticism. Possessions, marriage as well as any link with this world, are sacrificed for the sake of this new *qeiāmā* which God has established with His elect.

Such an estimate of Christian life is best reflected in the military terminology they employed. The terms adequate for their theology and practice were : 'struggle', 'fight', 'battle' and 'war'. This gives a taste of the military thought world in which these warriors of God lived. The important thing to notice is that these requirements were not reserved only to the consecrated heroes of the religious life, i.e. for the elite among the ordinary believers, but were made normative for the ordinary members of the ancient Syrian church. Only those who were ready for this radical manner of living were worthy of the sacramental life, and they alone could become *benai qeiāmā* and *benat qeiāmā,* i.e. the covenanters, as the full members of the church.

Further, there are the provoking possibilities created by the accession of the splinters from the earliest liturgy of baptism [31]. These precious remnants must be regarded as ancient strata which have been preserved as fossils in traditions of later formation. A safe guide like this is highly welcome on our excursion on a terrain with only very few landmarks.

These portions concern only the last episode in the procedure before the act of baptism, which the candidates had to undergo. But even this limited segment is very revealing. We are allowed to see what the covenant really meant — commitment for life in asceticism. We also are permitted to see how seriously these Christians took their vow. In repeated appeals, the candidates, for the status of the *qeiāmā* were exhorted to search their hearts as to whether

30 Pag. 69 ff.
31 Pag. 93 ff.

they had the strength to leave possessions behind, to renounce marriage for ever, and to accept the ascetic life. The candidates are even urged to go back if they are not ready for these consequences. Here in the light of these pieces of the baptismal liturgy the covenant conception in the context of asceticism is related to the idea of the sacred militia which determines the entire thought-world. The Covenanters are the fighters in the army of God. The ethos that stems from this is understood in terms of warfare. As the function of the priests is conceived so that this is to blow their trumpets signalling the engagement in battle with the enemy [32], so that of the fighters is to be in the harness to fight bravely in the heat of the battle in the army of God.

What we are able to see in the sources is not much. Nevertheless those observations which can be made are sufficient for the recognition that the primitive Christianity in the Syrian Orient was not of the ordinary shape as we know it in the development in the Hellenistic realm. In fact, asceticism has stood at its cradle. This factor in turn has impressed very peculiar features into its spiritual face.

3. THE PROBLEM AND AN ATTEMPT FOR SOLUTION

Now we come to the historical problem so impatiently awaiting explanation. This concerns the character of primitive Syrian Christianity, founded and built upon the Jewish Christian foundations. While many facets of ancient Syrian Christianity can be traced back to Jewish Christian origin, yet in the factor of asceticism, however, we encounter a phenomenon so astonishing that it seems to be entirely ouside of the Jewish mould which stands at the beginning of the development.

This phenomenon, the characteristic features of which we have briefly delineated, is highly strange and enigmatic. In fact, it puzzles the student of history. At the first glance such a physiognomy of primitive Syrian Christianity seems flatly to contradict everything we know of its Jewish Christian origins, since Judaism was not interested in asceticism.

Fortunately we are not left only to guesses, but we do have some

32 *Demonstrationes*, VII, col. 341.

evidence. To be sure the sort of literature which would have given us the desired information has perished along with its bearers, for who should have taken care of it? But one is grateful that these traces have not all perished like footprints in sand. Even the little we can gather from fragments, testifies to the existence of an ascetically orientated movement in Aramaean Christianity in Palestine.

When we put together what can be joined, we have the following picture.

An impressive array of witnesses emerges pointing to the role of abstinence in the lives of these Christians. This was so strong that in the climate of these convictions the portrait of the great biblical heroes was remoulded. Thus, these figures, John the Baptist [33], Peter [34], James [35] or Jesus Himself [36] became the paradigms of their observances.

In the light of these sources it also becomes understandable how the ascetic factor could permeate certain circles so intensely. Among the practices exercised by pious men in Judaism for the purpose of accelerating the coming of the Kingdom, abstinence with vows was an important means. Certainly the meaning of the older practices could be heightened among the Christian Nazirs [37]. In the

33 He does not use locusts, but oil-cakes, as this is laid down in their own gospel, EPIPHANIUS, *Panarion*, XXX, 13, v. I, p. 350.

34 Peter is depicted in the Pseudo-Clementine literature as a vegetarian who ate only bread and olives, *Ps.-Klementinische Homilien*, XII, 6, p. 176 f.; *Recognitiones*, col. 1357 f.

'Ich nährte mich von Rohr und Wurzeln und Holzspänen', JOSEPHUS, *Slavonic Bell. jud.*, p. 10. 'Grass and wild honey', *Life of John the Baptist*, p. 270.

35 He is depicted as a man who among other ascetic practices made a vow not to eat bread, HIERONYMUS, *De viris inlustribus*, p. 7 f. In Hegesippus, EUSEBIUS, *Hist. eccl.*, II, 23, 5, p. 166, James appears as the ideal of abstinence.

36 He appears as a confirmed vegetarian : *ἐποίησαν τοὺς μαθητὰς μὲν λέγοντες· ποῦ θέλεις ἑτοιμάσωμέν σοι τὸ πάσχα φαγεῖν, καὶ αὐτὸν δῆθεν λέγοντα· μὴ ἐπιθυμίᾳ ἐπεθύμεσα κρέας τοῦτο τὸ πάσχα φαγεῖν μεθ' ὑμῶν*, EPIPHANIUS, *Panarion*, XXX, 22, 4, v. I, p. 363. The Aramaic coloring of this piece is unmistakable. In the *Recognitiones*, I, 40, col. 1230 in Mt, XI, 19 'behold a glutton and a wine-bibber', the last word has been cut off since these Christians felt that it was entirely unthinkable.

37 A logion among the papyri found in Oxyrhynchus, 'if you do not fast (with regard to) the world, you will not find the Kingdom', is a good illus-

Pseudo-Clementine homilies Peter recommends fasting in such a way that we recognize the influence of a dualistic tension. Peter sees in fasting regarding things of the world an abdication of this possessions mean sin [39].

However few are the fragments of Aramaean Christian literature, they suffice to show that the observance of poverty belonged to their ascetic principles. In contrast with the contemporary Jewish views they felt a Christian should not possess anything because possession mean sin [39].

We also have traces, sporadic yet significant, of the fact that virginity was practiced in these circles. First of all, we mention a document which circulated among the ascetically minded Jewish Christians. This document was a letter ascribed to James of Jerusalem and was addressed to the virgins [40]. This important document permits us to see how James' authority had been used in the interest of the virtue of virginity.

Further, the patristic authors had at their disposal more data concerning the ideal of virginity among these Jewish Christian circles [41]. For instance on the basis of the sources available to him, Epiphanius concluded that a certain group of the Jewish Christians originally must have adopted the practice of virginity and sexual abstinence, but owing to later developments they had abandoned this practice and gradually had taken a negative attitude towards virginity [42]. Other data are of unknown origin [43].

What we have gathered from the scanty remains of the Jewish Christian sources is of such a character that it leaves the impression that the existence of an ascetic stream among other streams in the

tration : *ἐὰν μὴ νηστεύσηται τὸν κόσμον οὐ μὴ εὕρηται τὴν βασιλείαν*, *Oxyrhynchus Papyri*, I, p. 3.

38 *ὅθεν πρὸς τὴν τῶν δαιμόνων φυγὴν ἡ ἔνδεια καὶ ἡ νηστεία καὶ ἡ κακουχία οἰκειότατόν ἐστιν βοήθημα*, *Ps.-Klementinische Homilien*, IX, 10, p. 135.

39 *Ibid.*, XV, 5-11, p. 213 ff. Those who belong to the eternal world must abandon their possessions and everything in this world, *ibid.*, IX, 10, p. 135.

40 *ποτὲ γὰρ παρθενίαν ἐσεμνύνοντο, δῆθεν διὰ τὸν Ἰάκωβον τὸν ἀδελφὸν τοῦ κυρίου, καὶ τὰ αὐτῶν συγγράμματα πρεσβυτέροις καὶ παρθένοις γράφουσι*, EPIPHANIUS, *Panarion*, XXX, 2, 6, v. I, p. 335.

41 *Ibid.*

42 *Ibid.*, p. 334 f.

43 *Miscell. Coptic Texts*, p. 637.

primitive Christianity must be considered as established. It must be remembered that what we possess of the Aramaean Christian literature is very fragmentary. But it should be pointed out that nevertheless this scanty information radiates a strong and radical atmosphere which seems to have existed in different shades. Some suspicions pointing to the fact that the stream of asceticism must have played a greater role in the Aramaean Christendom in Palestine than was formerly thought [44], finds indirect support also by the new discoveries in the Dead Sea materials.

This would mean that the New Testament sources do not give us a full picture of the character of Aramaean Christianity in Palestine as the source of the first stimuli. But this we should have not expected from the New Testament writings, since their purpose was other than that of informing us about all the shades of primitive Christian movements in Palestine.

In such a situation it is imperative to look into the Jewish sources on the lookout for additional light.

This question becomes more urgent because of the information that has come into our possession now in unearthed scrolls and fragments concerning the infiltration of the ascetic trends in Judaism. Discoveries of these invaluable documents which began to flow in breathtaking speed into the treasuries of an astounded world, have opened new avenues also for our subject.

Abstinence from meat and wine was not new in Judaism. Since ancient times it was practiced by the pious men in the Nazirate. Ascetic movements put new life into these older observances [45].

The ideal of poverty — never understood in Judaism and bitterly criticized in the Talmud — exercised a great influence upon these groups that used various ways and means for its realization. Some settled this matter in a radical way, leaving everything that they

44 Vööbus, *Askees juudakristlaste juures*, p. 80 ff.

45 While some were more lenient and permitted fish and locusts, others adopted strictly vegetarian habits. Josephus tells of a rough ascetic, Banus, whom he had admired and once wanted to become his disciple. He followed a rigorous practice, living as a vegetarian, using only products which nature provided, *Vita*, II, p. 322 f. We also have a document from a group of severe spirit, who used only bread and juice, *Manual of Discipline*, VI, 5.6.

had [46]. Others, like the Essenes [47], settled this question by living in poverty but by surrendering their possesssions to the ascetic community which they entered [48].

Regarding the general ascetic spirit which filled all the facets of life, the Manual of Discipline, in describing the mood that lived in the community behind it, says that the ascetics practiced truth, unity, humility, justice and love, and adds : 'and asceticism in all the ways in which they walk' [49]. The latter reference conceals many other customs and habits which the ascetic mood created. Some need to be touched on briefly.

46 Josephus tells of the hermit Banus that he had abandoned everything and lived in the wilderness, *Vita,* II, p. 323.

47 It must not be forgotten that this term refers to a large stream of ascetic movements of different shades. It is obvious that Josephus has thrown together several cognate groups that are not identical and understood them as the third 'sect' in Judaism, over against other streams, *Antiquitates,* XIII, 5, 9, v. III, p. 182. His treatment of Judaism under the scheme of three 'sects' is certainly inadequate. The data regarding the various streams in Judaism, preserved in the patristic literature, show that the picture actually was far more complicated than Josephus' presentation. See particularly JUSTINUS MARTYR, *Dialogus,* p. 192; Hegesippus in EUSEBIUS, *Hist. eccl.,* IV, 22, 5-6, p. 370; *Constitutiones apostol.,* VI, 6, v. I, p. 313 f.; EPIPHANIUS, *Panarion,* I, XVIII, XIX, XXX LIII, v. I, p. 172 ff.; 215 ff.; 217 ff.; 333 ff.; II, 314 ff.; PS. HIERONYMUS, *Indiculus de haeresibus,* p. 283 f. Also the remarks in the Rabbinical sources confirm this impression. R. Johannan of whom we know that he had historical interests, speaks of a great number of streams in Judaism, Jer. Synh., X, 29 c, 57. This oversimplification of issues which we detect in Josephus makes one suspicious that he has given the Essenes the same treatment. This finds confirmation by his own presentation showing divergent views and practices among the Essenes.

48 Concerning the Essenes we are told that they hated riches and held a common treasury, JOSEPHUS, *De bello judaico,* II, 8, 3, v. VI, p. 177; PHILO, *Opera,* VI, p. 24. They used this common fund only for their most necessary needs that were estimated according to ascetic standards. They ate the most scanty meals an Oriental can eat. And they did not change their garments and shoes until they became rags. Regarding this discipline we possess an original document which gives a good insight into the observances held in the ascetic order which stands behind it. In this we see how everything had to be handed over to the community treasurer, *Manual of Discipline,* I, 12; V, 12. A technical term for this was עבר את הונו 'to mix his property'.

49 והצנע לכת בכול דרכיהם אשר לוא ילך, *ibid.,* V, 4.

The ascetic ethos manifested itself also in fasting [50] and in the reduction of sleeping time in order to study the Scriptures and meditate at the expense of nightly rest. We hear that there were communities of ascetics which organized vigils as a constant and regulated observance. We have one rule which reads : 'and let the many (i.e. the community) keep awake in community a third (part) of every night of the year to read in the book and to search the norm (of ordinances) and to bless in community [51].

The same ascetic attitude necessitated the neglect of bodily care. Josephus says that the Essenes did not use oil for anointing — considering this as dirt — and preferred a rough skin as more proper to their spirit [52].

Finally, the ascetic spirit was strong enough to break through even the strong positive disposition which marriage enjoyed in Judaism. Restrictions in this area also appear in groups that were not affected by the ultimate consequences, but still viewed marriage with a certain suspicion [53]. But in groups in which the ascetic spirit was developed consistently, virginity was made a norm in the ascetic code. Josephus [54] and Plinius [55] tell of Essenes that adopted the life in virginity. In this light other information becomes understandable, namely, that the Essenes were eager to accept children into their order so that they could educate them in their spirit. Doing so these ascetics took care of the future of their community

50 A rule in the *Damaskusschrift*, p. 21 : אל יתערב איש מרצונו בשבת 'let no man starve himself wilfully on the Sabbath' seems to reflect groups which went farther in their ascetic needs than this group. This tendency was against the Jewish practice which forbade fasting on Sabbath, see *Jubilees*, L, 12.

51 והרבים ישקודו ביחד את שלישית כול לילות השנה לקרוא בספר ולדרוש משפט ולברך ביחד *Manual of Discipline*, VI, 7.

52 *De bello judaico*, II, 8, 3, v. VI, p. 177. The same attitude appears also in *Megilloth genuzoth*, I, plate X.

53 In the rules for the 'congregation of Israel' it is stated that marriage is forbidden under the age of 20, *Qumran Cave*, p. 110. This corrects the current practice which according to the Talmud considers the 13th or 14th year of age mature for marriage. The motivation is significant: a person in advanced years is more able to distinguish between good and bad.

54 *De bello judaico*, II, 8, 13, p. 185.

55 Plinius, *Historia naturalis*, V, 17, v. I, p. 391 f.

which in itself was sterile [56]. Concerning the ascetics behind the Manual of Discipline it is not said explicitly that they lived in celibacy. The strict spirit of discipline for the warriors of God seems to have necessitated at least severe restrictions [57].

All this we have seen of ascetic practices on the periphery of Judaism gives clear testimony to ideas foreign to the Old Testament spirit. There is something which cannot be understood within the intrinsic development of Jewish traditions. Schürer's well-known definition which he gave to Essenism : 'Der Essenismus ist also zunächst der Pharisäismus im Superlativ' [58], fails entirely to explain the origin of this phenomenon. Even when full allowance has been made for the intrinsic possibilities, it is obvious that in the ascetic idea and practice we have seen one has to do with influences which must have come from outside. Only spiritual forces of that kind were able to substitute for the sacrifices their own rites of washings and ascetic practices, and only such could put beside the Torah their own literature which obviously served their needs and convictions better than the tradition of fathers [59].

The Slavonic *Bellum Judaicum* says bluntly that the Essenes had a great interest in foreign literature and borrowed from this literature what they found useful for their religious purposes [60]. And Josephus, after giving a description of their practices, reckoned with the reader's impression that there was something foreign here. He therefore felt the need of underlining the fact, for the reader's sake, that the Essenes were Jews [61].

56 καὶ γάμον μὲν παρ' αὐτοῖς ὑπεροψία, τοὺς δ' ἀλλοτρίους παῖδας ἐκλαμβάνοντες ἁπαλοὺς ἔτι πρὸς τὰ μαθήματα συγγενεῖς ἡγοῦνται καὶ τοῖς ἤθεσιν αὐτῶν ἐντυποῦσι, *De bello judaico*, II, 8, 2, p. 177.

57 The *Damaskusschrift*, p. 15 f. says explicitly that marriage was permitted in this particular group, but the explanatory note כסרך הארץ 'as the order of the country', or the same in an expanded form in the second fragment כסרך הארץ אשר היה מקדם 'as the order of the country, which has been since the beginning', *ibid.*, p. 29, sounds rather as though aimed against those who have taken a radical stand against marriage.

58 *Geschichte des jüd. Volkes*, II, p. 673.

59 *De bello judaico*, II, 2, 7, p. 161.

60 JOSEPHUS, *Slavonic Bell. jud.*, p. 256.

61 Ἰουδαῖοι μεν γένος ὄντες, *De bello judaico*, II, 8, 2, p. 176.

But even without these direct and clear testimonies one cannot fail to perceive the fusion of ideas and rites of different religions that had taken place within Judaism. This fact was recognized already by Bousset, namely, that Judaism is also a part of the problem of the general syncretistic religion of the Hellenistic period in which the Iranian influence has played an important role [62]. If this is so with the apocalyptic trends in regard to the ascetic movements, this recognition becomes even clearer. Even a superficial comparison reveals a large measure of similarity between the thought in the ascetic streams in Judaism as this appears particularly in newly discovered Hebrew and Aramaic documents and Iranian cosmogonic ideas.

A more careful study leads to the recognition that this similarity is both exceedingly close and curiously intricate. We learn to see that this mood in the ascetic streams of thought is an echo of the dualism found in the Gāthās, the archaic poems incorporated into the Avesta [63]. In heaven with God there is the prince of light and his army of angels who serve God, guide the battles of God, enlighten the hearts of men and lead them to good. There is also the prince of the underworld, with his army of demons, in revolt against God [64]. We can imagine how effectively the Iranian influence could work here and find receptive ground, for even in Palestine the archaic Semitic ideas about the battle between the Creator and Chaos were not unknown [65]. They had not entirely disappeared from the scene.

A look at the hybrid forms generated by the new trends helps to round off this survey. We see how dualistic elements have intruded into the Jewish milieu in such a fashion that they were able to introduce the non-Jewish idea of the world of two radically opposed camps. Furthermore, in some quarters these dualistic elements had penetrated so far that they degraded the body by making it a prison of the soul [66].

62 *Religion des Judentums*, p. 521.

63 *Yasna*, XXX.

64 Particularly the third hymn gives an insight into this battle, *Megilloth genuzoth*, II.

65 DUSSAUD, *Découvertes de Ras Shamra*, p. 65 ff.

66 *De bello judaico*, II, 8, 11, p. 183 f.

This last indication derives vital support from the recently unearthed Hebrew and Aramaean sources. We begin now to see better the strength of these trends in the realm of the relationship between flesh and spirit. It is quite understandable that non-Jewish elements break through here when we learn that flesh is what Satan uses to pull man down, and that spirit leads him to the battle-front. While the spirit guides the believer, flesh is made the spirit's antithesis by being placed in close relationship with evil — as close as the last restraint of Judaism would allow. In this connection it is highly instructive to note the epitheta connected with the term flesh. The flesh could be spoken of as 'flesh of perversity' [67], and 'guilty flesh' [68]. Human existence is described as the 'assembly of the flesh of perversity' [69]. All this speaks for itself. From all this evidence we gather that 'flesh' had become, in these ascetic circles, the sphere of the evil that was hostile to God and was the proper domain for sin [70]. This sort of dualism underlies ascetic trends, sometimes taking a form which comes close to late Gnostic speculations [71], and appears in all these documents under discussion as a framework for ascetic and mystical ideas that were able to transform the lives of these believers to a battle field. Thereby we have looked into the heart of the prime factor behind all these various ascetic trends. Thus, viewed from a general historical point of view the Judaism of the last centuries B.C. and of the first century A.D. belongs to the living stream of the fusion of ideas which has produced an extraordinary effect on religious practice. Such a condition stimulated new ascetic movements with new ideas and manyfold nuances in practice as well as having revitalized and expanded the older forms known in Judaism. Something of this is indicated also in the Talmudic tract Nazir [72]. And according to another tradition there was an increase in the number of those who

67 בשר עול *Megilloth genuzoth,* I, p. 19.

68 בשר אשמה, *ibid.*, I, p. 20.

69 סוד בשר עול *Manual of Discipline,* XI, 9.

70 Therefore every sin could be qualified as עוון בשר 'the sin of flesh', *ibid.*, XI, 12.

71 *Ibid.*, IV.

72 This text presupposes a lifelong Nazirate.

were attracted by the ascetic ideal and began to observe ascetic practices [73].

It remains for us to make some observations regarding important coordinates in this ascetic thought-world. This would bring us a decisive step closer to the purpose for which this excursion was made.

A concept which is of the greatest importance in the realm of ascetic thought, determining the consciousness of the communities, is the concept of the covenant. Whether the concept appears in a more exact form as 'the new covenant' [74] or simply 'covenant', in either case a new relationship with God is involved. On the basis of a consciousness of such a relationship a new community is formed which as the True Israel is distinct from the rest of the Jews. Of interest is the fact that the word Covenant in these texts has a fairly large breadth of meaning [75]. One is of particular concern to us at this point, namely the observation that even their community was designated by the same term. So, too, were its members called 'men of covenant', i.e. the covenanters.

Still another ray of light falls on their deep consciousness concerning their calling. This insight comes from their understanding of the functions which the community of 'men of the perfection of holiness' had to carry out. Concerning this fact the Manual of Discipline has the following to say : 'and they are for the (divine) favor (grace), to atone for the earth and prepare judgment for wickedness' [76]. Thus, this ascetic congregation claimed to possess an expiatory significance for the world outside. While the congregation exemplifies abstinence, privation, devotion in the study of the Torah and prayer along with its cultic practices, it exercised spiritual influence of cosmic amplitude.

Among the more notable aspects in the thought-world of these ascetic movements is the new understanding of the nature of life.

73 Baba Batra 60b says that the destruction of the temple contributed to this growth.

74 So in the *Damaskusschrift*, VIII, p. 14; Fragment B, *ibid.*; *Habakkuk Commentary*, plate LV, col. IIa.

75 See pag. 100 f.

76 והיו לרצון לכפר בעד הארץ ולחרוץ משפט רשעה *Manual of Discipline*, VIII, 9; cf. CIII, 6 . 7.

Certain sections from the prose and poetical texts of these movements bring us face to face with a new outlook. This peculiarity deserves a little further amplification.

In the rite of initiation the neophyte was made aware of the life ahead of him that was to be 'tried by the dominion of Belial'. It is worth taking a closer look at this statement, because it had a particular meaning for them, being a new ethos articulated in their own way. This peculiarity becomes manifest in the realm of metaphors in which they lived. Here is military terminology which has permeated all the aspects of their thought and life. The world and life was conceived of as a battle field, and they regarded themselves as warriors, as an army set up for warfare, in constant vigilance at the front. Several scenes from this imagery are preserved in their literature, and these help us to understand their feelings. One scene describes how the sound of the trumpet calls these warriors together for their gatherings [77]. Another depicts the priests holding the trumpets and the highpriest who delivers an exhortation to the warriors before the priests blow their trumpets and the battle begins with the enemy [78]. Still another scene describes the heat of the struggle telling of how the arrows fly, spears flash, and, in the vehemence of the fight, cries fire the warriors to do battle [79].

The same ethos is reflected also in the organizational forms. These ascetic movements regarding themselves as an army of God built themselves up as a sacred militia. This regard in its turn contributed to the permeation of their life and thought-world with a battle-atmosphere [80].

What we have seen in the preceding excursion brings us face to face with a phenomenon which in its substance reminds us the phenomenon of the primitive Syrian Christianity. All these features show that there is a common fund of thought behind them, and a chain of linked ideas. This is even more astonishing since besides the religious phenomenological form which both have in common, even

77 *Damaskusschrift*, XIV, p. 22; cf. *Megilloth genuzoth*, I, p. 25.

78 One such description appears in the 'Battle between the Children of Light and the Children of Darkness', *ibid.*, I, p. 21, 25.

79 The first hymn, *ibid.*, II.

80 The community is divided into formations with their heads and officers for the sake of its military functions in the war with Belial.

the detail features, unique in their character, appear as conspicuous in both, for instance the terminology used in connection with the function of the priests [81], the imagery employed to reflect their ethos [82], and the emergence of Scripture texts which bear a mark of distinct tenets [83].

The features of both phenomena, those of the covenanters in the primitive Syrian Christianity and those of the covenanters in the desert of Judah are so similar, indeed, so strikingly similar, that it is hard to resist the temptation to assume that they stand in a causal relation to each other [84]. The more so because all the premises we can recover about the beginnings of primitive Syrian Christianity point towards that solution. We have to reckon seriously with the possibility that the ascetic groups on the periphery of Palestinian Judaism, like the covenanters of Khirbet Qumran, also were influenced by the Christian message and they contributed to the formation of a distinct group in the Palestinian Aramaean Christianity.

In this connection, it is profitable for us to take into account observations which, to a certain extent at least, help us in illuminating our acute historical problem.

We begin with some instructive observations which can be made about the group of the first followers of Jesus. They were recruited from different spiritual climates. Thereby the movement at the very beginning shows centrifugal forces which only the person of Jesus could keep together.

81 In the description of the function of the priests, there is a striking feature. The function of the 'priests, scribes and sages', in the remains of an archaic baptismal liturgy, is described by the handling of trumpet, APHRAHAṬ, *Demonstrationes*, VII, col. 341. Regarding the same characterization see *Damaskusschrift*, XIV, p. 22 and *Megilloth genuzoth*, I, p. 25.

82 The imagery by which the religious ethos is reflected, namely war and battle, is strikingly similar. Compare particularly the remains of an ancient baptismal liturgy, APHRAHAṬ, *Demonstrationes*, VII, 18.20, col. 341 f., 345 with *Megilloth genuzoth*, I, p. 25.

83 Vestiges of a text of the Pentateuch which reflect tendentious modifications cast in the spirit and customs of the Covenanters so that these can best be explained in this way, emerge in the archaic Christian traditions close to Palestine or Syria, *De virginitate*, II, 14, p. 106 ff.; cf. VÖÖBUS, *Merkwürdige Pentateuchzitate*.

84 VÖÖBUS, *Significance of the Dead Sea Scrolls.*

The first followers of Jesus came from the baptist movement which seems to have played a far greater role than the tradition is willing to tell us. Among these followers we also see men from the Pharisees, Zelotes and those of Am-ha-arez [85]. The few notices which we have in the gospels show the variegated appearance of the group which Jesus had gathered. Here the variety of streams and trends in the contemporary Jewish religious milieu mirrors itself quite clearly. We also notice that these followers did not come with empty hands but brought with them a spiritual heritage in the light of which they understood the new message.

If men from all these different trends in Judaism were attracted by the person of Jesus, were those in ascetic movements the only exception? To be sure, the gospels are silent concerning them. Nevertheless the question remains, and we therefore have to consult other possibilities.

What we notice about the group that were the first followers of Jesus, should guide us when we begin to form ideas about the beginnings of primitive Christianity after the event of the Easter. In this further development the Palestinian milieu with its various trends must be taken into account — a fact which we have learned slowly.

To be sure the picture as it is painted in the New Testament writings shows only one congregation which gathered in the temple at Jerusalem. This was a congregation which was interested in the heritage of the Old Testament and was at pains to see to it that this heritage played its share in the shaping and perhaps re-shaping of the Christian tradition. The tradition laid down in the Gospel of Matthew is the best illustration here.

For a long time, this picture created an impression of the beginnings of the church which was not factual. And we still would have been under the influence of this impression if there had been no other

85 The early Christian tradition has preserved references that scribes as well as Pharisees, also, joined the Christian movement. One is reminded here cf the reading in John I, 47 in the Diatessaron : 'behold, indeed, a scribe, an Israelite'. In a list of the apostles and evangelists, obviously of Syrian origin, we read : ܢܬܢܐܠ ܪܫܐ ܕܣܦܪ̈ܐ 'Nathanael, the chief of the scribes', Ms. Sin. syr. 10, fol. 221 a.

light to help us. Owing to other sources, we now can see the actual conditions of the time somewhat better than formerly, and recognize the group in Jerusalem as only one stream among others in the earliest phase of the movement, namely a stream which according to all signs produced a form of the primitive tradition in the mould of the official Judaism. To-day we realize the impossibility of consulting the Acts of the Apostles for a realistic picture of the *whole* development. We should not even expect information here as to what happened outside of and parallel to the sphere of interest of the movement which was centered in Jerusalem.

The fundamental turning point in the re-orientation of our understanding regarding the character of Christian beginnings goes back to the new light which was thrown on the situation by the discovery of the Mandaean documents [86]. What stirs us here is the important bearing which these sources have for a deeper understanding of the spiritual milieu in which the Fourth Gospel has wrapped the Christian message. A calm and cautious use of this material [87] is of extreme importance for the quest of the substratum of the Johannine type of Christianity. Regardless of how other problems might be settled [88], we have no doubt that in these precious texts we come close to the same native soil of the moving ideas and concepts in that spiritual realm which provided the canvas for the 'spiritual gospel'.

The Fourth Gospel clearly reflects the message of Jesus and that about Jesus wrapped in the milieu of a cognate movement which had given its members as the first disciples of Jesus. This new insight compels us to reckon seriously with the possibility that this type of Christian tradition may be as ancient as the more judaized form of it, and that the later date of the composition of the gospel would have no bearing upon the age of the tradition it embodies. Thus,

[86] *Das Johannesbuch,* 1915; *Mandäische Liturgien,* 1920; *Ginza, das grosse Buch der Mandäer,* 1925.

[87] Lidzbarski's contentions regarding the dating of the extant materials, *Johannesbuch,* p. XVI ff., *Mandäische Liturgien,* p. XIX ff., cannot be followed. The material, in fact, is a conglomerate, containing texts which bear the marks of the influence of Manichaeism.

[88] An analysis of this material shows that there are strata which lead us to an older form of the Mandaean traditions embedded in a later formation.

we perceive that the germ of the gospel was placed not only into the soil of the tradition of the Pharisaic and official Judaism, but also into a milieu cultivated by various Jewish baptist movements on the periphery of Judaism.

Not only have new sources opened our eyes, but so has fresh research into the sources at our disposal. In this regard we come to Lohmeyer's study which has the merit of opening new and fruitful perspectives [89]. His investigation leads to conclusions which are of cardinal importance for the understanding of the formation of the tradition laid down in the Gospel of Mark. Its main thesis is that besides Jerusalem there was another important Christian community in Galilee. Moreover, Lohmeyer shows that its spiritual profile was entirely different from the Jerusalem tradition, being able to approach Christology, eschatology and ethics through its own theological outlook [90].

Whatever we think of some of the details in his arguments, Lohmeyer's investigation has thrown a new light on the research. And in this light, we recognize the existence of a new important mould of the primitive Christian tradition. The conclusion is inescapable. There was still another stream in the beginnings of primitive Christianity which drew its spiritual background from still different sources, from a milieu shaped by religious, non-nationalist, transcendental rather than by official theological and political interests.

Thus much new light has fallen on the period which gave birth to primitive Christianity, and this new light has gradually unfolded the actual picture of its beginnings. The thing which a historian learns to appreciate is the fact that the Palestinian religious and spiritual trends and streams played such an important role that they divided the Christian movement into various groups. Each group understood and interpreted the new message in its own way and shaped the oral and written tradition according to its own

89 'Galiläa und Jerusalem — aus diesem doppelten Ursprung ist die älteste Christenheit entstanden; wir verstehen dabei den Namen Galiläa in dem früher erörterten weiten Sinne, nach dem es im Osten das Land « jenseits des Jordans » und im Norden über den Merom-See hinaus bis an den Hermon, vielleicht bis nach Damaskus reicht', *Galiläa und Jerusalem*, p. 80.

90 *Ibid.*, p. 84 ff.

religious and theological outlook. We have slowly become cognisant of the fact that there was not only one stream from the beginning of the Christian movement. In its morphology, the early Christian movement must have resembled the delta of the Nile.

These observations form the necessary preparation in approaching our main question. It is time to consider the question we touched upon earlier, namely, whether the ascetic stream had its place in this picture of primitive Christianity too? We have already observed the pitfall connected with the argument that the New Testament writings are silent about this question. The veil over this question is being lifted, to be sure, very slowly but yet steadily. Thus we may cautiously surmise that what we know to-day is not yet the full picture. However, according to the signs which have come into view this picture of the beginnings in primitive Christianity must have been still more colorful than the sources and shreds of sources at our disposal now allow us to see.

In view of all this we have observed, we should expect that the spiritually alert groups in the ascetic movement had their place in the beginnings of Christianity. In the light of the observations we have made, indeed, we have to reckon seriously with the possibility that the ascetic groups like the Covenanters of Khirbet Qumran also were attracted by the Christian message and that they contributed to the formation of a distinct group in the Palestinian Aramaean Christianity. It would be strange, indeed, if a dynamic of such rich religious and spiritual life had no share in the process of the formation.

There is, of course, more than a mere postulation regarding this. In our sources we come across with vestiges which clearly speak of the existence of a segment in the Palestinian Jewish Christianity, colored by the tenets like those in the community of the Khirbet Qumran. Some of these we have already seen [91]. Here it should be mentioned that also the religious washings estimated by the Covenanters, emerge in the traditions laid down in Epiphanius [92], in the Pseudo-Clementine literature [93], and in some other sour-

91 See pag. 15 ff.

92 *Panarion* XXX, p. 333.

93 This document, which in its earliest stratum stems from a very ancient Jewish Christian tradition, is fond of ablutions which occupy a very important

ces [94]. Here we detect a chain of linked ideas in the Qumran texts and the remembrances regarding the ascetics and baptist factions of the Palestinian Aramaean Christianity, which have managed to escape oblivion.

In conclusion, all indications point to the possibility that this distinct group, the ascetically orientated faction in the Palestinian Aramaean Christianity, was destined to play an important role in history. It seems to have been transplanted into the lands of the Euphrates and Tigris and here constituted the first nuclei in the process of Christian expansion. If so, then the new discoveries in the desert of Judah have begun to lift the curtain of obscurity from the historical origin of Christianity in the Syrian Orient.

part in the system of religious tenets. According to these texts, the ablutions expel demons which cause not only sickness but also moral aberrations. These purifications, too, fill the heart with divine thoughts and internal purity. We do not only find here ritual acts similar to those of the Covenanters, but also a similar theology of purification which is regarded as a substitution for the sacrifices. These theologumena reveal many linked ideas which deserve to be investigated more closely.

94 The information in other authors like Justinus Martyr, Hegesippus and Hippolytus is decidedly less than satisfying.

CHAPTER II

THE PERIOD OF FIRST STIMULI

Whatever the actual situation might have been in these primitive Jewish-Christian communities in the lands of the Euphrates and Tigris, these Palestinian influences during the Aramaean period of Christianity have not been more than an arsis in the overture. As the study of the early period shows, powerful impulses, having a far deeper and more penetrating impact than those from Palestine, have entered the scene and taken over the further course of development into their hands. These impulses not only enlarged the first nuclei, expanding the Christian movement into dimensions which exceeded the ancient primitive frame, but developed them into a wider movement, covering these countries with a network of Christian congregations. But these impulses deserve our particular attention — seen from the aspect in which this study is interested. These impulses introduced or — in order to be more careful — perhaps revitalized ascetic factors which determined the whole direction and character of Christianity in the Syrian Orient, during the early phase when the Syrians could develop their church according to their own inherent forces and inclinations, far from Christian Hellenistic influence.

Because of the profound influence of certain men of great religious and spiritual force, Christianity was consistently crystallized in the countries of the Euphrates and the Tigris as a movement which to a large extent absorbed rigid and radical asceticism. A student of Christian history finds it very interesting to observe just how those outstanding spirits, who owing to their radicality were not successful in the West, made history in these areas.

1. TATIAN

a. His personal role

In the middle of the second century a man whose life and work has made the deepest impact upon Syrian asceticism was converted to Christianity. He was Tatian from 'the land of the Assyrians' [1], that is, from the land between the Tigris and Media on the west and east, and the Armenian mountains and Ctesiphon on the north and south. His home was probably in Ḥadiab. The patristic evidence is unanimous in saying that he was a son of Syriac-speaking parents [2].

Tatian found no solution for his needs in his home. If he stood in a military position, this did not satisfy him, and he resigned. We read of this in his own testimony : 'I do not like to rule, I do not wish to be rich, I decline military command' [3]. These auto-biographical remarks indicate clearly that Tatian was not contented. He had a propensity for spiritual riches, rhetoric, philosophical and historical studies, having been reared in a Hellenistic atmosphere since his youth.

Something drew him to foreign lands, and he turned his face to the west. This place was destined to become the scene of a far greater change in his life. We do not know where he went, but certainly the places which attracted him were the places of learning. He satisfied his philosophical needs, achieving a certain degree of reputation by his writings. He also was interested in different religions, examined their cults and rites and was initiated in their mysteries [4]. But he still felt the rule of demons in his life, as he himself says, the power of 'many lords and myriads of tyrants'.

Finally he found abroad what he did not find at home. He was attracted to the faith that was manifested in the attitude and life of Christians [5], and he was converted. He found what he needed in studying the 'barbarian writings' of the Christians : 'my soul was instructed by God, and I recognized that those teachings of the

1 *γεννηθεὶς μὲν ἐν τῇ τῶν Ἀσσυρίων γῇ*, *Oratio*, col. 888.

2 Tatian appears as **ὁ Σύρος**, in Clemens, *Stromata*, III, 12, 81, p. 232; Epiphanius, *Panarion*, XLVI, 1, v. II, p. 204, and in Theodoretus, *Haeret. fab. compendium*, I, 20, col. 369. Harnack's attempt to see in Tatian a Greek, *Überlieferung*, p. 199 ff., has failed.

3 *βασιλεύειν οὐ θέλω, πλουτεῖν οὐ βούλομαι, τὴν στρατηγίαν παρῄτημαι*, col. 829. The translation renders the last verb as a strong present tense, although the Greek text has perfect tense. It is not impossible that this perfect tense is chosen purposely. In this case it sounds so, that Tatian had actually served in the army.

4 *Ibid.*, col. 29.

5 *Ibid.*, col. 32, 33.

Greek lead to condemnation, but these barbarian teachings dissolve the slavery that is in the world and rescue us from the many lords and myriads of tyrants' [6]. As a result, he gave himself to the cause of Christ entirely and unconditionally.

Concerning the chronological questions we are uncertain. Some have suggested that this conversion took place before 150 A.D. [7]; others feel it occurred shortly before A.D. 165 [8]. However, we do not know where his conversion took place. Perhaps it was in Rome.

Tatian's stay in Rome and his activities there are wrapped in obscurity. Tradition brings him in contact with Justin Martyr, considering him one of Justin's disciples [9]. In fact Tatian refers reverently to him in his apology. Presumably Tatian himself became active as a teacher in Rome. This can naturally be expected of a man of his calibre. A note of Rhodon saying that he was instructed by Tatian in Rome [10] confirms the suggestion that Tatian perhaps established a school. The attempts, however, which have been made to interpret his apology as a sort of an inaugural speech in his school [11], cannot be taken seriously as an additional argument.

It also can be assumed that Tatian had relations with the Christians of his own race. The considerable Syrian element which appeared in the western communities existed also in Rome. This element was

6 *θεοδιδάκτου δέ μου γενομένης τῆς ψυχῆς, συνῆκα, ὅτι τὰ μὲν καταδίκης ἔχει τρόπον, τὰ δὲ ὅτι λύει τὴν ἐν κόσμῳ δουλείαν, καὶ ἀρχόντων μὲν πολλῶν, καὶ μυρίων ἡμᾶς ἀποσπᾷ τυράννων*, *ibid.*, col. 868 A.

7 HARNACK, *Chronologie*, I, p. 284.

8 BARDENHEWER, *Geschichte der altk. Literatur*, I, p. 264.

9 *ἀκροατής*, IRENAEUS, *Adv. haereses*, I, 28, 1, p. 259; EUSEBIUS, *Hist. eccl.*, IV, 29, 1, p. 390.

10 *Ibid.*, V, 13, 1. 8, p. 454, 458.

11 KUKULA, *Tatians sog. Apologie*, p. 16; PUECH, *Recherches sur le discours*, p. 42.

A proof against this view would be established if Tatian had written his Apology around the year 180, GRANT, *Date of Tatian's Oration*, p. 99 f. However interesting the arguments Grant brings forward, these are not cogent. The hard fact remains that this writing does not show an open break with the church. But when Irenaeus wrote the first book of his *Adversus haereses* around the year 180, then Tatian was already known as the chief heretic. The intrinsic evidence militates against the possibility that his Oration was written after the break with the church.

represented not only among the lower circles but also among the leading people. One should not overlook the Roman tradition that even the bishop of the Roman church, Anicet (ca 154-165), who ruled the Roman congregation while Tatian was in Rome, was a Syrian from Emesa [12].

Tatian was dissatisfied with what he found in the church. It annoyed him that he did not see enough enthusiasm and vigorism in what he saw as the manifestation of the Christian religion. According to the tradition Tatian articulated his radical views after the death of Justin Martyr [13]. This information certainly must be interpreted to mean that as long as Justin Martyr lived, great respect towards him kept Tatian under restraint so that he avoided an open conflict with Justin. For his dissatisfaction hardly came overnight. It had a longer history for even his apology shows that he had things on his heart that stood in opposition to the commonly shared views. According to the Chronicle of Eusebius Tatian's break with the church came in the twelfth year of Marcus Aurelius, i.e., in 172/3 [14], under Bishop Soter (ca 166-175).

The answer which Tatian found to his life's problems was a faith able to overcome all passions and to produce a rigorous life of the most extreme kind. He felt that after his conversion his eyes were opened to see that men who once were free had become slaves [15]. He was guided in his thoughts by the conviction that the soul by itself, being without God, tends downward towards matter [16], and having lost the heavenly companionship it hankers after communion with things which are inferior [17]. Because of this declivity all forms of life, customs and practices are corrupted. From this point of view, we can understand Tatian saying that everything in the world is madness [18]. On the other hand his experience showed that

12 Anicitus, natione Syrus, ex patre Johanne, de vico Humisa, sedit ann. XI m. IIII d. III, *Liber pontificalis*, I, p. 134.

13 Irenaeus, *Adv. haereses*, I, 28, 1, p. 259.

14 Eusebius, *Chronographia*, II, p. 173.

15 *Oratio*, col. 829.

16 πρὸς τὴν ὕλην νεύει κάτω, *ibid.*, col. 833; this ὕλη has desired to exercise lordship over the soul, *ibid.*, col. 840 f.

17 τῶν ἐλαττόνων μετουσίαν ἐπεπόθησεν, *ibid.*, col. 852.

18 *Ibid.*, col. 89.

the Christian faith is a deliverance from this slavery. This deliverance is possible only when man becomes a dwelling-place for God, when His spirit inhabits human beings [19]. But this possibility requires a restoration of lost conditions. For him all this meant that a Christian has only one way open to him. He must take a radical stand against all this which has taken shape in the process of corruption, everything which is common and earthly [20]. Christian faith takes on a completely new form of life : 'live to God, repudiating the old nature by apprehending Him' [21]. In other words this means : 'die to the world, repudiating the madness that is in it' [22]. The way of asceticism is the only form of life congruous with the new nature which rises above sinfulness and the rule of demons.

In another place Tatian says : 'we do not scatter ourselves' [23]. What the Christian should be concerned with in order to arrest this scattering, becomes clear in its seriousness when we see how Tatian applied this principle to practical life.

First, abandonment of possessions and an entirely negative attitude towards all earthy goods became imperative. 'If you are superior to the passions, you will despise all things in the world' [24].

Restraint must also be put on the needs and desires of the human body. Particularly the use of meat was prohibited [25]. Hieronymus is astonished that Tatian condemned 'meats which God has created for use' [26]. Also the use of wine was forbidden [27]. Whether Tatian derived this prohibition from the rules laid on the Old Testament Nazirate, as Hieronymus says, is another question.

19 *Ibid.*, col. 837.

20 λόγου γὰρ τοῦ δημοσίου καὶ ἐπιγείου κεχωρισμένοι, *ibid.*, col. 872.

21 ζῆθι τῷ θεῷ, διὰ τῆς ἑαυτοῦ καταλήψεως τὴν παλαιὰν γένεσιν παραιτούμενος, *ibid.*, col. 829.

22 ἀπόθνησκε τῷ κόσμῳ, παραιτούμενος τὴν ἐν αὐτῷ μανίαν, *ibid.*

23 καὶ μὴ σκορπιζόντων ἑαυτούς, *ibid.*, col. 868.

24 τῶν παθῶν ἂν ὑπάρχῃς ἀνώτερος, τῶν ἐν τῷ κόσμῳ πάντων καταφρονήσεις, *ibid.*, col. 849. Further Tatian makes a reference to the poison δηλητήριον in the natural productions, and to the sinfulness of man which aggravates the situation and calls for a negative stand.

25 A reference appears already in his *Oratio*, col. 857.

26 *Adv. Jovinianum*, I, 3, col. 223.

27 HIERONYMUS, *Commentaria in Amos*, col. 1010.

Another form of life which was considered corrupt is marriage with its carnal union. Again Hieronymus may be quoted here. He cites Tatian's rigid judgment on marriage and the procreation of children. He says that the most rigorous heresiarch of the Encratites used the passus : 'if one seeds on flesh, he will reap perdition from the flesh' as an argument and interpreted it as meaning that he who seeds in flesh is none else than a person who enters into union with a woman, and that whoever has intercourse with his wife will reap perdition from the flesh [28]. This is very plain language. Anathema is laid on the union of the flesh. Another reference in Irenaeus is in full conformity with this, namely, the remark that carnal intercourse is πορνεία. As a result of this condemnation, Tatian denied salvation to Adam [29].

Concerning Tatian's attitude towards marriage with carnal union several of his arguments appear in Tatian's works [30], showing how strongly he modified his interpretation in favor of this. But the strongest argument is used and quoted by Clement of Alexandria. He has preserved an instructive passage which brings us Tatian's exposition on 1 Cor. VII, 5 [31]. According to this Tatian said: 'fellowship in corruption weakens the prayer'. Then he called marriage fornication, relating it to Satan. His comment runs as follows : 'at any rate, by the permission he (i.e. Paul) certainly, though delicately, forbids it; for while he permits them to return to the same on account of Satan and incontinence, he exhibits a man who will attempt to serve two masters, — God by the 'consent', but by want of consent, incontinence, fornication and Satan'.

Tatian's influence must have been far-reaching. The fact that

28 Qui putativam Christi carnem introducens, omnem conjunctionem masculi ad feminam immundam arbitratur, Encratitarum vel accerrimus haeresiarchas, tali adversum nos sub occasione praesentis testimonii usus est argumento : si quis seminat in carne, de carne metet corruptionem; in carne autem seminat, qui mulieri jungitur : ergo et qui uxore utitur, et seminat in carne ejus, de carne metet corruptionem, *Commentaria in ep. ad Galatas,* col. 460.

29 *Adv. haereses,* III, 23, 8, p. 551.

30 So a fragment quoted by CLEMENS, *Stromata,* III, 12, 86, p. 236. The gospel word 'lay not up treasure on earth where moth and rust corrupt it', and the prophetic word 'you all shall grow old as a garment, and the moth shall devour you', Tatian applied to the procreation of children.

31 *Stromata,* III, 12, 81, p. 232.

he was declared a heretic, and the fact that after he returned to the Orient in the year 172 and disappeared entirely from the eyes of historiography[32] by no means can weaken the strength of this statement.

Some remarks need to be made concerning the first fact. The situation in the west and in the Orient must be taken into consideration. To be sure his picture, painted by the church fathers in the west, placarded him as the epitome of heretics. But the Syrians have preferred to hold their own opinion about him, and this tradition does not include him among the heretics in the company of Marcion, Bardaiṣan, Mani, Valentinus and others. It knows him only as the disciple of Justin Martyr and the author of the Gospel Harmony. According to the judgment of western standards his Christian outlook, together with his rigorous interpretation, was repulsive and abhorrent. But what seemed repulsive to the western mind, seemed normal to the Oriental taste. Moreover Tatian's radicalism might already have had contacts with the Christian thought and practice prevalent in Christianity in the Syrian Orient through the channels of the Syrian communities in the west.

With regard to the second fact it should be pointed out that there are observations which guide us when historiography becomes mute. These observations involve what we know of Tatian's personality and his qualifications.

One cannot overlook Tatian's spiritual and intellectual qualifications. Even before his conversion, he had attained a certain reputation as a thinker and scholar. These qualities he put in the service of the Christian cause as a teacher and author.

Besides these gifts Tatian must have possessed a powerful personality. Even though we have nothing but his apologetic Oratio, we can deduce this. It has been observed that his writing is difficult to understand, but through what he says one can observe a powerful man[33].

Along with all this his personality was fused with a passionate character. The pages of his Apology mirror something of his per-

32 Epiphanius' information that Tatian returned to the Orient in the 12th year of Antonius Pius, *Panarion,* XLVI, 1, p. 204, obviously must be understood so, that he has confused Marcus Aurelius with his predecessor.

33 Krüger, *Geschichte altchr. Literatur,* p. 72.

sonality. In all his boundless and reckless attacks upon everything Greek, we feel the fire which he had in his soul.

These observations constitute strong reasons for thinking that the developing young church could hardly escape the influence of such a vigorous promoter of the Christian cause.

We are also interested in the problem concerning the place in the Orient where Tatian continued his work and activity of spreading his interpretation of Christianity after he felt the call to return to the Orient.

As to this place opinions are divided. While Kukula sought this place in Asia Minor [34], Ponschab suggested Antioch in Syria [35]. It has also been thought that this place was the metropolis of Mesopotamia, Edessa. Zahn supported this view [36]. Harnack also supported this choice [37]. But this view that Tatian came to Edessa is merely presupposed by modern scholars. Behind the view is the feeling that such a great spirit should be linked with such a great place as the Mesopotamian metropolis. The sober fact is that there are no data in support of this argument. Fortunately, however, we are not entirely bereft of some guidance. We have a reliable source of information about conditions in Edessa and particularly about the men who were spiritual leaders there. The Chronicle of Edessa mentions the names of Marcion, Mani, and Bardaiṣan, as men closely connected with the spiritual past of Christianity in Edessa [38]. Tatian is not mentioned at all in this document. This is a sufficient ground for abandoning this conjecture and for looking for the place of Tatian's activity elsewhere.

Kahle proposed the view that Tatian returned to his home country and settled there [39]. This is far more probable than any other view that has been presented. And after all, Ḥadiab was also an important center. When Tatian returned to his land kindled by Christian faith, he must have found a considerable number of congregations there. For there were 20 bishoprics which existed

34 *Tatians sog. Apologie,* p. 3 ff.

35 *Tatians Rede,* p. 8 f.

36 *Tatians Diatessaron,* p. 282.

37 *Chronologie,* I, p. 289.

38 *Chronicon Edessenum,* p. 3 f.

39 *Cairo Geniza,* p. 198.

there in 224 A.D. [40], and these must have required considerable time for their growth and development.

Wherever it was that Tatian exerted his energy and devotion, his work constituted a major event in the growth and development of Syrian Christianity.

b. The role of the Evangeliōn da-Meḥalleṭē

Tatian's significance in the propagation of Encratite views is not limited to his personal influence and activity. Because Tatian has left his fingermarks on the text of the gospel harmony he composed, this influence reached far beyond the frontiers of the orbit of his activities. Therefore we have to mention also the services of the gospel text arranged by Tatian.

The gospel text prepared by Tatian was a harmony which was lost in the stormy history of Syrian Christianity. Tatian took sections out of each gospel and combined them into a more or less chronological whole. He combined the parallel pericopies, phrases and words in one gospel with those preserved in another. This procedure was guided by his meticulous care in including everything possible. Thus, a filigree-work came into existence which is a sort of Life of Jesus in running narrative. The Syrians called it the *Evangeliōn da-Meḥalleṭē* (the gospel of the mixed).

Soon after the work left Tatian's hands it started on a way which led it from triumph to triumph [41]. Its success among the Syrians was due to a combination of qualities which inhered in this document [42]. The national factor must have also promoted the prompt spreading of it. For the Syrians the author was their own countryman and most probably the gospel was composed originally in their own tongue. Moreover, it arrived on the scene at a suitable time, and thus it became the gospel of the Syriac-speaking communities. Thus Tatian's work continued to be used for several generations, serving the ecclesiastical and missionary needs of Syrian Christianity.

40 *Sources syriaques*, p. 30.

41 It was translated into many languages and used in many tongues, see Vööbus, *Early Versions*, p. 6 ff.

42 *Ibid.*, p. 22 ff.

This work which proved to be a real magnet for Syrian Christianity at the same time put Tatian's Encratite views into circulation and popularized them. Today we are much better informed about the extent of the ascetic elements woven into the narrative in his harmonistic work. Because of the fact that this important work was placed in the service of Christianity which gravitated towards the ascetic ideal, we have to examine the respective qualities of this work. This examination also helps us to supplement the picture presented in the preceding section.

Something of Tatian's views on possessions and property can be learned from his harmonistic work. There is a reading added to Mk. x, 30 which says something worthy of notice. The normal text affirms the recompensation promised by Jesus for the house, brothers, sisters, mother and father etc., for all that have been left for the sake of the gospel : a hundredfold in this time, 'houses and brothers and sisters and mothers and children and lands, with persecutions'. This μετὰ διωγμῶν invited Tatian to insert his own modification. The Persian text of the harmony reads 'all is affliction and anxiety' [43]. Here the life of possessions is depicted in its substance as nothing more than 'affliction and anxiety'. The same reading has found its way into the Persian gospel text [44].

The same attitude implied in this modification becomes clear when we examine other interpolations inspired by the tendency to delineate more clearly the character of the Christian life. An interesting case has been preserved in the Persian harmony. Here Mt. xiii, 52 has a form that is no longer seen in other texts in the stream of harmonistic traditions. In the normal text Jesus says that every scribe who has been trained for the kingdom of heaven is like 'a householder who brings out of his treasure what is new and what is old'. Thus, such a man is compared to a man with property. This statement was too much for the spirit cherished by Tatian.

[43] غم وغصه است *Diatess. persiano*, p. 157.

[44] A number of Persian manuscripts which have preserved a very interesting recension of the gospel text, offer here a reading which may stand even closer to the original Tatianic formulation : هم غم وغصه اند. وگدرنده 'all are affliction and anxiety and fleeting', Vööbus, *Studien zu den persischen Ev.-Texten*.

He felt it was misleading and therefore retouched the text [45]. This interpolation reveals Tatian's concept of the man who is trained for the kingdom of heaven. A Christian, a disciple of the gospel, cannot possess anything for the simple reason that he is called on to leave everything.

Concerning the practical consequences for Christian life, Tatian introduced formulations which have greater clarity. This clarity can be seen in a peculiar variant-reading of Lk. xɪv, 26. The reading 'every one who does not abandon his father and his mother' etc. [46], with which we come across in many authors who used the ancient text traditions [47], goes back to Tatian [48]. This means that Tatian discarded Mt.'s φιλῶν and Lk.'s μισεῖ and replaced them with a clearer expression that leaves no doubt as to how a Christian must act.

Several corrections reflect Tatian's strict attitude towards the use of wine which he condemned for Christians. Even the word 'wine' had to be stricken from the biblical vocabulary. We notice that the word in Jn. xv, 1 'I am the true vine' has been modified so that his text reads : 'I am the tree of the fruit of the truth' [49].

The same ascetic conviction appears in his handling of another passage. In the episode of the Last Supper Mt. and Mark report that after He gave bread and the cup, Jesus said that he will not drink again of this fruit of the vine until that day when he drinks it anew in his Father's kingdom (Mt. xxvɪ, 29; Mk. xɪv, 25), a statement which in a shorter form is placed after the first cup in Luke's account (Lk. xxɪɪ, 18). Again we feel the strength of the ascetic spirit when we notice how this passage annoyed Tatian. He deleted this statement from the text and excluded the idea that

[45] او بدیشان گفت همچنین هر نویسنده که شا گردی کند در ملکوت اسمان کشیده شود مانندست بخداوند خانه که از هرچه در خانهٔ حودست از کُهن واز نو بدر امده باشد 'He said to them : Thus every scribe who has been made a disciple and attracted into the Kingdom of heaven, is like a householder, who brings out from all what he has in his house, old and new', *Diatess. persiano*, p. 222.

[46] ܘܠܐ ܫܒܩ Peš., Syr-Sin, Syr-Cur.

[47] See Vööbus, *Celibacy*, p. 19 f.

[48] *Diatess. persiano*, p. 295.

[49] من درخت میوه راستی *ibid.*, p. 322.

wine will be drunk in the Kingdom. The text of the Diatessaron, as it appears in the Armenian translation of the commentary of Ephrem, runs : 'from now on I shall not drink from this generation of vine until the Kingdom of my father' [50].

Tatian's text also makes it clear that marriage with its carnal union has no place in the Christian life. This opinion stands out in several omissions and modifications which reveal his care in avoiding reference to Joseph as Mary's husband [51]. In Mt. I, 24, instead of the normal text 'he took his wife' Tatian rendered the text so that Joseph took Mary into his custody [52].

But the clearest demonstration of Tatian's attitude appears in Lk. II, 36 which shows how Tatian viewed the materialization of the Christian life. The ordinary text here speaks of the normal married life which the prophetess Anna lived with her husband seven years from her virginity. But Tatian corrected the text in the opposite direction and changed the married life mentioned into a state of celibacy : that she remained a virgin in her marriage [53].

One of the cleverest changes in the interest of the ascetic ideal emerges in a remote witness, in the Liège codex of the Diatessaron. This Dutch version offers the pericope in Mt. XIX, 4-9 with a very small gloss. Yet the alteration is able to change the whole meaning of the original text. In this pericope Jesus refers to the Old Testament narrative that concerns the creation of the first couple

50 *Յայսմ հետէ ոչ արբից յայսմ ծննդենէ որթոյս մինչև յարքայու-թիւն Հօր իմոյ·* *Srboyn*, II, p. 152. Redrafting of this passage is conspicuous in view of the Synoptic material. Tatian's reading suppresses the thought of a renewed drinking of vine in the Kingdom, expressed in Mark's *ὅταν αὐτὸ πίω καινὸν ἐν τῇ βασιλείᾳ τοῦ θεοῦ*, and Matthew's *ὅταν αὐτὸ πίνω μεθ' ὑμῶν καινὸν ἐν τῇ βασιλείᾳ τοῦ πατρός μου.*

51 This tendentious omission can be seen in the *Liège Diatess.*, p. 21 : eñ want hi en gherecht mensche was, 'and because he was a righteous man'; and also in the Diatess. Veneto; unde Iosep vecando co, cum ello fosse iusto et bono, *Diatess. italiano*, p. 27. Also Syr-Cur : ܕܟܐܢܐ ܗܘܐ ܓܒܪܐ 'because he was a just man'.

52 *Diatess. persiano*, p. 16. The same reading was known to Ephrem, *Srboyn*, II, p. 24.

53 خود هفت سال مانده بود بکر با شوهر خود 'she remained seven years a virgin with her husband', *Diatess. persiano*, p. 22. The same change 'in virginity' has been preserved also in the Dutch harmony in the Stuttgart Ms.

and the institution of marriage which, in the ordinary text, appears as a paraphrase of the text of Genesis. But Tatian divided this text into two parts by means of the gloss 'and Adam said' : 'when God had made male and female he joined them together; and Adam said: « because of this bond shall a man leave father and mother, and shall remain with his wife, and the two of them shall be joined in one flesh »' [54]. This 'Adam said' separates the thought into two sections in such a way that God's will covers only their joining together. Adam becomes responsible for the invention of the carnal link between husband and wife which joins them in one flesh. Thus this gloss suffices to degrade at one stroke the whole value of the conjugal life.

Finally, to take one more example, the answer of Jesus in the pericope in Lk. xx, 27-40 (and parall.) Tatian used to support his Encratite view. In the original text Jesus' answer refers to the state in eternity where one does not take a wife nor enter into marriage but where all are angels. The pericope takes on a completely different complexion if it refers to the Christian life in this world, as Tatian interpreted its meaning. In Tatian's understanding the people of this world marry, but Christians do not : 'the people of this world take a wife and make marriages; but they who shall be worthy of the life of that other world and of the resurrection of the blessed, will neither take wives nor make wedding feasts' [55].

It is interesting to notice that it did not demand very much of a capable man like Tatian to impart far-reaching implications to his gospel text. We are often surprised in finding how the simplest means were employed to the greatest effect : here a well-placed gloss, there a little change in word-order, sufficed to make it unmistakably plain that the prize of eternal life demands a radical renunciation of possessions, family life and marriage, i.e. the prize demands a life in abstinence and virginity.

54 Eñ ihs antwerdde hen aldus. Eñ hebdi nit ghelesen dat in den beghiñe doe goet man eñ wyf hadde ghe makt, dat hise tesamen gheuugde? eñ adam seide om me dese gheuugtheit so sal de mensche laten vader eñ moeder eñ sal bliuen met sinen wiue, eñ si tuee selen syn ghesament in eenen vleesche, *op. cit.*, p. 317.

55 Mar de ghene die werdech selen syn dis leuens van dire andre werelt eñ der opherstannessen der seleger die en selen noch wyue nemen noch brulocht maken, *ibid.*, p. 473 f.

Something more can be learned about the character of the Christian life as Tatian understood it. There are other modifications which help us see and understand his concept of Christian life more clearly.

There is one reading which testifies to Tatian's great interest in the Christian life as one of suffering. The Christian life finds an adequate expression in the notion of the 'cross'. It is instructive to observe that Tatian felt it necessary to insert this notion into the saying of Jesus concerning perfection. The word in Mt. XIX, 21 and parall. : 'if you would be perfect, go sell what you possess...' has been supplemented by the exhortation : 'and take your cross and come after me'. The Arabic Diatessaron has preserved this reading [56] along with the Persian version [57] as well as it has survived in the writings of those authors who were acquainted with archaic Syriac text traditions [58]. Tatian felt strongly that the concept of the Christian life is adequately depicted only by the term 'cross'.

There is still another observation which shows that Tatian understood the cross as the central motif of the Christian life. The saying of Jesus concerning the carrying of the cross must have been of such interest to Tatian that he wanted to emphasize it. In Mt. x, 38 and parall. the saying about taking or carrying the cross is supplemented by something which makes the saying more articulate, picturesque and concrete. Tatian added the word 'on his shoulder', preserved by a number of texts [59] and, in Syriac form [60] by authors who have used the archaic text traditions [61]. In this addition we once again see the direction of Tatian's thought which was greatly influenced by the meaning of suffering [62].

56 *Tatiani evang. harmoniae arabice,* p. 110.

57 *Diatess. persiano,* p. 155.

58 Vööbus, *Studies,* p. 200.

59 Opsinen hals, 'upon his neck', *Liège Diatess.,* p. 97; upon his back, *Pepysian Gospel,* p. 57.

The Persian version reads: بر ندارد 'on his back', *Diatess. persiano,* p. 208, and بگیرد 'upon his shoulder', *ibid.,* p. 134.

60 Ms. Laur. Orient. 308, fol. 34 a.

61 Vööbus, *Untersuchungen,* p. 16 ff.

62 This formulation became very important for the monasticism, Ms. Patr. Šarf. 66, cahier 16.

All this authentic material, which has come to light in various versions of Tatian's work, unveils the real extent of the penetration and permeation of his Encratite views into the gospel text that was proclaimed in the Syrian Orient during the first Christian generations. Together with the word of salvation a message was heralded that the Christian faith finds its realization only in rigid asceticism, which unites all those who bear the cross on their shoulders and follow their Master on their *via dolorosa.*

2. THE MOVEMENT OF MARCION

The patristic authors reveal clearly the growing concern with which they followed the progress of the Marcionite propaganda which seemed to know no barriers. Very rapidly Marcionite communities found ways to expand their mission. Already in the middle of the second century Justin Martyr could not conceal his astonishment over the elan of Marcion's movement which appeared everywhere [63].

Our information about the spread of the movement in Syria comes from several sources. The common source behind the Pseudo-Clementine Homilies and Recognitions, which originated at the beginning of the third century, was involved in a controversy with the Marcionite influence [64]. The oldest church inscription which we know of is an inscription on a lintel of a Marcionite church in Lebaba near Damascus. This inscription is dated 318/319 [65]. This fact is ominous. Something of the strength of the Marcionite church is revealed in the territory not far from Lebaba. Cyril of Jerusalem was much worried about the great danger which the Marcionite communities caused to the Catholic church in this area. In his catecheses he warns his believers concerning these dangers. On entering a strange town, he tells them, they must be careful not to step into a Marcionite church by mistake [66].

63 *Apologia,* I, col. 368 f.

64 *Pseudoklementinen,* II, 43; III, 38; III, 54 ff., p. 52 f., 70 f. 76 ff. Quomodo potest unum atque idem et bonum esse et iustum, *Recognitiones,* col. 1299.

65 WADDINGTON, *Inscriptions,* p. 582 f.

66 *Catecheses mystagogicae,* XVIII, 26, col. 1047.

In Palestine, under the victims of the persecutions, there were also those of Marcionite church. Regarding a Marcionite bishop under the victims, see EUSEBIUS, *De martyribus Palaest.,* X, 3, p. 931.

Another kind of evidence at our disposal comes from Laodicea in Syria. Towards the middle of the fourth century the Marcionite movement must have been a very acute problem. Even when the creed was formulated it was necessary for Christians to keep one eye on the ever-present Marcionite threat. We possess an interesting creed in which the first article is directed against the menace which came from these Marcionite quarters : 'we believe in one God... God of the law and the gospel, just and good' [67].

Besides this information, a summary statement is preserved by the Abercios-inscription which refers to a widespread influence the movement found in the communities in Syria [68].

But all this information about Syria, where the bishops kept guard over orthodoxy making great efforts in this battle with the Marcionite church is not comparable with the success which the Marcionite movement gained in the Syriac-speaking areas, for among these Syriac-speaking communities Marcionite propaganda found a particularly fertile ground in the Mesopotamian regions where its seed grew and spread rapidly.

We have some information about the Marcionite success in Osrhoene. Towards the end of the second century Bardaiṣan lived and flourished in Edessa. This interesting man who composed fascinating hymns and many-sided treatises was compelled to write dialogues against Marcion, composed in Syriac. Nothing of them has survived, although they did not circulate in Syriac alone but were translated into Greek by Bardaiṣan's disciples. But the remarks which Eusebius has made concerning these compositions, permit us to infer that Bardaiṣan saw the Marcionite movement as the greatest heretical danger in Mesopotamia at his time [69]. The anathemas from the orthodox Christian community provoked counter-measures from

67 The text is edited by CASPARI, *Alte und neue Quellen*, p. 20 : πιστεύομεν εἰς ἑνα θεόν... τὸν θεὸν τοῦ νόμου καὶ εὐαγγελίου, δίκαιον καὶ ἀγαθόν.

68 καὶ πρῶτα μέν τῇ 'Αντιοχέων ἐπιδημεῖ, εἶτα δέχεται τοῦτον 'Απάμεια, κἀκεῖθεν, ἐπὶ τὰς λοιπὰς μεταβαίνει πόλεις, καὶ στασιαζούσας διαλλάττει τὰς ἐκκλησίας· πάνυ γὰρ τότε τὸ τῆς αἱρέσεως τοῦ Μαρκίωνος κακὸν ἐνέμετο ταύτας. *Vita Abercii*, p. 512. πάνυ γὰρ τῷ χρόνῳ ἐκείνῳ ἡ αἵρεσις, τοῦ Μαρκίωνος ἐθορύβησε τὰς τῶν χριστιανῶν ἐκκλησίας, *Nouvelle récension de la vie d'Abercius*, p. 303.

69 *Hist. eccl.*, IV, 30, p. 392.

the Marcionites [70]. Thus the echo of the noise of this controversy remained in the air a long time.

We get a picture of the extent of the Marcionite penetration which seriously endangered the small group of orthodox Christians, desperately fighting for its life, in several sources [71]. Theodoret shows that Cyrrhestica was infected by the Marcionites even at the end of the fourth century [72]. Regarding Osrhoene particularly the numerous writings of Ephrem are illuminating. Here we read how the mind of this fearless champion was constantly vexed by seeing the shameful situation with which orthodoxy had to be content. Therefore Ephrem was compelled to deal with this powerful rival not only in his polemical writings, whether composed in poetry [73], or prose [74], but also in his commentary on the gospel [75]. He could not free himself from the influence under which this courageous fighter had to live.

The Marcionite church was no less successful in popularity in the districts of Persia, where it contributed to the Christian mission and moulded the spirit of primitive Christianity according to the pattern of a severe form of asceticism.

Probably the earliest Marcionite communities here were not much younger than those in Osrhoene, although the data are not conclusive. According to one tradition the Marcionite movement also received new contingents from Western territories because of measures taken to suppress their church [76]. These measures took place under Constantine the Great who at first allowed the Marcionites religious freedom, but later revoked the freedom of the heterodox groups.

As far back as we can see, the Marcionite movement was vigorous and powerful. On a short list of the heretics dangerous to the

70 A Syrian Marcionite Prepon wrote against Bardaiṣan, cf. HIPPOLYTUS, *Elenchus*, VII, 31, 1, col. 3333; THEODORETUS, *Haeret. fab. compendium*, I, 22, col. 372..

71 *Srboyn*, II, p. 321.

72 *Hist. eccl.*, V, 31, p. 331; *Historia religiosa*, col. 1440-44, 1452. Theodoret speaks also of the Marcionite villages and he claims that he had converted 8 such villages, *Epistola*, LXXXI, col. 1261.

73 *Contra haereses*; *Carmina Nisibena*, p. 124 ff.

74 *Prose Refutations*, I, p. 1 ff.; II, p. 50 ff.

75 See pag. 42.

76 Ms. Vat. syr. 11, fol. 231 b.

church in Persia of his time, Aphrahaṭ puts Marcion in first place[77]. The danger implied in this fact is confirmed by the Acts of Šemʿōn bar Ṣabbāʿē who, in the last admonitions he left as a legacy to the church, warned his fellow-believers of Marcionites in particular[78].

The correspondence of Papā, which is a free fabrication, contains something of value for our purpose : 'and we fear not only the pagans but also the Jews and Marcionites, who since they were suppressed by the rule of your kingdom in your territory, escaped to this region'[79]. This information imparts two facts of interest. First, besides the Jews and the Magi, their only Christian rivals were the Marcionites. Secondly, the Marcionites received new strength from the contingents that came from the West.

Also we hear how difficult it was to change the wellrooted traditions even later. The Marcionites were hard after orthodoxy, considering themselves the church and using the same customs as those used by the orthodox groups[80]. We are able to see the almost unbelievable position won by the Marcionite communities in Persia in a later document, the vita of 'Abā. There is an episode recorded in this document which happened at the Tigris and is inserted into the story of 'Abā's conversion. As a pagan 'Abā met a Christian ascetic and became involved in conversation with him. He asked the ascetic whether he was a Marcionite or a Jew. A remark at this point in the account is valuable for our purpose : 'for he called a Marcionite a Christian as (was) the custom of this place'[81]. This definition is confirmed in the witness given by the ascetic : 'I

77 *Demonstrationes*, col. 116.

78 *Acta martyrum*, II, p. 150 f.

79 ܘܠܐ ܗܘܐ ܒܠܚܘܕ ܡܢ ܚܢܦܐ ܕܚܠܝܢ ܐܠܐ ܐܦ ܡܢ ܝܗܘܕܝܐ ܘܡܪܩܝܘܢܝܐ. ܕܡܢ ܕܐܬܥܨܝܘ ܒܫܘܠܛܢܐ ܕܡܠܟܘܬܟܘܢ ܒܬܚܘܡܝܟܘܢ ܠܐܬܪܐ ܗܢܐ ܥܪܩܘ Ms. Vat. Borg. syr. 82, fol. 115 b.

80 *Histoire de Jabalaha*, p. 212 f. Perhaps the story of Aūgēn has borrowed its information about the manners of the Marcionites from an older source. Here too, it is said that the Marcionites used the same manners as the orthodox groups regarding hairdress and garments, *Acta martyrum*, III, p. 404.

81 ܩܪܐ ܓܝܪ ܟܪܣܛܝܢܐ ܠܡܪܩܝܘܢܝܐ ܐܝܟ ܥܝܕܐ ܕܐܬܪܐ *Histoire de Jabalaha*, p. 213.

am a Christian in truth, and not as the Marcionites who are deceiving and name themselves Christians' [82].

This episode is very instructive. It demonstrates how the Marcionites managed to hold to the position of currently being called 'Christians'. This account permits a certain sidelight on the conditions which must have prevailed in earlier times when the ratio of the numerical strength of the Marcionites was certainly stronger.

Radical asceticism characterized the life of the Marcionite type of Christianity that was established in the Aramaean Orient. The movement embodied a deep hatred against everything that is of the world. This attitude needs investigation.

The nature of Marcionite ethics is determined by a fundamental theological principle. The distinction between the God of the Law and God the Father of Jesus Christ caused the concept of the Christian life to assume a completely different complexion. Because the world was created by the God of the Old Testament, who loved deceit, violence, murder and other gruesome deeds, an imperative was given in Marcionite ethics to use his creation only in a minimum way in order to reject the work of this God and to insult him. Therefore the character of Marcionite ethics is primarily that of protest. These ethics are a witness and a proof that one does not stand in the service of the God of the Old Testament, but gives testimony to belonging to another God. These ethics have made the life and conduct of the Marcionite believers so hard and difficult that no Christian church has dared to approximate their position.

One of the institutions created by the God of the Law was marriage. Therefore the task of the Marcionite believers was the disparagement of this institution. Their duty was not to fill his world with children but to reduce it by their behavior as much as possible [83]. The practical application of the principle regarding wife and children can be seen in Lk. xxiii, 2 in the text of Marcion's redaction. This passage which gives the sum of the primary accusations brought against Jesus before Pilate, was supplemented by an additional statement, namely, that Jesus advised His followers

82 *Ibid.*, p. 214.

83 *μὴ βουλόμενοι τὸν κόσμον τὸν ὑπὸ τοῦ δημιουργοῦ γενόμενον συμπληροῦν*, Clemens, *Stromata*, III, 3, 12, p. 200.

to leave families, wives and children [84]. This was one of the few additions which Marcion deemed to insert into the text.

With regard to marriage Marcion demanded absolute continence. Marcionite communities consisted only of celibates who considered marriage as φθορά [85] and πορνεία [86]. Indeed, with unparalleled nausea the Marcionites spoke of marriage, family-life and of procreation of children. This fact is stated again and again by Oriental authors. Ephrem says that the Marcionites reviled marriage [87]. And a more ancient tract which once existed in Syriac, but has been preserved only in Armenian version, reports that the Marcionites dirty the bride and bridegroom saying that they are unclean [88].

According to Marcionite theology the body represents the element of Evil and is from the Evil One [89]. This principle they ascribed to Jesus, claiming that he had hated the body : 'because the body is polluted, hateful and abominable, our Lord despised it' [90]. The fact that the gospel says that Jesus healed the injured organs of the body did not mean anything to them [91]. For the redeemed ones, according to Marcion, there was only one aim : they were to rid themselves of the body and of bodily needs as much as possible. The Marcionites used the illustration of the shell and the young chicken, in which the latter does not need the former as soon as it is free and it begins its life [92]. There was, consequently, no room left for the body in the resurrection hope. Ephrem, describing this type of attitude and life, characterized Marcion as 'the hater of flesh' [93].

84 Epiphanius, *Panarion*, Scholion, LXX, col. 768.

85 Hippolytus, *Elenchus*, X, 19, col. 3436.

86 Irenaeus, *Adv. haereses*, I, 28, 1, p. 259.

87 ܐܝܟ ܕܓܕܦ ܠܙܘܘܓܐ 'for he who reviles marriage', *Contra haereses*, XLV, 6, p. 179; ܕܛܢܦܐܘ ܩܪܝܢ ܠܙܘܘܓܐ 'for they pronounce marriage unclean', XLV, 7, *ibid.*

88 *Srboyn*, II, p. 303.

89 *Prose Refutations*, I, p. 146 f.

90 ܡܛܠ ܕܛܢܦܐ ܦܓܪܐ ܘܣܢܝܐ ܘܢܕܝܕ ܫܛܗ ܡܪܢ *Contra haereses*, XLVII, 2, p. 183; ܦܓܪܐ ܕܛܢܦܐ ܗܘ 'body that is polluted', XLVII, 7, *ibid.*, p. 185.

91 Here Ephrem carries out his argumentation with ostentatious joy, *Prose Refutations*, II, p. 125 ff.; cf. also *Contra haereses*, XLII, 1 . 2, p. 168 f.

92 LII, 4, *ibid.*, p. 200.

93 XLIII, 15, *ibid.*, p. 173.

Under these circumstances it is not strange that the Marcionites did not hesitate to mutilate their bodies [94].

With regard to the nourishing of the body the same hatred existed. Marcionites were not to serve the creation of the Demiurge, and they have testified to this ethic in their practice of the strongest abstinence in eating and drinking. They rejected many kinds of food declaring them as being close to the Evil and therefore unclean [95]. The use of meat was particularly condemned. They felt that the smell of meat in the sacrifices delighted the Demiurge [96]. But they were allowed to eat fish, for the Lord Himself ate fish after His resurrection. Probably this was not the only argument they used [97]. Eznik's counter-argument that fish was not used for sacrifices and therefore it was inferior [98] missed the point. Just because fish had no relation to the sacrifices fish was acceptable.

We are not satisfactorily informed about the Marcionites' attitude towards the use of wine. And the references about the use of water instead of wine [99] find contradictory statements in the Orient [100].

Eating in general was, in the eyes of the Marcionites, something sinful, even a crime. This strict view manifests itself in the boldness with which Marcion made revisions even in the wording of Lord's Prayer. Instead of 'our daily bread' his corrected text reads : 'Thy daily bread give us each day' [101]. Everything in the prayer for daily nourishment revolted him.

94 Tertullian refers to eunuchs in connection with the baptism, *Adv. Marcionem*, IV, 11, p. 451; Origen, however, says that they did not practice castration, *Commentaria in Matth.*, XV, 3, p. 356.

95 In eating and drinking, the same radical purpose was carried through — to revolt against the work of the Demiurge : ad destruenda et contemnenda et abominanda opera creatoris, HIERONYMUS, *Adv. Jovinianum*, II, 16, col. 323.

96 *Opera omnia*, II, p. 522.

97 According to the Acts of Thomas there was a tradition regarding Jesus as a poor man who was catching fish for meals, *Apocryphal Acts*, p. 216.

98 *Etc ałandoç*, p. 281.

99 Epiphanius assures us that the Marcionites did not make an exception in their rigor even in the Eucharist and used water in the celebration of it : *ὕδατι δὲ οὗτος ἐν τοῖς μυστηρίοις χρῆται*, *Panarion*, XLII, 3, 3, p. 98.

100 Eznik is surprised that the Marcionites whom he knew permitted wine.

101 *τὸν ἄρτον σου τὸν ἐπιούσιον δίδου ἡμῖν τὸ καθ' ἡμέραν*, ORIGENES, *Fragmenta*, p. 254, no. XLVI.

The logical inference drawn from this fundamental principle was severe fasting, continuous and merciless in its nature [102]. On the Sabbath a total fasting was ordered, again, against the God of the Old Testament as a protest and contempt [103]. But this was only one among other regulations. In keeping their practices, the Marcionites felt that there was no real fasting as far as other religious groups were concerned. The Marcionites claimed that they fasted more than Ezechiel. It must have been painful for a critic like Ephrem not to be able to deny the extreme and severe form of the Marcionites' fasts [104]. In his rage Ephrem shouts that Marcion, as a personification of the movement, could fast as a serpent [105]. Only such a relentless mortification served to condemn and to destroy the works of the Demiurge [106].

With regard to the habits of dress, Ephrem depicts the Marcionites as dressed in sack-cloth, the classical garment of penitents [107].

The Marcionites held a similarly extreme view about the worthlessness of possessions. All possessions deserved nothing else but contempt. This renunciation was further guided by the conviction that the God of the Old Testament had promised luck for the rich ones but Christ had pledged His kingdom to the poor and needy.

The believers had to avoid as much as possible all dealings with the created world. The purpose was to allow the redeemed life to be emancipated from the created world and its embodied form. This idea was carried to the most extreme forms that the human body could sustain. Attaining this degree of emancipation, the Marcionites believed themselves no longer to be human beings, in the ordinary sense, but super-creatures. But the more they spiritualized the life the more they drew hatred, contempt and persecution upon themselves. Therefore they accepted condemnation in the consolation

102 Perpetua abstinentia, HIPPOLYTUS, *Elenchus*, VII, 39; X, 19, col. 3437; TERTULLIANUS, *De ieiunio*, XV, p. 293.

103 EPIPHANIUS, *Panarion*, XLIII, 3, II, p. 98.

104 *Prose Refutations*, II, p. 67.

105 ܡܪܩܝܘܢ ܕܐܝܟ ܚܘܝܐ ܗܘ ܨܡ ܗܘܐ 'Marcion was fasting as a serpent', *Contra haereses*, I, 17, p. 5.

106 THEODOR OF MOPSVESTIA, *In ep. Pauli Commentarii*, II, p. 139 f.; HIERONYMUS, *Adv. Jovinianum*, II, 16, col. 323.

107 *Contra haereses*, I, 12, p. 3.

that while the Demiurge is with the masses in their complacency, the Savior goes with the few elected ones on the path of suffering [108]. In this loneliness and in their bitter experiences the Marcionites believed they had found a criterion for disciples of Christ.

Of the religious practices of the Marcionites one, and indeed the most important, cannot be passed over without a remark. According to one section in Ephrem's refutations the Marcionites laid stress on the place which prayer held in their religious life. Ephrem has preserved even their own claim : 'we are praying the whole day' [109]. Ephrem does not dare to question the validity of their contention, but what he says is that regardless of their efforts, their prayers are not heard.

Finally a few words as to how their church life in the congregations was shaped according to these fundamental principles. All those who were not ready for the consequences of the Christian faith had to remain in the status of the catechumen. Only the ascetics were admitted to the congregation as full members. These members were celibates, and married persons who avoided carnal intercourse. Only these categories of persons deserved to be baptized. Tertullian says this clearly : 'the married he will not unite, the united he will not admit, for he deals only with the celibate and the eunuch, reserving baptism only to the dead or the separated' [110]. Marcion, however, did not demand that a marriage be dissolved once it existed — showing thereby respect to the gospel — but demanded a vow of continence and abstinence. Eznik says something about their habits and speaks of their vow before baptism took place. According to this report they promised to abstain from marriage and live an ascetic life : 'and they vow together with the lay-people for virginity..., and (they should) not (live) (i.e. the Chris-

108 Clemens, *Stromata,* III, 10, 69, p. 227.

The path of suffering led many Marcionites to self-destruction. Clemens speaks of heretics who, like the Indian gymnosophists, threw themselves into death in order to escape the hated creator, *Stromata,* IV, 4, 17, p. 256. Probably these were the Marcionites, cf. Harnack, *Marcion,* p. 188, note 4.

109 *Prose Refutations,* II, p. 68.

110 Marcion ecce legem tui quoque dei impugnas. Nuptias non coniungit, coniunctas non admittit, neminem tingit nisi caelibem aut spadonem, morti aut repudio baptisma servat, *Adv. Marcionem,* IV, 11, p. 451.

tians) as those who boast that « already since the basin (of baptism) we have vowed concerning meat and marriage »' [111].

Of course, as full members of the church only the ascetics could share the Lord's Supper [112].

This congregation of redeemed ones overcame the distinction between the sexes. Marcion's church established a community in which the Pauline ideal, that in Christ there is 'no male nor female', was concretized. This ideal became the basis on which Marcion made his last bold conclusion whereby a new understanding of the role of women was gained. They were permitted the right to teach, to exorcize and to baptize [113], although Marcion did not go extremes in this permission. He did not admit them to all the functions of the church. Nevertheless, Marcion went far enough to amaze his critics in the Catholic quarters.

3. THE MOVEMENT OF VALENTINUS

The adherents of the movement of Valentinus also found receptive ground in the Syrian Orient.

The earliest period of this movement lies in complete darkness. Whether Antioch served as an important channel which brought the movement in contact with the Syriac-speaking Christians is difficult to say. But the remark in Tertullian about the activity of Axionicus at Antioch is of interest anyway [114]. The earliest trace of the existence of the Valentinian movement in Edessa appears in the Vita of Bardaiṣan. According to this source it is presumed that the movement existed in Edessa already before the third quarter of the second century [115]. The value of this source is doubtful but the suggestion

111 *և ուխտաւորելք հանդերձ աշխարհականօքն ’ի կուսութիւն ... և ոչ որպէս նոքա, որք մեծամեծս կոտորեն՝ թէ մեք անդստին իսկ յաւազանէն ուխտաւորիմք ’ի մսակերութենէ և յամուսնութենէ,* EZNIK, *Etc ałandoc̣*, p. 288 f.

112 Quomodo tu nuptias dirimis nec coniungens marem et feminam nec alibi coniunctos ad sacramentum baptismatis et eucharistiae admittens nisi inter se coniuraverint adversus fructum nuptiarum? TERTULLIANUS, *Adv. Marcionem*, IV, 34, p. 534.

113 EPIPHANIUS, *Panarion*, XLII, 4, 5, v. II, p. 100.

114 *Adv. Valentinianos*, IV, p. 181.

115 *Biographie de Bardesane*, p. 12.

it contains may be not wrong. Something of the influence of the movement can be seen reflected in the fact that some of the characteristic formulations occur in the earliest liturgical traditions[116]. Through the letters of Julian Apostata we have information about the existence of their community in Edessa[117]. According to some indications the Valentinians must have been fairly active in Osrhoene. Ephrem also refers to their activity and complains about the flock which Valentinus has gathered from the church[118].

The movement also reached the territories beyond the Tigris, and continued to be an attraction in the religious scene under the Persian rule. We have direct reference to this characteristic of the movement in the treatises of Aphrahaṭ[119]. There are also traces left behind that can only mean that the movement must have played a considerable role[120].

The erratic journeys which have taken place in the interpretation of the Valentinian gnosis show that in order to understand the structural role of asceticism in it, one has constantly to refer to certain premises. This is important also because the sources concerning the Valentinians' practical Christianity do not flow freely. And what does flow is fused with waters darkened by interests other than objectivity and honesty.

In Valentinianism religious life on the higher level is understood philosophically and moves between two poles. On the one hand the psychical being has to take on a proper figure and it must be educated towards good in order to be able to receive the pneumatic seed. On the other hand this pneumatic seed must take root until man becomes a pneumatic man. Thus both poles belong together

116 The Acts of Thomas have preserved a prayer of baptismal liturgy, a sort of epiclesis, which *inter alia* says : ܬܐ ܓܠܝܬ ܐܪ̈ܙܐ ܟܣ̈ܝܐ ܬܐ ܐܡܐ ܕܫܒܥܐ ܒܬ̈ܝܢ ܕܬܡܝܢܝܐ ܒܝܬܐ ܗܘܐ ܢܝܚܟܝ 'come, revealer of secret mysteries; come, mother of seven houses, thy rest was in the eighth house', *Apocryphal Acts,* p. 193.

117 *Juliani imp. opera,* I, 2, p. 196.

118 *Contra haereses,* XXII, 3, p. 78 f.

119 *Demonstrationes,* I, col. 116.

120 It seems that certain traditions behind the *Liber graduum* stem from ideas popularized by the Valentinians, particularly the speculation about Syzygies, see pag. 190 ff.

according to the fundamental principle of Syzygy [121]. Through this union the psychical substance will be accommodated and the pneumatic seed will take root and develop, because this seed needs physical and sensual means for its development [122].

The sphere of psychical life is identified now with the church and here there is a place for good works. But the pneumatics by gnosis and its mysteries reach the height of perfection, and on this level everything is centered around the pneuma. Thus, to the gnostics the church became a hotbed from which they recruited those fit for perfection. But the gnostics also wanted to maintain relations with the church, because they have to live in 'the mystery of Syzygy' [123]. The Valentinians were annoyed that the church severed relations with them and condemned them as heretics [124].

This premise is very important in understanding Valentinian ethics correctly. The ecclesiastical fathers in their apologetic zeal simply misunderstood the issue. They inferred too hastily that if good works belong to the psychical sphere, i.e. to the church members, the Valentinian perfect Christians discard all ethical norms. Nevertheless much groundless talk in Irenaeus [125], taken over in a summary fashion by Tertullian, has not entirely overshadowed the truth. Thus, we have to separate the facts from the tendentious myth.

In the light of the fact that the sphere of pneumatism cannot stand alone but must be coupled with the psychical one characterized

121 Clemens, *Excerpta ex Theodoto*, XXI, 1-3, p. 113. Here one is the male or angelic, and the other is female or seed; both form a couple, a *συζυγία*. The thought that the pneumatic believers are yoked together with the psychic Christians in the process of spiritual growth means that the pneumatic believers are tied to the obligations regarding the ethical conduct of the psychic Christians, and must observe these in order to attain greater and deeper maturity.

122 Irenaeus is very clear about the thought that, in the process of education, the pneumatic believers are yoked together with the psychic Christians : *τὸ δὲ πνευματικὸν ἐκπεπέμφθαι, ὅπως ἐνθάδε τῷ ψυχικῷ συζυγὲν μορφωθῇ, συμπαιδευθὲν αὐτῷ ἐν τῇ ἀναστροφῇ. Καὶ τοῦτ' εἶναι λέγουσι τὸ ἅλας καὶ τὸ φῶς τοῦ κόσμου. Ἔδει γὰρ τῶν ψυχικῶν καὶ αἰσθητῶν παιδευμάτων. Δι' ὧν καὶ κόσμον κατεσκευάσθαι λέγουσι, καὶ τὸν Σωτῆρα δὲ ἐπὶ τοῦτο παραγεγονέναι τὸ ψυχικόν, ἐπεί καὶ αὐτεξούσιόν ἐστιν, ὅπως αὐτὸ σώσῃ*, *Adv. haereses*, I, 6, 1, p. 70.

123 *μυστήριον τῆς συζυγίας*.

124 *Ibid.*, III, 15, 2, p. 501 f.

125 *Ibid.*, I, 6, 2 f., p. 73 ff.; see also Tertullianus, *Adv. Valentinianos*, XXX, p. 205.

by good works, it becomes clear that in this process towards perfection — called education — asceticism has its very important place. Thus asceticism which conquers the nature, purifies it and liberates it appears along with the factor of revelation, and the means of grace.

Concerning the continence practiced by the Valentinians, one information is particularly valuable regardless of the difficulties with which it is beset. The passage is quoted as one which the Valentinians used to cite [126] : 'whosoever, being in the world, did not love a woman as to have dominion over her [127] is not of the truth and not shall attain to the truth; but whosoever, being of the world is [128] dominated by a woman, shall not attain to the truth, because he has been conquered by woman in concupiscence'.

This text speaks clearly of two categories of Christians and we recognize here the perfect ones, and the ordinary ones who belong to the church : those 'in the world' are the pneumatics and those 'of the world' are the psychic believers, as Irenaeus has rightly noticed. So far the text offers no problem because these categories are distinguished by phrases taken from the language of the Fourth Gospel [129].

The difficulties arise in the interpretation of the meaning of the text. We begin with the more difficult part of the passus in the first sentence. Older interpretations have seen in this sentence a blunt statement that carnal intercourse cannot harm the perfect one because he is on a level above all these things. This is an explanation which, as we shall see, is contradicted by Irenaeus himself. Surely, Irenaeus understood the text in this sense. This,

126 *ὅς ἂν ἐν κόσμῳ γενόμενος γυναῖκα οὐκ ἐφίλησεν, ὥστε αὐτὴν κρατηθῆναι, οὐκ ἔστιν ἐξ ἀληθείας καὶ οὐ χωρήσει εἰς ἀλήθειαν· ὁ δὲ ἀπὸ κόσμου ὢν [μὴ] κρατηθεὶς γυναικὶ οὐ χωρήσει εἰς ἀλήθειαν διὰ τὸ ἐν ἐπιθυμίᾳ κρατηθῆναι γυναικός*, EPIPHANIUS, *Panarion*, XXXI, 21, 9, I, p. 418 f.; cf. IRENAEUS, *Adv. haereses*, I, 6, 4, p. 76 f.

127 The Latin text has : ut ei coniungatur (= *αὐτῇ κραθῆναι* of *κεράννυμι*). It seems that the reading in the Greek text is correct, and not the reading in Latin. Holl suggests *αὐτῆς* instead of *αὐτὴν*.

128 In this part the Latin text which omits the negation has preserved the original. This [*μή*] is supported by the editions of Holl, Harvey and Massuet.

129 The perfect Christians like the Apostles are : 'in the world' but they are not 'of the world', as the psychic Christians are.

understanding, however, is not worthy of our confidence. On the contrary, as the text stands, its meaning can only be that a love which is not checked and balanced by discipline over one's wife, is forbidden for Gnostics. A union without watchful control would degrade a perfect Christian.

This result is confirmed by the rest of the text. It says that a Christian in the church, i.e. a psychic believer, who is conquered by a woman and lives in sexual intercourse with her, although in a legitimate marriage, is not fit 'to attain to the truth', i.e. to become a perfect Christian.

Fortunately we have other means of controlling the correctness of our interpretation. One is theoretical, another practical. Both point in the same direction.

According to the principle of Syzygies the degree attained in the psychical sphere not only is necessary, but also is the only way in which the whole process of 'education' towards perfection is conceivable.

Further, we have important references regarding the practice of virginity among the Valentinians. The Valentinians have been known as those who reject marriage[130]. There is however still something more that clearly shines through the distorted report in Irenaeus. We observe that he contradicts himself. In the same chapter

130 JOANNES CHRYSOSTOMUS, *De virginitate*, col. 536 ff. This harmonizes with the concept of holiness in the Valentinian sources. Thus the gospel of the Valentinians contains the following significant statement : ⲛ̄ϩⲣⲏï ϩⲛ̄ ⲟⲩⲥⲁⲩⲛⲉ ⲉϥⲛⲁⲥⲱⲧ̄ϥ̄ ⲙ̄ⲙⲁϥ ⲁⲃⲁⲗ ϩⲛ̄ⲛ ⲟⲩⲧⲟ· ⲛ̄ⲣⲏⲧⲉ ⲁϩⲟⲩ̄ ⲁⲩⲙⲛ̄ⲧⲟⲩⲉⲉⲓ ⲉϥⲟⲩⲱⲙ ⲛ̄ϯϩⲩⲗⲏ ⲛ̄ϩⲣⲏï ⲛ̄ϩⲏⲧ̄ϥ̄ ⲙ̄ⲡⲣⲏⲧⲉ ⲛ̄ⲛⲟⲩⲥⲉⲧⲉ ⲁⲩⲱ ⲡⲕⲉ ⲕⲉⲓ ϩⲛ̄ ⲟⲩⲁⲉⲓⲛ ⲡⲙⲟⲩ ϩⲛ̄ ⲟⲩ ⲱⲛ̄ϩ̄ ⲉⲓϣⲡⲉ ⲁⲛⲉⲉⲓ ϭⲉ ϣⲱⲡⲉ ⲙ̄ⲡⲟⲩⲉⲉⲓ ⲡⲟⲩⲉⲉⲓ ⲙ̄ⲙⲁⲛ ⲟⲩⲛ ⲡⲉⲧⲉϣϣⲉ ⲁⲣⲁⲛ ϭⲉ ⲛⲧⲛ̄ⲙⲉⲩⲉ ⲁⲡⲧⲏⲣ̄ϥ̄ ϣⲓⲛⲁ ⲉⲣⲉⲡⲓⲏⲉⲓ ⲛⲁϣⲱⲡⲉ ⲉϥⲟⲩⲁ· ⲁϥ· ⲁⲩⲱ ⲉϥⲥϭⲣⲁϩ̄ⲧ̄ ⲁϯⲙⲛ̄ⲧ ⲟⲩⲉⲉⲓ 'by means of a Gnose, he shall purify himself of diversity with a view to Unity, by engulfing the Matter within himself like a flame, obscurity by light and death by life; certainly, if these things have happened to each one of us, we should then, above all, take care that the House be holy (and) silent for Unity', *Evangelium veritatis*, p. 25.

It is also significant that in the Gospel of Thomas, used in these circles, the following logia are ascribed to Jesus : 'Blessed are the single ones (celibates) and the elected ones — for you shall find the Kingdom because (you come) from it, and you shall enter in again', *Coptic Gnostic Papyri*, p. 89; 'many are standing at the door, but these are the single ones (celibates) who shall enter the bridal chamber', *ibid.*, p. 94.

from which we took the above-mentioned text, Irenaeus makes the remark : 'but others of them, again, at first claim to live together as with sisters venerably...' [131].

If we pay full attention to this last statement, we must admit that what we have here most probably is spiritual marriage which has been practiced among the perfect Christians in this movement. Moreover, what Tertullian includes for the sake of polemics, agrees with this recognition. He says that castration was known and practiced among the Valentinians [132]. This statement is something which is quite understandable in the light of these circumstances. If castration was practiced by them in the West, there is no doubt that the practice found an even more receptive climate in Syria and Mesopotamia where the ground certainly was prepared for this custom.

As to how asceticism penetrated their lives in other questions we have to be contented with very general remarks. Clement of Alexandria has preserved further information with regard to the meaning of life in the pneumatic sphere. According to this source the nature of this life is a disengagement from matter and by this act a dissociation from the inferior world [133]. So we have to conclude that those perfect Christians who were admitted to the elite were believers who were ready to kill their flesh and practice mortification in every respect [134]. In a fragment left over from a homily of Valentinian origin the perfect Christians are addressed exactly in this sense : 'you are the lords of the creation and of all corruption' [135].

131 *ἄλλοι δὲ αὖ πάλιν σεμνῶς κατ' ἀρχὰς ὡς μετ' ἀδελφῶν προσποιούμενοι συνοικεῖν...* *Adv. haereses*, I, 6, 3. Further Irenaeus raises suspicions as to the purity of their life. Here he certainly speaks as a prejudiced judge, thinking that their eventual slips were worse than those which happened in the Catholic quarters.

132 *Adv. Valentinianos*, XXX, p. 206.

133 Clemens, *Stromata*, III, 102, 3-4, p. 243, cf. II, 10, 2-3, p. 118.

134 See also some remarks in Irenaeus, *Adv. haereses*, III, 15, 2, p. 502 f.

135 *Οὐαλεντῖνος δὲ ἔν τινι ὁμιλίᾳ κατὰ λέξιν γράφει· «ἀπ' ἀρχῆς ἀθάνατοί ἐστε καὶ τέκνα ζωῆς ἐστε αἰωνίας καὶ τὸν θάνατον ἠθέλετε μερίσασθαι εἰς ἑαυτούς, ἵνα δαπανήσητε αὐτὸν καὶ ἀναλώσητε, καὶ ἀποθάνῃ ὁ θάνατος ἐν ὑμῖν καὶ δι' ὑμῶν· ὅταν γὰρ τὸν μὲν κόσμον λύητε, ὑμεῖς δὲ μὴ καταλύησθε, κυριεύετε τῆς κτίσεως καὶ τῆς φθορᾶς ἁπάσης»*, Clemens, *Stromata*, IV, 89, 1-3, p. 287.

The gaps in our information are unsurmountable as to the exact role this movement played in the religious milieu in Mesopotamia. Whether some stimuli were present in the movement which Irenaeus called 'like the Lernaean hydra' and called forth other Gnostic ramifications of which we have a number in cryptic names, we do not know. The only case which we are able to trace produces a negative result. The movement of Bardaiṣan is not an offspring of Valentinus.

To be sure the Vita of Bardaiṣan asserts that the movement of Valentinus won Bardaiṣan [136]. This is a view which is repeated by many other sources which have popularized the view that Bardaiṣan belonged to the Valentinian Gnosticism [137]. Of the reliable sources in our possession, we do not have any that reveals elements which resemble those of the Valentinian system.

But in the area of ethics this assertion is completely defeated. At first sight some authentic pieces containing the cosmogony might leave the impression that there is a certain similarity in the premises. A hymn from Bardaiṣan himself speaks of the mixture caused by the creation and of the process of purification and liberation from the elements of darkness which the soul has to make [138]. But only in appearance does this give a theological basis for a possible ascetic approach to life. Over against this, another remark preserved by Mōšē bar Kēphā, seems to refer to a quite different explanation [139]. But the most valuable piece of information is given by a contemporary of Bardaiṣan, Sextus Julius Africanus. He saw Bardaiṣan in the court of King Abgar IX (179-216) in Edessa as a

136 *Biographie de Bardesane*, p. 15.

137 EUSEBIUS, *Hist. eccl.*, IV, 30, 3, p. 393; HIERONYMUS, *De viris inlustribus*, XXXIII, p. 24; PHILOXENOS, *Hérésies christologiques*, p. 248.

138 THEODOROS BAR KONI, *Liber scholiorum*, II, p. 308; see also Ephrem's remark that the body is from the Evil one, and therefore there is no resurrection, *Contra haereses*, LIII, 4, p. 203; also Iwannīs of Darā about Bardaiṣan, Ms. Vat. syr. 100, fol. 3 b.

We cannot find out from which sources Šahrastānī has taken the tradition that Bardaiṣan was a champion of ascetic tenets, *Kitāb al-milal wa ăl-niḥăl*, p. 194 f.

139 ܟܕ ܡܬܕܟܐ ܘܡܨܛܠܠ ܒܚܕ ܒܛܢܐ ܘܝܠܕܐ ܥܕܡܐ ܕܢܫܬܠܡ 'as it is being purified and filtered by one conception and birth until it is completed' Ms. Par. syr. 241, fol. 17 b.

man of important social position. And it is remarkable that the only thing he knows to report about Bardaiṣan is his admiration of his skill in archery! [140] Besides, the way Ephrem treats Bardaiṣan and his followers leaves no doubt that this form of Gnosticism had nothing to do with the ascetic movements [141]. Thus all the information seems to support the view, presented by Jaʿqōb of Edessa, that the Gnosis of Bardaiṣan had no predecessors but actually was an independent branch in the Gnostic Pantheon [142].

140 *Veterum mathem. opera*, p. 300.

141 Speaking of Bardaiṣan he finds that in comparison with Marcion and Mani his personified movement appears as worldly, adorned with garments and beryls, *Contra haereses*, I, 12, p. 3 f.

142 ܗܠܝܢ ܕܝܢ ܕܒܪܕܝܨܢ: ܠܐ ܗܘܐ ܦܘܠܓܐ ܡܢ ܗܠܝܢ ܕܡܢ ܩܕܡܘܗܝ, ܐܝܬܝܗܘܢ, 'with regard to the followers of Bardaiṣan, these were not a schism of those that were extant before him', JAʿQŌB OF EDESSA, Two *Epistles*, p. 434.

CHAPTER III

THE ROLE OF ASCETICISM IN THE THIRD CENTURY

1. SOURCES

a. The Odes of Solomon

First of all we have to treat a document which has been in the center of a long controversy, the Odes of Solomon [1], found in a Syriac manuscript in 1909 by Harris, in a codex which came from the banks of the Tigris [2].

Everything in these texts suggests the second century Eastern Christianity. But the question regarding their home and original language has found no agreement among the students. The chief rival contentions are Syrian [3] and Greek [4]. Since I first studied these texts I became very dubious regarding their Greek origin and studies which have tried to produce arguments in favor of Greek origin have not cured me from this scepticism. The hand of the early Syrian Christianity is clearly noticeable. The thought-pattern, religious ring, mystical speech, the influence of the Targumim in biblical text and method of interpretation, Semitic character in style and rhythm, all this seems to demand a solution

1 *Odes and Psalms of Solomon*, I.

2 Ms. J. Ryl. Syr. 9, ca. 16th cent. Another codex, Ms. Br. Mus. Add. 14,538, of the 10th cent., has preserved only the last part of the cycle.

3 See Bernard, *Odes of Solomon*, p. 1 ff.; de Zwaan, *Edessene Origin*, p. 285 ff.

4 Frankenberg, *Verständnis der Oden*; Connolly, *Original Language*, p. 530 ff. See the full bibliography in Quasten, *Patrology*, I, p. 167 f. The Odes occur in the stichometry of Nicephorus, Patriarch of Constantinople at the beginning of the 9th century. Here the Odes together with the Psalms of Solomon are mentioned as containing 2100 verses. He must have had in his hands a list of the canonical books which included also these texts. It also must be mentioned that 5 of the Odes appear in the Gnostic work known as the *Pistis Sophia*, p. 1 ff. It has been suggested that these texts were translated from the Greek.

which sees in these poetical texts a product of the ancient Syrian Christian community.

An examination of the linguistic appearance of the Odes reveals how thoroughly Semitic they are — and not Greek. And certain terms which have appeared to be translations from the Greek, lose their significance when it is observed that the Syriac Psalter had already made these expressions common property. An analysis of the metrical scheme, the style and the rhythm shows that here we are not dealing with Greek phenomenon, but all we see here is fundamentally Semitic. These poems reflect a Syriac cast everywhere we look.

What speaks particularly strongly in favor of the primitive Syrian Christianity, is the religious and theological character of these poetical texts. This includes a singular amalgam of the covenant consciousness, baptismal imagery and heightened awareness of ethos in asceticism which shows the clear mark of the primitive Syrian theologumena.

The find of a section of the primitive baptismal liturgy in a homily of Aphrahaṭ (see part II, chapter I) opens a new perspective for our problem. Such an ancient and precious text preserved by a Christendom not touched by Hellenism is a deposit of information most pertinent to our problem, because it reveals the provenance of the Odes. The spiritual milieu in both is astonishingly interrelated to such a degree that their congruity becomes manifest. The portion of baptismal liturgy focuses the main features of a peculiar Christianity : the centrality of the covenant, baptism, ethos designated as 'war', and salvation as a result of the contest. This peculiar scheme appears also in the Odes. The most excellent demonstration appears in the Ode IX. This speaks of 'the true covenant of the Lord', of baptism as putting on 'the crown', of the ethos as 'the wars on account of the crown' where none 'may not fall in battle', and of the reward in salvation for those who have conquered and reached the victory and 'shall be inscribed in His book'. Once again the same scheme recurs in the Ode XI which crystallizes the main co-ordinates. Baptism is reflected by the imagery of water. This requires the abnegation of 'vanity', 'the madness thrown over the earth' as a precondition for 'the rest without corruption'. That by the 'war' asceticism is meant, is also shown by the Ode XXXIII.

These are impressive evidences of an archaic Syriac baptismal liturgy and the Odes of Solomon have a common substratum marked by its distinctiveness. These observations make it possible to answer the question of the provenance of the Odes of Solomon with a measure of confidence.

Finally, it is not impossible that these texts give even some hints as to their particular point of origin in Syrian Christianity [5].

Our conclusion regarding the Syriac provenance of the Odes of Solomon appears quite natural in the light of our knowledge regarding the history and pre-history of hymnology. Important stimuli were created in the Syrian communities which very early laid a particular stress on singing as a means of expression of faith and its propagation. These were so important that the Syriac texts translated into Greek became creative even for the Greek hymnography.

b. Pseudo-Clementine *De virginitate*

The next document, *De virginitate,* is beset with perplexities. The text of these two letters has been preserved in a Syriac manuscript of the year 1470, which brings these letters as an appendix to the text of the Apostolos [6]. An analysis of these texts [7] leads to the conclusion that they cannot represent the original. There is no other way than to see in these few fragments in Greek, which have been preserved in Antiochus of St. Saba [8], the remnants

5 Some Odes make allusions which seem to fit in with what we know about the situation in Edessa. The most interesting appears in the Ode VI which speaks of a stream that 'became a river great and broad for it flooded and broke up everything and brought (it) into the temple, and the restrainers of the children of men were not able to restrain it, nor the arts of those whose business is it to restrain the waters, for it spread over the face of the whole country, and filled everything', *Odes of Solomon,* VI, 8-9, p. 12. Indeed, the Chronicle of Edessa knows enough to tell about the frequent inundations of the tricky river of Daiṣan which so frequently threatened the city and destroyed also the church, *Chronica minora,* p. 3. These allusions and some others may point to Edessa, DE ZWAAN, *Edessene Origin,* p. 296 ff.

6 See GWYNN, *Older Syriac Version,* p. 281 ff.

7 *De virginitate,* p. 20.

8 Πανδέκτης τῆς ἁγίας γραφῆς col. 1421 ff.

of the original. The content of these texts, however, has persuaded the students to look for their place of origin in Syria or Mesopotamia. Unfortunately no further light has been shed on the question of origin. The remark in a Coptic translation discovered recently [9], that these two letters came from Athanasius' pen, cannot be taken seriously on the grounds of internal evidence. For this we know well enough the views of Athanasius.

It has long been felt that the document must have originated in Syria or in Mesopotamia. A hint which seems to merit our confidence is this, that the document was known in the Eastern provinces. Epiphanius knew these letters, and during his time they enjoyed an enviable reputation in Palestine, for they were cited and used publicly in the churches [10]. Moreover the other authors, who reveal a knowledge of and interest in the document, are also from Palestine or Syria. We are therefore encouraged to conclude that the place of origin was in the vicinity of ancient Syrian Christianity.

There is something else that seems to hint in this direction. Namely, this document has preserved some singular scriptural traditions. If these texts originated in a milieu which had close relations with the primitive Syrian Christianity, this would present the most natural explanation [11].

If we assign it with other scholars to the early Christianity in Syria we hope that we shall not be very far wrong. But we also must confess the feeling that we are on a rather uncertain road in all the questions of place and origin.

c. A lost Syriac treatise in Armenian

The next document is in Armenian and has been preserved among the texts ascribed to Ephrem [12]. Certainly Ephrem cannot be the author of it. Further, Schäfers noticed discontinuity and internal chasms in the text which make it necessary to cut this longer

9 *Ps. Cl. 'De virginitate' coptice*, p. 249 ff.; *Nouveaux fragments de la pseudo-clémentine*, p. 265 ff.; *Une citation copte*, p. 509 ff.

10 *Panarion*, XXX, 15, I, p. 352 f.

11 Vööbus, *Merkwürdige Pentateuchzitate.*

12 *Srboyn*, II, p. 261-345.

13 Schäfers, *Altsyrische antimark. Erklärung*, p. 205 f., 225 f.

treatise into sections [13]. One section is the source we are interested in [14]. The Syrian idiosyncracies which stand out in our text make it clear that the Armenian form is only a translation and that the text was originally composed in Syriac. This recognition is corroborated by the biblical text used here. Thus we find our way back from the Armenian text to the underlying Syriac. Besides this the internal evidence of this text shows that we have a document before us which must be very early. This is the impression everyone has gained who has examined it. It seems to belong, if not to the second, then to the third century. The view proposed by Harris, that this treatise is the lost work of Tatian himself [15], is far from having been proven, and must be dismissed.

d. The Acts of Thomas

Fortunately we possess a document which cannot only be used with greater assurance that it leads us into the Mesopotamian milieu but which also helps to fill undesirable gaps which the sources available to us, leave in the picture of the character of these primitive conditions at this early time. The Acts of Thomas in Syriac [16] have been preserved in several codices of which only one reaches back to the last century of the first millennium [17]. All others are very young. In only a very fragmentary portion the literary tradition can be traced back into the fifth or sixth century [18] by means of a palimpsest codex.

These Acts exist also in Greek [19]. The question which of these languages is the original must be decided in favor of the Syriac. The Syriac cast, supported by linguistic, stylistic and the character of the biblical text used here, is so conspicuous that it does not permit another verdict [20]. But this judgment does not silence all

14 *Srboyn*, II, p. 314-323.

15 HARRIS, *Tatian*, p. 44, 51, note 2.

16 *Apocryphal Acts*, p. 173 ff.

17 Ms. Br. Mus. Add. 14,645, written in 935/6 A.D.

18 Ms. Sin. syr. 30, fol. 141 a ff. These fragments have been edited by BURKITT in SSin, IX, p. 27 ff.

19 *Acta apostolorum apocrypha*, II, p. 99 ff.

20 The Greek translation is sometimes very puzzling since it follows slavishly the original text. For instance, the phrase *ἐλθὲ ἡ κοινωνία τοῦ ἄρρενος, ibid.,*

the problems pertinent for the use of this source of information. An analysis of the Syriac texts signals a warning. A comparison of the earliest codex with the palimpsest fragments — also the fragments of an Arabic translation made from Syriac are different [21] — shows the fact that the text has been submitted to revision which has replaced archaic elements not acceptable to the later theological taste. What we begin to see in the palimpsest fragments becomes manifest when this analysis is extented to the Greek texts. The Syriac text-form which once served as the basis for the Greek translation, represented a form much more archaic. Thus, although Syriac was the original language, there is the need to consult the Greek text which so often mirrors what the Syriac texts have lost.

As was already indicated, we have in this document to do with a source that originated in ancient Syrian Christian circles. It was probably composed in the first half of the third century. The place of origin is hinted at in the Acts. For in telling us that one of the disciples of Thomas had brought his body to the West [22], the author inadvertently reveals it. It must have been east of Edessa for the remains of Thomas were supposed to rest in Edessa.

e. A lost Syriac treatise in Greek

Help comes from quite an unexpected corner. Fortune sometimes smiles upon the depressed scholar even under the most adverse circumstances. A new source of information emerges in the realm of Greek literature. This is a homily on virginity which attracts a special attention. Only the beginning of this document was made known long ago [23], its entire text was made available in edition recently, and as the title shows, as a document whose origin is

p. 142, 166, can be explained as an exact translation but meaningless into Greek. A retranslation of this phrase into Syriac discovers here the source for this curious rendering : ܒܪܗ ܕܓܒܪܐ, which is another term for 'Son of Man' known in early Syriac texts.

21 Regarding the codex in Katalog of K. W. Hirsemann 16, see BAUMSTARK, *Geschichte syr. Literatur*, p. 344 f.

22 *Apocryphal Acts*, p. 332.

23 *Analecta sacra*, V, p. 75.

shrouded in mystery [24]. A number of problems raise their heads and with importunity demand attention. What becomes clearer as we probe for the genesis of the document is the recognition that originally it cannot be of Greek origin, but a translation work. This becomes plain already in the first reading which gives a good enough hint. This impression is intensified by examination. A number of features indicate where we have to seek for their home. A few most important ones must be singled out.

These facts are briefly these. The apparent Syriac cast of the document springs to the eye of the reader. Particularly the Christological terminology is conspicuous. The favorite term is that Christ is the Bridegroom, the veritable Bridegroom [25]. All this thought-pattern has the same ring as the early Syriac documents in which the message is focused in the Savior as the Bridegroom [26] and salvation as the 'bridal chamber' — terms which emerge surprisingly frequently here [27]. In the same vein is the archaic term 'Servant' for Christ [28] which was erased from the liturgical and theological use. These theologumena as well as the Encratite ideals which have percolated this document [29] savor of the early Syrian traditions.

The extent of the canon, too, is an indication. This text uses the Acts of Paul as a part of the canon and inspired Scriptures [30]. All this accords well with what we know of the early Syrian Christianity.

24 *Une curieuse homélie grecque*, p. 35 ff.

25 *Ibid.*, p. 37, 39, 49, 57, 63.

26 See regarding the ܚܬܢܐ 'Bridegroom', EPHREM, *Prose Refutations*, II, p. 172 *et passim*; *Carmina Nisibena*, p. 74, 76, 141; Ms. Vat. syr. 247, fol. 243 a; Vat. syr. 543, fol. 87 b; Br. Mus. Add. 17,172, fol. 282 b. A good illustration is offered by the Idiomela of Cosmas and their Syriac translation. Μηναῖον II, p. 14 reads : *καὶ ὑπόδεξαι τὸν βασιλέα Χριστόν*. But the Syriac version of it had to be made palatable to the Syriac taste adding the term 'Bridegroom' : ܦܘܩܘ ܠܐܘܪܥܗ ܘܩܒܠܘܗܝ ܠܡܠܟܐ ܚܬܢܐ ܡܫܝܚܐ, as this is found in a Menaion of the Melkite rite, Ms. Vat. syr. 342, fol. 21 b.

27 *Une curieuse homélie grecque*, p. 49 *et passim*.

28 *τῷ παιδὶ κυρίου τοῦ θεοῦ*, *ibid.*, p. 39.

29 VÖÖBUS, *Syrische Herkunft*, p. 70 f.

30 *Op. cit.*, p. 61.

The most tangible evidence, however, lies in the biblical text quoted in this document. We have now reached the very crux of the argument. This material is of quite unusual interest. An analysis of the Old Testament passages, of those of the gospels and the Apostolos brings us face to face with phenomena which unmask this scriptural material as Syriac, being influenced by the Targumic traditions in the Old Testament [31], and by the ancient Syriac textual inheritance in the gospels and the Pauline corpus [32]. It is in place, here to underline the irresistible force of this evidence.

The document, then, is by provenance not Greek but Syriac. Thus it ceases to be a puzzle. And before us is a lost document in Syriac literature which must be, judging from its archaic character, an early one. It is too much to expect that such an archaic work has escaped revision. In the present form it is certainly a work of several hands. But it is not difficult to see the original archaic stratum in it.

2. THE IDEAL OF VIRGINITY

a. The rôle of continence

It would certainly be a false assumption to believe that the doctrine and practice of the Syrian Christianity of the third century can be woven into a neat and uniform pattern. But there are certain underlying tenets which remained the same however complicated may have been the ramifications of the Christian movement.

All the available sources are unanimous in their testimony that the fundamental conception around which the Christian belief centered was the doctrine that the Christian life is unthinkable outside the bounds of virginity.

The 'Odes of Solomon' offer some unmistakable allusions to the intimate fusion between the Christian message and the proclamation of virginity. It is a matter of regret that the mystical character of speech often hinders us from getting a clear understanding of what is said. Regardless of how one might interpret the details in Ode XXXIII — we shall probably never discover its exact

31 Vööbus, *Syrische Herkunft,* p. 71 ff.

32 *Ibid.,* p. 73 ff.

meaning — the identification of the Christian message with the ideal of virginity is beyond a doubt reflected here. Both aspects appear identical here [33]. This view also appears in other traditions the value of which we cannot assess any longer.

The document which, among others, renders us a great service is naturally the Acts of Thomas which, as we have already seen, have come to us in two versions, the Syriac and the Greek.

The hero in the Acts of Thomas offers many illuminating arguments which acquaint us with his rigorous message. In his arguments we recognize pieces of popular mission propaganda in the service of asceticism. Through them we are permitted to see some salient elements which echo the archaic preaching in Mesopotamia.

When we inquire about the alliance between the religious and ascetic thought, our attention is caught by the strongest and most violent declarations regarding the evaluation of marriage.

In these didactic sections intercourse in the marriage is called 'the deed of shame', 'this deed of corruption' [34], 'dirty and polluted pleasures' [35], and 'filthy intercourse' [36]. It is a union which is not of divine will and origin but 'founded upon earth' [37] and therefore is the 'veil of corruption' [38]. This is something from which man must be rescued before he has access to the gifts of everlasting value. The body must be cleansed, the 'veil of corruption' must be taken away, before the divine life can enter as the spirit enters the temple. In a hymn this thought is expressed in the form of beatitudes : 'blessed are the bodies of the holy (chaste) ones, which are worthy to become clean temples in which the Messiah shall live' [39]. Thus the sexual phenomenon is an obstacle to the higher level of life, and only its removal opens the way to eternal life. In a prayer a converted one says : 'And Thou give me that I may

33 See pag. 87.

34 ܥܒܕܐ ܕܒܗܬܬܐ *Apocryphal Acts*, p. 183; ܥܒܕܐ ܗܢܐ ܕܚܒܠܐ, *ibid.*, p. 288.

35 *Ibid.*, p. 288.

36 *Ibid.*, p. 257.

37 *Ibid.*, p. 294.

38 ܬܚܦܝܬܐ ܕܚܒܠܐ, *ibid.*, p. 182.

39 ܛܘܒܝܗܘܢ ܠܦܓܪܝܗܘܢ ܕܩܕܝܫܐ ܕܫܘܘ ܕܢܗܘܘܢ ܗܝܟܠܐ ܕܟܝܐ ܕܢܥܡܪ ܒܗܘܢ ܡܫܝܚܐ, *ibid.*, p. 261.

preserve the holiness (continence) in which Thou hast pleasure, and through which I shall find eternal life'[40].

There is another line of thought and argument in the preaching which keeps closer to the biblical foundation. This appears in the instructions which purpose to discredit marriage by different means, namely by pointing out its futility. There is also here something of the contemporary propaganda means by which the proclamation operated.

The instructions declare that the alleged happiness of life in marriage and in having children is nothing but a fiction which conceals bitter realites. To have children in fact means to have heavy cares that end in bitter sorrow. We observe an example of these admonitions which describe the many disillusions and pains caused by children : 'either the king falls upon them, or a demon seizes them, or paralysis falls upon them; and if they be healthy they are corrupted either by adultery or theft, or fornication or by covetousness or by vain-glory; and through these crimes you will be tortured by them'[41].

But this contingent of grief and torture is not all which falls to the lot of the married couples. This propaganda knew other effective means by which to appeal to the conscience of the converted ones. Prospects for more dangerous and fatal results were in store for these missionaries. They warned that married life and children affect the moral character of parents. They described how the children cause a change in the ethical and religious behavior of their progenitors and how parents become oppressors, reckless and greedy for the sake of their children[42].

Over against all this trouble, sorrow and grief the primitive Kerygma dwelt heavily on the prospect of a careless and sorrowless life that was completely free. With full orchestration the promise which belongs to those who choose this freedom is presented by this triumphant finale : 'and you shall be hoping when you shall see the wedding feast which is the true one; and you shall be praisers

40 ܘܐܢܬ ܗܒ ܠܝ ܕܐܛܪ ܩܕܝܫܘܬܐ ܗܝ ܕܐܢܬ ܐܬܪܥܝܬ ܒܗ̇ : ܘܐܝܟܐ ܚ̈ܝܐ ܒܗ̇ ܐܢܐ ܡܫܟܚ ܕܠܥܠܡ, *ibid.*, p. 264.

41 *Ibid.*, p. 181.

42 *Ibid.*, p. 181 f.

in it; and you will be counted among those who enter the bridal chamber' [43].

Thus, all in all, the Christian proclamation was tied to the propaganda of virginity. Both were so inextricably interwoven that the Christian message and virginity were identified. In a hymn-like section this fusion is brought into focus : 'holiness (continence) is the messenger of the peace which the gospel of salvation brings' [44].

The reference just made leads us to another observation which is highly significant since it reveals an indication from the linguistic area which, in its turn, testifies to the peculiar religio-ascetic climate in ancient Syrian Christianity. This indication comes in the striking usage of the word *qaddīšūtā* 'holiness' and *qaddīš* 'holy' in archaic Syrian terminology. This word refers to sexual continence so that 'holy' is used as a synonym for chastity and purity [45]. But it also must be observed that this term is distinctly separated from *betūlūtā* 'virginity' which expression is reserved to those women and men who have kept their virginity and have not married. The term 'holiness', then, refers to married couples who have not preserved their virginity but practice continence [46]. This practice can be noticed clearly in *De virginitate* [47] as well as in other ancient documents [48]. This practice definitely says something important. We have to see the community's experience in using words this way. This is something which makes it possible to construct *ex*

[43] *Ibid.*, p. 182.

[44] ܩܕܝܫܘܬܐ ܐܝܙܓܕܐ ܗܝ ܕܫܝܢܐ ܕܣܒܪܬܐ ܕܚܝܐ, *ibid.*, p. 255.

[45] *De virginitate*, p. 20. So it is used also in the *Odes of Solomon*, p. 25, 45, 55, cf. 75 f.

[46] ܩܕܝܫܐ ܗܘ ܕܙܟܐ ܠܙܘܘܓܐ 'holy is the one that conquers marriage', Ms. Br. Mus. Add. 14,592, fol. 75 a.

[47] ܒܬܘ̈ܠܐ ܘܒܬܘ̈ܠܬܐ 'male-virgins and virgins' are put in juxtaposition with ܕܐܙܕܘܓܘ ܒܩܕܝܫܘܬܐ 'that have been united (in marriage) in holiness', *De virginitate*, p. 18 ff.

[48] As to the careful distinction with which Aphrahaṭ has used these two terms, see SCHWEN, *Afrahat*, p. 131 f : 'Ich möchte nun annehmen, dass bei Afrahat « Jungfräulichkeit » im eigentlichen Sinn, von dem Mann oder dem Mädchen gebraucht wird, die geschlechtlichen Umgang überhaupt noch nicht gepflogen haben, während « Heiligkeit » sexuelle Abstinenz bereits Verheirateter bedeutet'. See pag. 105.

ungue leonem the peculiar religio-ascetic climate, even if there were no other facts to come to our aid.

There is yet another source awaiting discussion. This is in a lost Syriac document, recovered in its Greek translation. Here one finds himself in the midst of a milieu quite congenial. It clings to the conviction that Christ, the true Bridegroom came for the purpose of gathering and elevating only those who followed his call with the vow of virginity. How deeply such recognition lies at the heart of this Christianity, is shown by the implications developed in the document. The further we carry our inquiry here the more impressive the body of far-reaching inferences does become.

The true believers who are betrothed to the celestial Bridegroom will inherit the bridal chamber [49]. Regarding the latter, it is stated that there is no room for corruption and it therefore belongs only to the virgins. Those who are not virgins, do not receive the crown of the kingdom of heaven, and do not enter into fellowship with the eternal Bridegroom [50].

Among other interesting texts, there is one paragraph which must here find mention by reason of its importance, since it reflects the bearing of the statement just quoted. This portrays the situation in the eternal world. The virgins, clad in garments of immortality, sing the triumphal hymn of virginity, wear the crowns of everlasting life and dance in the presence of Christ being accompanied by the angels, and enjoy heavenly bliss. From the brightness of joy, this picture turns to the fate of married women. This is painted in dim colors. Regardless of their repentence in this life and in the next, they experience humiliation. They discover bitterly what they have done. But now all their lamentation is useless. They remain excluded from paradise precisely because they had entered married life [51]. Data such as these allow us to estimate the weight of Encratite principle current at that time.

49 *Une curieuse homélie grecque*, p. 39.

50 καὶ εἰς ἄφθαρτον νυμφῶνα οὐκ ἔφθασαν καὶ παστὸν αὐτῶν οὐκ ἐξέτειναν, καὶ διὰ τοῦτο βασιλείας οὐρανῶν στέφανον οὐκ ἐδέξαντο, καὶ τῷ ἀθανάτῳ νυμφίῳ οὐχ ὡμίλησαν πρὸς αὐτὸν γὰρ οὐκ ἔφθασαν, *ibid.*, p. 57.

51 ὅταν Χριστὸς ὁ νυμφίος τὴν στοργὴν ἐνδείξηται, ὅταν στεναγμῷ στενάξῃ, τότε πάλιν μέμψεται ἑαυτήν, τότε πολλὰ μεταμεληθήσται καὶ ἀνωφελὴς ἡ μετάνοια αὐτῆς ἔσται, *ibid.*, p. 49.

Up to this point we have found valuable allusions and statements concerning the place of virginity in the message of the primitive phase of Syrian Christianity. But as to how this ideal was applied, we found ourselves still in the region of uncertainty. Fortunately we possess in the Acts of Thomas data which, to a certain extent, help to fill this undesirable gap in the picture of the Christian life at that early time. These data treat the practices of the Syrian Christians of the third century so explicitly that a portion of this ancient milieu becomes alive. The data unfold a particular form of Christianity which thoroughly was under the influence of the doctrine of virginity.

In the Acts of Thomas virginity is a theme which recurs again and again with new variations in the frame of the narrative. It is certainly not necessary to say that here we are not disturbed by the legendary character of the stories when we investigate the religious ethical principles which determined the type of Christian life.

The effect of the archaic Christian preaching is revealed in an episode of a young man who kills his bride. The reason stated by the narrative is highly important for our purpose : she had been so deterred by the Christian preaching and admonitions that she had refused to marry him [52].

The effect of the archaic Christian preaching recurs in another story which takes place in a royal palace on the wedding night. This time a couple that was just married comes under the influence of the Christian message and is won to the Christian faith. Through a vision of Jesus they are warned about the sexual intercourse, being admonished that only if they abandoned all intimacy could they become clean internally and become temples for the spirit. The text says : 'and the young people were persuaded by our Lord, and gave up themselves to Him, and were preserved from filthy lust and passed the night in their places' [53]. The prayer which follows is no less revealing. The young husband pours out his gratitude in prayer being thankful that he has escaped an almost incurable disease and everlasting punishment, that he now feels new health

52 *Acta apostolorum*, p. 168.
53 *Apocryphal Acts*, p. 182.

has come through virginity, and that now he is on the way to eternal life [54].

What has been mentioned up to now concerns persons whom the Christian message, and the decision to follow it, reached at the point when they were making preparations for marriage. The Christian Kerygma found them before it was not too late. The effect of preaching on the people already married also is depicted in various episodes. These episodes show that the demand for virginity was by no means less valid for those who already were united in marriage, although these found themselves in a much more difficult situation. In the case of married people acceptance of the Christian faith practically meant giving up their marriage.

An episode concerning Migdōnia is particularly illustrative in sketching the influence of the primitive Christian message on married life. Through Thomas' preaching Migdōnia was won to the Christian faith. We are particularly interested in the religious-ethical program which Thomas gives to his convert, which demands that she abandon luxury and comfort. Then he says to her : 'degrade not yourself to this filthy intercourse, and be deprived of the true fellowship' [55]. This last demand is not as clear in the Syriac text which has undergone a revision. But the Greek text states clearly that this filthy intercourse which deprives anyone of the true fellowship, is just legitimate marriage with her husband [56]. In addition to this Thomas declares : 'intercourse passes away with much contempt; Jesus alone abides and those who hope in Him; and take refuge (with Him), and give themselves up for Him' [57].

Further it is told that Migdōnia acts accordingly. As a Christian she acknowledges that her marriage relationships are now invalidated. She refuses to come together with her husband, and since the conversion she sleeps in a separate place. She throws into the face of her husband : 'do not remind me of your dirty and polluted

54 *Ibid.*, p. 183 f.

55 ܘܠܐ ܬܬܬܚܝܢ ܠܫܘܬܦܘܬܐ ܗܕܐ ܨܐܝܬܐ ܘܬܬܓܠܙܝܢ ܡܢ ܗܝ, ܫܘܬܦܘܬܐ ܫܪܝܪܬܐ, *ibid.*, p. 257.

56 οὔτε ἡ κοινωνία ἡ ῥυπαρὰ ἡ πρὸς τὸν ἄνδρα σου, *Acta apostolorum*, p. 203.

57 *Apocryphal Acts*, p. 357.

pleasures, and your evil and fleshly deeds — your deeds of shame, those which I was doing with you when I did not believe' [58].

In addition to this we have another instance in which the same consequences are told bluntly. Here the Christian preaching reached a couple, Ṣīfōr and his wife who decide to become Christians. The consequences of their decision we hear from Ṣīfōr's lips. Again to the Syriac version an element has been added which makes Ṣīfōr's statement more general and vague [59], and in one manuscript the distorted word-order has helped to eradicate its primitive meaning [60]. But the Greek text has preserved more faithfully what once stood in the ancient Acts in Syriac : 'I and my wife and daughter, for the rest (of our life) shall live in holiness, in chastity and in one sentiment' [61]. Thus we see that originally the Syriac text spoke of a clear promise of abstinence as an essential pre-condition to becoming a Christian.

Finally, the endeavors of the ancient preachers in Mesopotamia seem to be summarized in a verdict given by Karīš about the activities of Thomas : 'he teaches them the new God and establishes new laws, those which have never been heard of by us; and he says : « you cannot become children of eternal life, which I teach, unless you are torn away, a man from his wife, and a woman from her husband »' [62].

All these episodes mentioned here give concreteness to the doctrine regarding the intimate connection between religious and ascetic thought. The Christian Kerygma was proclaimed along with the propaganda of virginity in such a way that both were so inextricably interwoven that Christian faith and sexual continence were identified.

Moreover, there are other criteria which aid us in assessing the real significance of the ideal of virginity in the thought and life of the ancient Syrian Christians. A criterion lies in the observation that documents which came from the Greek hellenistic milieu and

58 *Ibid.*, p. 288.

59 *Ibid.*, p. 301.

60 'My daughter' has been inserted between 'I' and 'my wife'.

61 ἐγώ τε καὶ ἡ ἐμὲ γυνὴ καὶ ἡ θυγάτηρ ἐν ἁγιωσύνῃ οἰκήσομεν λοιπόν, ἐν ἁγνείᾳ καὶ μίᾳ διαθέσει, *Acta apostolorum*, p. 239.

62 *Apocryphal Acts*, p. 268.

were translated into Syriac, show what adjustments were necessary before this material could be made palatable to the needs of the ancient Syrian communities [63]. It also should be mentioned that repercussions of these archaic views shine through in some later documents, characterized by the symbiosis of the archaic and later traditions [64]. Finally, something of these archaic traditions can

63 For instance we take a section of a prayer of John spoken shortly before his death. Its Greek text is in Acta Joannis CXIII, in *Acta apostolorum*, II, 2, p. 212. Its Syriac recension under the title 'An account of the decease of John the Apostle and Evangelist' is to be found in *Apocryphal Acts*, I, p. 70.

ὁ θέλοντί μοι ἐν νεότητι γῆμαι ἐπιφανεὶς καὶ εἰρηκώς μοι· Χρῄζω σου Ἰωάννη· Ὁ καὶ ἀσθένειάν μοι σωματικὴν προοικονομήσας· ὁ τρίτον μου βουληθέντος γῆμαι παραυτίκα ἐμποδίσας μοι, ἔπειτα δὲ ἡμέρας ὥρᾳ τρίτῃ ἐν θαλάσσῃ εἰρηκώς μοι· Ἰωάννη, εἰ μὴ ἦς ἐμός, εἴασα ἄν σε γῆμαι·	ܗܘ ܕܐܬܚܙܝܬ ܠܝ ܒܛܠܝܘܬܝ ܟܕ ܨܒܝܬ ܠܝ ܕܐܣܒ ܐܢܬܬܐ. ܘܐܡܪܬ ܠܝ ܕܣܢܝܩ ܐܢܬ ܠܝ ܝܘܚܢܢ. ܗܘ ܕܠܐ ܡܦܪܘܫܘܬܐ ܦܓܪܢܝܬܐ ܨܒܝܬ ܠܝ ܟܕ ܬܠܬ ܙܒܢܝܢ ܟܕ ܠܐ ܡܫܬܡܥ ܐܢܐ ܨܒܝܬ ܠܡܣܒܗ̇. ܗܘ ܕܒܝܡܐ ܐܡܪܬ ܠܝ ܕܣܢܝܩ ܐܢܬ ܠܝ ܝܘܚܢܢ. ܘܐܠܘܠܐ ܠܐ. ܫܒܩܐ ܗܘܝܬ ܠܟ ܕܬܣܒ ܐܢܬܬܐ ܠܡܬܐܒܠܘ ܘܠܡܒܟܐ.

'he who appeared to me in my youth when I desired to take to myself a wife, and said to me : « You are needful to me, John »; who desired for me the bodily sterility when three times when being not obedient I wished to marry; who on the sea said to me : « you are needful to me, John, and if not I would let you take a wife to mourn and weep ».'

64 In a poem on the chorepiscopus of Nisibis, ascribed to Ephrem the activities of this cleric are ascribed as changing the believers into virgins : ܘܗܦܟ ܐܢܘܢ ܠܒܬܘܠܘܬܐ ܘܩܕܝܫܘܬܐ ܗܝ ܕܙܟܝܐ ܠܙܘܘܓܐ ܘܡܫܚܠܦܐ ܟܝܢܐ ܒܦܘܝܣܐ

'and he changed them to virgins — sanctity that conquers marriage and alters nature by persuasion', Ms. Br. Mus. Add. 14,592, fol. 75 a. These archaic traditions emerge in a more tangible form in a work which definitely belongs to Ephrem. The most interesting, among others, appears in his hymns on the Paradise. The seventh hymn speaks a language which, by its roughness and harsness, compells us to listen : ܘܒܬܘܠܬܐ ܕܣܢܬ ܟܠܝܠܐ ܕܡܬܚܒܠ : ܒܓܢܘܢܐ ܕܢܗܝܪܐ ܕܪܚܡ ܒܢܝ ܢܘܗܪܐ : ܒܗ ܬܨܡܚ ܕܣܢܬ ܥܒܕܐ ܕܚܫܘܟܐ 'and a virgin who has hated the crown (of wedding) that is corrupted, shall radiate in the illuminated chamber that loves the children of light, because she has hated the works of darkness' EPHREM, *De Paradiso*, VII, 15, p. 28-29. It is clear that marriage and procreation of children are here equated with 'the be seen in the formulas in which the ancient Syrians have reduced their archaic Kerygma to the fundamentals[65].

In connection with the recognition of virginity as the fundamental requirement, a co-ordinate in the structure of the primitive Christian message in the Syrian Orient, another interesting observation presents itself. This concerns the reflexion of the archaic Kerygma in the theological terminology. In the earliest sources Christ's epithet is 'Bridegroom'. We come across formulations which seem to stem from ancient creedal formulas[66]. Quite conspicuous is the role that this term plays in the Syrian usage of a later time. The role of this theologumenon becomes more understandable only after one has stood at its real sources.

b. Contest between the forms of continence

All that is said in the previous chapter makes it sufficiently clear that the practice of spiritual marriage came to Syria, Mesopotamia and Persia through various channels. If we take the sources like the Acts of Thomas or even later sources into account we can imagine what happened when Christian preaching gained success here. The existing marriages were converted into spiritual marriages. On the track of a lost Syriac document resuscitated in its Greek recension, one can penetrate deeper into the ascetically dominated outlook in these circles. Weapons for the view that Christian morals opposed married life, were derived from the armory of the gospels. As a result the only form of marriage for the redeemed community is a status in which wife is treated as though she is not wife but a sister. This document comments further that in such a marriage the matrimonial ties are not dissolved, but incontinence is suffocated[67]. Thus the only

works of darkness' and the virtue of virginity is made the prerequisite for the bliss of salvation.

65 For example : 'Maʿnā... was preaching to them virginity and holiness', Ms. Br. Mus. Add. 14,601, fol. 164 a.

66 For instance a formula like : ܡܫܝܚܐ ܐܠܗܐ ܕܝܠܢ ܗܘ ܚܬܢܐ ܫܪܝܪܐ 'Christ, our God is the true Bridegroom', Ms. Vat. syr. 247, fol. 243 a.

67 These duties in the interest of the virginity, including also the supervision over daughter and son, are described as the function of 'the priest of

form of Christian marriage is this which is not in opposition to virginity [68].

Also single people found others with whom they decided to live in this kind of life. Cases in which people entered this form of marriage in early youth and remained in it all their lives, living as a sister and brother, as Hieronymus observed these among the Syrians in the desert of Chalkis, belonged to the Christian scenery in the third century. In fact, in the middle of the third century this institution must have been in its vigor in Syria. We see for instance Bishop Paul of Samosata surrounded by these ascetics [69]. We have reasons to think that it blossomed more exuberantly in the territories farther East. This form of life was constantly sustained and matured by powerful movements which shaped early Christianity in these territories. It was kept and cultivated in the context of other archaic customs and practices [70].

The only way to get an idea of its role is through later sources and documents which are from the fourth century and later. These deal with the eradication of the custom which in the eyes of the church had come into disrepute. However tenacity of the practice permits to draw some inferences about the situation in earlier times when this form of Christian life was a part in the archaic Christian Kerygma.

But this recognition does not mean that the practice of *syneisaktoi* held a monopoly or remained unchallenged at the time under discussion. There has probably always been a contest between the different groups concerning the highest form of virginity. We do not know anything about the development of the institution, but even without explicit evidence it is fair to suppose that certain phenomena of decline must have been appeared during the epoch which followed the first enthusiasm. These phenomena of decline in

God of the Most High', *Une curieuse homélie grecque*, p. 39, 63, 65. οὐ τὴν δέσιν λύων, ἀλλὰ τὴν σωφροσύνην σπείρων, ἵνα τὴν ἀκρασίαν πνίξῃ, *ibid.*, p. 65.

68 οὐδ' ἕτερον δὲ ἑτέρου ἀλλότριον, *ibid.*, p. 37.

69 *Vita Malchi*, II, col. 53 f. About Paul of Samosata see EUSEBIUS, *Hist. eccl.*, VII, 30, 12, p. 710.

70 The term ܙܘܘܓܐ ܕܥܠܡܐ ܗܢܐ 'the marriage of this world', Ms. Šarf. Patr. 38, fol. 119a seems to be a reflection of the conditions in which there existed a form of marriage congenial with the spiritual world.

turn must have arosed criticism and opposition to the practice of *syneisaktoi*. We know this to be true from other similar phenomena in the history of religions. Hardly the complications of the development were different in the Syrian area. We also may suppose that this opposition grew hand in hand with the consolidation of the groups which developed into the so-called orthodox movement. If our sources do not betray us, the question became more acute earlier in the areas closer to the Western standards of Christian life and practice. This is all we can say about the controversy, and we may only guess that this milieu produced an attitude which developed into the contempt of everything female.

In the absence of other documents we have to dwell heavily on a document which comes from a neighboring area of Syrian Christianity, or possibly even from an area closer — from Syria. This we have in the so-called Pseudo-Clementine letters *De virginitate*. The spiritual milieu which unfolds itself here helps us to get an idea about the trends which clashed with each other.

It is a pity that we have to use a source whose time and place of origin, regardless of studies and new materials which have come to light, is still obscure. However the question of place of origin might be decided, this document allows us an important glimpse into the life and activity of those Christians who as baptized celibates belonged to the membership of the church. This source leads us into a milieu of rivalry and contest. On the one hand the document shows the institution of spiritual marriage, rooted deeply in the Christian practice, under attack. It is accused of misuses, maculas and disrepute. It is said in the accusations that there are those 'who live with virgins with the pretext of fearing God, and throw themselves into danger, and wander with them alone on the way and in the desert — a way that is full of dangers and full of scandals, and of snares and of pits; it is utterly not right for the Christians and the fearers of God that they conduct themselves so' [71].

On the other hand the document shows how the opposition had seized the initiative, reshaping views and creating devices, means and arguments. Thus this document lifts the veil from an important

[71] *De virginitate*, I, 10, p. 44.

milieu of the past. What we discover here is a valuable addition to our scanty knowledge.

Kerygmatically, the document proclaims the view that there is only one form of virginity capable of earning the promised bliss, and that this virginity is kept in the form of separated life of the sexes. This separation is proclaimed as the only legitimate form of the Christian life in the service of virginity, and it stands high above the virginity practiced in the form of spiritual marriage. The Syriac text reads here : 'and He will give virgins (among men) and virgins (among women) a reputable place in the house of God... which is more excellent than (the place) of those who are joined together (married) in holiness (continence) and whose beds are not polluted. For God will give to the virgins (among men) and virgins (among women) the Kingdom of heaven as to the holy angels because of this great and powerful witness' [72]. The Coptic version of the document offers a different text in which eunuchs are added to the mention of virgins. Here we read : 'for He gives in His home a place more excellent than that of sons and daughters to eunuchs and virgins; for they are more excellent than those who dwell in honorable marriage and in a pure bed; God will give an incorruptible kingdom of angels to those who have made themselves eunuchs, and to virgins, because of this great witness' [73].

This marriage 'in holiness' with beds 'not polluted' mentioned in our text cannot refer to ordinary marriage when we take Syrian concepts and the theological contents of the document into consideration. The mention refers to those who live in spiritual marriage. Above these in spiritual marriage stand the real virgins as

72 ܘܢܬܠ ܠܒܬܘ̈ܠܐ ܘܠܒܬܘ̈ܠܬܐ ܐܬܪܐ ܡܫܒܚܐ ܒܒܝܬܗ ܕܐܠܗܐ... ܘܡܝܬܪ ܡܢ ܗܢܘܢ ܕܐܙܕܘܓܘ ܒܩܕܝܫܘܬܐ: ܘܠܐ ܐܬܛܢܦܘ ܡܫܟ̈ܒܝܗܘܢ. ܢܬܠ ܠܗܘܢ ܓܝܪ ܐܠܗܐ ܠܒܬܘ̈ܠܐ ܘܠܒܬܘ̈ܠܬܐ ܡܠܟܘܬܐ ܕܫܡܝܐ ܐܝܟ ܠܡܠܐܟܐ ܩܕ̈ܝܫܐ. ܡܛܠ ܣܗܕܘܬܐ ܗܕܐ ܪܒܬܐ ܘܚܣܝܢܬܐ, *De virginitate*, I, 4, p. 18 ff.

73 ϥϯ ⲅⲁⲣ ⲛ̄ⲛⲉⲥⲓⲟⲩⲣ ⲙⲛ̄ⲙ̄ⲡⲁⲣⲑⲉⲛⲟⲥ ⲛ̄ⲟⲩⲙⲁ ⲉϥⲥⲟⲧⲡ ϩⲙ̄ⲡⲉϥⲏⲉⲓ ⲉϣⲏⲣⲉ ϩⲓϣⲉⲉⲣⲉ· ⲉⲩⲥⲟⲧⲡ ⲡⲁⲣⲁⲛⲉⲛⲧⲁⲩϣⲱⲡⲉ ϩⲙ̄ⲡⲅⲁⲙⲟⲥ ⲉⲧⲧⲁⲉⲓⲏⲩ ⲙⲛ̄ⲡⲙⲁ ⲛ̄ⲛ̄ⲕⲟⲧⲕ ⲉⲧⲧⲃ̄ⲃⲏⲩ. Ⲡⲛⲟⲩⲧⲉ ⲛⲁϯ ⲛ̄ⲛⲉⲛⲧⲁⲩⲁⲁⲩ ⲛ̄ⲥⲓⲟⲩⲣ ⲙ̄ⲙⲓⲛ ⲙ̄ⲙⲟⲟⲩ ⲙⲛ̄ⲙ̄ⲡⲁⲣⲑⲉⲛⲟⲥ ⲛ̄ⲟⲩⲙⲛ̄ⲧⲉⲣⲟ̄ ⲛ̄ⲁⲧⲧⲱⲗⲙ̄ ⲛ̄ⲧⲉⲛⲁⲅⲅⲉⲗⲟⲥ, ϩⲓⲧⲛ̄ⲧⲉⲓ̈ⲛⲟϭ ⲛ̄ϩⲟⲙⲟⲗⲟⲅⲓⲁ, *Ps. Cl. de virginitate coptice*, p. 256.

'the city of God, and the dwelling-places and temples in which God stays and in which He dwells, and in which He acts (literally : walks) as in the holy city that is in heaven'[74].

This stream of thought discovered some interesting ways to give sanction to its positions. The document uses the Old Testament text portions that are different from the canonical tradition and with its interpolation show the ascetic tendency to keep men and women separated. Yet, the document uses these texts as Scriptural evidences, and with complete assurance the author says 'for behold the Sacred Scriptures testify to my words'. We have already treated these texts[75].

The document also gives detailed advices on how to put the ideal of virginity into practice. In doing this it is careful not to be satisfied with general admonitions but gives rules of behavior in various concrete situations.

Great caution is required of the brethren in Christian communities in avoiding any direct contact with women. The men do not deal with the virgins and have nothing in common with them. They do not eat or drink together with virgins. They do not permit virgins to wash their feet or to anoint them[76].

An interesting episode from the liturgical practice deserves to be mentioned since it leads us to the heart of an attitude hardened by the milieu of contest. The worship service consists of an admonition and prayer followed by the liturgical kiss which takes place among men. Concerning the women and virgins the text states : 'but women and virgins have to wrap their hands in their garments; we also in watchfulness and in all chastity, as we direct eyes above, modestly and in all decent manners wrap our right hand in our garments; and then they (virgins) may come and give us (the kiss of) peace on our right hand'[77].

In general the ascetics do not accept any service of hospitality from women, regardless of whether they are virgins, single or married, Christian or heathen, the ascetics accept service only from men[78].

74 *De virginitate*, I, 9, p. 40.

75 *Ibid.*, II, 14, p. 106; see also Vööbus, *Merkwürdige Pentateuchzitate.*

76 *Ibid.*, II, 1, p. 70.

77 *Ibid.*, II, 2, p. 76.

78 *Ibid.*, II, 2, p. 74.

Only in exceptional cases in which the travelling ascetics come to a small community where there is no man and where there are only women to serve them, can they stay overnight if they keep the strict regulations given by the document. After service has been rendered and night is at hand, the women have to select the oldest and the most chaste from their group who shows to the retiring ascetic his sleeping place. She has to bring a lamp and all else necessary for a hospitable reception for a travelling brother. But the warning regarding the selection of this woman is repeated here with much concern : 'but (she should be) an old one, who through much intelligence and years has been proved, whether bringing up children, whether receiving strangers, whether washing the feet of the holy ones' [79].

But the ascetics do not stay in a place where there is only one woman, although she be Christian. They do not even pray or read the Scripture, but they 'flee as from before the look (literally : face) of a serpent and as from before the look (literally : face) of sin' [80].

As it was mentioned previously, this struggle between the forms of virginity seems to conceal important development. In order to change the deeprooted practice of spiritual marriage, drastic measures were demanded. Such an insight helps us perhaps better to understand the ways in which woman became — according to the propaganda of evangelization — an instrument of Satan [81]. She was depicted as someone whose body is fire [82] and whose appearance is something that pollutes the eye [83]. This judgment held even if the woman was an ascetic's own mother. All these trends, which ended in misogyny, were gradually coming into vogue and had a great future ahead.

79 *Ibid.*, II, 4, p. 82.

80 *Ibid.*

81 APHRAHAṭ, *Demonstrationes*, I, p. 265.

82 Ms. Berl. Sach. 329, fol. 268 a.

83 *Early Judaeo-Christian Documents*, p. 46.

3. OTHER FACETS OF ASCETICISM

a. Ascetic practices

The documents we have already consulted on the practice of virginity, unfold the religious milieu in such a way that we see something of how the ascetic Kerygma put restrictions on all bodily needs.

Thomas himself exemplifies a model for Christian life. His food is very scanty. His menu consists only of bread and salt [84]. Bread and water also appear as the food of ascetics in the Pseudo-Clementine letters. Concerning the hosts it is said : 'and they bring bread and water and something that God has provided' [85]. The absence of meat is evident, and abstinence from wine is also beyond doubt. A demon is reputed to have said that wine is something in which he takes pleasure as in libations on the altar [86]. There were movements in which this practice was not broken even during the celebration of the Eucharist. The recensions of the Acts of Thomas give various readings concerning this latter point. While in the Syriac texts Migdōnia asks her nurse for a loaf of bread and 'a mingled draught in a cup' for the Eucharist [87], in the Greek recension in the scene of Eucharist we see that bread and cup of water were the elements upon which blessing was invoked [88]. Here it is clear that the process of correcting by later ecclesiastical practice has left its marks.

Further, fasting takes an important place in the practice of Christian life. Thomas fasts constantly [89]. His enemies characterize him as one who fasts much and prays much [90]. We see him starting his fasting at dawn, continuing it throughout the whole day and refraining from taking his scanty meal until the evening comes :

84 *Apocryphal Acts*, p. 271.

85 *De virginitate*, II, 2, p. 74.

86 *Apocryphal Acts*, p. 246.

87 *Ibid.*, p. 291.

88 ὡς δὲ ἐβαπτίσθη καὶ ἐνεδύσατο, ἄρτον κλάσας καὶ λαβὼν ποτήριον ὕδατος κοινωνὸν ἐποίησεν αὐτὴν τῷ τοῦ Χριστοῦ σώματι καὶ ποτηρίου τοῦ υἱοῦ τοῦ θεοῦ, *Acta apostolorum*, p. 231.

89 *Ibid.*, p. 243, 171.

90 *Apocryphal Acts*, p. 188.

'and he eats nothing at all but bread and salt from evening to evening'[91].

The same ascetic orientation permeates the whole Christian outlook we meet in the Acts of Thomas. It takes a hostile attitude to all that is in the world. Possessions are not allowed place in this ethics. Thomas declares : 'His laborers must serve Him in holiness... and must be free from the heavy care of wealth, and from the trouble and vanity of riches'[92]. On another occasion Thomas testifies : 'and I glory in poverty and in asceticism and in contempt, and in fasting and in prayer and in great faith (witness)'[93].

Thomas also exemplifies how the Christian life really looks. He has no possessions at all[94]. He confesses : 'Behold, my Lord, that we have left our possessions for Thy sake that (we might gain) Thee, the possession of life'[95]. He is so poor that he has not even bread for his daily needs and wears only one garment regardless of seasons and conditions[96]. He also refuses to receive anything from others, and what he happens to have he gives to others. Repeatedly he says that all these things of the world including the most desirable, are of no use to a believer.

Thomas also is homeless. He confesses with others he had converted : 'and behold, my Lord, that we have left our homes and these (our) people, and for Thy sake have become stangers'[97]. Thomas' critics characterize his habits in the following words : 'and he teaches them the new doctrine of holiness, and teaches and says : « a man cannot live unless he separates himself from all that he has and becomes an anchorite and a vagrant like himself »'[98]. The latter habit appears on the positive side in the interest of Christian work and mission. Thomas is a wanderer and traveller

91 *Ibid.*, p. 271.
92 *Ibid.*, p. 296.
93 *Ibid.*, p. 308.
94 *Acta apostolorum*, p. 242.
95 *Apocryphal Acts*, p. 231.
96 *Ibid.*, p. 264.
97 *Ibid.*, p. 231.
98 ܘܡܠܦ ܠܗܘܢ ܝܘܠܦܢܐ ܚܕܬܐ ܕܩܕܝܫܘܬܐ. ܘܡܠܦ ܘܐܡܪ ܕܠܐ ܠܡ ܚܝܐ ܐܢܫ ܐܠܐ ܐܢ ܐܬܦܪܫ ܡܢ ܟܠ ܕܐܝܬ ܠܗ: ܘܗܘܐ ܡܟܣܢܝܐ ܘܡܫܢܘܪܐ ܐܟܘܬܗ, *ibid.*, p. 267.

who rescues the souls for the army of the Great General and Athlete.

The vagrancy of the ascetics also appears in another document which once existed in Syriac but is now available only in an Armenian translation. This document states that those who decide to become ascetics agree 'to go forth from his home and his relationship, to depart into other regions and to throw himself into the combat of the war of death' [99].

There is another place in the Acts of Thomas which gives an interesting bird-eye summary of his life and habits. This account describes a standard that was laid down for the primitive Syrian Christians to follow : 'I give thanks to Thee, my Lord, that for Thy sake I have become... [100] and an ascetic and a pauper and a vagrant'.

b. The structure of the ethos

After having discussed the ascetic practices in the primitive Syrian Christianity we have a reason to pause for a while and to glimpse at the ethos, the 'Weltgefühl' which stimulated all these practices. Thus, we will be able to understand better the role which asceticism played in the earliest Syrian Christianity.

We could begin recognizing the heightened awareness of the dissociation from corruption, i.e. from the world. This is a feeling which shines through every account, sermon and prayer, which escaped oblivion. In the Acts of Thomas a bride who was saved for the faith in the last minute on her wedding-chamber, tells her mother happily that 'the veil of corruption is taken away from me' [101]. Another saved man says gratefully : 'I have been set free from evil cares and from deeds of corruption' [102].

99 *որ ցանկացեալ կամի զինուորել, և գրել զինքն 'ի թիւս համարոյ զինուորաց աստէն յերկրի, նախ զայս դնէ 'ի մտի իւրում՝ ելանել 'ի տանէ իւրմէ և յազգատոհմէ իւրմէ, հեռանալ նմա յայլ գաւառս, և անկանել նմա 'ի մարտ պատերազմի մահուան*, *Srboyn*, II, p. 318.

100 *Apocryphal Acts*, p. 273. The term 'reclusus', suggested by Wright, is a conjecture, the original word is corrupted.

101 *Apocryphal Acts*, p. 182.

102 *Ibid.*, p. 203.

In the 'Odes of Solomon' we have some useful references. It is true we cannot approach this document with too great expectation because the religious lyric developed here exuberantly tends to veil the more sober outlook, wrapping the actual conditions in nebulous speech. However not everything fades out of perspective. In one of the odes this heightened awareness is apparent : 'but there stood a perfect virgin, who was proclaiming and calling and saying, O you sons of men, return you, and you daughters of men, come, and forsake the ways of that corruption and draw near unto me, and I will enter unto you, and will bring you forth from perdition'[103].

There is a concreteness in all these thoughts which arrests our attention. We discover a selfconscious ethos which draws clearly the demarcation line between spiritual life and corruption that roots in physical existence. A didactic section in the Acts of Thomas leads deeper into these sentiments. In a sermon Thomas describes the nature of the life in corruption, i.e. in the world. Here he says that sexual intercourse blinds the intellect, darkens the eyes of the soul and makes the body sick; that covetousness agitates the soul and that the service of the belly causes the soul to live in care[104].

Only the eradication of these phenomena releases man from bondage and prepares the heart as a dwelling-place for God[105]. Thus life in asceticism becomes 'His fellowship in incorruption'[106]. In the Armenian texts the nature of this new form of existence, detached from corruption, is defined as a 'spiritual mode of life'[107], a phrase repeatedly emphasized. It obviously must have had a peculiar sound in the ears of these Christians.

This tension in the 'Weltgefühl' of the ancient Syrian Christians

103 ܐܠܐ ܩܡܬ ܒܬܘܠܬܐ ܓܡܝܪܬ. ܘܡܟܪܙܐ ܘܩܪܝܐ ܘܐܡܪܐ ܒܢ̈ܝ ܐܢܫܐ ܐܬܗܦܟܘ. ܘܒܢܬܗܘܢ ܬܐܝ̈ܢ. ܘܫܒܘܩܘ ܐܘܪܚܬܗ ܕܚܒܠܐ ܗܘ ܘܐܬܩܪܒܘ ܠܝ. ܘܐܥܘܠ ܒܟܘܢ ܘܐܦܩܟܘܢ ܡܢ ܐܒܕܢܐ, *Odes of Solomon*, XXXIII, 5-7, p. 75 f.

104 *Apocryphal Acts*, p. 194.

105 *Ibid.*, p. 281.

106 *Odes of Solomon*, XXI, 5, p. 44; they 'rest in incorruption', *ibid.*, p. 30.

107 The hallmark of the believers is that they are separated from the world *հոգեւոր գնացիւք* 'through spiritual mode of life' or 'spiritual way', *ibid.*, p. 315, 3; 9-19. The last word means *πορεία, ὁδός*, *Thesaurus armeniacus*, I, p. 564.

makes itself manifest in a remarkable vocabulary. What we notice in the terminology taken from contest, struggle and war, deserves our interest for more than one reason. In a sermon Thomas makes a pregnant statement about the positive contents of this life, mentioning a thought which recurs often in variations : 'holiness (purity) is the athlete who is not overcome'[108]. This statement brings us face to face with a peculiar mood in the consciousness of this Christianity. A Christian is an athlete, a fighter, a warrior. The consciousness of being a tireless warrior was the hallmark of the Christian life. This ethos is constantly nourished by looking to Christ as 'our true Athlete' and 'our holy General'. A prayer, which radiates the glow of these warriors, reads : 'Thou who art a help to Thy servants in the contest, and throwest down the enemy before them; who standest in contests for us and grantest us victory in all of them — our true Athlete, who cannot be hurt, and our holy General, who cannot be conquered'[109]. The terms 'contest' and 'war' which find expression in both sermons and prayers, describe the proper sentiments in the service of Christian perfection.

The same description of Christianity is brought to focus in the 'Odes of Solomon'. In these poems the choice of terms, words, the phrases along with the whole tenor of the presentation draw attention to the fact that the Christian life was something constantly characterized by 'war'[110]. In this 'war' Christians persevere and thus gain the victory[111].

Further, the document in the Armenian version helps to supplement this picture of the Christian life as one of 'war' and Christians as 'warriors'. These Christians are those who throw themselves into battle in such a way that, along with their companions as other warriors, they do not see anything but the glitter of weapons and the storm of the battle and hear only the voice of the trumpet[112]. Such a 'Weltgefühl' is the only one which deserves the name Christian, since its creation is the only reason why Christ

108 *Apocryphal Acts*, p. 254 f.
109 *Ibid.*, p. 209, cf. p. 218.
110 *Odes of Solomon*, VIII, 7; IX, 6, 9, p. 27, 29.
111 *Odes*, IX, 12; XVIII, 6; XXIX, 9, *ibid.*, p. 29 f., 72.
112 *Srboyn*, II, p. 318.

came into this world[113]. As a new confirmation and consolation for these warriors a word of Jesus is quoted that is not found in the canonical writings : 'whoever approaches me, approaches fire'[114]. This 'fire' is interpreted to mean the heat of battle.

It was necessary to unfold this terminology in order to apprehend more of the real extent of asceticism and its penetration into Christian thought and practice. The place of asceticism in the earliest Syrian Christianity is no longer viewed as accidental, depending more or less on individualistic and subjective inclinations. Its place is structural. Moreover this understanding of the fundamentals which stand behind our quoted documents is shared fully with other groups such as Marcionites, Valentinians and various branches of Encratites. As the investigation shows, early Syrian Christianity in the Roman as well as in the Persian territory was a melting-pot in which various rigorous influences were blended into a particular mixture through mutual competition and cross-fertilization. But regardless of the variety of stimuli we may say that a homogeneous character of Christianity was consolidated in so far as the predominant and the structural role of asceticism is concerned. Thus what distinguishes asceticism in the early Syrian Christianity from others, is not only the circumstance that here the Encratite and enthusiastic stream was much broader and far more potent, but the integral part which asceticism occupied in the Christian Kerygma.

There are reasons for pausing here before we conclude this paragraph.

To be sure, to-day this phenomenon appears strange. At first glance it might look as if the key to its understanding has been lost. But its real meaning becomes clear when we examine carefully the contemporary ideas and feelings which inspired these earliest Christians in the lands of the Euphrates and Tigris. Close inspection leads us to recognize that these Christians possessed their own views concerning the meaning of the faith and life of the believer. The active nature of the Christian life meant something peculiar to these ascetics. In their 'war' and 'contest' they saw something

113 *Ibid.*, p. 314.
114 *Ibid.*, p. 318.

which was working towards the consummation of the cosmic upheaval, something which helped to accelerate the realization of the coming of the Kingdom of God. The same basic conviction, for instance, lies behind the Acts of Thomas. This conviction explains why the document is so much concerned with women who repudiate their marriage and the procreation of children. These steps taken by women represent their major contribution towards the acceleration of the great cosmic events. This is the grandiose mission in which these Christians found their place. And it is in this mission that we see the final meaning of earliest asceticism. All the Christian factions were striving for this goal, inspired by the consciousness of taking a real part in the reduction of the dominion and duration of the present world. When one desires to understand the early phase of asceticism this aspect must not be overlooked. In this aspect one gets closest to the heart of the 'Weltgefühl' among the primitive Christians in the Syrian Orient.

4. THE BEARING OF ASCETICISM UPON THE CONCEPT OF CHURCH

a. The structural rôle of asceticism

It is not surprising that this type of Christianity also influenced the concept of church in ancient Syrian Christianity. For if the ascetic way of life was the only reason for which Jesus came into the world then it is natural that only those who were ready to follow this rigorous way in 'His fellowship in incorruption' and 'the form of a new person', constitute the church.

To be sure, to-day one might gaze upon this phenomenon as a curiosity, but in the eyes of the ancient Syrians only a church with such qualities could be an instrument working towards the consummation of the cosmic upheaval and the expansion of God's dominion in the world. Such a concept of church naturally meant to these Christians that the sacraments were the privileges of the assembly of ascetics.

With regard to sacraments, baptism became the prerogative of the ascetic elite only. It became the sign of those who had courage to make the radical decision to turn their backs decisively upon the world and walk in conformity with new standards. A passus in which the ascetic and sacramental elements are interwoven, appears in a section in the Acts of Thomas which seems to have preserved ancient liturgical formulations : 'blessed are the spirits of the holy ones (chaste ones) who have taken the crown and gone up from the contest' [115]. Since 'crown' in the Syrian traditions refers to baptism [116], this archaic formula shows the fundamental elements, asceticism, baptism and contest in their relationship.

Similar ancient formulas seem to have been preserved also in the Odes of Solomon. Reading, for instance, statements like : 'and there have been wars on account of the crown' [117], it is difficult to escape the impression that the same fundamental relationship is implied.

These more or less evident formulations find confirmation by the narratives in the Acts of Thomas. Migdōnia was won to Christian faith, and we can read of the preparations she had to make for her reception into the church. On the occasion of her reception we read that Thomas gives her as a catechumen his conditions. He demands that she abandons not only luxury and comfort, but also her marriage [118]. Wīzān, a young male convert reveals his enthusiastic intention to be baptized and confesses to the Apostle that he has kept his virginity during his whole marital life since he had been compelled to marry [119]. Thus he feels that he is entitled to receive baptism because he has already shown himself capable of keeping his virginity, the condition laid down as a prerequisite for the reception of baptism.

And in the episode of Ṣīfōr, as we have already seen, he makes a promise before he is baptized [120].

Baptism was understood also as a definite sanction for the decision to live the ascetic life from which it seems there was no

115 ܛܘܒܝܗܝܢ ܠܪ̈ܘܚܬܗܘܢ ܕܩܕ̈ܝܫܐ ܕܢܣܒܘ ܟܠܝܠܐ ܘܣܠܩܘ ܡܢ ܐܓܘܢܐ *Apocryphal Acts*, p. 261.

116 The baptized persons were dressed in white robes and crowns were placed on their heads. 'Crown' in the liturgical hymns refers to baptism, *Breviarium chaldaicum*, I, p. 426; III, p. 431 f.

117 ܘܩܪ̈ܒܐ ܗܘܝ ܡܛܠ ܟܠܝܠܐ ܗܘܘ, *Odes of Solomon*, IX, 9, 9, p. 29.

118 See pag. 75 f.

119 *Apocryphal Acts*, p. 317 f.

120 See pag. 76.

turning. It must be said that this opinion does not rest on any definite text. But there is an episode which can be interpreted only on this assumption. In this episode a woman urges Thomas and says to him : 'Apostle of the Most High, give me the sign of my Lord, that the enemy may not come back again upon me' [121]. This 'sign' clearly is baptism because immediately Thomas leads her to a river and baptizes her.

In the light of these narratives we come to the same conclusion we have already made. Baptism was put in the service of ascetically orientated Christendom as a means of producing new men for the assembly of ascetics. This we find summed up in a section in which Thomas explains the meaning of the sacrament : 'this is the baptism of remission of sins; this is the procreator of the new man; this is the renewer of minds, and the mingler of soul and body' [122].

All the terms used here had a very concrete meaning understood from the perspective of the new wholeness provided by ascetic Christianity.

We have been looking around for vestiges which might lead us to archaic conditions as these existed in the communities of the Syrians in the second and third centuries. As we have seen, all these have not been vestiges in sand which could by swept away. Because of these vestiges found we were able to catch a glimpse of a peculiar milieu which was created by the message of various Christian movements and inspired by the sacred texts adjusted by the hands of Marcion, Tatian and Valentinus.

It also seems that something of the archaic liturgical traditions has survived in such sources as Ephrem's discourses. The critic who would maintain that Ephrem has incorporated these allusions will have arguments to defend this opinion [123].

121 *Apocryphal Acts*, p. 217.

122 *Ibid.*, p. 301.

123 Many passages which combine virginity, baptism and salvation, have a peculiar ring, *Prose Refutations*, II, p. 170. By baptism the body becomes renewed as a dwelling-place and there is no room for the old practices, Ms. Br. Mus. Add. 14,623 fol. 23a. Virginity keeps alive the pure ones, *Prose Refutations*, II, p. 177.

Some tones are very conspicuous since these seem to have followed older

So far no allusion was made to another important channel which helps us to get still better orientated in this remote period. We now turn to the evidence preserved like a fossil in a younger document which we possess in the treatises written by Aphrahaṭ. As a result of another study [124] the seventh treatise of this work which has appeared as an enigma to everyone who examined it, turns out to be a hidden treasure, particularly important for studies in this remote period. As a closer scrutiny shows in this treatise we find portions from a pristine liturgy of baptism in Syriac idiom [125].

Of course, the remnants are not extensive, but when we recall that we thought we possessed nothing of this kind, we consider them very valuable. Here we could not wish for a better conclusion to this chapter. These remnants disclose the last acts in the preparation for baptism as it was in use before Aphrahaṭ's days. Here we are permitted to see the candidates for baptism before us and to listen to what was told them on this occasion in the archaic Syrian Church. These who were called for 'contest' are addressed and admonished with the following words : 'anyone who is afraid, let him retreat from the struggle, that he might not break the heart of his brothers as (well as) his (own) heart. And anyone who plants a vineyard, let him retreat from its work, that he might not think of it and would be conquered in the war. And anyone who has betrothed a wife and wills to take her, let him retreat and rejoice

exegetical traditions. Particularly noteworthy is an allegory of Exod. XII, 21 ff. applied to the church, which in this case can be only a society of virgins : ܗܐ ܗܟܝܠ ܝܚܝܕܗ ܕܡܐ ܐܚܝܕܝܐ ܠܕܡܐ ܒܬܘܠܬܐ ܕܒܗ ܚܬܝܡ ܬܪܥܟ. ܒܕܡܘܬ ܬܪܥܐ ܕܐܬܚܬܡܘ ܗܘܘ ܒܕܡܐ ܪܣܝܣܐ ܕܠܓܘ ܡܨܪܝܢ. ܒܡܐ ܕܠܒܪ ܕܗܘ ܗܘ ܕܡܐ ܥܠܝܗܘܢ ܕܬܪܥܐ ܪܫܝܡ ܗܘܐ ܡܢ ܠܒܪ. ܚܝܐ ܕܠܓܘ ܒܛܘܦܣ ܒܬܘܠܘܬܐ ܒܫܝܢܐ ܫܪܝܢ ܗܘܘ 'behold, therefore the unique (special) blood bought the virgin blood with which your door is sealed in the likeness of doors which were sealed with the blood sprinkled within Egypt; for as much as that same blood was marked upon the doors outside, life within was dwelling after the type of the virgin state in peace', *ibid.*, p. 182. Archaic exegetical traditions in connection with Mt. xxv, 1-10 seem to have preserved in Ms. Ming. syr. 190, fol. 133 b.

[124] VÖÖBUS, *Celibacy*, p. 52 ff.

[125] See pag. 177.

with his wife. And anyone who builds a house let him retreat to it, that he might not remember his house and would not fight wholly. The struggle is suitable for solitaries, because their faces are set for that which is before them, and they do not remember something that lies behind them, for their treasures are before them; and anything that they spoil, all (belongs) to themselves, and they receive their profit abundantly'[126].

This liturgical text also draws the curtain revealing the second scene of the baptismal rite. We learn that it was expected that after this urgent exhortation the hesitating ones leave and the servants of the church gather those who remain at their decision and are convinced that they have been 'recruited for war'. These have to stand the second test when their readiness is submitted to a new screening. The admonition which follows takes place shortly before the rite of baptism : 'anyone who has set his heart to the state of marriage let him marry before baptism, lest he will fall in the struggle and will be killed. And anyone who fears this part of the contest, let him retreat, lest he will break the heart of his brethren like his own heart. Anyone who loves possession, let him retreat from the army, lest when the battle becomes hard for him, he will remember his possessions and retreat. And anyone who retreats from the struggle — shame belongs to him. Everyone who has not chosen himself and has not yet put on the armor, if he retreats he is not blamed. But every one who chooses himself and puts on the armor, if he retreats from the struggle, laughter belongs to him (i.e. will be laughted at). To him who renounces (lit. empties) himself the contest is suitable, because he does not remember something which is behind him and does not retreat to it'[127].

126 ܡܢ ܕܕܚܝܠ ܢܦܢܐ ܠܗ ܡܢ ܐܓܘܢܐ ܕܠܐ ܢܬܒܪ ܠܒܐ ܕܐܚ̈ܘܗܝ، ܐܝܟ ܠܒܗ. ܘܡܢ ܕܢܨܒ ܟܪܡܐ ܢܦܢܐ ܠܦܘܠܚܢܗ ܕܠܐ ܢܬܪܐ ܒܗ ܘܢܚܫܘܒ ܒܟܪܡܐ. ܘܡܢ ܕܡܟܪ ܐܢܬܬܐ ܘܨܒܐ ܕܢܣܒܝܗ ܢܦܢܐ ܠܗ ܘܢܚܕܐ ܐܢܬܬܗ ܫܢܝܐ. ܘܡܢ ܕܒܢܐ ܒܝܬܐ ܢܦܢܐ ܠܒܝܬܗ ܕܠܐ ܢܬܕܟܪ ܒܝܬܗ ܘܠܐ ܢܬܟܬܫ ܟܠܢܐܝܬ. ܠܝܚܝ̈ܕܝܐ ܗܘ ܝܐܐ ܐܓܘܢܐ ܡܛܠ ܕܠܩܕܡܝܗܘܢ ܦܢܝܢ ܐܦ̈ܝܗܘܢ ܘܠܐ ܡܬܕܟܪܝܢ ܡܕܡ ܕܒܣܬܪܗܘܢ ܡܛܠ ܕܣܝ̈ܡܬܗܘܢ ܩܕܡܝܗܘܢ ܐܝܢ ܘܡܕܡ ܕܒܙܝܢ ܟܠܗ ܠܢܦܫܗܘܢ ܗܘܐ ܘܫܩܠܝܢ ܡܘܬܪܢܗܘܢ ܡܢ ܣܓܝܐܘ *Demonstrationes*, col. 341, 344.

127 ܕܡܢ ܕܠܒܗ ܣܡ ܠܙܘܘܓܐ ܕܐܢܬܘܬܐ ܢܬܢܣܒ ܡܢ ܩܕܡ ܡܥܡܘܕܝܬܐ

After these admonitions and exhortations the determined candidates are admitted to the act of baptism.

Not less significant is the fact that baptism in these texts is called 'the water of proof'[128]. Moreover, it is said explicitly that 'everyone who is valiant — the water proves him (i.e. is proved by water); who are slothful are excluded (separated) from thence'[129]. Once more the same fact is repeated that the water of baptism will prove those who are selected and fit for combat. All these precious remnants of archaic terminology show unmistakably that they stem from the formulations of the baptismal liturgy in use at a time when the sacrament was not a rite for all Christians but a seal for those aspirants who were expected to forsake marriage, possession and life in the world[130].

Like baptism, the Eucharist was put into the service of the ascetic Christians. In the narratives the act of baptism was followed by the sacramental meal. Besides this, when Thomas recapitulates his doctrine and practice comparing them to the manners of the world, he says : 'I boast in poverty and in asceticism, and in the communion of the brethren and of the spirit of holiness; and in the intimacy of brethren who are worthy for God'[131]. The last term obviously refers to participation in the sacramental life of the

ܕܠܐ ܢܦܠ ܒܐܝܩܪܐ ܘܢܬܦܠܠ. ܘܡܢ ܕܕܚܠ ܡܢ ܗܕܐ ܡܠܬܐ ܕܬܬܒܥܐ ܢܦܘܩ ܠܗ ܕܠܐ ܢܬܒܪ ܠܒܗ ܕܐܚܪܢܐ, ܐܝܟ ܠܒܗ. ܘܡܢ ܕܡܣܟܢܐ ܪܢܝܗ ܢܦܘܩ ܡܢ ܚܝܠܐ ܕܠܒܐ ܒܪ ܢܨܚܢܗ ܘܡܐ ܢܬܒܪ ܡܣܝܢܘܬܗ ܘܢܦܘܩ ܠܗ. ܘܡܢ ܕܡܢ ܐܝܩܪܐ ܗܦܟ ܗܘܐ ܠܗ ܣܟܠܐ. ܘܡܢ ܕܢܦܫܗ ܠܐ ܐܝܟ ܘܪܝܐ ܒܕܚܠ ܠܐ ܠܒܪ ܐ̱ ܗܦܟ ܠܗ ܡܬܠܬܐ ܐܠܐ ܒܠ ܕܡܥܢܝܐ ܢܦܫܗ ܘܠܒܪ ܘܠܐ ܐ̱ ܗܦܟ ܡܢ ܐܝܩܪܐ ܗܘܐ ܠܗ ܒܝܫܬܐ. ܠܡܢ ܕܢܦܫܗ ܡܫܪܪ ܐܝܟ ܠܗ ܬܬܒܥܐ ܡܛܠ ܕܠܐ ܡܬܕܒܪ ܡܢܗ ܕܒܥܬܝܪܗ ܘܗܦܟ ܠܘܬܗ, *ibid.*, col. 345.

128 ܡܝܐ ܕܒܘܚܪܢܐ *ibid.*, col. 344.

129 ܟܠ ܕܚܠܝܨ ܡܝܐ ܒܚܢ ܠܗ ܘܐܝܠܝܢ ܕܚܒܝܢ ܡܢ ܬܡܢ ܡܬܦܪܫܝܢ, *ibid.*, col. 344.

130 *Ibid.*, col. 348.

131 ܘܐܢܐ ܡܫܬܒܗܪ ܒܡܣܟܢܘܬܐ ܘܒܚܣܝܢܘܬܐ ... ܘܒܫܘܬܦܘܬܐ ܕܐܚܐ ܘܒܪܘܚܐ ܕܩܘܕܫܐ. ܘܒܟܢܝܫܐ ܕܐܚܐ. ܐܝܠܝܢ ܕܫܘܝܢ ܠܐܠܗܐ *Apocryphal Acts*, p. 307 f.

Eucharist. This 'intimacy of brethren' belonged to those who according to the standards of asceticism were considered 'worthy for God'.

All these observations bring out a different concept of church and congregation which consists only of the ascetic aristocracy. But it may be assumed that the practical life itself made room for a circle of those not qualified for higher efforts to be gathered around this nucleus. We see the same phenomenon in the movement of Marcion and Valentinus. In this case the ascetics had some functions with regard to these catechumens, or penitents [132]. The Acts of Thomas do not speak much of this relation, but in a poetical piece at least some of these function are alluded to.

> 'Blessed are the spirits of the holy ones (chaste ones)
> who have taken the crown and gone up from the
> contest to what is given up to them.
> Blessed are the bodies of the holy ones
> which are worthy to become clear temples
> that the Messiah shall dwell in them.
> Blessed are you, holy ones
> for unto you (belongs) the power to ask and to receive.
> Blessed are you, holy ones
> for you are called judges.
> Blessed are you, holy ones
> for you are empowered to forgive sins' [133].

132 In the Pseudo-Clementine *De virginitate* the ascetic elite constitutes the church, but others are called 'companions'. The proemium says that the letter is written ܠܪ̈ܚܡܝ ܐܚܝ̈ܗܘܢ ܘܠܪ̈ܚܡܝ ܩܪ̈ܝܒܝܗܘܢ 'to those who love brethren, and to those who love their neighbors', *De virginitate*, p. 2, 4. In other documents, the non-baptized members are called ܬܝ̈ܒܐ *taiābē* 'penitents'.

133 ܛܘܒܝܗܝܢ ܠܪ̈ܘܚܬܗܘܢ ܕܩ̈ܕܝܫܐ. ܕܢܣܒܘ ܟܠܝܠܐ
ܘܣܠܩܘ ܡܢ ܐܓܘܢܐ ܠܡܕܡ ܕܐܬܝܗܒ
ܠܗ ܠܗܘܢ.
ܛܘܒܝܗܝܢ ܠܦܓܪ̈ܝܗܘܢ ܕܩ̈ܕܝܫܐ. ܕܫܘܘ
ܕܢܗܘܘܢ ܗ̈ܝܟܠܐ ܕܟ̈ܝܐ
ܕܢܥܡܪ ܒܗܘܢ ܡܫܝܚܐ.

The *De virginitate* depicts the obligations of the ascetics towards others in prayer, exorcism [134] and confirmation of faith [135]. They also are responsible for missionary, evangelistic and pastoral work. They traverse the cities and villages as travelling missionaries, expanding the gospel and strengthening the small communities [136].

We have glanced at the concept of church which, historically speaking, has played a very significant role in ancient Syrian Christianity. It has given a peculiar shape to the features of early Syrian communities. Besides, when the church adopted a different position during the course of its development, the strength of the earlier did not run out immediately. On the contrary its influence still continued in concealed regions in Mesopotamia and Persia. The rise and rapid expansion of Manichaeism seems to be partly due to the attractiveness of these archaic traditions. But we do not need to stop here. This ancient concept fascinated many Syrians within the church even later when conditions had changed and the primitive phase had retreated before new and advanced views. There were circles, as we shall see, which turned their back upon the advanced development time after time and took recourse to the same agelong concept of the church. Thus even later this concept had strength enough to become the heritage from the past which troubled the church of later generations again and again.

b. *Qeiāmā*

In connection with the archaic concept of church a term must be studied which on its part helps to throw additional light on the

ܛܘܒܝܟܘܢ ܩܕܝܫܐ. ܕܠܟܘܢ ܗܘ ܫܠܝܛ
ܠܡܫܐܠ ܘܡܣܒ.
ܛܘܒܝܟܘܢ ܩܕܝܫܐ. ܕܐܝܬܘܢ
ܕܝܪ̈ܐ ܐܬܬܪܝܬܘܢ.
ܛܘܒܝܟܘܢ ܩܕܝܫܐ ܕܬܫܒܩܘܢ
ܚ̈ܛܗܐ ܐܫܬܠܛܬܘܢ.

Apocryphal Acts, p. 261.

134 *De virginitate*, p. 56.

135 *Ibid.*, p. 66.

136 *Ibid.*, p. 72, 78, 80, 82, 88.

inner structure of the ascetic church. This is the term *benai qeiāmā* or *benat qeiāmā*, resting on the vocable *qeiāmā* with the fascinating problems which it offers. In translation this vocable has been rendered as 'sons (resp. daughters) of the covenant', 'ascetics' and 'monks'.

An attempt has also been made to understand this term from the meaning of the root 'rise up' and 'stand'. Wensinck has suggested that *qeiāmā* means 'stand', and in this case *benai qeiāmā* would be those who belong to the holy stand [137]. Maude agrees with him with a slight variation, explaining the basic meaning of the word *qeiāmā* to be 'rising up' to a higher and stable level, whether this level was the baptismal state or the state of monks [138].

The examples in the synagogical practice have been brought into the discussion. In another study Wensinck suggested that *qeiāmā* is a derivation from the institution of Judaism [139]. Indeed, the Mishna knows such an institution of the men who stood by at the sacrifices in the temple. This institution existed also in the synagogue where they read the scripture [140].

137 *Qejama*, p. 561. This 'Stand' or 'Bestand' is taken over also by BARDENHEWER, *Geschichte altk. Literatur*, IV, p. 331. Wensinck asserts : '... ich meine, dass « Stand, Bestand » die richtige Übersetzung ist an vielen Stellen in der älteren syrischen Literatur', *op. cit.*, p. 562. Perhaps Wensinck was too much influenced by PAYNE SMITH, *Thesaurus syriacus*, II, col. 3533 f. where the meaning of the vocable is given in the following terms : 1) statio, 2) statutum, 3) foedus, pactum. BROCKELMANN, *Lexicon syriacum*, p. 653 renders its meaning in a similar way : 1) stare, 2) status, statio, 3) resurrectio, 4) praesidium, 5) foedus. However the word for status, statio is ܩܘܡܐ *qaūmā*.

138 MAUDE, *B'nai Q'yama*, p. 14. A similar attempt was made by ADAM, *Grundbegriffe*, p. 226 where he asserts : 'Dann wäre der Ausdruck so zu übersetzen : « diejenigen, die zu dem Aufrechtstehen gehören »... also « die Stehenden ». Das setzt voraus, dass die Stelle (Lk. 2, 34) in ihrer Anwendung nicht mehr auf Israel beschränkt, sondern in vollem Sinne der christlichen Gemeinde zugeeignet wurde'. He brings this idea in relation with the angels.

139 *Weiteres zu Qejama*, p. 812.

140 אנשי מעמד, Taanith 4, 2 . 3. Further it is told here that these men had greater obligations in fasting, fasting 4 days a week, from Monday to Friday. Another parallel is found in a letter of Gaon 'Amram bar Šašna : ומן בני קיומי שהם במקום סנהדרי קטנה 'and from the *benē qeiūmē*, who are in the place of the little Sanhedrin'. In this document, this group stands between the ordained scholars and the great mass of ordinary Rabbis in the ranks of the

The latter suggestion is certainly far-fetched. This group in the temple and the synagogue consisted of devote men within the congregation. As we shall see, the *qeiāmā* originally must have had an exclusive meaning, and only later did it lose this meaning. Besides this there are other serious difficulties. The term *qeiāmā* claims richer connotations than those derived from the root 'to stand'. Thus, it would be useless to pursue the subject any further in those directions.

A careful approach to this question, which should undertake to bend back the misleading suggestions, would first gather the elements of the meaning of this term preserved in the later sources. These gleanings are necessary because they prevent the study from seeing these matters out of focus and help to assess better the facets of meaning. As the examination of the sources shows the term had a fairly large breadth of meaning. There is need of at least a brief review of the principal aspects involved.

First of all the *qeiāmā* is a word which has been used to render the term covenant which God has made with men, although this is not always the case. In this sense the word renders the new covenant [141].

Further the meaning of the term *qeiāmā* became popular in connection with the oath and vow as these were practiced in the church and in monasticism [142]. In this sense the essence of monasticism is defined as *qeiāmā* [143]. Another nuance of the same meaning appears as a solemn promise in God's name [144].

Finally, depending upon the width and quality in the meaning

academy of Talmud in Babylonia in the 9th or 10th century, KITTEL, *Eine synagogale Parallele*, p. 235.

141 *Liber graduum*, col. 452. ܐܩܝܡ ܩܝܡܐ means 'to establish a contract', 'to make a pact'. As in every contract, the obligations are mutual. On the part of God, this is His gracious attitude, on the part of His elected, the religious and ethical injunctions required in order to be eligible for the benefits of the pact.

142 ܘܐܩܝܡ ܗܘܐ ܩܝܡܐ ܠܐܠܗܐ 'and he established the *qeiāmā* to God', *Legends of Eastern Saints*, I, p. 9; ܩܝܡܐ ܕܐܩܝܡܬ ܠܐܠܗܝ 'the *qeiāmā* that I have established to my God', *Neṣḥānā*, p. 579.

143 Ms. Br. Mus. Add. 14,493, fol. 176; Add. 17,262, fol. 72.

144 *Acta martyrum*, IV, p. 532; *Story of Euphemia*, p. 69.

of the *qeiāmā* the term also meant the company of persons whom the covenant or vow brought and knitted together. In a still wider sense the term meant not the institution of ascetics but the clergy [145] and even the congregation and church [146].

As this glimpse of the usage of the term *qeiāmā* shows the crucial point in its whole meaning is apparent. There can be little doubt where the weight of the term lies. This is not simply a 'state' or 'stand' but in the covenant idea, that includes the idea of oath and vow. A secondary meaning of the term is a group of persons who keep the vow or covenant.

If in this argumentation there should be some loose strands, they will be bound together by other evidence of surprising strength. This evidence is found in the text of the Dead Sea scrolls.

The concept of the covenant is deeply impregnated into the consciousness and life of the ascetics behind the Dead Sea literature. To them the word 'Covenant' also had a fairly large breadth of meaning but there is no doubt that the weight of the term lies in its first and primary meaning. All the texts say that this is God's covenant, a covenant which God takes care of [147] in his goodness and grace [148]. Men can enter into this relationship [149] through a new form of life. The Manual of Discipline says concerning the neophytes that : 'all those who enter into the order of the community shall pass over into the covenant in the presence of God' [150]. One other point is worth noticing. There are passages which show that the term 'covenant' was also used in the meaning of vow. One passage says : 'he establishes by a covenant on his soul to separate himself from all men of wickedness' [151]. Thus it is of interest to observe that so far as the concept of covenant is concerned, man's responsibility is taken as seriously as God's grace [152]. The covenant

145 *Julianos der Abtrünnige,* p. 3.

146 *Ibid.,* p. 12, 142.

147 *Megilloth genuzoth,* I, p. 24 f.

148 ברית חסד 'the covenant of grace', *Manual of Discipline,* I, 8.

149 הבא בברית, *ibid.,* II, 12; V, 20.

150 וכול הבאים בסרך היחד יעבורו בברית לפני אל, *ibid.,* I, 16.

151 ואשר יקום בברית על נפישו להבדל מכול אנשי העול, *ibid.,* V, 10.

152 With regard to the ascetics it is said המחזקים בברית 'who hold firmly the covenant', *ibid.,* V, 3.

requires commitment. It is told in plain words that the ascetics are those 'who are eager in the community to establish (realize) his covenant'[153]. And in a metrical section which deals with the profoundest meaning and purpose of the ascetic community, it is stated that one of the purposes is 'to establish the covenant according to the eternal ordinances'[154].

This what has been stated up to now constitutes the real and basic elements in the 'covenant'. All other ramifications in the meaning of the term are simply derivations. And one is which concerns us here particularly. Much importance attaches to the observation that the ascetic community, too, could be designated by the same term. If we give full value to certain passages it is fairly evident that the whole community could be identified with the term 'covenant'[155], and its members could be called as 'men of the covenant'[156].

That is what we have been seeking for. These finds from the literature of the Jewish Covenanters are highly important for more than one reason. This analogy helps us in dealing with our question and with the similarity of both phenomena which is so striking that it is difficult to resist the impression that there must exist an organic relation between both. It is to the foci of the first Aramaean Christian communities in Mesopotamia that we should naturally look for the appearance of these conceptions in the Syrian Orient.

With that working principle we shall turn back to the question of *qeiāmā* of the ancient Syrian Christians. All its facets now receive meaning and life.

153 המתנדבים ביחד להקים את בריתו, *ibid.*, V, 20-22.

154 להקם ברית לחוקות עולם, *ibid.*, VIII, 10.

155 There is particularly one passage which deserves to be quoted : וכול איש מאנשי היחד ברית היחד, 'and any man of the men of the community of the covenant of the Community', *ibid.*, VIII, 16 . 17. Another observation can be made in ¬onnection with the curses in the liturgy of the initiation. One phrase runs : ידבקו בו כול אלות הברית הזות ויבדילהו אל לרעה 'may all the curses of this covenant cling to him, and may God single him out for evil', *ibid.*, II, 15 . 16. As the text and the context show the covenant here means the community of the ascetics.

156 אנשי בריתם, *ibid.*, V, 9; VI, 19.

It becomes fully conceivable that in the young Aramaean Christian movement which cherished the awareness of newness with regard to the covenant relation, the term in this sense must have played an important role in abrogating the Jewish concept of the covenant. A priori it can be well imagined that apologetics and polemics took care of placing the covenant-idea in the forefront of the debate and at the heart of the new self-consciousness. These reflections seem to have been transplanted into the thought world of the ancient Syrian Christians who : 'put on the crown in the true *qeiāmā* of the Lord'[157].

As with the Covenanters, the life of the primitive Syrian Christians was focused in the vow. The evidence in the remnants of the ancient baptismal liturgy is conclusive[158]. Also the ancient Syriac treatise in Armenian translation comes to our aid. There is a passage which refers to the Enemy who tries to allure the 'warriors' in order to destroy their 'stand of the vow'[159]. This is a translation text, and such a text has its disadvantages. Nevertheless for our question this disadvantage is not serious. In this case it is safe to assume that the original Syriac contained only one word, namely the *qeiāmā,* because the Armenian phrase as it stands in the text cannot be translated into Syriac. We would need to repeat the term *qeiāmā,* and this repetition would not make sense. Therefore we have before us an ancient explanation of the technical term *qeiāmā* given by the Armenian translator.

Even more can be seen, namely, the relation of this *qeiāmā* with baptism. Hymns of an ancient baptismal liturgy which have been preserved by the Acts of Thomas can guide us in these steps. Here

157 ܘܣܝܡܘ ܟܠܝܠܐ ܒܩܝܡܐ ܫܪܝܪܐ ܕܡܪܝܐ, *Odes of Solomon*, IX, 11, p. 29.

158 It is told that the officers of the church have to admonish : ܠܟܠܗ ܩܝܡܗ ܕܐܠܗܐ ܩܕܡ ܡܥܡܘܕܝܬܐ ܠܐܝܠܝܢ ܕܩܪܒܘ ܢܦܫܗܘܢ ܠܒܬܘܠܘܬܐ ܘܠܩܕܝܫܘܬܐ 'the whole *qeiāmā* of God before baptism, those who have vowed themselves to the virginity and holiness, young men, and virgins and holy ones', APHRAHAṬ, *Demonstrationes*, col. 345.

159 *Եւ է զի տեսանէ նա զոք զի զգեցեալ է զէն, եւ մարտնչի ընդ նմա, եւ գրոց մտաց, զի լուծցէ զուխտաւորութիւն եւ կործանեսցէ զնա*, 'and sometimes he (i.e. Satan) sees one that he has put on the armor, and he fights against him and the meaning of the Scripture in order that he might cancel the stand in the vow, and may destroy him', *Srboyn,* II, p. 316.

the link between the *qeiāmā* and the baptismal rite is recognizable in such statements as : baptism is 'the establisher of the new man' [160]. Here the same verbal root as in the term *qeiāmā* appears.

Finally, as the Covenanters in their terminology identified the covenant with their society so also did the ancient Christians. We refer here to a document which has preserved all these archaic elements side by side : 'for the whole *qeiāmā* of men and women they were abstinent and chaste and they were holy and pure and they dwelt singly and abstinently' [161]. And according to the Semitic usage the *benai qeiāmā* and the *benat qeiāmā* are those who participate in the vow and are members of the body of the *qeiāmā*.

On the basis of a careful induction of many strands of evidence the investigation of the structure of the archaic concept of church gains new and valuable perspective.

5. TERMINOLOGY

a. *Betūlā*

In the earliest documents, we find several terms which later fell into disuse, or which were transformed in their meaning. These are worthy of more extended comments. Here, too, we have a chance to enter a path that permits us some significant glimpses of the archaic form of Syrian Christianity. A study of these would focus all the previous investigation to a burning-point.

In the first place, the terms *betūlā* 'virgin' (masculine), *betūltā* 'virgin' (feminine) and *betūlūtā* [162] 'virginity' come into consideration. These are the most natural to explain, in view of the previous discussions, and would not detain us long. Since the virtue of virginity was for the ancient Syrians the anticipation of resurrection [163], and as such the prerequisite for the adoption of the

160 ܘܡܩܝܡܢܘܬܐ ܒܪܢܫܐ ܚܕܬܐ, *Apocryphal Acts*, p. 301.

161 ܩܝܡܐ ܕܝܢ ܟܠܗ ܕܓܒܖ̈ܐ ܘܕܢܫ̈ܐ ܢܟܦܝܢ ܗܘܘ ܘܕܟܝܢ ܘܩܕܝܫܝܢ ܗܘܘ ܘܕܝܪܝܢ ܘܝܚܝܕܐܝܬ ܘܢܟܦܐܝܬ ܥܡܪܝܢ ܗܘܘ *Doctrina Addai*, p. 50.

162 ܒܬܘܠܐ : ܒܬܘܠܬܐ : ܒܬܘܠܘܬܐ

163 Ephrem has preserved a tradition which states bluntly that virginity was exactly the reason why Elijah was transported to heaven with his body, *De paradiso*, VI, p. 24 f.

Christian faith and for the inclusion into the Christian fellowship, and since the whole message could be brought under the denominator of virginity [164], so it was natural to call the adherents *betūlē* [165]. In the 'History of John the Son of Zebedee', the hero is called simply *betūlā*, reflecting this primitive usage of the term [166]. The best source, here, is the Pseudo-Clementine *De virginitate* which calls Christians *betūlē* and *betūltē* [167].

We also notice that something of the ancient usage of the term is reflected in the early Syriac literature, particularly in Ephrem [168], where archaic traditions stand amicably side by side with younger formations.

b. *Qaddīšā*

Another term which is certainly as ancient as the previous one is *qaddīšā* 'holy', and *qaddīšūtā* [169] 'holiness'. In the Syriac domain, this term received a new meaning over against the Greek ἅγιος as it was used in the primitive church of Hellenistic origin. The particular cast of the Kerygma in the Syrian Christianity caused modification in the meaning of this term, giving it an entirely new signification.

Since marriage was regarded as a 'bitter tree' which has no place in the Paradise [170], and since the requirement of the Kerygma is : 'wipe off the filth from your face and love His holiness and clothe yourselves therewith' [171], the *qaddīšūtā*, in the first place, means sexual purity as a prerequisite for the renewal and indwelling spirit. In the Acts of Thomas, it is said that : 'His servants should serve Him through holiness and purity' [172]. Then it is explained

164 Ms. Br. Mus. Add. 14,601, fol. 164 a.

165 Ms. Br. Mus. Add. 14,592, fol. 75 a.

166 *Apocryphal Acts*, p. 5.

167 See pag. 72.

168 *De Paradiso*, IV, 12, p. 15.

169 ܩܕܝܫܐ : ܩܕܝܫܬܐ : ܩܕܝܫܘܬܐ

170 *Odes of Solomon*, XI, 21, p. 32.

171 ܘܫܘܘ ܛܢܦܘܬܐ ܡܢ ܐܦܝܟܘܢ : ܘܪܚܡܘ ܩܕܝܫܘܬܗ ܘܠܒܫܘܗ̇ XIII, 3 *ibid.*, p. 34.

172 ܕܢܦܠܚܘܢ ܠܗ ܦܠܚܘܗܝ ܒܩܕܝܫܘܬܐ ܘܒܕܟܝܘܬܐ *Apocryphal Acts*, p. 296.

what is meant thereby, namely: 'to serve Him ...through abstinence and through virtue and chastity, and that all these fleshly (lusts) should be strange to us' [173].

That we are on the right trace is indicated by some observations in Ephrem, where older traditions have survived. Particularly traditions embedded in hermeneutic knowledge handed down from earlier times have a good claim to have stemmed from archaic legacy. One such tradition speaks of the ark of Noah and states that 'the women sanctified themselves in the ark of Noah' [174]. Owing to the context this tradition speaks a clear language since these wives of Noah's sons had to abstain from sexual intercourse.

Further, there are certain clues which point to another interesting idiosyncrasy in the use of these terms among the ancient Syrians. This manifests itself in the usage of these terms in Aphrahaṭ who seems to have been faithful toward archaic terminology. Always, when Aphrahaṭ speaks of Joshua [175], Elijah [176] and of Adam at a period before Eve was created [177], he uses consistently the term *betūlā*, and *betūlūtā* to characterize them. Also, Mary appears always as *betūltā* [178]. However, for the persons with marital status, Aphrahaṭ never employs *betūlūtā*, but always uses the term *qaddīšā* and *qaddīšūtā*. Speaking of Moses, Aphrahaṭ always uses the term *qaddīšūtā* [179]. This is the case in connection with Israel at the Sinai [180]. The priests in the sanctuary also are qualified by the *qaddīšūtā* [181]. This demonstration points to the fact that the term *qaddīšā* and *qaddīšūtā*, in the earliest usage, designated a distinct group of the believers, namely those who did not bring their natural virginity to Christian life — but they, as married

173 ܕܢܦܠܚܝܘܗܝ... ܘܒܚܢܝܦܘܬܐ. ܘܒܡܗܝܪܘܬܐ. ܘܒܩܕܝܫܘܬܐ. ܘܗܘܝ، ܢܘܟܪܝܝܢ ܡܢ ܟܠܗܝܢ ܗܠܝܢ ܦܓܪܢܝܬܐ *ibid.*, p. 296.

174 ܢܫ̈ܐ ܢܫ̈ܐ ܕܐܬܩܕܫ ܒܗ *Carmina Nisibena*, I, 9, p. 3.

175 *Demonstrationes*, col. 832.

176 *Ibid.*, col. 833.

177 *Ibid.*, col. 837.

178 *Ibid.*, *passim.*

179 *Ibid.*, col. 261, 825, 832.

180 *Ibid.*, col. 825, 832.

181 *Ibid.*, col. 261.

persons, had abandoned married life and started to observe sexual purity as holiness required by the Kerygma [182].

c. *Īḥīdaiā*

Īḥīdaiā [183] is a term which has played a very important role, even in the later history of monasticism long after the conditions had changed. It appears, already, in connection with the remains of an archaic baptismal liturgy [184].

With regard to the origin and meaning of *īhīdaiā*, the views are divided and various opinions have been expressed [185].

Recently, Adam has proposed that, as far as the origin of this term is concerned, the Syriac *īḥīdaiā* is original and the Greek μόναχος only secondary [186]. However of greater importance would be the implication of this postulation. In this case, its meaning would appear in a quite different light. Adam supposes that the basic vocabel, from which the term stems, must be found in the Syriac counterpart of the Greek μονογενής 'the only begotten' [187], rendered by the Syriac version of the gospels by *īḥīdaiā* 'sole', 'only', 'singular' [188] Indeed, if all this would be true, then a quite new vista would open itself. In this case, the meaning of *īḥīdaiā* would be not less — than that the ascetics have appropriated the title of honor of Christ and applied it to themselves as those who became the followers of Him, in the truest sense of the word [189]. By

182 Ephrem speaking of three degrees, marriage, continence and virginity, says clearly that the second is ܩܘܕܫܐ *qūdšā*, *Contra haereses*, L, 10, p. 180.

183 ܝܚܝܕܝܐ

184 ܠܝܚܝܕܝܐ ܗܘ ܝܐܐ ܐܓܘܢܐ 'for solitaries is the struggle suitable', Aphrahaṭ, *Demonstrationes*, VII, 18, col. 341.

185 See pag. 220.

186 *Grundbegriffe*, p. 218.

187 'Dass *iḥidaja* im syrischen Sprachgebrauch genau dem griechischen μονογενής entspricht, steht fest und kann nicht bezweifelt werden', *ibid.*, p. 219.

188 The Pešitta renders μονογενής in John I, 14, 18 and III, 16 by *īḥīdaiā* 'sole', 'only', 'singular', 'special'. The Old Syriac version in the form of the Curetonian text, renders this vocable by *īḥīdā* 'only', 'special'. The Sinaitic text is extant only in the last passage where it reads similarly.

189 'Von hier aus ist es zu begreifen, dass es zu der Übertragung des Prädikates *iḥidaja*- μονογενής von dem Gottessohn auf die Kinder Gottes kommen

the way, such an identification would not be very strange and would not be an innovation, since we know instructive parallels for this phenomenon in Judaism [190]. It would be a corollary that mysticism which was generated by Syrian asceticism, had its cradle already in its earliest stage of development.

However, an explanation like this raises acute historical problems. It is very doubtful whether one can follow Adam in these pathways. There is some justification for doubt as to whether the Syriac term *īḥīdaiā* is a translation from the Greek μόναχος as this has been suggested [191]. The Syriac term, more probably, is original and does not go back to the Hellenistic but to the Palestinian Aramaean Christianity. However, granted that this assumption is admissible, it does not, thus, need to lead us to far-fetched speculation. For it is a guesswork, regardless of the striking impression left by the first look, and regardless of the fact that sometimes the term *īḥīdaiā* has been brought together with the term μονογενής 'the only begotten one', so in Aphrahaṭ [192], and also in some cases in the Greek patristic literature [193]. A closer look, however, tends to pour cold water over these fascinating suppositions.

It is time to give the proofs. There are several reasons which stand in the way. In the first place, we have to listen to what the Syrians themselves have to tell about the background of the μόναχος. In this respect, we are grateful for a text which deals with just the problem under discussion. This text shows, unmistakably, that the Syrians themselves did not explain *īḥīdaiā* by μονογενής, but they

konnte. Die *iḥidaja* sind die wahren Nachfolger des Messias Jesus, und die Bezeichnung *iḥidaja* wurde der hohe Ehrentitel seiner Getreuesten. Ein Würdename Jesu ist also auf seine wahren Jünger übertragen worden... das ist das Geheimnis der Mönche', *Grundbegriffe*, p. 220.

190 See MARMORSTEIN, *Nachahmung Gottes in der Agada*, p. 7.

191 VAN DER PLOEG, *Oud-syrisch monnikslcven*, p. 23.

192 ܟܠܗܘܢ ܝܚܝ̈ܕܝܐ ܡܚܕܐ ܠܗܘܢ ܝܚܝܕܝܐ ܕܡܢ ܥܘܒܐ ܕܐܒܘܗܝ،
'the *īḥīdaiā* from the busom of His Father shall gladden all the *īḥīdaiē*', *Demonstrationes*, VI, 6, col. 269.

193 τὸ γοῦν πρῶτον τάγμα τῶν ἐν Χριστῷ προκοπτόντων τὸ τῶν μοναχῶν τυγχάνει. Σπάνιοι δὲ εἰσιν οὗτοι· διὸ κατὰ τὸν 'Ακύλαν μονογενεῖς ὠνομάσθησαν ἀφωμοιωμένοι τῷ μονογενεῖ υἱῷ τοῦ θεοῦ, EUSEBIUS, *Commentaria in Psalmos*, col. 689.

saw its equivalent in μόναχος[194]. Moreover, this passage shows that the Syrians did not claim that the μόναχος is of secondary character In view of the fact that the Syrians gladly took an opportunity to glorify their language and its importance[195], this modest explanation is more than instructive.

Further, another important observation comes into consideration. 'Unique', 'the only begotten' is not the only meaning of our vocable. The term *iḥīdaiā*, in the form of an adverb, is connected in the Syriac usage with the verb 'to live' and this definitely does not mean something mystical at all, but 'to live singly', 'to live solitarily' and is attested in the early Syriac literature. The most remarkable occurrence appears in the Doctrine of Addai[196]. Here, we have to see the source of the meaning of *iḥīdaiā* : 'a person who lives singly', a 'celibate'. Thus, in this term, too, the powerful factor of virginity manifests itself.

Finally, there are less adventurous ways for the explanation of the fact that the term *iḥīdaiā* has been brought together with the term 'the only begotten one'. The reason lies close at hand. The term *iḥīdaiā* was ambiguous and it would be a surprise, indeed, if these rich hidden possibilities would have been left unnoticed and unused, particularly in prayer. We have traces regarding this. In the solemn formulations, this was done in the form of prayer[197]. This usage is the most natural and the most satisfactory way of a solution to the above-mentioned phenomena.

[194] ܘܗܝܕܝܢ ܟܕ ܚܣܢ ܠܗ ܛܟܣܐ ܘܪܒ ܐܬܟܢܝܘ ܠܗܘܢ ܥܡܐ ...... ܘܐܬܩܪܝܘ ܡܘܢܟܘ ܘܥܡܪܝܗܘܢ ܡܘܢܣܛܪܝܐ ܕܡܬܦܫܩܝܢ ܣܘܪܝܐܝܬ ܡܥܪ̈ܐ ܕܝܚܝܕ̈ܝܐ , 'and at that time when the order (i.e. the institution) gained strength and grew large they were called...... in Greek *μοναχοί*, and their dwelling-places *μοναστήρια*, which are interpreted in Syriac as the caves (or cells) of the *iḥīdaiē*', Ms. Vat. syr. 501, fol. 23 b. The word which is lost in the text is obviously *iḥīdaiē*. This is attested also by the Arabic recension which has preserved the word المتوحدين = *iḥīdaiē*, Ms. Vat. arab. 153, fol. 189 b.

[195] Concerning the claim of the Syrians that the Syriac language was the language from which all other languages stemmed, and that God Himself talked to Adam in Syriac, see *Schatzhöhle*, p. 122.

[196] ܘܝܚܝܕܐܝܬ ... ܥܡܪܝܢ ܗܘܘ 'and they dwelt singly', *Doctrina Addaei*, p. 50.

[197] Ms. Vat. syr. 304, fol. 140 a.

CHAPTER IV

MANICHAEAN MONASTICISM

It was on the 20th of March, 242, during the coronation festival of King Shahpuhr I, that the crowds in the streets and bazaars of Seleucia-Ctesiphon heard the message of the new religion. Many heard it from the mouth of its prophet, a youthful man, named Mani. Indeed, for him, this was the inauguration of his proclamation. What started here reaped success after success with such breathtaking speed that his movement soon deeply affected the Syrian Orient. As in the history of Syrian Christianity one cannot pass by the momentous role the Manichees played in the Syrian Orient — where to many observers it seemed not impossible that the new movement could win over Christianity — so can their influence not be overlooked in the history of asceticism and monasticism. For just as Manichaeism left its deep footprints upon the religious development of the Syrian Orient [1], just so did it leave an indelible impression upon the area of asceticism. Therefore it is necessary for us to devote an entire chapter to monasticism as it was shaped by Manichaeism.

1. FOUNDATIONS

While ideological principles form the premise for practice, we must try to get a glimpse of the ideological background in order to understand the practice. Therefore, before investigating the ascetic phenomenon created by Mani and its forms and manners of life, it is necessary to cast a brief glance over the fundamental structure of the system. Only in this way will the range and structural role of the ascetic phenomenon become manifest in its sharpness.

The fundamental theme, deeply spreading its roots everywhere into the Manichaean system, stands in relation to the cosmogonical

1 Vööbus, *Manichaeism and Christ. in Persia*, p. 7 ff.

mythologumena. The mythos of the origin of the universe is based upon the essential fact that there the demoniac forces played an active role. The evil principle has become the forerunner of everything in existence. The *Škand-vimānīk vičār* comments : 'furthermore, this, that the world is a bodily (literally, 'embodied') formation of Ahriman, an altogether bodily formation, (is itself) a creation of Ahriman' [2]. If, now, particles of light have been forcibly imprisoned in this mass of demonically formed material, a tragic situation has been called forth which creates the possibility of far-reaching results. It is thereby determined that the creation of the whole universe as such is only something negative which already, at the moment of its birth, must have borne the mark of degeneration. Life, the world with its cosmic events, the continuation of the universe, sowing and reaping, the continuing life of mankind — all this is a process which has only a negative quality [3]. In essence it is nothing else but the attempt of the Power of Darkness to hold back forever the particles of light which are imprisoned here by the continuation of the life of mankind, and to hinder by every means their return to the world of light.

From this basic theologumenon there follows immediately the radical asceticism which alone allows the particles of light imprisoned in the body to be liberated, and to return unhindered from the lower world into their home of light.

The corollary of this hostile attitude involves more than a cosmic process. Just as the whole physical universe, the macrocosm, is full of tension, so analogically the microcosm. Man, too, is a creation of the Dark Power, and compared with the macrocosm he is its exact replica. The tension between the cosmic antipodal forces reaches even into his being and causes him to be torn and rent. Mani, in borrowing from the Christians (as, indeed, he borrowed many other elements) the trichotomy that man is made up of body, soul, and spirit, modified the Christian position by dividing these parts between the two dualistic principles. This gave rise to especially violent polemics among Christian authors who found utterly impossible the idea that man is a created product of the evil principle.

2 *Škand-gumānīk vičār*, p. 7.

3 JOANNES CHRYSOSTOMUS, *In ep. ad Galatas comm.*, col. 618.

According to the ecclesiastical [4] and Iranian [5] authors, the creator of the body is called literally 'demon' and 'devil'. To the ecclesiastical authors a characteristic complement may be found in a cosmogonic hymn of Manichaean origin. Concerning the creation of the body, this text says : 'from the dirt of the demons and the faeces of the demonesses she (Āz) formed this body and she herself entered it' [6]. Thus the human body was fully compromised in the eyes of the Manichees. The various names given to the body — e.g. 'bitter likeness', 'creature of Hades', 'dark house' — in the psalms of the Manichees are full of disdain for the subjection of the body to deterioration [7].

These perspectives will enable us adequately to understand how deeply the foundations of asceticism were laid into the groundwork of theological principles. Thereby asceticism became a structural element in Manichaeism. When everything visible and corporeal represents the evil principle, an opposing and complete abstinence from the world and rigorous mortification are the only ways leading to liberation and salvation.

But, however much Mani's thoughts may have been theoretically consequent, the practical life made its own reservations. Experience taught and dictated well in advance that it would be impossible to demand of all believers complete abstinence from the world. This practical factor forced Mani to create an inner team, a special category of men and women who were ready to give up their earthly benefits and devote themselves to the higher ideals of salvation and service. These were the Electi who constituted the monasticism of the Manichees.

In the *Kephalaia* Mani dedicates some lines to the origin of the monastic ideal, which he ascribes to a revelation. He says that during the reign of Ardashir (226-241), in a certain year — he is not more specific — the 'living paraclete' came to him and imparted

4 EPHREM, *Prose Refutations*, I, p. 5, 122; SERAPION OF THMUIS, *Against the Manichees*, p. 34; HEGEMONIUS, *Acta Archelai*, p. 99; *Sacr. conciliorum nova collectio*, VI, p. 431, cf. V, p. 1286. Cf. ALEXANDER OF LYCOPOLIS, *Contra Manich. opiniones*, p. 5 f.

5 *Dēnkard*, V, p. 244.

6 *Manich. kosmog. Hymnus*, p. 217.

7 *Manichaean Psalm-Book*, p. 54, 99.

to him the revelation of the mystery of monasticism, as well as certain cosmic and cosmogonic ideas. That particular revelation had caused Mani to call monasticism into being [8]. This pathetic remark, however, must be subject to criticism; for it is difficult to see on which points Mani really could claim originality. It is more sober to apply to the origin of monasticism the same principle he considers valid for other aspects of his religion. He himself admits that he has borrowed elements from other religions and specifically mentions Buddhism, Christianity, and Zoroastrianism [9]. The milieu from which he himself came also had certainly exerted its influence [10].

We are more or less certain as to the names of monks in various languages. As is known, Mani wrote most of his principal works in the Syriac language. In Syriac it is likely that he used the term *zaddīqā* — a word which means 'righteous' [11] — for monks and *zaddīqtā* for female ascetics [12]. We know positively which word Mani used in Persian — for it is known that other parts of his works were written in that language — to denote monks. Owing to a fortunate coincidence, among a series of valuable documents discovered in Turkestan there is a leaf in the Southwest Iranian language the text of which most certainly goes back to Mani himself. It contains the name for the monks : *wiṣīdagān*, meaning someone who has been elected [13]. In an extensive work written in the Persian-Parthian language this term appears quite often [14]. As a technical term, it became popular in other languages in the Orient and the West.

8 *Kephalaia*, p. 15.

9 'The writings, the wisdoms, the apocalypses, the parables, and the psalms of the previous churches are united from all directions in my church into the wisdom which I have revealed to you. As a river joins another river to form a mighty current, so these ancient books have joined one another in my writings', *ibid.*, p. 2.

10 See pag. 122.

11 As δίκαιος is used in the Greek and Coptic, *Manichaean Psalm-Book*, p. 11, 28; 37, 8; 81, 23; 99, 31 etc.

12 ܙܕܝ̈ܩܬܐ, *Prose Refutations*, I, p. 128.

13 *Mitteliranische Manichaica*, II, p. 296.

14 *wcydg['n] Bet- und Beichtbuch*, p. 24.

As may be seen from these data, Mani brought forth his monasticism in connection with the idea of having a body of the Elect. But besides this concept there is another word, *din-dar,* evidently used quite frequently, and particularly as a loan-word in many Oriental languages[15]. This term, which means *qui observat religionem* in the Northern Persian language, does not appear in the West Iranian Turfan fragments. Another word which has spread far outside [16] is *dinaver,* meaning, in the language of central Persia, 'believer'.

Besides these more usual names there were some other terms in use, some of which were given by others and some of which were used only among themselves [17]. The term 'virgin' appears often in the Oriental fragments and hymns, having been immortalized by an inscription in Greek [18].

The entry into monastic life was preceded by an act of reception which, while established from the very beginning, seems later on to have been complemented with new elements. How this took place during the earliest period, we do not know in detail. We know only that the most important part of the reception act was an oath by which the aspirant had to commit himself to higher demands.

We know more of the vow taken by the monks upon being admitted to the company of the Elect. The higher obligations to which the monk was ready to submit were summed up into a compendium of prescriptions handed down over many generations. We have reason to think that the gist of its character has been preserved in later documents. It is true that Mani himself gave prescriptions to his monks; this work, however, has not yet appeared — to our distress. It is possible that he already had divided these requirements into certain parts — i.e., five commandments and three seals [19].

15 It appears in the Soghdian sources, *ibid.*, p. 50, and through the medium of this language it came into the Uigur and Turkish languages.

16 In the Soghdian, *ibid.*, p. 43 f., and as '*tien-na-wu*' also in the Chinese sources, *Traité manichéen,* p. 554.

17 The term 'brother' and 'sister' belongs to older terminology, *Kephalaia,* p. 37; *Handschriftenreste,* II, p. 33; *Mahrnāmag,* p. 22. A remnant of the term 'brother' in Syriac has been survived in a fragment in Br. Mus. Orient. 6201 C.

18 Βάσσα παρθένος Λυδία Μανιχέα, KUGENER-CUMONT, *Recherches,* III, p. 175.

19 The work is lost which, according to its title — πραγματεία — seems

With regard to the three 'seals', Augustinus informs us that they were *signaculum oris, manuum et sinus.* An original fragment found in Turfan corroborates this. It speaks of three seals — the seal of hands, mouth, and thoughts [20]. As to the meaning of these seals there is no doubt. The first *signaculum* prohibited impure speech and lies; the second prohibited deeds, and the third thoughts, which were not in harmony with the nature of the world of light. Attention repeatedly has been directed towards the fact that these three fundamental prescriptions in the asceticism of Mani were borrowed from Buddhist traditions.

The situation with the commandments is not so simple. Newly discovered texts have shed some light upon the problem; but, because these texts are still at a stage in which their translation is disputed, they have raised new problems. The first of the commandments contains a prescription for truthfulness; the second, abstention from errors (which, however, may have been either moral or ritual); the third demands an attitude suitable for religion; the fourth, purity of speech; the fifth, poverty [21]. These commandments contain spiritual-ethical elements as well as others of a completely physical character. From the ethical prescriptions there is quite a series of demands behind these few clues : the monk is obliged to abstain from falsehood, wrath, revenge, malicious joy, and all other low passions. Instead of that, he must live so that wrath might be superseded by love, suspicion by confidence, and rashness by patience. Among the practical virtues, humility was

to have discussed the questions of practical life and to have been a sort of compendium of ethical and ritual norms. Unfortunately, also, Fihrist's report has a lacuna here and does not offer us information about the content of this document. We receive, however, an impression from different directions that Mani established extensive ordinances and rules. It is also noteworthy that Mani appears in the Christian tradition as ܣܐܡ ܢܡܘܣܐ 'the law-giver', SEVERUS, *Homilia*, CXXIII, p. 137.

20 *Handschriftenreste*, II, p. 63; AUGUSTINUS, *De moribus Manichaeorum*, X, col. 1353 f.

21 *Bet- und Beichtbuch*, p. 14 translates the Soghdian terms : 1. Wahrhaftigkeit; 2. Nicht-Verletzen; 3. Religionsgemässes Verhalten; 4. Reinheit des Mundes; 5. Glückselige Armut. WALDSCHMIDT-LENTZ, *Manichäische Dogmatik*, p. 548 translate the same terms : 1. Wahrheit; 2. Sündlosigkeit (?); 3. Religiöses Äusseres; 4. Reinheit des Mundes; 5. Glücklich sein (und) doch Arm sein.

considered as one of greatest importance [22], since it must replace pride and haughtiness with self-discipline, and offenses with patience. This may be illustrated by the miniatures of the Manichees, from which it can be seen how the Manichaean monks already attempted to stress their humility through their gestus [23].

On the other hand, the monastic commandments also contained a series of ascetic rules. It is not necessary to go into the contents and order of the separate rules in great detail, since certain prescriptions very often were divided between several rules and combined with elements of a spiritual-ethical nature. The main reason, however, is that we have to look deeper into the ascetic practices, basing this study on a wider bulk of all available sources.

2. ASCETIC PRACTICES

One of the first ascetic practices of the monks, which sometimes gave them the name, is virginity. To understand this, a glance at the cosmogonic conception will suffice. In Adam particles of light dominate, whereas Eve is filled with elements of darkness. The attitude toward women becomes especially clear when one recalls that the story of the Bible regarding the creation of woman is decorated with elements which have the purpose of introducing a tendency to belittle and discredit womankind [24]. This indicates why, in practice, their behavior developed into misogyny among at least part of the monks. In their contacts with women, Manichaean monks treated them a inferiors [25].

With womankind the whole sexual complex has fallen into disgrace. Certain Pahlavi texts allow us an insight into the feelings of these circles : 'and as the producer and maintainer of the bodily formations of all material existence is Ahriman, for the same reason it is not expedient to induce birth and to propagate lineage; because it is cooperating with Ahriman in the maintenance of mankind and cattle, and in causing the exhaustion of the life and

22 Augustinus, *Contra Faustum*, V, p. 273 ff. A Middle-Persian text describes this virtue more closely, *Mitteliranische Manichaica*, III, p. 254.

23 Le Coq, *Buddhistische Spätantike*, II, Tafel 8 b.

24 Cf. *Traité manichéen*, p. 523.

25 See also *Türkische Manichaica*, III, p. 22; *Traité manichéen*, p. 583.

light within their bodies'[26]. If, due to circumstances, reservations were made here for common believers, the monks were naturally those who could in no way become collaborators with Ahriman. It is not difficult to understand why many practised castration[27].

After virginity, poverty takes an important place. The Manichees saw great danger in riches : whoever is rich in this world shall be punished upon leaving the body by being sent into the body of a poor man, there to lead the life of a beggar[28]. The monks therefore developed the principle of poverty in a very radical way. They were not allowed to own anything and had to live in complete poverty. All that was desirable for any ordinary man in earthly life had to lose every significance for them. In their practical admonitions, the danger of possessions was placed on the same level as the danger of a wife[29].

But this poverty had to penetrate even deeper. All earthly ties between men which nature has set up between families and tribes were to be annihilated[30]. This ideal was conceived in its special meaning among the Manichaean monks as 'holy' poverty[31], with which they further associated thoughts of happiness and joy as celebrated in high melodies[32].

The same rigorism which demanded radical poverty becomes manifest in the fact that the monks had to surrender all duties and services, even those of an ecclesiastical nature. They also gave up continuously peaceful life and permanent domiciles and were compelled to live as vagrant ascetics. This brought a characteristic feature into Manichaean monasticism : they became untiring wanderers[33]. The ideal of the poor, wandering monk appears in late

26 *Pahlavi Texts*, III, p. 245 f.; see also *Greek and Latin Papyri*, p. 38 ff.

27 Joannes Chrysostomus, *Commentarius in ep. ad Galatas*, col. 668. Another reference appears in ar-Rāzī who reports that the Electi are ready to mutilate themselves in order to eradicate concupiscence, *Livre de la conduite*, p. 329 f.

28 Hegemonius, *Acta Archelai*, X, p. 16.

29 See the Estrangelo fragm. S. 9, in *Manichaica*, III.

30 Faustus says : « I have left my father and mother, my wife, my children, and everything the gospel orders to leave », Augustinus, *Contra Faustum*, V, 1, p. 272.

31 *Manichaean Psalm-Book*, p. 33, 157.

32 The same thought was carried over into the fifth commandment, pag. 114.

33 ... quia peregrini et alienigenae mundo, *Manuscrit manichéen*, p. 65.

documents as a primary monastic duty. The practice remained characteristic of Manichaean monks even in the days of al-Džāḥiẓ, who mentions travelling as their characteristic practice [34].

The travelling could be done only on foot, since, according to their views, to hire an animal was forbidden. The use of a horse, other riding animals, or a carriage meant that one was cherishing and cultivating the body [35]. When among the reproaches made on the occasion of the schism to Mihri by the Miklāṣia, it was said that he had been on the back of a mule [36], this must have been a most serious offense against ascetic standards.

The ascetic taste, of course, controlled one's nourishment, which played a great part in the fight against the body. While choosing one's food was not made a problem for the common believer, certain fixed principles were valid for the monks. It is known already from the sixth catechesis of Cyril of Jerusalem that Manichaean monks were allowed to use only select food [37]. Meat and all animal food was prohibited most severely. Only vegetarian food was permissible, since the priority of vegetable life was already rooted in the cosmogonic beliefs of the Manichees [38].

The monks' most natural food was bread, which was sometimes eaten with salt [39]. Mostly, this menu consisted of fruits. The Latin anathema formula enumerates a whole series of fruits [40]. Owing to some chance, the menu of the monks has been preserved on a miniature which shows, on the occasion of their *bema* festival, a three-legged platter placed before a platform on which one can

34 *Risāla*, p. 20. The rule never to pass two nights in the same place, AL-DŽAHIZ, *Kitāb al-ḥajavān*, IV, p. 147, seems to have been imposed by such scrupulous circles as those of Ruhbān al-Zanādiqa, and were not, therefore, a general regulation.

35 See the formulas in their prayer- and confession book, *Bet- und Beichtbuch*, p. 33.

36 EN-NADIM, *Kitāb al-Fihrist*, p. 99.

37 *Catecheses mystagogicae*, VI, col. 596.

38 CUMONT, *Recherches*, p. 39 f.

39 *Manichäische Homilien*, p. 57.

40 Creditur pars Dei polluta teneri in cucumeribus et melonibus, et rediculis, et porris, et quibusque vilissimis herbulis, *Commonitorium*, III, col. 1155.

clearly recognize melons, grapes, and before that a table covered with heaps of loaves of bread or bigger cakes [41].

Among drinks, wine and all other intoxicating drinks were naturally strictly prohibited. Wine was, in the eyes of the Manichees, like the choler of the prince of darkness [42]. Milk, too, was prohibited [43]. Besides unfermented fruit juices, only water was left for their use. Outsiders have gained the impression that water was their prevailing drink. In the Codex Theodosianus the monks are even given a name corresponding to such a limitation [44].

The monks were allowed to use even the permitted food to only a very limited extent and must have felt daily want. They could not have any stores of food, and it was their duty to use only minimally what they received. The information in later sources that the monks could not possess more than one day's supply of food [45] rests firmly on older traditions. They were only permitted to have food for one meal, just as the Buddhist monks.

Besides these restrictions, fasting occupied an important place in bodily mortification. Mani ordered fasting even for common believers, who were obliged to keep the minimal fasting time. This, according to the Chuastuanift, amounted to 50 days a year [46]. The monks naturally had to be masters in that, leaving common believers far behind [47]. Indeed, the Manichaean monks won general admiration and attention by the intensity of their fasting and achievements in this respect. Titus of Bostra, Cyril of Jerusalem, and Marūtā

41 Le Coq, *Buddhistische Spätantike*, II, Tafel 8 b.

42 Augustinus, *De moribus Manichaeorum*, col. 1362 ff.

43 Augustinus, *De haeresibus*, XLVI, col. 37; cf. *Traité manichéen*, II, p. 265 ff.

44 *Codex Theodos.*, XVI, 5, 7; cf. also *Traité manichéen*, II, p. 266.

45 وتحريم أُقتنا شى خلا قوت يوم واحد ولباس سنة 'and he forbade them (i.e. his ascetics) to obtain any possession except food for one day and garment for one year', al-Biruni, *Chronologie orient. Völker*, p. 208.

46 This rule, in the Chuastuanift, finds substantiation by the *Kephalaia*, XCI, p. 233 which states that the catechumens must have 50 fast days and adds that these are 50 Sundays. See also LXXXI, *ibid.*, p. 193.

47 *Kephalaia*, LXXIX, p. 191 f. has a chapter which deals with the question of fasting among the 'holy ones', i.e. the Electi. Here it is said that the Electi fast daily and exception is made for these who do not endure this degree

of Maipherqaṭ [48] speak of their ruthless and unrelenting fasting. Whether they went as far as the Buddhist monks, who are reported to have fasted so rigorously that it brought on their death, we do not know. Yet these monks did become remarkably conspicuous. Information concerning their figures, lean and bony from fasting, has been preserved in several sources. Ephrem, in his *mēmrā* against the heretics, says that the Manichees attracted attention because of their pale complexions [49]. In Augustinus mention is made that they are even as partakers of the promises of the gospel, the hungerers and thirsters, and already outwardly recognizable for their leanness and their pale complexions [50].

Naturally, the ascetic mentality also controlled the monks' dress. Reports have remained in several sources that the monks evidently had a prescription according to which they had to be content with what they actually wore. We do not know whether the regulation, found in the late sources, that they were allowed to change their dress only once a year [51] goes back to Mani himself.

The monks' garments had to correspond to the monastic mentality. Their material could by no means be smooth or comfortable, and appearance and work had to conform to the principle of modesty. Ornamented garments were condemned [52]. The usual Manichaean monastic dress was a long garment reaching to the ground : thus the monks are often called 'the long-garmented' [53]. Like the Manichaean clergy, they preferred white robes; thus in their hymnology

of mortification. Once, again, Mani states this in *Kephalaia*, LXXXI, p. 193, where he develops his idea that fasting of the Electi generates angels : 'I have heard from you, my Lord, as you said: seven angels are born out of the fasting of each single Elect', *Kephalaia*, p. 193. Further the Soghdian fragments found in Turfan, published by Henning, bring additional light in this question.

48 *Contra Manichaeos*, I, 34, p. 22; Cyrillus, *Catecheses mystagogicae*, VI, 31, col. 596; *Studia syriaca*, IV, p. 71.

49 *Contra haereses*, L, 6, p. 195.

50 ... exsanguis corporibus..., *De utilitate credendi*, col. 92; cf. *Vie géorgienne de S. Porphyre*, p. 198.

51 al-Biruni, *Chronologie*, p. 12; cf. Abū'l-Ma'ālī, *Il Bayān*, p. 607. This is confirmed by the Turfan fragments, *Handschriftenreste*, p. 33; *Traité manichéen*, I, p. 576.

52 en-Nadim, *Kitāb al-Fihrist*, p. 99.

53 *Chuastuanift*, p. 14; *Türkische Manichaica*, III, p. 22, 38.

they sometimes appear as 'those dressed in white', 'bright lambs', and 'doves with white plumage'. The monks may be seen also on the Manichaean miniatures. Among numerous figures they are easily distinguishable from the priests, who are decorated with wreaths and abundant ornaments. The monks are clad in white dress and bear caps of the same color on their heads [54].

As to the color of their dress, the Manichaean monks were not so absolutely firm as statements have suggested. Remarks in the Oriental sources indicate that they also wore black robes [55]. In such cases the need of accommodation evidently was stronger than tradition and custom, and certain situations made it necessary not to differ outwardly.

There are remains in the sources which make it seem possible that the monks at least partly adopted the custom of dressing themselves in robes sown up carelessly from rags and tatters. There are no evidences of this in the documents of the Manichees themselves, but the casual remarks made by ecclesiastical authors cannot lightly be cast aside. Such a hint appears in Mārī, who, obviously, has taken it from a narrative connected with the life of Mār Bābōi, who became catholicos in 457 [56]. In addition, there appears another nint in the codex of the Law of Theodosius. Here the term *saccophores* occurs, and it follows from this that the Manichaean monks

[54] Le Coq, *Buddhistische Spätantike*, II, Tafel 8 b.

[55] Mari, *De patriarchis*, p. 41; Michael Syrus, *Chronique*, II, p. 248.

[56] Bābōi, being himself a Mazda-believer met one day a man وعليه برة خلقة 'and on him a garment of rags', Mari, *op. cit.*, p. 41. He thought that this man was a Manichaean monk.

In addition to this, another episode is also of interest. What is told in the biography of Porphyrius, bishop of Gaza, written by Marcus the Deacon, seems to point in the same direction. While the Greek text is mute regarding the garment of the Manichaean ascetics introduced here, *Vita Porphyrii*, LXXXVIII, p. 68 f., its Georgian recension adds an interesting feature by saying that these ascetics were clothed with the garment of the მძოვართათა, *Vie géorgienne de Porphyre*, p. 198. This Georgian term is not very clear, but seems to refer to the *βοσκοί* 'shepherds', described by Sozomenus, *Hist. eccl.*, VI, 33, col. 1393. In this sense the Georgian term appears also in Ms. Jer. Patr. georg. 3, fol. 71 b; see also a note by Peeters in *Vie géorgienne de Porphyre*, p. 198. These 'shepherds' who rejected all civilization must have used the most primitive sort of covering.

were conspicuous for their miserable and ragged clothes [57]. It seems that their spirit of accommodation made itself manifest here, too.

Keeping the foregoing in mind, and particularly the views of the Manichaean monks with regard to the body, we naturally cannot expect any grace from them as to bodily care. Since the body is a worthless organ, it is superfluous to try to save it in case of illness. The monks were especially forbidden to use medicine. The tradition embedded in a text of confession certainly rests upon ancient practice. Here the monk enumerates, among forbidden deeds, that of having used medicine [58]. Only mortification was the body's due. Since no proper food was necessary for it, it was unnecessary to cover it carefully with clothes or even allow it a bed to rest in, or accord it some other cherishing care even in the event of sickness.

In the dust and glare of the Oriental sun, washing was a necessary measure for bolidy cleanliness and hygiene. Frequent washing was prescribed for the Buddhist monks to keep the body clean as well as the clothes. We suspect, for more than one reason, that the monks of Mani, along with other measures for bodily care, threw aside hygiene also. In the dogmatics of Mani, water belonged to the five sacred elements [59]. There were special prescriptions for respecting sacred elements. A fragment, M 49, contains a warning that the auditors must keep away from water and touch and defile it as little as possible [60]. If, then, it was necessary to lay down such warnings for common believers, of whom it was known in

57 *Codex Theodos.*, XVI, 5, 7.

58 *Bet- und Beichtbuch*, p. 33.

There is a special chapter about the significance of chastisement of the body of the holy ones. In the first place, it is said : **ⲡⲣⲱⲙⲉ ⲉⲧⲟⲩⲁⲃⲉ ϭⲁⲓⲟ ⲡⲉϥⲥⲱⲙⲁ ϩⲛ̄ ⲧⲛⲏⲥⲧⲓⲁ [ⲉϥⲗⲁ] ⲙⲁⲍⲉ ⲛ̄ⲧⲁⲣⲭⲟⲛⲧⲓⲕⲏ ⲧⲏⲣⲥ̄ ⲉⲧϣⲟⲟⲡ ⲛ̄ϩⲏⲧϥ̄** 'the holy man chastises his body through fasting, and overcomes (or restrains) the whole body of the archonts that is in him', *Kephalaia*, p. 191.

59 The Greek anathema formula speaks of water as an animated element, *Formula ant. receptionis manichaeorum*, p. 88.

60 *Mitteliranische Manichaica*, II, p. 307. In another text which comes from Turkestan, the influence of the demons upon men is seen not only in their moral decline, avidity, revenge, and mercilessness, but also in their rude behavior toward water, which they beat along with other holy elements, *ibid.*, I, p. 199.

advance that it was difficult for them to keep the rules so it seems quite a matter of fact that the monks were the very ones obliged to be much more careful and pedantic. This would have hindered the monks from washing. It is interesting to note that Mani, taking this radical stand, repudiated those views and practices regarding water with which he had grown up [61].

If running water did not come into consideration for washing, might they not have used rainwater? It certainly did not belong to the category of sacred elements, since in the cosmogony the origin of rainwater was explained not with the principle of light, but as a work of the demons [62]. But there have arisen other difficulties which did not allow standing water or rainwater to be used for washing, at least among the monks. The imaginations concerning the origin of rainwater were appalling enough to make one avoid the use of this product. Rainwater was the excretion of the demons who were fixed to the firmament. The mythologumenon tells how female demons appear before male demons, causing excitement and therefore rain [63]. To those who were pure and spiritualized, a product with this origin was hardly acceptable for any use. They must have held it for something which they painstakingly avoided.

61 This milieu is clearly shown by an interesting section in the Kephalaia which under mythological figures represents different religious movements, dangerous to the existence of the young religion. Besides the figures which point to Mazdaism, Hellenism and Mantics, there appears also a fourth figure : **ⲡⲡ̄ⲛ̄ⲁ ⲁⲛ ⲙ̄ⲡⲣⲣⲟ ⲛ̄ⲛ̄ⲁⲣⲭⲱⲛ ⲙ̄ⲡⲙⲁⲩ ⲡⲉ ⲡⲉⲓ ⲉⲧⲟ ⲛ̄ⲣ̄ⲣⲟ ⲙ̄ⲡⲟⲟⲩⲉ ϩⲛ̄ ⲛ̄ⲇⲟⲅⲙⲁ ⲛ̄ⲧⲉ ⲧⲡⲗⲁⲛⲏ ⲛⲉⲓ̈ ⲉⲧ [ϯⲱ]ⲙⲥ̄ ⲙ̄ⲡⲃⲁⲡϯⲥⲙⲁ ⲛ̄ⲙⲙⲟⲩⲉⲓ̈ⲉⲧⲉ ⲉⲣⲉ ⲧⲟⲩϩⲉⲗⲡⲓⲥ [ⲙ̄ⲛ̄] ⲡⲟⲩⲕⲁϩ[ⲧⲏϥ] ϩⲙ ⲡⲃⲁⲡϯⲥⲙⲁ ⲛ̄ⲙⲙⲟⲩⲉⲓ̈ⲉⲩⲉ** 'the spirit of the king of the archonts of water is that who today rules in the sects of superstition, who baptize by water-baptism, because their hope and trust (is placed) on water baptism', *Kephalaia*, p. 33. It is very surprising but significant to see that these baptist sects, retired and living quietly, have taken away Mani's peace. In another place this movement is called **ⲧⲟⲩⲙⲟⲩⲧⲉ ⲁⲣⲟⲩ ϫⲉ ⲛ̄ⲕⲁⲑⲁⲣⲓⲟⲥ** 'those being called *καθαροί*, *ibid.*, p. 44. Bar Bahlul renders this Greek term, *Lexicon syriacum*, p. 1941 by ܐܒܝܢܐ which is just the same term that appears in the tradition as the baptist sect in which Mani grew up, Theodoros bar Koni, *Liber scholiorum*, p. 311.

62 Titus of Bostra, *Contra Manichaeos*, p. 60.

63 The appearance of the female demons calls forth the *ejaculatio seminis*, *ibid.*, p. 28 ff. Cf. Ephrem, *Contra haereses*, L, 5, p. 194.

A book of confessions states that it is a sin for the monks to touch rain, snow, or dew [64].

On these premises, the terse reports and warnings against washing which are preserved in our sources become comprehensible. According to Augustinus, Mani condemned even bathrooms [65]. The *Acta Archelai* brings up a clearly motivated prohibition : washing must be avoided because it burdens the soul with faults [66]. Thus life in dirtiness and filthiness became inevitable [67]. According to the Christian sources urine could be used when washing became unavoidable [68].

In the question of the prohibition of washing, Mani evidently turned his eye from the Buddhist monks, who despised dirtiness and kept themselves clean, to those figures who, ever since primeval times, could be seen in India walking around wildly with long hair and dressed in filthy rags, having long fingernails, and covered with dirt and dust — features against which Buddha already had protested as being outward manners not benefitting the soul of man, but which again and again influenced others to imitate them.

The culmination of all these means of giving pain to the body as a demon realm is seen in the attitude toward dangers to life which are presented by human hands or by wild animals. These bring life to a premature end and free the soul from the bondage of the 'vile body'. Ephrem refers to this in an important passage among

64 *Bet- und Beichtbuch*, p. 35.

65 *De moribus Manichaeorum*, XVIII, col. 1374.

66 εἴ τις λούεσθαι, εἰς τὸ ὕδωρ τὴν ἑαυτοῦ ψυχὴν πήσσει, si quis laverit se in aqua, animam suam vulnerat, HEGEMONIUS, *Acta Archelai*, p. 16; cf. *Bet- und Beichtbuch*, p. 33.

67 Ephrem speaks of the filthiness of the Manichaean ascetics declaring this to be something which reflects their internal status ܕܚܠܘ ܡܢܗܘܢ ܐܚܝ ܘܠܐ ܬܘܒ ܬܛܥܘܢ ܒܗ̇ : ܒܗ̇ : ܒܗ̇ܝ ܐܝܬܝܗܘܢ ܕܠܒܪ : ܕܕܡܘܬܐ ܗ̇ܝ ܘܛܠܠܐ ܕܗ̇ܝ ܐܝܬܝܗܘܢ ܕܠܓܘ 'be afraid of them, my brethren, and do not err again by it (let not be deceived by it), i.e. by their outward filth which is a likeness and shadow of their inward filth', EPHREM, *Contra haereses*, L, 8, p. 195.

68 *ἀναθεματίζω τοὺς τοῖς οἰκείοις οὔροις ἑαυτοὺς μιαίνοντας καὶ μὴ ἀνεχομένους τὰς ῥυπαρίας αὐτῶν τῷ ὕδατι ἀποπλύνειν ἵνα μὴ μολυνθῇ φασὶ τὸ ὕδωρ*, *Formula antiqua receptionis*, p. 88; cf. *Traité manichéen*, tr. Chavannes et Pelliot, II, p. 349.

his polemical arguments : 'and if the followers of Mani do not flee before a robber, and do not take refuge in fortress or wall, let us ask : is it because their bodies cannot be injured? And if they are looking forward to this, that they could be killed and could escape from the body...' [69].

3. RELIGIOUS PRACTICES

Until now we have observed the ascetic side of the Manichaean monastic life. Now let us turn to the question of the occupation of the monks and nuns, and how these passed their time.

The monks devoted such a great part of their time to prayer that to a certain extent one may speak of the cult of prayer which replaced all other cultic acts. It was not allowed even for common believers to act here according to their own discretion, for prayer is mentioned in the first place as an effective measure for the liberation of the particles of light for their separation and resurrection. The Chuastuanift cites four fixed prayer times which the auditors had to keep every day [70]. To what could be demanded from common believers only to a very limited extent, the monks must certainly have submitted themselves in much greater measure. To the minimum just cited, three prayer times were added which fell during the night and were connected with vigils. We shall have occasions to recall this later.

It is important to observe that the length of the prayers is conspicuous. Stress was laid here upon long and lasting prayer. Titus of Bostra alludes to long prayers which occupied much of the monks' time [71]. The Soghdian texts especially allow us a glimpse of the importance with which prayer was regarded among the

69 *Prose Refutations*, I, p. 38.

70 *Laien-Beichtspiegel*, p. 159.

71 *Contra Manichaeos*, I, 34, p. 22.

En-Nadīm knows to tell us that Mani had imposed the commandment of 4 or 7 prayers. Doubtlessly, Mani himself had composed prayers for the use of his monks. Nothing, however, has survived of these texts. Incidentally, there existed one work with the title *περὶ εὐχῶν*, mentioned among the Manichaean writings by TIMOTHEUS CONSTANTINOP., *De receptione haeretic.*, col. 21, and AUGUSTINUS, *Contra Faustum*, XIV, p. 411.

monks. We observe the figure of monks, tired and weak in body, who struggle with themselves and their drowsiness to comply with the prayer times which were to be kept under all circumstances, either when stationary or when on the move. In one confessional text the monk, confessing his errors, mentions occasions on which, because of sleep or some accident or illness or pain, he somehow neglected his prayers and hymns, whether in the morning or in the evening, at night or in the daytime, on a journey or in town [72].

Among the Manichaean monks prayers came in connection with acts of repentance and prostration which were developed into a system of specified acts. Prostrations consisted of throwing oneself to the earth and were connected with doxologies which were pronounced while one lay prostrate. They differed in the course of the prostrations [73].

The monks devoted another part of their time to the recitation of hymns, which, in connection with praying, have been mentioned as the most important monastic occupation. Mani himself furnished his monks with certain appropriate materials. In the *Kephalaia* he counts, besides his chief works, the psalms and prayers which he has composed [74]. The abundance of fragments and texts of hymns and psalms, preserved in various Central Asian languages, shows what an extensive literature of this kind must have been in existence.

We know also that at least some of the hymns were sung aloud, for in the Manichaean psalms the 'virtuous assembly of the righteous', i.e. the monks, is characterized as sweet and pleasant singers [75]. Mani himself laid stress upon melodies. Among the items in his corpus of letters, one writing appears concerning the importance of religious music [76]. Besides the hymns and psalms, other works of Mani were also recited in a loud voice [77].

Enough space was allotted in the daily program of the monks for meditation. In later texts it is even said that the monks did not

72 *Bet- und Beichtbuch*, p. 39.

73 EN-NADIM, *Kitāb al-Fihrist*, p. 96 speaks of 12 acts.

74 SCHMIDT, *Mani-Fund*, p. 30.

75 *Manichaean Psalm-Book*, p. 99.

76 EN-NADIM, *op. cit.*, p. 105.

77 For later time this custom is clearly confirmed by the fragments in the Uigur language, *Handschriftenreste*, II, *Nachträge*, p. 109.

allow a single moment to pass in vain and used the rest of their time for meditation. After reciting hymns, the monks repeated them in their minds and were, in this fashion, obliged to fill the time between reciting and prayer. Meditation was as obligatory as prayer. That a pure *dindar* must remain in meditation is a maxim which appears frequently.

The contents of the meditations may be approximated by way of hints we find in the documents. Of course, the great cosmogonical drama occupied a great part in their thinking, also the episodes of their rich mythology, but particularly those full of the continuous struggle which went on in the universe for the liberation of the particles of light. Those who stood in the midst of this process were most naturally attracted by these mythologumena which helped to fire them with devotion. From here it is only a step to the thought of the evil enemy that he might secretly have seduced him and loaded him with faults and guilt despite his monastic garment.

Some observations make it evident that the *meditatio mortis* which appears as a characteristic motive in later sources [78] always had the same role. In these hours the thought of transitoriness was the impulse which brought meditation upon abstract things, psychologically closer, and gave it flesh and blood through introspection. The demand is deeply rooted in the ascetic tradition that the monks must keep death in mind, meditate upon the day of death, and think of the moment in which they would stand before the god of death. This trembling compelled them to ponder over that terrible and dangerous day, which perpetually had to be kept before their eyes.

There are solid affirmative points, however, as to the opinion that meditation was connected with sadness and weeping, which was the custom known in some religions. That Mani himself moved in this atmosphere and was acquainted with these customs may be seen from a quotation of his, inserted in Persian into a text in the Soghdian language, in which he orders prayer because of sins, and

[78] There is in M 4 a collection of 'death-hymns' as the opening lines of this text show. These obviously were for the use of the Elect, for they assume that the dead man is perfect in virtue and that he will ascend to heaven.

commands weeping and sadness[79]. This gives us a right to assume that the emphasis laid upon this practice, as preserved in later documents, rests on older traditions. In the Middle Iranian texts it is said that the monks must always tremble, weep, and be full of sorrow[80]. In the Coptic homilies there are exhortations to weep and be sad because of one's companions and those who will remain in the body[81]. Chinese translations have preserved some hymns which make the role of weeping manifest. On a hymn scroll we read : 'I am, O great Saint, a lamb of the light; I shed tears, suffered, wept, and wailed'[82]. Other such passages may be found in addition to this one. Surveying the hymnology of the Manichees, one sees how often sorrow appears and what a place tears occupied in monastic piety.

How closely monasticism must have been connected with weeping and sorrow may be seen by one passage which has survived in the Middle Iranian texts and which speaks of these phenomena as being among the essential activity of the monks. This passage states that all pure monks, who are compared to doves having white feathers, wail and lament and are full of sorrow[83]. Another fact is especially important. The monks (it is said) have grown so familiar with sorrow and tears that they have come to be known as those who are sad and weep, and are called accordingly. One fragment from a celebrated hymnbook has preserved a passage concerning monks in which they repeatedly appear as 'the sad'[84].

79 Henning renders this passage as follows : '... seiner eignen Seele soll er sich erbarmen, und soll weinen und trauern, beten und flehen, und den Sündenerlass erbitten', *Bet- und Beichtbuch*, p. 36.

80 Henning translates : 'Sei eingedenk... und Du sahst die Erlöser, die (?) zu Dir kamen, (von Dir) ersehnt. Sei eingedenk des Zitterns, des Weinens und der Trauer...', *Mitteliranische Manichaica*, III, p. 876.

81 [..]ⲣⲓⲙⲉ ϭⲉ ⲛ̄ⲧⲛ̄ⲣϩⲏⲃⲉ. ⲛ̄ⲧⲛ̄ϣⲱⲛⲉ ⲛϩⲏⲧ ϩⲁ [ⲛⲁ]ⲧⲛ̄ⲣⲉⲓ̈ⲧⲉ : ⲣⲓⲙⲉ ⲛⲉϥ ⲡⲉⲧⲁϭⲱ ϩⲙ̄ⲡⲥⲱⲙⲁ [ϣ]ⲁⲧϥⲛⲟ ⲁⲡⲓⲛⲁϭ ⲙ̄ⲡⲟⲗⲉⲙⲟⲥ : 'thus weep and let us mourn and let us pity our adherents; weep about him who will remain in the body until he sees this great war', *Manichäische Homilien*, p. 15.

82 *Stellung Jesu im Manichäismus*, p. 108, 65; cf. *Mitteliranische Manichaica*, II, p. 325, no. 4.

83 *Ibid.*, II, p. 325.

84 It is a pity that this fragment has suffered very much. Yet its substance

In the Persian-Parthian language the monks are similarly described, since *āmustān* denotes someone who is sad and mourning as well as a monk [85].

Speaking of the religious duties of the monks, one cannot neglect their services of worship. They assembled among themselves for corporate worship service. While the auditors held their services on Sundays, the monastic service of worship took place on Monday, a day of radiant joy [86]. In a confession book some references to the cultic acts of the monastic worship service have survived. According to this text, their service was simple and consisted of prayers, hymns, and a sermon. Finally the confession of sins came in which the monks mutually asked forgiveness and imparted it to each other [87].

The relation of monasticism to the literary culture should not be overlooked. What Basil emphasized in Greek monasticism had already been brought out by Mani and set up as a tradition obligatory for his monks — that of interest in, and devoted care of, books [88]. Books accompanied their religious exercises and satisfied their intellectual needs. The monks had to read incessantly and were not permitted to tire in their diligence.

But those in whose hands books were inseparable companions had to contribute themselves to the spread of books and literary culture. Here Mani's own directives and personal example became decisive for the future, combining literary interest permanently with the

seems to be clear regardless of its damaged condition. Müller translates the remains as follows : 'Kommet, Brüder... Es kam den Betrübten Belehrung... Es kam Kunde von der Götter göttlichstem... Vergib mir grosser Gott... Versammlung der Betrübten, einer dem andern... Brüder, betrübte, Lichter... Betrübte, herbei, wir wollen segnen...', *Mahrnāmag*, p. 26.

85 *Bet- und Beichtbuch*, p. 26.

'But there was a difference between the inner attitude of the Manichee ascetic and the orthodox Christian monk. The latter, whether hermit or coenobite, had retired from the world with a consciousness of sin and a sense of personal unworthiness... The Manichee Elect does not appear to have been a « mourner »', BURKITT, *Religion of the Manichees*, p. 46. In the light of the evidence of the original sources presented above, Burkitt's statement needs correction.

86 *Mahrnāmag*, p. 26.

87 *Bet- und Beichtbuch*, p. 40.

88 Cf. *Türkische Manichaica*, III, p. 22.

ascetic life. Ephrem says that according to the testimony of Mani's disciples, Mani painted scrolls in colors, and quotes his motivation : 'As he said : « I have written them in books and pictured them in colors; he who hears them in expression also would see them in an image, and he who is not able to learn them from... (one word is corrupted) might learn them from pictures »' [89]. What was known from the secondary sources — i.e., that with regard to the production of books Mani emphasized calligraphy and ornamentation, including miniatures — is confirmed by his own words in the *Kephalaia,* where he says that he has written his own works calligraphically and decorated them artistically, thus pursuing his belief that the inner value of a thing becomes more evident when stress is laid also upon its exterior features. At the same time Mani admonishes the bearers of his inheritance to copy the manuscripts correctly [90].

Of course this instruction of Mani concerned, in the first place, those who were called in the highest degree to watch over his spiritual inheritance. The obligation thereby was laid upon monasticism to take care of the creation and cultivation of a literary culture.

Thus the monks have been active in reproducing and multiplying manuscripts. In this activity, the master's example in calligraphy lived on in the monks; and the reports of Greek and Arabian authors concerning the remarkable elegance of Manichaean manuscripts, as well as those manuscripts and fragments which already have been discovered, confirm unanimously that these admonitions were not in vain. Although we want to know more about that side

89 ܐܝܟ ܕܐܡܪ ܕܟܬܒܬ ܐܢܝܢ ܒܦܢܩܝܬܐ ܘܨܪܬ ܐܢܝܢ ܒܣܡܡ̈ܢܐ ܗܘ ܕܫܡܥ ܠܗܝܢ ܒܡܠܬܐ. ܢܚܙܐ ܐܢܝܢ ܐܦ ܒܨܘܪܬܐ ܘܐܝܢܐ ܕܠܐ ܡܨܐ ܕܢܐܠܦ ܐܢܝܢ ܡܢ... ܢܐܠܦ ܐܢܝܢ ܡܢ ܨܘܪܬܐ *Prose Refutations,* I, p. 127.

90 SCHMIDT, *Mani-Fund,* p. 42. Augustinus cannot conceal his admiration for the amount of beautiful and elegant codices he found in use among the Manichees : haesitantibus vobis et quid respondeatis non invenientibus conspiciuntur tam multi et tam grandes et tam pretiosi codices vestri et multum dolentur labores antiquariorum et saccelli miserorum et panis deceptorum, *Contra Faustum,* XIII, 6, p. 384; incendite omnes illas membranas elegantesque tecturas decoris pellibus exquisitas, ut nec res superflua vos oneret..., *ibid.,* XIII, 18, p. 400.

of their activity, the sources are generally reticent. We therefore appreciate all the more a Soghdian text which shows that among the monks the eagerness and care in this area of spiritual culture achieved special significance. Here we find that the neglect of the art of writing was considered a grave error. The piety with which the monks submitted themselves to this task is shown by a confessional text in which a monk asks forgiveness for having neglected the art of writing, for hating or despising it, and for having damaged or injured a brush, a writing-board, or a piece of silk or paper [91]. In the case of such reverence for the art of writing and manuscript production, one can hardly err in assuming that outstanding merits in the development of literary culture must be ascribed to the writers and painters in monastic garb.

4. RELATIONSHIP BETWEEN THE MONKS AND THE AUDITORS

Finally, we must touch upon the religious significance of the Manichaean monks and upon their role in the Manichaean communities.

In one of his letters Mani himself called those who comply with the eternal prescriptions *sancta ecclesia* [92]. In other words, upon monasticism as an 'inner team' Mani built up the congregations of auditors. The very same thought is expressed in the Manichaean homilies — i.e., that the church will not waver so long as the Elect resist [93]. With Mani the concept of the church coincides with the number of those who have become perfect in the monastic ranks.

Mani has entrusted to the hands of the Elect the tasks of carrying out missionary work and confirming the believers in their faith. Only those perfect and spiritualized, those who have submitted themselves to the demands and implications of the Manichaean doctrines were competent to function as the spiritual elite. In this task the monks were perpetually stimulated by an order of Mani

[91] Henning translates : 'wenn ich der Schreibkunst abgeneigt, sie hassend oder verachtend, einen Pinsel, eine Schreibtafel (?), ein Stück Seide oder Papier in den Händen gehalten (und dabei) viel Schaden und Beschädigung angerichtet habe', *Bet- und Beichtbuch*, p. 33 f.

[92] EVODIUS, *De fide*, V, col. 1141.

[93] *Manichäische Homilien*, p. 28.

himself, stated in a chapter of the *Kephalaia,* admonishing the monks never to tire in this work [94]. This team, monks and nuns alike, must always have been in missionary service. Nuns, indeed, kept space with the monks.

Owing to the immense authority of the monks, it was one of the religious duties of the auditors to respect and honor them without reservation. All of the texts in the different languages demand that the auditors strive with all their hearts to gain the favor of the monks and to become as dear to them as if they were relatives. They are bound to the monks through two ties : love and fear. They must respect the monks as their masters and rulers and fear to transgress their ordinances. This means that Mani adopted the same view that is found in Buddhism — i.e., that the monk takes the central position in religious life and others are as his servants whose duty is to be useful to him and do good to him.

To be sure, there was actually a certain mutual giving and receiving between the monks and the believers. The texts put it bluntly that laymen and monks both support each other, each in his own way : the auditors give alms and the monks support the auditors with the heavenly treasures [95]. Through that ancillary service the auditors had an opportunity to cling to the substance of the congregation, i.e. the Elect, and enter into a certain communion with spiritual gifts.

One method of obtaining communion with the monks was through the institution of the confession of sins. Since the forgiveness of sins was delegated to the monks [96], the Manichees had to confess to the monks. The believers came to confession privately, knelt before the monks, and asked to be touched with their hands [97]. They relieved their hearts and received pardon for their sins. Besides this, a part of the worship service was reserved for the confession of sins. This was true even of the worship service held on their great *bema* festival, when Mani himself was expected to descend from Paradise and take his place among the believers [98]. A Soghdian

94 *Kephalaia,* LXXXI, p. 193 ff.

95 *Manuscrit manichéen,* p. 67.

96 *Contra haereses,* II, 2, p. 6.

97 AUGUSTINUS, *Epistulae,* CCXXXVI, col. 1033.

98 *Manichaean Psalm-Book,* p. 34.

text contains the *bema* liturgy, determined for the auditors. The order of all the single acts is not very clear; but, from as much as becomes apparent from the inserted Parthian hymns and doxologies to Mani and from the lessons, we know that the veneration of Mani, together with his monks, belonged to this order and was followed by the confession of sins [99]. We have no detailed information about the worship services held by the monks, but presumably after these services the same ritual took place, since Mani himself ordered the monks to assemble at any time and pardon sins [100]. Indeed, the fragment M 1 begins with the words: 'come together', addressed to the monks, the auditors appearing only as taking part silently [101] and assuming the role of those who relieved their consciences and received forgiveness.

The auditors also turned to the monks for the fulfilment of their prayers. From those whose allotted share was religious truth and who, through self-denial, had found the way into the world of knowledge and experience, the lay people sought assistance with their problems and difficulties as though it came from higher beings [102].

Among the Manichees the idea of mediation also played an important part. The souls of the monks rose unhindered into the realm of light and eternal glory together with the angels [103], but the soul of a common auditor had the misfortune of confronting all kinds of obstacles on its way. This was a source of fear and trembling among the lay people, who were always in need of an

99 *Bet- und Beichtbuch*, p. 46.

100 *Ibid.*, p. 40.

101 *Mahrnāmag*, p. 20 f.

102 Hegemonius, *Acta Archelai*, X, p. 16 f.

In this connection, it must be observed that the Manichaean monks were regarded as the incarnation of the godhead. What Augustinus, *Contra Faustum*, V, 10, p. 283 says regarding this has found confirmation by the original Manichaean texts. In the Coptic homilies, it is stated that, in the monks, the godhead is visibly among the believers, naked, hungry, suffering, homeless and vagrant, giving them opportunities to clothe him, to feed him and to assist him, *Manichäische Homilien*, p. 38. Also, in the Kephalaia, the Electi are spoken of as those on whom the godhead has descended and in whom he dwells, *Kephalaia*, LXXXVIII, p. 220.

103 *Manichaean Psalm-Book*, p. 81.

advocate before the Eternal Judge. We have a picture of a heart-rending moment in which the sinner falls down before the monk and implores him in his last plight [104]. Most certainly the monks themselves caused pangs in the hearts of their listeners by not being stingy in painting fantasies of very dim colors. The idea that the monks could function as advocates of the auditors who had helped and honored them [105] was advantageous to the nimbus of the monks in Manichaeism. This expectation must have inspired the auditors to look up to the monks as their helpers.

By seeking from the monks forgiveness, the fulfilment of their prayers, and their role as mediators, the community of lay people established close relation with those who had given up the world. These were the chief factors which made the communities of auditors dependent upon the monks. There is a characteristic passage in a hymn which relates that just as the eye is necessary for the foot in walking, and the hand for the mouth when eating, so the elect are indispensable for other people in attaining to spiritual purification and salvation [106].

Another side of this relationship involved the temporal existence of the monks. Mani, in establishing his monasticism, tried to isolate it completely from that which would be worldly, dangerous, and morally harmful, and to do this in such a way that the very physical existence of the monks was dependent upon the help of the auditors.

The monks were impelled to be careful by their fear of somehow hurting or injuring even the smallest living being. It was a crime to think evil of wild beasts, birds, reptiles, and the like. To err against any animal or bird was to sin against the soul residing in them [107]. Since this was the same sin as killing a man, it must have caused the monks much sorrow.

It was not different with the vegetation which was one of the five forms of existence [108]. Therefore, whoever was guilty of injuring a tree or breaking a fruit from it suffered a severe punishment [109]. To

104 EN-NADIM, *Fihrist*, p. 102.

105 *Manuscrit manichéen*, p. 71.

106 *Manichäische Hymnen*, p. 37.

107 TITUS OF BOSTRA, *Contra Manichaeos*, p. 63; *Bet- und Beichtbuch*, p. 32 f.

108 See BANG und GABAIN, *Uigurisches Fragment*, p. 251.

109 AUGUSTINUS, *De moribus Manichaeorum*, XVII, col. 1368 f.

tear a plant out of the ground was a crime tantamount to homicide [110]. It has remained incomprehensible to the ecclesiastical fathers as to how tilling the soil, which ought to be the most innocent of all professions, came to be regarded by the monks as a crime equal to murder [111].

The multitude of prescriptions imposed on the monks was not limited solely to living organisms. One must also consider the elements : air, earth, wind, pure light, water, and fire [112]. It was forbidden to dig in garden and field or even to touch the buds and blossoms of the trees and the roses on a spring morning, or to tread on the earth where something grew, lest a plant be trodden into the mud [113].

It is evident that such meticulous caution made every work and labor impossible. The Manichaean monks went even farther than the Buddhist monks, who held that physical work was unessential and even a hindrance in the development of a higher life, since it disturbed the monks in their compliance with their ascetic customs and meditations. For the Manichees work and labor became a crime. It was even forbidden for a monk to build himself a shelter, even the most primitive hut. Thus Ephrem scoffs at those monks, and calls them sick dogs, who refuse to do any kind of work [114].

Thus it became impossible for the monks to obtain any living for themselves. Not to speak of obtaining food, the monks were not allowed to prepare themselves a meal of the foodstuffs they had received, fearing that they might thereby harm the particles of light [115]. Besides this, the use of fire was prohibited. By frying and cooking one would only increase his trespasses.

Monasticism under these limitations had no other possibility — excluding death by starvation — than to employ those who, because

110 THEODORETUS, *Haeret. fab. compendium*, col. 380.

111 AUGUSTINUS, *De haeresibus*, XLVI, col. 35 f.

112 καὶ εἴ τις περιτατεῖ χομαί, βλάπτει τὴν γῆν · καὶ ὁ κινῶν τὴν χεῖρα βλάπτει τὸν ἀέρα, ἐπειδὴ ὁ ἀήρ ψυχή ἐστι τῶν ἀνθρώπων, HEGEMONIUS, *Acta Archelai*, X, p. 17; cf. *Handschriftenreste*, II, p. 98.

113 *Bet- und Beichtbuch*, p. 35.

114 *Contra haereses*, II, 2, p. 6; see also his *Prose Refutations*, I, p. 127.

115 'They are not even willing to break bread lest they would pain the light that is mixed in it', *ibid.*, p. 4.

they stood lower than the monks, could take upon themselves additional misdoing in order to help the monks. As the latter were helpless and unable to live by themselves, they needed attendants, especially in countries in which they appeared as missionaries and Manichees were small in numbers. In such cases the attendants who accompanied them were indispensable. It may indeed be noticed from the travels of the monks and nuns that they always appeared with companions who obviously took care of the ascetics as servants. Boys, too, were given to them as attendants, as may be deduced from a certainly wrong reproach which implied that the Manichees had practised pederasty [116].

It was especially the duty of the auditors to look after the feeding of the monks. This was a reward of the self-denial and pains which the monks had taken upon themselves. The duties of both parties were thus separated and regulated under the principle that the monks should devote themselves to their duties and the auditors to their alms [117].

In the point under discussion Mani was not fully satisfied with merely giving exhortations. The wish to be sure that this obligation should be carried through forced him to employ a very peculiar auxiliary device which is not at all in harmony with his consistent line of thinking. This lies in the idea which holds that the monk, by virtue of his organism, is thrust very physically into the process of the liberation of the particles of light. Through eating, the parts of light were not at all harmed by the monks, but — on the con-

116 AL-BIRUNI, *Chronologie orient. Völker*, p. 208.

With regard to the servants as companions, an interesting episode appears in the biography of Porphyrius. The Greek original reports here : *τῇ δὲ ἐπαύριον παραγίνεται ἡ γυνή, ἔχουσα μεθ' ἑαυτῆς ἄνδρας δύο καὶ τοσαύτας γυναῖκας· ἦσαν δὲ νεώτεροι καὶ εὐειδεῖς, ὠχροὶ δὲ πάντες*, MARCUS, *Vita Porphyrii*, LXXXVIII, p. 68 f. The Georgian recension, however, supplements this account with additional features: მაშინ მოვიდა დედაკაცი იგი. და მის თანა ორნი ჭაბუკ-ნი. და დედანი მრავალნი სასითა მძოვართათა : და ორნი მათგანნი ყვთელ იყუნეს ვითარცა ღმრთის მოშიშნი, 'then the woman arrived, accompanied by two young men and many maids, in the garment of the 'shepherds'; two of them were pale as the ascetics (lit. the fearers of God)', *Vie géorgienne de Porphyre*, p. 198.

117 *Manichäische Homilien*, p. 30.

trary — by being eaten they would be liberated from their imprisoning matter and collected into the pure bodies of the monks, where, being purified, they would concentrate into a body of light.

By such an auxiliary device, on the one hand, an inconsistent thought was introduced; while on the other hand the care of monks was assured in the Manichaean communities so long as religious instruction invented means of a punitive nature for those who were not sufficiently interested in this work.

From these premises Mani drew the right to employ strong terms with regard to the duty of almsgiving, in order to lay it down upon the shoulders of the auditors as a complicated burden. As to how complicated this must have been, we get a glimpse in the Chuastuanift, which in one place mentions as many as seven kinds of alms [118]. In fact, in all of the Manichaean literature which is concerned with the auditors, the discussion goes no further than their duties of almsgiving.

We also learn that the neglect of this duty was threatened with eternal punishment. In the *Acta Archelai* it is stated more circumstantially that the lot of those who have sinned in this matter will be the torments of Gehenna and incarnation into lower beings [119]. Other texts offer additional information on the same question. Those who do not prepare food and a hut for a hungry and thirsty monk who lacks shelter are condemned [120]. This duty was so great that even the last bit belonged to the monks. In a Turkish text it is said that the auditors must bring alms to monks even when they, in so doing, give away their last and are themselves forced to starve [121].

Owing to Mani's auxiliary device, eating by the monks became something more than the ordinary and was surrounded by religious secrecy. The author of the *Acta Archelai* describes such a scene in which a monk receives food and consumes it. Before he begins to eat bread, he says, after an appropriate prayer excusing himself before the bread, that it was not he who reaped it, ground it, and

118 *Laien-Beichtspiegel*, p. 161.

119 HEGEMONIUS, *Acta Archelai*, X, p. 16.

120 *Türkische Manichaica*, III, p. 29.

121 AUGUSTINUS, *De moribus Manichaeorum*, XVI, col. 1367; THEODOROS BAR KONI, *Liber scholiorum*, II, p. 313; cf. *Türkische Manichaica*, III, p. 11.

baked it in the oven, but that it was someone else who did these things and brought it here; he therefore may eat it in innocence [122]. This rite, which formerly was known only through the document just mentioned, becomes especially clear in the Soghdian texts, which have preserved additional features regarding the preparations of this act. Thus, in one passage, a monk describes very interestingly the way in which daily alms ought correctly to be used. Preparation for eating forms an indispensable part of this almost mystical action. At first the monk thinks with grateful heart of God and Buddha. It becomes evident from the text that he has certain mythological scenes of the primeval struggle before his eyes. Then he thinks of what it is that he eats. Although the text is deplorably obscure, it is clear enough that two thoughts were connected with this : the guilt caused by the preparation of the food, and the part which the monk had to perform in the process of liberating the particles of light which were hidden in the food [123].

122 καὶ ὅταν μέλλωσιν ἐσθίειν ἄρτον, προσεύχονται πρῶτον, οὕτω λέγοντες πρὸς τὸν ἄρτον, οὔτε σε ἐγὼ ἐθέρισα οὔτε ἤλεσα οὔτε ἔθλυψά σε οὔτε εἰς κλίβανον ἔβαλον· ἀλλὰ ἄλλος ἐποίησε ταῦτα καὶ ἔνεγκέ μοι· ἐγὼ ἀναιτίως ἔφαγον. καὶ ὅταν καθ' ἑαυτὸν εἴπη ταῦτα, λέγει τῷ κατηχουμένῳ, ηὐξάμην ὑπὲρ σου· καὶ οὕτως ἀφίσταται ἐκεῖνος, HEGEMONIUS, *Acta Archelai*, X, p. 16 f.

123 *Bet- und Beichtbuch*, p. 41.

CHAPTER V

IN SEARCH OF THE ORIGIN OF MONASTICISM IN MESOPOTAMIA

1. THE AUTOCHTHONOUS CHARACTER OF SYRIAN MONASTICISM

So far we have been concerned with the treatment of the history of asceticism in its primitive phase, that is to say, a pre-history of monasticism. It is now proposed that we carry the subject further by conducting an inquiry into the origin of monasticism in Mesopotamia.

Whence came this fruitful and important phenomenon in Syrian Christianity?

To pose this question is to raise one of the most intricate problems in the history of Syrian asceticism. Too often, church historians have taken it for granted that there is no problem at all, assuming that the origin of monasticism in Mesopotamia must be regarded as a part of the general movement which started in Egypt under the influence of Anthony and Pachomius. It has become a habit to speak of, and to look at, Egyptian monasticism as the hotbed of the monachal movement which furnished germs to be transplanted into other countries, including the Syriac-speaking territories [1]. But is that so? Is that not an oversimplification of an onerous problem? In order to attempt to wrestle with the answer, let us leave the current view where it stands and try to learn what can be learned of this problem from the earliest possible sources.

It must be said at the outset that this problem goes back to an era which offers little in the way of trustworthy sources. In the Syriac

1 'Syria was one of the first parts to which monasticism spread from Egypt, and the type of monastic life in vogue in Syria was in all respect that of Egypt', O'LEARY, *Syriac Church*, p. 60; see also VAN DER PLOEG, *Oud-syrisch monniksleven*, p. 14 f.; LASSUS, *Sanctuaires chrétiens*, p. 264; cf. KHAYYATH, *Syri orientales*, p. 183 f.

literature we possess some documents which pretend to know more than they really do, and to give sounder information than they can possibly give.

There is a history of Mār Aūgēn which is devoted to events contemporary with the origin of Syrian monasticism. According to this document it was the influence of Pachomius which caused monasticism to be transplanted to Mesopotamia. Mār Aūgēn himself is said to have been a pupil of Pachomius : the companions with whom he appeared in Mesopotamia were the ones he had gathered around himself in Egypt [2]. This document does not stand up against criticism. On closer acquaintance with the text one gets a very bad impression, because the author does not seem to have had any idea of what actually happened. These texts give the impression of being a conglomerate composition drawn up from many sources and relating to remote events, so that Mār Aūgēn himself is often overshadowed. A critical examination shows that the whole story cannot be earlier than the 11th century [3].

If it is granted that this is a fabrication of later origin, do some correct historical data still exist regarding this man with whom the introduction of monasticism has been connected? This, too, must be denied. It is a well-known fact that liturgies have preserved the memory of the most important persons through diptychs, and documents of that kind are not usually altered. In the liturgical traditions of the Syrians we find the names of many famous old monks other than the fathers of Egyptian monasticism, including several pioneers of whom we know nothing more. Yet a name of even remote resemblance to Mār Aūgēn's cannot be found [4]. It is out of the question that the name of one of the most meritorious founders of monasticism in Mesopotamia could have been omitted from all the other names in the tradition — the more so because the latter does not show traces in these matters of a deliberate attempt to forget everything connected with Egypt.

There is a series of documents in the Syriac language which attempt to narrate the events of the early fourth century. This

2 *Acta martyrum,* III, p. 383.

3 See pag. 217 ff.

4 *Ṭaksa dekahnē,* p. 279.

series, however, originated many centuries later, and its desire to reveal exact information and data betrays at once the fact that it is of no value. All documents of this kind which, like these, deal with legend more than with history may be put aside without reservation.

With regard to the origin of Syrian monasticism, Hieronymus is anxious to provide some remarkable information. He tells us about Hilarion, a pupil of Anthony [5], who settled in a desert south of Majuma. Hieronymus alleges this man to have become the founder of monasticism among the Syrians, of whom he remarks that until that time monks and monasteries had been unknown to them [6]. Indeed, in the Syrian tradition after Hieronymus, Hilarion maintained the reputation of being the founder of monasticism in Syrian Christianity.

Of course it must be stated that we have no reason to disbelieve Hieronymus, who, during his sojourn in the desert of Chalkis, received his information from Syrians scarcely one generation after the event. It is, however, evident that with this report Hieronymus has merely touched the periphery of the problem. As we shall see later, this information can better be utilized in dealing with the development of monasticism among the Syrians rather than with its origin. Hieronymus lived far from those Mesopotamian districts in which a dense and active Christian population could be found — and Mesopotamia, it must be said, had remained almost untouched by Hellenism and contacts with the West. Here, the question arises as to whether monasticism, in those parts where Christendom did have a Hellenistic character and an orthodox face, owed its origin to the great examples from Egypt; and whether in those areas in which the process of Christianization had taken a distinctly different road, there may not have been other factors operative in producing the monastic movement.

Thus, since the sources have preserved no direct information

[5] *Vita Hilarionis,* col. 30.

[6] Quod postquam auditum est, et longe lateque percrebuit, certatim ad eum de Syria et Aegypto confluebant : ita ut multi crederent in Christum, et se monachos profiterentur. Necdum enim tunc monasteria erant in Palaestina nec quisquam monachum ante sanctum Hilarionem in Syria noverat. Ille fundator et eruditor hujus conversationis et studii in hac provincia fuit, *ibid.,* col. 34 f.

about the origin of monasticism, this question cannot be traced from the surface.

We move on more secure ground for our investigation when we turn to the information preserved by Theodoret, whose valuable work on monasticism also furnishes a short historical survey. Since he was at home with the Syriac language, was highly interested in monasticism, and had close contact with Syrian monks, it is natural that he may have known the traditions of older times. Thanks to these circumstances, he is able to tell us some data which are of great significance. First, it is significant that he does not know of the Egyptian provenance of monasticism in Mesopotamia. Moreover, his information positively points in a quite different direction. The trend which underlies his information goes from the Orient toward the West, not from the West toward the East.

At the beginning of his work, as an introduction to other monks, Theodoret places the figures of two of the oldest monks. These naturally attract our attention. It is regrettable that he does not say anything about the source of his information. He never reveals where he obtained these data. Perhaps they may have been oral reports, but it is not absolutely impossible that he also used some written documents. However it came, his information seems to give some important hints with regard to the oldest period of Syrian monasticism.

One remarkable figure at the beginning of Theodoret's work is Jaʿqōb of Nisibis. Some details given here are irreplaceable. We shall examine them more thoroughly later. He describes Jaʿqōb as a monk who left the community and chose a life in the mountains — i.e., the highest peaks in the neighborhood of Nisibis. Far from the community and civilization, he lived as an anchorite, a living protest repudiating everything connected with civilization [7].

The figure of Jaʿqōb of Nisibis is not only most interesting and remarkable as to what is said about his ways of living, but also attracts our attention from a chronological standpoint. Because his was a household name among the Syrians, the historical place of this peculiar monk does not remain hopelessly obscure. He was included in the ancient martyrology preserved in a codex written

[7] *Hist. religiosa,* col. 1294.

in 411 A.D., although he was not a martyr himself [8]. His name figures in the subscriptions of the acts of the Synod at Nicea in 325 [9]. According to the Chronicle of Edessa he died in 338 A.D. [10] Another chronicle, that of Mešīḥāzekā, links Jaʿqōb with Šerīʿā, bishop of Arbēl. During Šerīʿā's episcopate Jaʿqōb is reported to have been a famous monk in the neighborhood of Nisibis, whom Šerīʿā often visited in order to receive a blessing from him [11]. The episcopate of Šerīʿā can be dated from 304-316 [12].

There is another source which is connected with the local traditions of Nisibis. In the diptychs of the church of Nisibis, Elīiā bar Šīnaiā found certain data about Jaʿqōb which he used in his chronicle — namely, that he became bishop of Nisibis in 308, succeeding Bishop Babū [13]. The last data, however, are not very trustworthy as long as there are no other sources to substantiate this information. In our case, indeed, a witness who is in close connection with events in Nisibis enables us to take a big step forward. Ephrem, in his poems, gives us very valuable hints that Jaʿqōb was actually the first bishop in the row of Jaʿqōb-Babū-Wālāgeš-Abrāhām [14] and not the second to succeed Babū as Elīiā reports. Thus the beginning of his episcopacy may go back to the first years of the century if we avoid surpassing the century limit, and even that cannot be impossible [15].

Now, by supposing that this approximate date is useful and that around 300 Jaʿqōb rose to the bishopric of Nisibis, we might conclude that he must have had behind him a period of monastic life during which he gained fame as a monk before becoming the 'head of Mesopotamia'. To fix the time when he began his monastic life far from the population centers and communities, we may safely go back to the penultimate decade of the third century. There

8 *Martyrologes et ménologes*, p. 19.

9 *Patrum Nicaenorum nomina*, p. 20 f., 64, 84, 102, 150.

10 *Chronicon Edessenum*, p. 4.

11 *Sources syriaques*, p. 46.

12 SACHAU, *Chronik von Arbela*, p. 15.

13 *Opus chronologicum*, p. 98.

14 *Carmina Nisibena*, XVII, 106-108, p. 30; cf. p. 20 f.

15 In the poem XIII, 15, *ibid.*, p. 21 Ephrem gives a clue in saying that peace with the Persians, made by Diocletian in 297, took place under Jaʿqōb. If this contains a kernel of truth, then his episcopacy reaches back to 297 A.D.

is also nothing in these sources to suggest that he was regarded as the first monk. On the contrary it is assumed that there were monks before Ja'qōb.

Here it might be mentioned that Peeters has subjected the stories concerning Ja'qōb to a critical examination and denies, as a result, that the episodes told in his story have any historical value. He shows that Theodoret has fused stories and persons, or that these had even reached him in such a condition [16]. Peeters' arguments concerning the components of the compilation are cogent but do not necessarily controvert the essential point. It is still quite possible that our documents, in spite of their vague character and worthless legends, have preserved one authentic element — the monachal background of Ja'qōb. This may be accepted as historical without violating any canon of critical investigation. It is difficult to see how this essential point can be confuted by criticism, since it is confirmed by the poems of Ephrem, which tell us of the character of the first three bishops in Nisibis. Indeed, among his colleagues Ja'qōb is noted for his ascetic reputation. In his hymns, obviously written in 358, Ephrem refers reverently and repeatedly to certain ascetic labors [17]. Some historical elements may also be in the tradition preserved by Faustus of Byzantium, which is earlier than that of Theodoret. Here also Ja'qōb is described as dwelling in the mountains and the desert area [18].

Thus, if all this is not misleading, we may conclude that the few trustworthy reports about Ja'qōb of Nisibis seem to cast some rays of light on the beginnings of Syrian monasticism. About 280 A.D., if not somewhat earlier, anchoritism which was related to the ecclesiastically organized Christianity, was to be found in the mountains around Nisibis.

This finding is seconded by similar observations, although not of the same quality. It is possible to make some additional obser-

16 'Il n'est pas besoin d'un long examen pour se convaincre que ce récit est brossé d'imagination ou d'après des sources légendaires, en dehors de toutes les attestations positives qui viennent d'être rappelées. Aux rares endroits où il se rapproche de l'histoire, c'est pour la noyer sous des développements fantastiques', *La légende de S. Jacques*, p. 291.

17 *Carmina Nisibena*, p. 22, 24.

18 *Patmowt'iwn Hayoç*, p. 20 ff.

vations regarding some of the early monks in Mesopotamia. The figure of the next monk after Ja'qōb belongs to a somewhat later era. This one-time celebrity, Jūlianā Sabā, is also one of the most prominent figures mentioned by Theodoret [19]. The Syrian sources furnish us with some data not given by Theodoret. This monk was well-known to Ephrem, who composed hymns to his memory. It is a pity that he did not think it necessary to include biographical material in more than one of these poems. In that one poem, however, he says that his monastic life lasted for about 50 years [20]. Since the Chronicle of Edessa places his death in 678 A.G. = 367 A.D. [21], Jūlianā Sabā must have become a monk about the second decade of the fourth century. But again, even in Ephrem, who was well informed about monastic matters, we find no mention of Jūlianā Sabā's having been one of the first monks. Ephrem depicts his life and manners in the knowledge that he adopted the monastic way of life from earlier predecessors. This observation is certainly very important.

One may make some further observations about other earliest monks [22] which would yield about the same results — namely, that the beginnings of Syrian monasticism seem to reach back at least to the end of the third century. Although it would be a very bold undertaking to accept every single item in these sources as proof in the strict sense of the word, since there is no possibility of checking these approximate data, there is still a question as to whether all these hints *en bloc* can be easily waived with the assertion that there is no historically correct crumb of any kind of reminiscences. That would seem to be an apodictic verdict. We need not believe everything these authors assert, but it may well be that some hints are not far from the truth. In any event we meet several authors interested in the history of monasticism who, on the basis of their information, felt that the beginnings of Syrian monasticism should be dated to the period before the end of the

19 *Hist. religiosa*, col. 1305 ff.

20 *Hymni et sermones*, III, col. 873.

21 *Chronicon Edessenum*, p. 5.

22 Compare what Theodoret writes about Acepsimas whom he places at the end of the reign of Valens, *Hist. eccl.*, IV, 28, p. 268 f. The same can be observed about Halas, SOZOMENUS, *Hist. eccl.*, VI, 34, col. 1396.

third century. We may assume that they knew what they were talking about. Without being able to put the finger on any particular date which deserves preference, the impression remains from a number of figures of the early monks (among whom none pretends to belong to the pioneers) that our conclusion has received some corroboration. If strong probability, opposed by no known facts, is to guide us, it must be concluded that monasticism existed in Mesopotamia during the first decades of the fourth century. This epoch, however, must have been preceded by an earlier era in which monasticism undoubtedly originated.

As to the spread of monasticism about 300 A.D. something, although very little, can be said. The fact shines through all the early sources that the earliest monasticism in Mesopotamia shows no connection with Egypt. Rather, the sources open up to a new perspective. At that time monasticism must have existed not only in the Roman area of Mesopotamia, but also in the Persian territory; for just as Christianity in these two countries was in a state of mutual giving and receiving, so it must also have been with monasticism. As far as the eye can see, we find monasticism in Mesopotamia linked with monasticism beyond the frontiers [23].

That is all that can be said about the earliest period in the light of the sources mentioned above. These observations from this elusive period do not permit us to connect the origin of monasticism in Mesopotamia with Egyptian influences. The sources available to Theodoret, which knew nothing of these influences, deserve our trust if we cannot put faith in other similar documents.

Anthony is known to have appeared in Egypt about 280-290 A.D. and to have achieved fame later on as the 'star of the desert' and the 'father of monks'. Of course the Syrians themselves subsequently believed their monasticism to have come from Egypt; however, the oldest reports indicate that Egyptian influences upon the beginnings of monasticism in Mesopotamia cannot be reckoned with seriously. On the one hand the phenomenon of monasticism seems to appear too early in Mesopotamia and Persia; on the other hand the spread of monasticism from Egypt took place in comparatively slow fashion. The latter observation is suggested by the information

23 THEODORETUS, *Hist. religiosa*, col. 1296; *Sources syriaques*, p. 46.

preserved in Hieronymus, who, speaking of Hilarion, states that until then monks and monasteries had been unknown to the Syrians [24]. That means that when this pupil of Anthony settled in Majuma in 306 A.D., monasticism from Egypt had not even reached Western Syria.

Therefore, upon the supposition that some data concerning Jaʿqōb of Nisibis and some other monks may at least be considered as partially trustworthy, we have hints to justify the inference that monasticism originated independently among the Syrians in Mesopotamia and Persia and can thus be looked upon as an autochthonous phenomenon.

Finally some other original Syriac sources which point in the same direction should not be overlooked. They cannot, to be sure, boast of their great historical value, but they are sources older than all the sources which have adopted the later view of Egyptian origin of the Syrian monasticism. These texts regard the rise of monasticism as an inner Syriac development, whether they derive the monastic movement from the days of Mār Mārī [25] or from time immemorial [26].

Our documents do not allow us to look further backward and thus approach nearer to the time of the actual origin of monasticism, for even this period is enshreuded in a semi-darkness which dims any clear perspective that we might have. Earlier developments are shut off by a curtain which seems impenetrable. We know only that it conceals some very important factors and events connected with the origin of Syrian monasticism.

2. CONSIDERATIONS REGARDING SOME INTRINSIC FACTORS IN THE ORIGIN OF SYRIAN MONASTICISM

Is there no way of peering through that curtain? We must try to find one, for it is highly desirable to supplement what sporadic hints we have received.

24 See pag. 140.

25 The scanty historical data incorporated into the legendary deeds of Mārī bring the founding of monasticism into relation with Mār Mārī, and do not know anything of the Egyptian influences, *Acta S. Maris apostoli,* p. 50.

26 Or monasticism in Mesopotamia was regarded as from time immemorial, Ms. Borg. syr. 82, fol. 13 a. Another survey of Syrian monasticism, found in Ms. Vat. syr. 159, fol. 162 a, testifies to the same. See also traditions embedded in Ms. Berl. Sach. 241, fol. 2 a ff.

First come some general considerations which may help clarify the direction in which we must proceed.

Against the contention that monasticism in Mesopotamia originated independently, nothing of significance can be asserted *a priori*. On the contrary, this seems extremely probable. In quest of the conditions and circumstances which may have evoked monasticism, the simplest assumption is that it could well have arisen in circles inspired by a devout perusal of the Scriptures, these being taken literally. Possibly the New Testament passages which speak of those who are no longer 'of this world' may have played a part. In early Christendom — and here we find an analogy to other cases which display a similar stiffening process — a downward curve may be detected, showing how its ethos waned and how something which was primarily conceived of as an inner spiritual freedom and independence from worldly things later came to be interpreted as the visible renunciation of the world, one's home, and society.

Several figures in the Old and New Testament could furnish tangible models for life in the desert, or the homeless life which afforded no place to lay one's head. The idea which later prevailed among the Syrian monks that biblical models had been their prototypes may not entirely have arisen from thin air. In Ephrem such prototypes are more frequently John the Baptist and, from the Old Testament, Elijah or Elisha [27]. Perhaps these models evoked anchoritism in Mesopotamia as spontaneously as, according to the existing reports, Anthony conceived this idea in Egypt under the inspiration of Matthew xix. The apocryphal literature includes other elements which may have exerted [28] an influence in that direction [29]. That Hebr. xi, 37 f., 'they were... wandering over deserts and mountains, and in dens and caves of the earth — of whom the world was not worthy', had caught the attention of ascetics for this we have a direct reference [30]. There is no proof

27 *Opera selecta*, p. 113; *Monumenta syriaca*, I, p. 4; *Hymni et sermones*, IV, col. 150; Ms. Šarf. Patr. 302, fol. 222 b.

28 See how the manners of Thecla were imitated by a monk Jōḥannan, *Vitae virorum celeb.*, p. 43 f.

29 In Ms. Vat. syr. 520, fol. 120 b Ephrem speaks of the imitation of the Apostles.

30 Ms. Vat. Borg. syr. 82, fol. 24.

of a similar origin — we know too little of conditions for that — but what Eusebius relates about Narcissus of Jerusalem at the beginning of the third century [31] is something that might also have happened in Mesopotamia. This becomes particularly probable if one recalls the 'Weltgefühl' which animated the ancient communities in the Syrian Orient.

Furthermore, outward conditions may have increased the number of similar cases and even made this kind of life necessary under the circumstances. This would especially be the case in Persia as a result of the enmity of the followers of Mazdaism, who made the life of any ascetics in a congregation full of trouble. Under these conditions the idea of leaving the community to lead an undisturbed ascetic life in solitude may have presented itself naturally [32]. Persecution, too, may have had a certain influence. During the persecutions Bishop Blasius of Sebaste left his residence and lived in the grottos of the mountains [33]. One also might refer to Hippolytus, who writes of a Syrian bishop who, during the persecutions, exhorted his congregation to take refuge in the desert in the name of Christ [34]. The congregation gathered around this bishop, being (as was frequently the case) a group which could be assembled conveniently in one room, could easily have formed a colony of ascetics in the desert. This took place in the Roman territory. When persecutions later broke out in the Persian area, most of the Christians fled to the mountains [35], while others sought shelter in the desert and other far off places [36]. It is cogent to assume that when they returned, some could have preferred to remain and pursue a quiet, solitary life.

Still another factor comes into consideration, i.e., the belief that there is to be found behind all tempting thoughts and desires not

31 *αὐτός γε μὴν τὴν τῶν εἰρημένων μεδαμῶς ὑπομένων μοχθηρίαν καὶ ἄλλως ἐκ μακροῦ τὸν φιλόσοφον ἀσπαζόμενος βίον, διαδρὰς πᾶν τὸ τῆς ἐκκλησίας, πλήθος, ἐν ἐρημίαις καί ἀφανέσιν ἀγροῖς λανθάνων πλείστοις ἔτεσιν διέτριβεν*, *Hist. eccl.*, VI, 9, p. 538.

32 See *Acta martyrum*, IV, p. 172.

33 *Synaxaire arménien*, XXI, p. 21 f.

34 *Kommentar zum Daniel*, p. 230 ff.

35 *Sources syriaques*, p. 59 f.

36 *Synaxaire arménien*, p. 472.

only the human heart, but the Devil himself with all his army of evil spirits. Those who lived perpetually in the world of the New Testament and received their incentive from it [37] could resolve to go forth and fight the demons. In fact, the earliest monks lived and acted according to such ideas. According to the ancient Semitic belief which had wide popularity in the Orient and is still deeply rooted, all wild and uninhabited places, ruins, cliffs, ravines, and bare rocks [38] are the dwelling places of demons. The same ideas were prevalent in the environment of Parseeism : whereas useful plants, cultivated land, and inhabited areas deter the demons, barren soil and uninhabited areas conversely encourage the demons to take up their residence [39]. From this aspect it becomes understandable that the 'athletes of Christ' felt the incentive to appear in those places in which ordinary mortals were afraid to appear and settle down. Thus, they started to combat the demons in their own quarters. It is interesting that a brief survey of monastic history takes this view. Here it is explained why the monks were called *nāphqē*, i.e. anchorites : 'they were called *nāphqē*, first, because they went out of the world during their life; and secondly, because they went out in order to make war with the Enemy' [40]. Ephrem repeats an ancient tradition regarding the character of an anchorite : 'on his departure from the world the power of the spirit accompanies him and anoints him as an athlete for combat with the Mighty one' [41]. Thus equipped, anchorites went forth unto the war with the 'demons, the sons of the desert' [42], and 'spirits and demons on

37 Cf. *Luke* x, 19 f.

38 ܚܘܪܒܐ ܕܥܠ ܛܘܪ̈ܐ 'wilderness on the mountains', Ms. Br. Mus. Add. 12, 160, fol. 136 a.

39 *Videvdat*, III, 4-10, p. 326 f.

40 ܐܬܩܪܝ ܢܦܩ̈ܐ. ܚܕܐ ܐܝܟ ܕܢܦܩܘ ܡܢ ܥܠܡܐ ܒܚܝ̈ܝܗܘܢ. ܘܐܚܪܬܐ ܬܘܒ ܐܝܟ ܕܢܦܩܘ ܠܡܥܒܕ ܩܪܒܐ ܥܡ ܗܘ ܕܒܥܠܕܒܒܐ., Ms. Vat. syr. 501, fol. 23 b.

41 ܥܡ ܡܦܩܗ ܕܡܢ ܓܘ ܥܠܡܐ ܚܝܠܐ ܕܪܘܚܐ ܢܦܩ ܠܗ ܘܡܫܚ ܠܗ ܐܝܟ ܐܬܠܝܛܐ ܠܐܓܘܢܐ ܕܥܡ ܚܣܝܢܐ *Sermones duo*, p. 4, col. 1. Narsai says the same thing, Ms. Ming. syr. 55, fol. 98 a.

42 ܫܐܕ̈ܐ ܒܢ̈ܝ ܚܘܪܒܐ *Opera selecta*, p. 10.

the mountains' [43] in the latter's own residence, using prayer and any other necessary instruments [44]. This subject is of such vital importance that Ephrem has devoted lengthy treatments to it [45]. There is no doubt that this was the principal task in the oldest monasticism [46]. With massive beliefs of this kind [47] and premises regarding the spirit of 'warriors of God' discussed in preceding chapters, it would not be stange if such incentives played a part in the genesis of monasticism among the Syrians.

3. EXOTIC PHYSIOGNOMY OF THE PRIMITIVE SYRIAN MONASTICISM

We have been able to say little thus far about the origin of monasticism, but we still have said enough to indicate that we must search further. Although it is possible that these factors actually were operative — i.e., that Christians left their communities under the influence of the impulses they received from biblical examples, and with the intention of fighting the demons in their lairs — it must nevertheless be admitted that all this is an inadequate explanation of the origin of monasticism's earliest phase in Mesopotamia. We are faced with new and inexplicable obstacles of a serious nature.

43 Ms. Cambr. Add. 1982, fol. 228 a.

44 The gong, *naqōšā*, was an old attribute, and here the monks displayed a practice similar to those of various other nations among whom the drumming played great role. One Syriac document on the *naqōšā* says : 'this is the sound which the Satan fears and by which his enemy calls the anchorets to fight. This is the voice which summons the armies like a trumpet, so that everybody may rise against the Evil and conquer his army... the hidden demons are thereby driven away from their councils', Ms. Berl. Sach. 352, fol. 113 b, 114 a.

45 Ms. Vat. syr. 202, fol. 229 b ff.

46 See an extract from a discourse of Ephrem about the warfare with the Satan, Ms. Br. Mus. Add. 14,614, fol. 75 b ff. Archaic features seem to have been preserved in narratives like that of Mar Pīnhas, *Acta martyrum*, IV, p. 210; or that of Mār Abḥai, *ibid.*, VI, p. 609; and in the story of Mār Mārī, *Acta Maris Assyriae*, p. 81; *Légende d'Aaron*, p. 712, 722 f.; Ms. Ambr. A 296 inf., fol. 87 a ff.

47 For instance, Ms. Par. syr. 235, fol. 168 a describes how an ascetic assails a mountain occupied by the demons who regard it as their dwelling place. Thus the community of monks is called 'the conqueror of the demons', Ms. Par. syr. 160, fol. 397 a; see also Ms. Ox. Bodl. Or. 412, fol. 59 b.

By these deliberations we could possibly make more tenable the idea of an independent origin of monasticism, but we could hardly make this explanation tally with the manifestations of the peculiar aspects of Syrian monasticism in Mesopotamia and its environs.

The horizon recedes somewhat when we try to approach our problem from another direction. Something very important will appear before our eyes when we gather together all of the oldest sources concerning the physiognomy of primitive monasticism and submit them to investigation.

The Greek fathers already had regarded the earliest form of Syrian monasticism as something very peculiar. To mention only one example : Gregory Nazianzus speaks with astonishment of the Syrian monks who fasted for 20 days together, wore iron fetters, slept upon the bare ground, and stood immovable in prayer in the rain, wind, and snow [48].

Gregory is not alone in this respect. Theodoret also cites Jaʿqōb of Nisibis, drawing his figure in lines which present very plastically the whole appearance of primitive monasticism. This monk cast off all vestiges of civilization. He chose as his dwelling place the solitude of the highest mountain tops and the thickets in the woods. In summer heaven was his roof, in winter he abode in a cavern which offered him poor shelter. He abstained from the use of clothing, fire, and a dwelling. He also rejected labor and ate no food earned by work, but sustained himself upon what nature offered him from the natural products of herbs and fruits [49]. Even if we grant to Peeters that the description of these ascetic manners is derived from other sources which have been compiled arbitrarily into the life story of Jaʿqōb, who thereby has become adorned with foreign feathers, not all the value of this picture withers away.

For precaution's sake we must not be satisfied merely with the data recorded by Gregory and Theodoret. These peculiarly radiant fragments from primitive monasticism can be fitted into a fairly

48 *Poemata historica*, col. 1455.

49 ἐν ἔαρι μὲν, καὶ θέρει, καὶ μετοπώρῳ ταῖς λόχμαις χρώμενος, καὶ ὄροφον ἔχων τὸν οὐρανόν... τροφὴν δὲ εἶχεν, οὐ τὴν μετὰ πόνου σπειρομένην καὶ φυομένην, ἀλλὰ τὴν αὐτομάτως βλαστάνουσιν... τὴν τοῦ πυρὸς παραιτούμενος χρείαν, *Hist. religiosa*, col. 1293 f. A similar account in Armenian, *Varkʿ ew vkayabanowtʿiwnkʿ*, II, p. 84 f.

amplified picture if evidence from ancient Syriac, as well as from ancient Armenian literature is taken into account. We are fortunate in possessing documents which lift the curtain enough so that the investigation can catch a better glimpse of the countenance of primitive monasticism.

Especially precious data about the character of the archaic Mesopotamian monasticism are to be found in Ephrem of Edessa, in documents which, indeed, are irreplaceable.

A letter of Ephrem, the authenticity of which is beyond doubt [50] with the exception of the last half of its text [51], introduces us to a particular type of monasticism. These monks abandoned their communities and civilization and lived a life which reduced them to the state of wild animals. They lived with animals, ate grass with them, and perched on the rocks like birds. A further remarkable characteristic of these primitive monks is that their only activity was prayer [52]. But what particularly arouses our amazement is their thirst after mortification and self-annihilation. Not only did they persist in severe fasting and extreme self-deprivation, they actually went so far as to despise life itself. Ephrem refers to their attitude by saying that they did not take any precautions against savage animals and snakes [53].

This highly interesting description in Ephrem's letter finds a desirable supplement in his other writings. In a treatise which passes critical examination [54], some of the same features occur. The earliest monks are introduced as figures hidden in squalor, with wild visages and long hair — men, indeed, who remind one rather of eagles than of men, and whose bodies are dreadfully disfigured by hunger : 'your long hair (looking) like (that of) an eagle, furnishes you with wings (of flight) on high; your filthiness, which was your clothing, weaves for you a garment of light; the sultry heat which ate you during the day, satiates you with a chamber of light; the cold by which you were punished, revives you like (with) new wine; hunger that ate from your flesh, leads

50 BURKITT, *Ephraim's Quotations*, p. 24.

51 VÖÖBUS, *Letter of Ephrem*, p. 6 ff.

52 *Opera selecta*, p. 120.

53 *Ibid.*

54 VÖÖBUS, *Beiträge zur krit. Sichtung*, p. 51 ff.

you to the bliss of Eden; thirst (so strong) that your veins were dried up, flows to you as the source of life' [55].

In another authentic [56] *mēmrā* Ephrem introduces the monks whom their ruthless acts of chastisement and mortification have made them wrecks [57]. These wild monks, and their way of life in the wilderness, are described by the author as living close to the world of the animal kingdom. In this tract Ephrem invites his readers 'to become companions to the mountaineers and neighbors to the anchorites' and adds : 'behold they mingle themselves with animals and take pleasure with birds; they mix themselves always with stags and are leaping with fawns' [58].

Particularly, there come to our aid two ascetic treatises which stand the test of critical scrutiny [59]. It is pleasing to gain, in this manner, a clearer picture of archaic monasticism as seen in supplementary features which these two metrical texts describe.

In the first treatise the ascetics are described as monks who have given up work and urban life. They roam in deserts like animals, wandering from place to place and eating grass and roots. They pass the night in narrow caves, climb and live like birds on rocks, and dig holes for themselves on mountain peaks [60]. Their appearance is wild, repulsive, and matted with filth and dirt. 'They bear the burden of their hair and the sufferings (caused by) their garments; there are those who dress in rags, and there are those

55 ܣܒܪܟ ܕܒܪܐ ܐܝܟ ܕܢܒܐ ܐܟܪ̈ܐ ܠܢܘܒܗܐ ܬܗܘܐ ܠܟ ܀ ܠܐܬܝܟ ܕܗܘܬ ܬܠܒܫܬܟ ܐܣܛܠܐ ܕܗܘܪܐ ܘܬܗܘܐ ܠܟ ܀ ܥܘܒܐ ܕܐܟܠܟ ܒܐܒܕܡܐ ܠܒܘܣܡܐ ܕܗܘܪܐ ܡܐܪܘܐ ܠܟ ܀ ܟܦܢܐ ܕܟܦܢܟ ܐܬܗܦܟ ܣܒܪܗ ܚܕܬܐ ܡܪܘܬ ܠܟ ܀ ܨܗܝܐ ܕܐܟܠ ܗܘ ܒܣܪܟ ܠܓܘܫܡܐ ܕܚܝܢ ܐܝܟ ܠܟ ܀ ܗܘܐ ܕܐܬܥܘܕܪܬ ܥܫܝܢ ܡܒܘܥ ܚܝ̈ܐ ܕܡܪܘܐ ܠܟ ܀ *Hymni et sermones*, IV, col. 153.

56 VÖÖBUS, *Literary Critical Studies*, p. 47.

57 Ms. Šarf. Patr. 302, fol. 221 a.

58 ܢܗܘܐ ܚܒܪܐ ܠܛܘܪ̈ܝܐ. ܫܒ̈ܒܐ ܠܡܕܒܪ̈ܝܐ. ܕܗܐ ܡܬܚܠܛܝܢ ܥܡ ܚܝ̈ܘܬܐ ܘܡܬܦܪܓܝܢ ܥܡ ܦܪܚܬܐ ܀ ܡܬܚܠܛܝܢ ܟܠܥܕܢ ܥܡ ܐܝ̈ܠܐ ܘܡܫܘܪܝܢ ܥܡ ܒܢ̈ܝ ܐܝܠܐ *Ibid.*, fol. 222 b. Ms. Šarf. 19/1, fol. 81 a reads : ܡܬܚܠܛܝܢ ܟܠܥܕܢ ܥܡ ܪ̈ܐܡܐ 'they mix themselves always with (wild)bulls'.

59 VÖÖBUS, *Untersuchungen*, p. 4 ff., 25 ff.

60 *Monumenta syriaca*, I, p. 5, cf. p. 7 f.

whose covering is straw'[61]. Some of these monks are actually naked[62]. Filthiness is characteristic of their way of life[63]. Ephrem adds once again that they thirst for mortification[64] and that their activity consists only of prayer[65].

At some points the second treatise affords us a better insight into the same singular milieu. We find the same characteristic features, but with some expanded remarks. These monks have given up work and renounced every kind of civilization. They live like animals, eat grass and roots, persist in severe fasting, and wander from place to place. Their appearance is described as wild and dirty : their hair is wild and unkempt, they are dressed in rags, and, regarding their only activity, it is stated again that this was prayer[66]. But our source is willing to tell us even more, for luckily some traits are pointed out with still more distinctness — especially their contempt for life and the extent of their mortification. What is only hinted at here and there in the sources previously mentioned, is frankly told in this document. We are shown the greatest aim of these monks — to be destroyed through sufferings and torments for the sake of Christ. Ephrem relates that there were several groups of monks who were unwilling to die a natural death[67]. They killed themselves through severe fasting and starvation or through other kinds of hideous torture[68]. It is expressly related that the monks delivered themselves over to wild animals and snakes and gave themselves to the flames : 'and others set firmly that they might not fall; in their minds they decided to die; and they were zealous and risked (every) horror; some of them prepared themselves as food for serpents and savage animals; they delivered their bodies to the serpents and prepared themselves for savage

61 ܠܚܣܝܢ ܘܩܘܪܐ ܕܡܣܝܪܗܘܢ ܘܐܘܠܨܢܐ ܕܠܒܘܫܗܘܢ ܘܐܝܬ ܕܠܚܡܝܢ ܒܪ̈ܕܝܬܐ ܘܐܝܬ ܕܣܘܪܚܢܬܐ ܡܢ ܚܠ̈ܠܐ *ibid.*, p. 7.

62 *Ibid.*, p. 5.

63 *Ibid.*, p. 5, 7.

64 *Ibid.*, p. 8.

65 *Ibid.*, p. 12.

66 *Sermones duo*, p. 5 f., 8, 10. Cf. Vööbus, *Monachisme primitif réfléchi dans les écrits d'Éphrem.*

67 *Ibid.*, p. 22.

68 *Ibid.*, p. 22.

animals; others of them burned their bodies in the fire that consumed (them) in their zealousness'[69].

Besides Ephrem, there are other sources at our disposal[70]. The chief authority among the Syrians[71] upon whom we base our knowledge of archaic monasticism is Isḥaq of Antioch. Besides other information regarding the manners of the primitive monks, as these already have been discussed, the tradition has survived in one of his original tracts[72] that they ignited their own bodies[73].

Finally, one should not overlook the possibility of an approach to the primitive phase of monasticism from another direction. Since the Syrian monasticism was transplanted with its traditions very early into Armenia, could it perhaps be that recollections of the earliest phase of Syrian monasticism have survived here, also? Indeed, not all the reminiscences are dimmed. In Armenian the most important accounts of the primitive phase of monasticism are those preserved by Faustus of Byzantium in his prominent historical work written at the end of the fourth century. It is very instructive to read his last chapter concerning the monk Gind and his fellow monks, Syrians by birth, and their ascetic manners and customs of chastising themselves. We are told that these monks, in their appearance and manners, were like wild animals, living together with animals: 'they retired to the grottos, caverns, clefts of the earth; they had only one piece of cloth, (were) wandering bare-footed, they mortified themselves, ate herbs, vegetables and roots; as wild animals they wandered on the mountains (clothed) in

69 ܘܡܢܗܘܢ ܡܟܣܬ ܕܠܐ ܢܦܠܘܢ ܒܣܘܣܐ ܒܪܚܡܝܗܘܢ ܕܢܣܒܘܬܗܘܢ ܘܦܠܓܘ ܘܣܡܘ ܥܠ ܕܚܫܝܢ ܀ ܡܢܗܘܢ ܠܢܘܪܐ ܘܡܥܪ̈ܬܐ ܦܠܓܘ ܢܦܫܗܘܢ ܪܘܚܬܐ ܘܥܒܕܘ ܢܘܪܐ ܥܠ ܦܓܪ̈ܝܗܘܢ ܘܢܦܫܗܘܢ ܚܕܪܘ ܠܡܥܪ̈ܬܐ ܀ ܡܢܗܘܢ ܐܘܩܕܘ ܦܓܪ̈ܝܗܘܢ ܒܢܘܪܐ ܕܐܘܩܕܐ ܒܛܢܢܗܘܢ *ibid.*, p. 20 f.

70 Ms. Šarf. Patr. 143, fol. 254 b shows that these traditions were known among the Syrians in Persia. A monk found in a cave horrified the visitors by his wild appearance: ܘܡܠܒܫ ܘܡܟܣܐ ܟܠܗ ܒܣܥܪܐ ܕܦܓܪܗ 'and he was clothed and covered entirely with bodily hairs'.

71 Probably the source of a poem which circulated under the name of Gīwargīs, the bishop of the Arabs, *Poemi siriaci*, p. 34 ff., was not independent, but was borrowed from Ephrem, see Vööbus, *Untersuchungen*, p. 25 ff.

72 Vööbus, *Beiträge zur krit. Sichtung*, p. 54 ff.

73 *Homiliae*, I, p. 40.

skins and hides; they chastised and tortured themselves; they were in constant insecurity, they roamed in the desert's cold and heat, in hunger and thirst — out of love towards God'[74].

Also, excessive fasting and the custom of mortification by self-destruction through starvation were features of the primitive monasticism which was transplanted into Armenia. Consequently, we perceive how this picture which has been sketched in distinct lines coincides accurately with that portrayed by Ephrem and Isḥaq.

Besides Faustus, we have valuable information which has survived in a collection of homilies in Armenian, composed by Yovhan Mandakowni (d. ca 460). One particular homily affords us suitable material for studying the close connection between the ascetic traditions of Mesopotamia and Armenia[75] and contains proof that self-destruction also occurred among those primitive monks on Armenian soil who, throwing themselves into the fire or delivering themselves over to the wild animals, reached the highest degree of mortification. He states : 'they went even into the fire out of obedience, and toward the savage animals'[76].

In conclusion we may say that acquaintance with the documents which contain information about the primitive phases of the monachal movement among the Syrians, preserved in the most ancient sources in Greek, Syriac, and Armenian, is highly illuminating. Particularly, the findings in the Syriac and Armenian sources stand out with startling vividness. Thanks to these data, we are able to form a definite idea about the particular physiognomy of primitive Syrian monasticism.

If we give full attention to the findings which we have encountered, we have to admit that they make it impossible to escape the following conclusions.

74 'ի քարանձաւս ամրացեալք յայրս և 'ի քարածերպս երկրի, և միահանդերձք բոկագնացք զգաստացեալք խոտաճարակք ընդաբուտք արմատակերք, զօրէն գազանաց 'ի լերինս շրջէին՝ լեշկամաշկօք և մորթօք այծենեօք, նեղեալք տառապեալք և տարակուսեալք, յանապատի մոլորեալք, 'ի ցուրտ և 'ի տօթ, 'ի քաղց և 'ի ծարաւ վասն սիրոյն այ, *Patmowtʿiwn Hayoç*, p. 230 f.

75 *Čarkʿ*, p. 30 ff.

76 և վասն հնազանդութեան 'ի հուր եւ մատնէին, և 'ի գազանս դիմէին, *ibid.*, p. 33.

First, we find new confirmation of the conclusion already reached — that the origin of monasticism in Mesopotamia cannot be looked upon as a transplanting of the monachal ideas from Egypt into the lands of the Tigris and Euphrates. Primitive monasticism in Mesopotamia is too different from what we know of monasticism in Egypt.

Second, an important aspect comes up which teaches us how properly to evaluate the deliberations made in the previous section. The origin of monasticism in Mesopotamia cannot be explained satisfactorily by means of the biblical examples or the primitive idea of a mission to fight the demons. We see how every thought along these lines reveals its inherent weakness and inability to explain fully the very phenomena which need to be explained.

Third, in spite of their fragmentary condition, the features of the primitive monasticism which we have encountered leave no doubt that they are in reality a fusion with elements derived from a source which claims a very different inception. These reports, fortunately transmitted from several directions, give evidence that they are elements of exotic provenance. Every time one examines the data concerning archaic monasticism, one cannot suppress the intrusive impression that asceticism and the beginnings of Mesopotamian monasticism must have been subjected to a certain intervention owing to which the ascetic traditions undoubtedly underwent a fundamental change. Obviously, this was due to some foreign influence. It cannot remain unnoticed that contact with radical tendencies of heterogeneous character must here have exerted an influence which interrupted the direct line of development inspired by the genuine Christian principles. It must certainly have been a strong outward influence which succeeded, even at the very vital points for which biblical faith had to offer unmistakable answers, in replacing the Christian conception of the value of manual toil with a directly contrary view, which reduced everything in Christian worship to prayer, and which brought with it such deep enmity toward the world, life, and the body as to make faith in God the Creator Himself questionable.

As we are confronted with this situation the question arises : how can we explain this peculiar intervention?

4. THE ROLE OF MANICHAEISM IN THE ORIGIN OF SYRIAN MONASTICISM

It is tempting to connect these findings made in the preceding section with the ascetic ideas and manners of the Manichees. When we search for further vestiges, we find some indications which make this thought especially relevant.

First of all, these peculiarly glistening ingredients of primitive Syrian monasticism fit in excellently with those which characterize the life of the Manichaean monks. As we have already seen [77] the Manichees were so antagonistic to everything physical that they destroyed all earthly ties brought about by nature between people, family, and kinsmen, extinguished the natural human desires to plant and sow and till the soil, and uprooted every kind of work. Everything that had any connection with civilization was destroyed. Manual labor was damned as a sin. The use of fire was forbidden. The only meager nourishment permitted was vegetarian. Besides all this, all physical existence was in their eyes the work of the Devil; and the body, conceived as dirt, deserved corresponding treatment. Therefore, they wrecked their bodies by the most severe fasting. The similarity of both phenomena is extremely fascinating. Indeed, reports concerning the earliest monks give a picture which is astonishingly congruent with the portrait of the monks of the Manichaean type.

If we keep this in mind and try to take a closer look at the Mesopotamian milieu, our problem takes on new light.

First, an investigation into the circumstances of early Mesopotamian Christianity is instructive. We have already seen that Manichaeism spread chiefly among the Syrians. Not only were most works of Mani written in the Syriac language for Syrians, but there are traces of activity in Mesopotamia by Mani himself. Many discussions and guesses as to whence Mani moved had to be silenced when the *Kephalaia* was discovered. It is told by this source that Mani, after having received permission from Shahpuhr to preach, went to Persia, Parthia, Adiabene, and the frontiers of the Roman

77 See pag. 115 ff.

Empire [78]. By this time the first Manichaean congregations in Mesopotamia already had come into existence. To these, he wrote letters [79]. Soon the movement captured the first place at the front of the rivals to the orthodox groups [80]. It is important to note that this sweep was continued in such a manner [81] that the movement, acquiring great significance [82], was able to take over the leadership in the process of Christianization to a marked degree.

78 ϩⲛ̄ⲣⲙ̄ⲡⲉⲩⲉ ⲉⲛⲁϣⲱⲟⲩ ϩⲛ̄ ⲧⲡⲉⲣⲥⲓⲥ ϩⲛ̄ ⲧⲭⲱⲣⲁ ⲛ̄ⲛ̄ⲡⲁⲣⲑⲟⲥ ϣⲁϩⲣⲏⲓ̈ ⲁⲇⲓⲁⲃ ⲙⲛ̄ ⲙ̄ⲙⲉⲑⲟⲣⲓⲟⲛ ⲛ̄ⲛ̄ⲧⲟⲩϣⲉⲩⲉ ⲛ̄ⲧⲙⲛ̄ⲧⲣ̄ⲣⲟ ⲛ̄ⲛ̄ϩⲣⲱⲙⲁⲓⲟⲥ '(I spent) many years in Persia, in the country of the Parthians up to Adiabene and the confines of the territory of the empire of the Romans', *Kephalaia,* p. 15 f.

79 A corpus of 76 letters was known to en-Nadīm and others. About the codex of letters discovered in Egypt, written in Coptic, see SCHMIDT-POLOTSKY, *Mani-Fund,* p. 24 f.

80 The Manichees appear at the head of the lists of dangerous movements, see for instance *Narratio de Simeone,* col. 823; Acts of martyrdom of Šemʿōn bar Ṣabbāʿē, *Acta martyrum,* II, p. 150; THEODOR OF MOPSVESTIA, *On Baptism,* p. 169; see also Ms. Br. Mus. Add. 14, 726, fol. 1 a ff.; Ms. Vat. syr. 100, fol. 3 b.

81 From this impact we have an echo in the history of Karkā de Bēt Selōk, which shows how all other infiltrating movements faded away with the coming of this real danger. The chronicle offers the following telling note: ܘܡܢ ܙܒܢܗ ܕܒܠܫ ܡܠܟܐ ܘܥܕܡܐ ܠܫܢܬ ܥܣܪܝܢ ܕܫܒܘܪ ܒܪ ܐܪܕܫܝܪ : ܕܗܘܝܢ ܬܫܥܝܢ ܫܢܝܢ : ܚܩܠܐ ܗܘܬ ܒܪܝܟܬܐ ܟܪܟܐ : ܘܠܝܬ ܗܘܐ ܒܗ ܙܝܙܢܐ 'and from the time of the King Bālāš until the 20th year of Šābor bar ʾArdāšir, these are 90 years, Karkā was a blessed field, and there were no weeds in it', *Acta martyrum,* II, p. 512. Then the report goes over to tell of the arrival of Mani's disciples Addai and ʿAbzakia or ʿAbdakia. Since Shahpuhr I started his rule in 241, the arrival of these men falls in the year 261. This important event could indeed have been impressed indelibly into the memory of the congregation in Karkā.

82 With horror the Christian sources mention the great Manichaean danger, which caused an endlessly tenacious wrestling. However these would like to report success in suppressing the danger, the facts reveal the opposite. In Karkā Bishop ʿAqeblāhā who ruled under Vahram IV (388-399) was wrestling with them successfully in uprooting the movement, as the source narrates, *Acta martyrum,* II, p. 517. But his successor Bishop Šābōrberaz had to do the same thing! *ibid.,* p. 518. — In Edessa the development of the early Christianity is connected also with Mani's name, as the Chronicle of Edessa shows, *Chronica minora,* p. 3. Bishop Rabbūlā did what he could to uproot them, *Opera selecta,* p. 193, but they continued to remain on the scene, and this even for centuries. For as the biography of Theodorus, archbishop of Edessa, *Vita*

This recognition, however, needs to be stated more precisely. For a deeper grasp of the milieu in which Mesopotamian monasticism originated we must not overlook either the idiosyncratic ability by which Manichaeism was able to assume such a role, or the peculiarity of the atmosphere which permitted such a response.

We must first take into account the idiosyncratic ability which presents itself in the operation of the Manichaean movement. One of the most notorious features of the movement was its elasticity. It had an enormous adaptability and power of accommodation in which lies, at least in part, the secret of its success. Beliefs and forms of spiritual culture were absorbed from the environment in such a way that it seemed to make the dualistic content of Manichaeism much more palatable for local conditions. In the Hellenistic environment it borrowed from Hellenistic sources, in the Orient it made use of whatever spiritual resources the local conditions afforded. No one can study the Manichaean fragments from Turkestan without becoming attentive to the Buddhist ideas and mythology here adapted [83]. The same hybrid process may be noticed in documents of Manichaeism produced in China [84] and in Tibet [85] where the ideas, conceptions, and even formulas are taken over from the environment and successfully utilized in the expansion of the movement's own ideas. As elsewhere, so also in Mesopotamia, Manichaeism certainly adapted itself to the spiritual milieu which existed there.

Secondly, with regard to the Mesopotamian and Persian milieu, we need to recall the observations previously made. We have seen that the primitive Christian environment was brought about by various movements and groups congenial to asceticism. Here the Marcionites, who constituted in the ancient movements one of the most antagonistic to the world, played an important part. Then came the Valentinians, various kinds of Encratites, and others, as well as various shades of all of them. All these movements displayed a

Theodori, p. 71 f., 78, 80, 81, 91, shows Edessa could not get rid of them even in the 9th century! In Persia there were villages completely under the spell of the Manichaean influence, Ms. Vat. syr. 472, fol. 93 a.

83 See *Soghdische Texte*, II.

84 *Traité manichéen.*

85 GRÜNWEDEL, Legenden des Na-ro-pa.

uniform hatred toward the world and the body. Mesopotamia thus became a veritable playground for extremely radical ascetic ideologies which evoked mutual competition.

During the third and fourth centuries the real spiritual and religious strength lived precisely in these movements. The same is true for numerical strength. Ecclesiastically organized Christianity was a mere minority group in comparison. In Edessa, according to Ephrem, the majority which bore the name of 'Christians' consisted of groups shaped by Marcion and Mani, while the ecclesiastically organized minority had to be content with the humiliating situation of being called a sect after the name of its leader Palūṭ [86]. Ephrem was constantly distressed by its defensive position, a situation echoed by the last sigh in his testament [87]. The situation elsewhere could not have been any different. This judgment from the mouth of a mournful contemporary is by no means an exaggeration. Still later, Marūtā complains about the same situation when he surveys the situation in ecclesiastical Christendom which reminded him rather — using his words — of 'a single ear of wheat on a huge field full of weeds which the Devil has sown full of heretics...' [88].

Naturally, all these various ascetic movements were in a state of mutual give-and-take. In this respect the sources afford us some indications which enable us to discern something of their propaganda methods and the means which were necessitated by a climate of competition. Ephrem laments the adaptation of Christian features and the methods of disguise used by the Manichees for their own advantage : 'for their works are similar to our works, as their fasting is similar to our fasting, but their faith is not similar to our faith' [89]. The testimony of the same witness in his 22nd poem against the heretics, which vividly depicts the actual conditions, shows what attraction their rigorism and the efficiency of their policy of adaptability afforded, and thus permits us a deeper insight. He says : 'Marcion separated his lambs, then Mani fell over

86 *Contra haereses*, XX, 5, p. 79.
87 *Testament*, p. 100.
88 Ms. Vat. Borg. syr. 82, fol. 29 b.
89 *Prose Refutations*, I, p. 184.

them and robbed them from him; one insane bit the other one' [90]. These vitriolic words of Ephrem refer to a process initiated by Manichaeism and displaying a strength greater than that displayed by any other religion as to the penetrating power of its asceticism.

From the Persian area some direct evidences of the relations between Manichees and Christians have come down to us. They may be found even in the annalistic literature. A few brief remarks seemingly afford a hint as to what troubles befell the Manichaean movement under Vahram I (273-276) and seemingly also afflicted the Christians, so that Catholicos Papā had to make efforts to prove that there was no connection between the ecclesiastical group and the dangerously compromised followers of Mani [91]. These relations must have had such a far-reaching effect if, even at the time of Catholicos Aḥai (410-415), the local situation sometimes was so strained that the struggle gives the impression of having been a desperate one. One drastic step is particularly mentioned among all other measures : a number of the religious buildings had to be burned in the attemps to obtain more separation between the Manichaean infiltrations and the 'ecclesiastical' Christian groups. The lack of a clear line of demarcation between Manichees and Christians was alarming. It is said that these groups were so intermingled in their customs and ways that they could not be distinguished from one another : 'for the Christians were intermixed with Marcionites and Manichees and made things from their works' [92]. This means that if ecclesiastically orientated Christendom could not come to the surface without employing such drastic and violent measures at the beginning of the fifth century, the process of intermingling must have been more serious approximately one century earlier.

This conclusion is very significant for our investigation. Under these conditions nothing is more natural than to infer that Mani-

90 ܒܢܘܢ ܒ̈ܢܘܗܝ ܚܛܘܦ ܗܘܐ : ܢܟܠ ܕܡܐܢܝ ܘܫܢܝܐ ܡܢܗ ܫܢܝܐ ܠܫܢܝܐ ܢܟܬ ܗܘܐ *Contra haereses*, XX, 3, p. 79. The Marcionites and the Manichees appear together also in other documents, see Ms. Vat. Borg. 82, fol. 7 b.

91 Mari, *De patriarchis*, p. 8.

92 لان النصارى كانوا قد اختلطوا مع المرقيونيّة والمانويّة ويعملوا شيئاً من افعالهم *Histoire nestorienne* V, p. 325; cf. Amr, *De patriarchis*, p. 26.

chaean monasticism secured a significant place for itself in Persia and Mesopotamia. This is not only a guess, it is a fact proved by original sources. It finds special and immediate confirmation in the homilies of the Manichees. These tell us that many monks and nuns went to the Mesopotamian provinces, propagated their way of life there, and found adherents [93]. There is one important original Manichaean text of an historical nature which also includes a report of the earlier expansion of Manichaean monasticism in Mesopotamia. According to this document, even the first efforts of one Mani's chief apostles, Addā [94], were crowned in such a way that many were won over to monasticism in the western provinces [95]. This last point cannot be exaggerated. The same may clearly be seen from a *mēmrā* of Ephrem in which it may readily be perceived that the situtation caused the pious man much sorrow. The severe and manysided monasticism of the Manichees had captured the people and thus won great sympathy. He grieves over its infiltration and influence, which embraced even women : 'and also today he (the demon) seduces the simple women through diverse pretenses : he catches one by fasting, the other by sackcloth and leguminous plants' [96]. He makes desperate efforts to warn men and women who felt

93 ... ⲁ ⲭⲱⲣⲁ.ⲛ̅ⲧⲥⲧⲁⲩⲣⲱⲥⲓⲥ ⲛ̅ⲧⲟ... ⲧⲡⲉⲣⲥⲓⲥ ⲁⲃⲁⲗ ϩⲛ̅ⲧⲙⲁⲓ̈ⲥⲁ-ⲛⲟ[ⲥ] ... ⲙⲛ̅ⲕⲧⲏⲥⲓⲫⲱⲛ : ϩⲙ̅ⲡⲕⲁϩⲛ̅ⲛⲟ[ⲍⲉ] [ⲟⲥ ⲙⲛ̅ⲧⲃⲁ]ⲃⲩⲗⲱⲛ ⲕⲁⲧⲁ ⲡⲟⲗⲓⲥ ⲡⲟⲗⲓⲥ : ⲟⲩⲏⲣ ... ⲧⲃⲉ ⲁⲩϣⲉ ⲁⲃⲁⲗ ⲛ̅ϩⲏⲧⲟⲩ ⲕⲁⲧⲁ ⲣⲁⲙ [ⲡⲉ ⲣⲁⲙⲡⲉ ⲙ̅]ⲡⲁⲣⲑⲉⲛⲟⲥ ⲙ̅ⲛ̅ⲛⲉⲅⲕⲣⲁⲧⲏⲥ '(in every) country (spread) the news of the crucifixion... Persia until Mesene... and Ktesiphon, in Susiana and Babylonia in every town. How many have... and have gone forth yearly from them, the virgins and the ascetics', *Manichäische Homilien*, p. 76.

94 About the same Addai see THEODORETUS, *Haeret. fab. compendium*, col. 380 f.; according to the history of Karkā de Bēt Selōk Addai came to Karkā, accompanied by ʿAbzakiā, or ʿAbdakiā, *Acta martyrum*, II, p. 512. See also *Chronicon Maroniticum*, p. 60.

95 'Sie gingen ins Römerreich, sahen (erlebten) viel Lehrstreitigkeiten mit den Religionen. Zahlreiche Erwählte und Hörer wurden erwählt. Während eines Jahres war er dort, kam (dann) zurück vor den Gesandten. Darauf schickte der Herr drei Schreiber, das Evangelium und zwei andere Schriften dem Adda. Er befahl (ihm) : « Bringe (dies) nicht weiter weg, sonder bleibe dort, wie ein Kaufmann, der (seinen) Schatz öffnet ». Adda verwandte viel Mühe auf jene Gegenden, er gründete viele Klöster, er erwählte zahlreiche Erwählte und Hörer', *Mitteliranische Manichaica*, p. 301 f.

96 *Contra haereses*, XXIII, 7, p. 88.

deeply attracted toward this form of ascetic life and urges them : 'flee from them, brethren! Do not let yourselves be deceived by exterior color, for this is the color of poison' [97]. It is a pity that the other numerous expressions into which he has poured out his sourness of heart are too vague and elusive to be of much value to quote individually, but in general they bear witness to how deep the interflowing of Manichaean and Christian elements must have been. Similar conclusions may be reached from the spell which the Manichees even later exercised in generating new forms [98].

These facts appear to be of great historical importance. They leave little escape from the supposition that Mesopotamian monasticism could not primarily be anything else but monasticism formed along Manichaean lines.

Investigation of religious conditions in Mesopotamia shows that a wide and extensive movement existed in that area, ranging from Manichaeism of a Christian hue to a Christianity of Manichaean elements [99] which took unto itself every intermediate shade imaginable. Similarly, we have to picture for ourselves the primitive stage of monasticism there, where the line of demarcation between the Christian and Manichaean elements vacillated considerably. As certainly as we find the pure Manichaean monasticism with all its colorings and connotations, we must also postulate several modified forms in which many an existing line and much pedantry were mellowed by the local coloring which drew its strength from the Christian elements. Here especially must be mentioned the prohibition of gathering the fruits of plants and trees, a prohibition which made living alone impossible. Proof that a change must have taken place is not wholly missing, but such evidence is not of the age in which we could wish to find it. As may be seen from the Soghdian documents, different consuetudes were still preserved among the

97 L, 6, *ibid.*, p. 195.

98 See the remarks about a movement founded by Baṭai under the rule of Peroz (457-84), making a new combination of Marcionite and Manichaean elements, THEODOROS BAR KONI, *Liber scholiorum*, II, p. 343 ff. In this connection it is interesting to see how these influences lingered on tenaciously. This movement of Baṭai apparently was a semi-Manichaean one.

99 It is interesting to observe that the Manichaean term ܙܕܝܩܐ *zaddīqē* appears as a term for the ascetics among other terms, Ms. Vat. syr. 92, fol. 72 a.

Syrians later on. Specifically, we hear that complaints arose in the Soghdian communities about those who had recently come from Mesopotamia into the local congregations and who were given the name of 'damned Syrians' because they had softened many a practice of the Manichees [100]. The instructive lesson given by this document is that Manichaeism among the Syrians had indeed made some changes in adapting itself to local conditions. These traditions seem to belong to the effects of the process of assimilation which started when the movement first appeared on the scene. But, if pure Manichaeism was subject to various shadings, this was all the more true of its variations, into which Christian elements had made deeper inroads.

Now if, indeed, Manichaean monasticism had a share in the origin of Syrian monasticism in Mesopotamia, it is important to observe several new and productive elements which it introduced into the environment of Mesopotamian asceticism. Here we need to touch upon some elements which deserve special attention.

In the first place, the immense authority, complete autonomy, and independence of the monks deserve notice. At a time when the role of the congregation of believers began to rise at the expense of the archaic concept of the ascetically structured church, Manichaeism must have revitalized the archaic forces which clung to the fundamental conviction that ascetics stand far above ordinary believers [101]. Manichaeism must have brought fresh winds into the falling sails of the ascetics' efforts towards their independence. It does not require much mental strain to visualize that monks who took upon themselves such rigorous renunciations could be encour-

100 '... sie haben etwa persönlich Bäume gefällt oder im Garten ein bisschen umgegraben, oder gar sich in fliessendem Wasser gewaschen... Sie bekommen unter andern das Prädikat « die verdammten Syrer »', HENNING, *Neue Materialien*, p. 16. What we learn from the letters of Mani, preserved in Coptic, arouses our particular curiosity. It is interesting that in one of these we hear about Sisinnios, one of Mani's chief lieutenants, who under the title ὁ διάδοχος appears in PHOTIUS, *Contra Manichaeos*, col. 41, cfr PETRUS SICULUS, *Historia Manichaeorum*, col. 1265. Further we learn that he had sent complaints to Mani about the attitude of the 'brethren in Mesopotamia'. According to these gravamina, these 'brethren in Mesopotamia' did not follow the ordinances given by him. See the preliminary remarks made by SCHMIDT, *Mani-Fund*, p. 24.

101 See pag. 90 ff.

aged to make themselves independent of the wider circles of believers who rallied behind their own ecclesiastical organization, worship, and hierarchy. How far the practical attitude of the Manichaean monks toward these simple believers showed its hand in the changes brought about in the Christian atmosphere is naturally difficult to say. But the feeling of, and the need for, independence in a changing situation, and the hatred which existed for the world and everything in it, could be sufficient to send the ascetics, who up to now lived in the communities, into permanent solitude. In any case Manichaean monasticism, entering as it did upon the scene of Mesopotamian asceticism, must have spread and popularized the idea that the ascetics as an elite corps are free from the congregations.

There is a second new factor which must have revolutionized Mesopotamian religious thought and practices. Manichaeism, as we have seen, reduced worship to prayer alone [102], and this became a substitute for all religious acts and cultic institutions. Probably we cannot adequately evaluate the implications arising from the idea that the ascetic is no longer bound to the church with its institutions and sacraments.

The third productive factor may be found in the introduction of esoteric forms and manners into ascetic practice, thereby enriching the Mesopotamian ascetic climate. It must be considered an important merit of Manichaeism that it brought the fertile and and receptive ascetic movements of Mesopotamia into contact with various forms and manners of Indian asceticism. It is apparent that already Mani had Buddhist monks as paradigms before his eyes, and it is also possible that he and his companions knew still other models from India. This does not stand merely as a possibility, something more can be said. New discoveries have antiquated earlier disputes and guesses as to whether Mani had been in India and met monks there. Excavations in modern times have proved that a journey to India to see the Buddhist monks was not indispensable, because Buddhist colonies have been found in eastern Persia [103]. It is natural that a religious spirit such as Mani's must

[102] See pag. 124 ff.

[103] See the finds of the Buddhist monasteries in Gandhāra founded in the first centuries, FOUCHER, *L'art gréco-bouddhique*, I-II.

have had an interest in, and found an attraction in learning about, the ascetic life of these groups.

Even the disputes about Mani's possible stay in India now belong to the past since the *Kephalaia* was discovered. Here Mani tells us about his journey to India [104]. No serious doubt can exist that Mani found models here and borrowed from them. A far-reaching resemblance between Manichaean monks and Indian phenomena testifies to this. Moreover, the first adherents from these traditions certainly helped to secure a place for their traditions in Mani's monasticism. When Mani, according to his own witness, made a good selection of ascetics while in India [105], these latter certainly did not come with empty hands but brought along with them their previous manners and habits. Here, even in its beginnings, Manichaean monasticism had adopted monastic forms and manners from the monastic armory of India. Thus also, through the medium of Mani's monasticism, these assimilated forms were transmitted to the Mesopotamian milieu. Consequently, the spiritual life and manners in that area received manifold stimuli toward the fertilization of the ascetic atmosphere. In this connection a statement made by Ephrem is too precious to be discarded. Here, keeping his eye on the Mesopotamian situation, he gives an estimate : 'in Mani the lie from India has again come to domination' [106]. One ventures to think that such a diagnosis of Manichaean monasticism at this point is, in essence, more correct than the opinion offered by many a modern scholar.

Through the channels of Manichaeism, such unique influences were directed into Mesopotamia that the well prepared ascetic environment must have been enriched by the elaboration of the pattern of ascetic life with its new elements. When Manichaeism, which had seen other types of monks in India and eastern Persia, joined with the fanaticism and enthusiastic psyche of the Syrians, energies must have been released for new formations in the ascetic movement.

104 *Kephalaia*, p. 15.

105 ⲁⲓ̈ⲥⲱⲧⲡ ⲙⲡⲙⲁ ⲉⲧⲙⲙⲉⲩ ⲛ̄ⲟⲩⲙⲛⲧⲥⲱⲧⲡ ⲉⲥⲁⲛⲓⲧ 'and there I chose a good selection', *ibid*. The Coptic word for 'selection' is an equivalent for the Greek ἐκλογή — a term which Mani used as a synonym for 'church'.

106 ܘܡܠܟ ܒܡܐܢܝ ܬܘܒ ܫܘܩܪܐ ܕܡܢ ܗܢܕܘ *Contra haereses*, III, 7, p. 12.

In view of all that has been said, it does not appear strange that we meet with features in the archaic form of Mesopotamian monasticism which were by no means inspired by the spirit of the New Testament and Christian tradition. Reports of the primitive monks give us a picture which is astonishingly congruous with the familiar portrait of the monks in India.

The picture of the ascetics, who have sacrificed their homes and families, as well as a life in civilization, as given in the Dasabrāhmaṇa-Jātaka, depicts them as wild beings. These monks appear with long nails and wild bodily hair, with filthy teeth, dusty hair, covered with dirt and filth and travelling around as beggars [107]. Moreover, their reckless chastisement and mortification of the body was developed into a craving for self-destruction. They did not even shrink back from the last consequence — self-annihilation [108]. This is the *agnipraveśa,* the voluntary death of the ascetic virtuosi, as the peak of the ascetic accomplishment. Ancient texts tell us that this *agnipraveśa* was accomplished by fasting [109], by precipitation from a rock [110], by going into water [111], or fire [112]. Especial value was attached to voluntary death in the flames [113]. According to Brahmanic wisdom, this form of *agnipraveśa* is described as a secure entrance into the world of Brahman [114].

With regard to the spread of the features which are particularly characteristic of Indian monasticism — e.g., ceaseless vagrancy, dressing in rags, nakedness, dirtiness, savage hairdress [115], self-

107 *Mehāvagga,* VIII, 28, p. 217 f., 220, 245 f.; *Dhammapada,* X, 141, p. 38 f.; *Anugītā,* XXXIV, 7, p. 375; *Kullavagga,* V, 10, p. 89; *Jātaka,* IV, p. 362; the ascetics live as wild animals : *Buddha-Karita,* p. 70 ff.; *Fo-sho-hing-tsan-king,* p. 72 ff.

108 See an episode in the Pātimokkha where a monk advises his companion to commit suicide : 'Ho! my friend! What good do you get from this sinful, wretched life? Death is better for you than life', *Pātimokkha,* p. 4.

109 *Jābāla-Upaniṣad,* p. 247 ff.

110 The Tsa-pao-tsang-king was translated into Chinese in the year 472 A.D. CHAVANNES, *Cinq cents contes,* III, p. 141 ff.; see also *Laws of Manu,* VI, 32, p. 204.

111 *Jābāla-Upaniṣad,* p. 247 ff.; *Laws of Manu,* VI, 32, p. 204.

112 *Ibid.,* p. 248 f.

113 *Vāsishtha,* XXIX, 4, p. 136.

114 So the commentary of Nārāyaṇa on the *Jābāla-Upaniṣad,* p. 248.

115 See pag. 152 ff.

destruction through fire [116], there is no puzzle. These were introduced by the medium of Manichees, just as Manichaeism played the same role of medium between India and Mesopotamia in matters of literary narratives and motives [117].

Through this enlightenment, then, the silhouette of the primitive Syrian monks begins to emerge from semi-darkness into the daylight. If we knew more about the archaic monks in Mesopotamia than that which tradition affords us, certainly other traits which now may only be guessed at would become more visible.

Finally, in these conclusions we may have an answer to the question of why Syrian Christianity forgot the genesis of its monasticism. Its short memory at this point should surprise us no longer.

Although ecclesiastically organized Christendom preferred to forget the beginnings of its monasticism and later sought to paint over them with an ecclesiastical brush, since it was more pleasant to claim that monasticism had been derived from Egypt, the influence of Manichaeism remained in monasticism as a constitutive element which may be perceived unerringly even in its later stages. What had penetrated it in earlier times never vanished — e.g., the restless and vagrant life which despised work and had as its aim only untiring prayer and meditation, and severe mortification through the destruction of the human body. This perspective will help explain many a factor in the peculiarity of Syrian monasticism in both its earlier and later stages. Without this aspect archaic Syrian monasticism, together with its diverse aspirations and eccentric trends, would remain completely incomprehensible to us.

116 Ibn Hazm, *al-fisal*, II, p. 74.
117 Bang, *Der manichäische Erzähler*, p. 1 ff.

PART II

ASCETICISM AND MONASTICISM IN PERSIA

CHAPTER I

ASCETICISM IN A CHANGED SITUATION

1. SOURCES

a. Treatises of Aphrahaṭ

The edition of the treatises of Aphrahaṭ, sometimes called homilies, opened up a wealth of information about early Eastern Syrian Christianity. All these treatises are exactly dated. His first ten treatises were composed in 337, the following in the year 344, to which a year later was added one which rounded off the cycle. By means of an alphabetic acrostic all the treatises are tied together. All this invaluable material has been preserved by ancient Syriac manuscripts of the 5th and 6th centuries [1]. In addition the greater part of the treatises are also in an ancient Armenian translation [2], and one treatise is in Georgian [3] and in Ethiopic [4]. Frequently, this source speaks of ascetics — a milieu in which the author, according to his own words, was at home. In understanding the history of asceticism in Persia it is of great importance to clarify the testimony of this source of so venerable age.

When one views all the sections and passages which are of interest for the history of asceticism and examines them carefully, he stands face to face with a highly interesting phenomenon. What arouses attention is a rift in the lute which goes through the treatment of several important questions.

1 The earliest codex Ms. Br. Mus. Add. 17,182 which contains the first ten treatises is written in 473/4 A.D. The second part of the same codex with the rest of his treatises was written in 511/12. The next earliest codex, Add. 14,619, belongs to the 6th century.

2 Falsely ascribed to Jaʿqōb of Nisibis, *Jacobi ep. Nisibeni Sermones.*

3 A manuscript of the Shatberd monastery, see BONWETSCH, *Unter Hippolyts Namen überl. Schrift*, p. 3 f.

4 Ms. Par. aeth. 146, fol. 245 b ff., falsely ascribed to Jaʿqōb of Nisibis.

First we notice how Aphrahaṭ speaks of women. In several occasions he talks about woman in such a way that she is not considered lower than man. His examples gathered from the Old Testament which demonstrate how woman is equal to man, enumerate the great women invested by God with high office [5]. But over against this evaluation other sections and passages speak entirely different language. Aphrahaṭ says bluntly that Adam is better than Eve [6]. One manuscript even reads — and this is certainly original — that Adam is much more beautiful and better than Eve [7]. Bolder tones are evident in pronouncing woman as the instrument of Satan since the days of Adam. This dim verdict, too, gathers biblical examples showing how much Eve's hand has caused failure and downfall even among those standing in the Nazirate [8]. Repeatedly the treatises come back to this theme showing in horror what a calamity has been prepared by women [9].

The same strange rift can be seen in sections and passages which treat marriage. There are passages which speak frequently of marriage as something good, established by God. In his treatise on the 'virginal life and sanctity' we read a statement about marriage, namely, that 'it is something very good' [10]. Aphrahaṭ says that he is far from those who want to debase marriage and bring some criticism or blame because the institution is created by God [11]. But there are perplexing statements which imply the very opposite : in its substance marriage is negative, something which paralyzes all the religious needs and presses man into the grip of this world [12]. Marriage is therefore an institution in the order of nature. But if Christians would correct the creation-order, no doubt is left as to what they should do. A strongly biased interpretation presses itself

5 *Demonstrationes*, I, col. 596; he gives a list of prophetesses who were equal to men, *ibid.*, col. 657; cf. *ibid.*, II, col. 49.

6 *Ibid.*, col. 837.

7 *Ibid.*

8 *Ibid.*, col. 256 ff.

9 *Ibid.*, col. 265.

10 *Ibid.*, col. 837.

11 *Ibid.*, col. 836.

12 One section says bluntly that marriage has only one purpose — procreation of children, but it has no ethical or spiritual value, *ibid.*, col. 825, 837, 1017.

into the forefront[13]. An exposition of Gen. II, 24 about man who leaves his father and mother and remains with his wife, speaks a language which cannot be clearer : 'this is the sense : when man has not yet taken wife he loves and honors God his father and the Holy Spirit his mother, and he has no other love; and when man takes a wife he abandons his father and his mother, these that (were) previously mentioned, and his mind is captured by this world, and his mind, and his heart and his thought are dragged from God into the world'[14]. Thus, according to this view virginity would be normal for Christians.

The same discrepancy appears in the concept of church. An examination of Aphrahaṭ's treatises leaves no doubt that at his time the archaic concept of church had given place to a development which made it possible for non-ascetic believers to become eligible for its membership[15]. Over against this clear picture a different and not less clear view is represented which cannot be harmonized with all this just depicted. This view involves a special problem connected with certain sections in Aphrahaṭ's seventh treatise. Here we see the candidates for baptism before us making their final preparations for the reception of baptism. In these two admonitions they are warned that baptism belongs only to ascetics, and if the candidates do not feel ready for this struggle, they should simply go back to their former life[16].

This strange discrepancy leads us to an old problem. Indeed, this treatise has appeared as a riddle to Koch[17], Müller[18], Richter[19],

13 Noah is introduced as the master example of the ideal of virginity; for 500 years Noah did not approach his wife; owing to his virtue mankind is indebted to him for its deliverance, *ibid.*, col. 549, 552. Concerning Moses it is said that it would be blasphemy to think that Moses had a marital life : 'if he had served (marital) communion, he could not have served the majesty of his Lord', *ibid.*, col. 825.

14 *Ibid.*, col. 840.

15 See pag. 186 ff.

16 These texts are quoted on page 94 f.

17 *Taufe und Askese*, p. 54.

18 *Ehelosigkeit*, p. 21.

19 He thinks that celibacy is dragged into the controversy only rhetorically *Älteste Auseinandersetzung*, p. 112.

Duncan[20], and to everyone who has examined it. How are we to explain these disparate phenomena, and this quandary created by contradictory data? Can these be brought to come to terms with one another?

As we search for a way out, an observation comes to our aid which, in fact, leads us out of this impossible circle. It would involve too lengthy a digression here to go into the full study of the question. Besides it is not needed to unfold the observations in detail, since this investigation has been carried out elsewhere[21]. But the gist of it must be given here.

An investigation of the seventh treatise, on the one hand, and the other material, on the other hand, gives a perspective which helps one to recognize the existence of traditions of quite different provenance laying side by side : these accepted in Aphrahaṭ's contemporary church and those of its past. By this recognition the study can proceed from the point at which it has stood. Then we learn to realize the real meaning of a quite different religious atmosphere in the seventh treatise, a milieu in which rigorous ascetical requirements enjoy their unrestricted validity.

A closer look detects unmistakable signs of very archaic character in these texts in the seventh homily. Special mention should be made of the very significant fact that in these sections baptism is called 'the water of proof' [22], and it is explained by archaic Old Testament typology [23] not applicable to Christian standard of Aphrahaṭ's time. In addition the terminology regarding the officers of the

20 *Baptism*, p. 100.

21 Vööbus, *Celibacy*, p. 49 ff.

22 ܡܝ̈ܐ ܕܒܘܩܝܐ, *Demonstrationes*, col. 344 $_{6}$. The meaning of this is given in a clear statement : ܟܠ ܕܚܠܝܨ ܡܝ̈ܐ ܒܚܢܝܢ ܠܗ ܘܐܝܠܝܢ ܕܡܚܝܠܝܢ ܡܢ ܬܡܢ ܡܬܦܪܫܝܢ 'everyone who is valiant the water proves him; and those who are slothful are excluded (separated) from thence', *ibid.*, col. 344 $_{7-8}$; see also col. 348 $_{2-4}$.

23 The episode with Gideon in Judges vii, 4-5 is used for this purpose : ܪܒ ܗܘ ܕܝܢ ܗܢܐ ܐܪܙܐ ܚܒܝܒܝ ܕܩܕܡ ܓܕܥܘܢ ܘܚܘܝ ܛܘܦܣܐ ܕܡܥܡܘܕܝܬܐ ܘܐܪܙܗ ܕܐܓܘܢܐ ܘܕܡܘܬܐ ܕܝܚܝ̈ܕܝܐ 'for, beloved, great is that mystery that Gideon anticipated and showed a typos of the baptism and the mystery of struggle and the likeness of the solitaries', *ibid.*, col. 344.

church is revealing. In our section the official persons appear under the names 'priests', 'scribes' and 'sages'[24]. These terms appear only in our texts, but not in other places where we would expect them to appear. In the fourteenth treatise, which includes a synodical letter written by Aphrahaṭ to the Mesopotamian bishops, he employs repeatedly quite different terms such as 'bishops', 'presbyters' and 'deacons'[25], which were certainly the terms in contemporary use. Further Aphrahaṭ repeatedly says that these admonitions quoted by him, are those used by the official servants in the church[26]. However, it should be kept in mind that the seventh treatise is not a circular to the clergy in general but was written to a single person[27]. All this can mean only that Aphrahaṭ has quoted a source.

Being confronted with this evidence one finds it difficult to resist the impression that in this seventh treatise Aphrahaṭ is quoting a source which in origin and historical background must have been quite different — a primitive baptismal liturgy. Thus this enigmatic homily turns out to be a hidden treasure.

This recognition gives a new perspective to the right understanding of discrepancies and contradictions regarding other traditions, too. Our confidence in the soundness of this conclusion is fortified by the observation that exegetical, ethical-paraenetical and theological traditions of an older period naturally must show themselves in an author who was living in an epoch of transition. What, for instance, might seem to us a curiously arbitrary treatment of the Scriptures — as the example quoted previously — can more naturally be simply a different exegetical tradition quite legitimate in an earlier period, a tradition which had not yet adjusted itself to the changing church.

The fact that the ancient liturgical texts were still in use during Aphrahaṭ's time in the Eastern Syrian church is not curious at all. It is a law in the history of religion that such liturgical texts last much longer than the conditions which have produced them. This is the privilege of sacred texts. Only the interpretation changes

24 *Ibid.*, col. 341.
25 *Ibid.*, col. 573.
26 *Ibid.*, col. 341_{12-14}; $345_{6-7\ 11}$.
27 *Ibid.*, col. 356.

from time to time. In this way the difficulties of these texts can be overcome and finally be not recognized. Regarding this situation Aphrahaṭ himself has given a good example.

Naturally, it was gratifying when Baumstark, an expert of liturgical research, gave his approval to this recognition [28] and when scholars like Draguet [29], Spuler [30], Van Roey [31], von Campenhausen [32], and others gave their consent also.

The upshot of this discussion is obvious enough. A closer acquaintance with these texts leads to discoveries which turn out to be guides in solving the problem which has beset scholars. These positive results prove to be historically important for the new insight that the wealth of the traditions in Aphrahaṭ's treatises is not from the same mould. The literary heritage of Aphrahaṭ is rather a convolution in which different layers of traditions are embedded. The presence of these strata in the traditions adds to this work a particular value for the history student. This discovery is particularly encouraging in light of the scarcity of documents for the early period. This insight gained by source-criticism also makes it imperative that the only methodologically correct way to approach such sources is to interpret and understand each tradition on the basis of its own testimony.

b. *Ketābā demasqātā*

An extensive document in the ancient Syriac literature *Ketābā demasqātā* [1], 'the Book of Degrees', made available in print as long as 1926 [2], has not found the attention which it really deserves. When it does find mention, then it is in connection with the Messalians (Euchites). But its real significance and contribution to church-historical study has not been realized. As these lines will

28 See Vööbus, *Celibacy*, p. 56 note 21.

29 *Le Muséon*, LXVII (1954), p. 208.

30 *TLZ*, LXXVIII (1953), col. 425.

31 *RHE*, XLVIII (1953), p. 567 f.

32 TR, NF, XXII (1954), p. 344 f.

1 The earliest codices are Ms. Br. Mus. Add. 14,578 and Add. 14,612 (6/7 cent.), but contain only single treatises; also Add. 18,814 and Add. 12,160 (7/8 cent.). Ms. Par. syr. 201 (12 cent.) offers the largest cycle.

2 *Liber graduum*, PS, I, 3.

show, they certainly lie elsewhere. This study is reopening a question that was widely thought to be closed.

When the learned editor, Kmosko, was preparing this text for publication, other important discoveries were moving the scholarly world. Villecourt found that certain passages in the 'Spiritual Homilies' preserved under the name of Macarius coincided with the Messalian phrases quoted by Timothy of Constantinople and John of Damascus; and on the basis of these observations he came to the conclusion that all this material ascribed to the name of Macarius must be of Messalian origin [3]. These and the subsequent studies [4] gave a real incentive for a new approach and created a feeling that the long lost 'Asceticon' of the Messalians, known by name through the Acts of the Ephesian Synod, has been finally exhumed. It certainly is not without bearing that Kmosko's preparation for his edition fell within this period of excitement. These new winds together with all that was in the air, could hardly leave untouched a scholar who was working on this unknown ascetical work from an anonymous author. It is not a cause for wonder that here, too, Kmosko began to see positive connections between the *Ketābā demasqātā* and the Messalian movement. He felt that the milieu suggested by this document points to an early stage in the development of this movement [5].

All this is quite understandable. But it is surprising that in all later research this document has found attention only from this aspect with surprisingly confident freedom. Rücker took Kmosko's views for granted [6]. In 1935 Hausherr wrote an article on the date of the composition of this document in which he strengthened Kmosko's view by an apodictic statement : 'Messalianismi aliquam speciem in Libro Graduum exiberi nemini dubium esse poterit' [7]. And this has been restated by the same scholar [8]. In a study

3 *Date et l'origine des 'Homélies spirituelles'*, p. 250 ff.

4 Wilmart, *L'origine véritable des 'homélies pneumatiques'*, p. 361 ff.; *Fausse lettre latine de Macaire*, p. 411 ff.

5 'Hinc non est mirum in L.G. quoque inveniri semina eiusdem doctrinae perversae ex qua antinomismus periculosus Messalianorum germinavit', *Liber graduum*, Prefatio, p. CXLIV.

6 *Zitate im syrischen « Buche der Stufen »*, p. 342.

7 *Quanam aetate prodierit 'Liber Graduum'*, p. 497.

8 *L'erreur fondamentale du Messalianisme*, p. 328 ff.

published in 1938 he says : 'L'encratisme du Liber Graduum est messalien aussi bien que l'immoralisme que signale Saint Jean Damascène et Theodor' [9]. Assertions like these invite interrogation [10].

To put it bluntly, it is strange that Kmosko's view has not invoked a critical re-examination. There are reasons enough for this. Here, I venture to point out some very serious flaws that go hand in hand with this whole supposition.

One reason is that the typical attitude and practice, which gave the movement its name, does not appear in the *Ketābā demasqātā*. It is evident that prayer is not the only means for perfection — as in Messalian doctrine — but only one among others. The document says very clearly that asceticism in its several forms is an integral factor [11] in this process towards perfection. Consequently, one must ask, with what right, then, are Christians in the *Ketābā demasqātā* called Messalians?

Further, the Messalian doctrine of the indwelling demon, which appears in all the heresiological sources as a fundamental doctrine, is absent in the *Ketābā demasqātā*. Original sin in our document is not caused by the demon which enters man after his birth [12], but by concupiscence [13]. And Kmosko's treatment of certain passages which refer to Satan who occupies man [14], is too far-fetched; he does not pay attention to the role played by Satan and demons in popular ascetic literature beginning with the Acts of Thomas. By pressing this language too far all monks and ascetics could be made to appear as Messalians [15].

9 *Messalianisme*, p. 6.

10 Vööbus, *Liber graduum*, p. 108 ff.

11 Particularly fasting and vigils are the most important means of mortification, *Liber graduum*, col. 845, 853, 908 *et passim*. It is represented as a radical practice so that from the frequency of fasting the body is affected greatly and made sick.

12 *ἕλκειν γὰρ ἕκαστον τῶν τικτομένων ἔλεγεν ἐκ τοῦ προπάτρος, ὥσπερ τὴν φύσιν, οὕτω δὴ καὶ τὴν τῶν δαιμόνων δουλείαν*, Theodoretus, *Hist. eccl.*, IV, 10, 17, col. 1144; cf. *Haeret. fab. compendium*, IV, 11, col. 429, 432, also Timotheus Constantinop., *De receptione haeretic.*, col. 48.

13 *Liber graduum*, col. 536.

14 *Ibid.*, Praefatio, p. CXLIV.

15 When, for instance, the biographer of Rabbūlā of Edessa says that Rabbūlā, after his conversion and trip to the holy places in Palestine, returned and

A CHANGED SITUATION 181

Finally, the negative stand taken by the Messalians against the sacraments and the institutions of the church cannot be found in the *Ketābā demasqātā* [16].

These are the main difficulties to be faced by anyone who tries to uphold the Messalian origin of our document. It should mean something that of those four points which Hausherr enumerates as characteristic of the Messalians [17] not a single one can be found in the *Ketābā demasqātā*.

But far more important than the absence of essential Messalian doctrines is the positive content of the *Ketābā demasqātā*. We take here the central question which permits us to look into the heart of the religious thinking and feeling in this milieu — the relation of these ascetics to the church and its institutions.

In the twelfth treatise on the ministry of the hidden and visible church we have the most important information, although these questions are touched upon also in other treatises.

It is said here, concerning the origin of the church, that the Lord Himself established it. Owing to its divine birth the church is 'the blessed mother who educates all children' [18]. Also, the ecclesiastical institutions, its altar, baptism, and priesthood, go back to the same divine source [19]. Moreover, the author is not satisfied with these general statements, but comes to speak more explicitly about their role in practice. So the document teaches its readers to respect the servants of the church [20]. Against the practice of the Messalians [21] it is said expressly in two treatises that the

went into the desert in order to fight as an athlete, it is told here that : he fought : ܘܥܡ ܪ̈ܘܚܐ ܒ̈ܝܫܬܐ ܡܢ ܠܓܘ ܘܡܢ ܠܒܪ 'with evil spirits within and without', *Opera selecta*, p. 167, does it mean that this anonymous writer was a Messalian?

16 See pag. 192.

17 1. L'inhabitation du démon dans l'âme. 2. Inefficacité du baptême et des sacrements pour purifier l'âme de cette présence diabolique. 3. Efficacité exclusive de la prière. 4. L'effet obtenu, qui est double : l'apathia et la venue du Saint-Esprit, *L'erreur fondamentale du Messalianisme*, p. 329 f.

18 *Liber graduum*, col. 292.

19 *Ibid.*, col. 292 f.

20 The author advises that priests be called 'my master and patron', *ibid.*, col. 389.

21 Besides containing information about the Messalians, the sixth canon

monks take part in the worship service [22]. And concerning the sacrament of baptism it is said that : 'we believe in and stand firm that the visible baptism of the spirit and the propitiation and the forgiveness of sins are due to him that believes in it' [23].

All this, the author says, leads to the conclusion that a separation from the visible church means guilt : 'if a man separates himself from it (i.e., the visible church) and serves on the mountain he is guilty and goes astray' [24]. Our document admits that there are monks who actually separate themselves from the visible church, and 'serve on the mountain'. But the verdict here is : those are guilty and go astray [25].

This information speaks for itself. But fortunately this is by no means all we are permitted to hear. The document enlightens our question from an even more important angle when the author pushes the question into the focus of theological fundamentals. In the twelfth treatise he says : 'if we doubt and show contempt for this visible church and this visible priesthood and this absolving baptism, our body becomes not the temple, our heart not the altar and the castle of praise; and the exalted church and its altar and its light and its priesthood do not appear to us (at all)' [26]. In other words, both forms of the church are inseparable. The same theological principle appears in connection with baptism. The document says that without the visible baptism no one can attain to the higher

of the Acts of the Synod at Gangra states that these ascetics have despised the church-buildings as the οἶκος τοῦ θεοῦ, *Sacr. conciliorum collectio*, II, p. 1101.

22 *Liber graduum*, col. 261, 288.

23 ܢܗܝܡܢ ܘܢܫܪܪ ܒܗܕܐ ܡܥܡܘܕܝܬܐ ܕܡܬܚܙܝܢܐ ܕܪܘܚܐ ܗܝ, ܘܚܘܣܝܐ ܘܫܘܒܩܢ ܚܛܗܐ ܗܝ, ܠܟܠ ܕܡܗܝܡܢ ܒܗ *ibid.*, col. 288.

24 ܕܐܢ ܐܢܫ ܐܬܦܪܫ, ܠܗ ܡܢܗ ܘܦܠܚ ܒܛܘܪܐ: ܚܝܒ ܗܘ ܐܘ ܛܥܐ ܗܘ *ibid.*, col. 296.

25 *Ibid.*, col. 296 f.

26 ܐܢ ܗܘ ܕܡܬܦܠܓܝܢܢ ܘܡܫܝܛܝܢܢ ܠܗܕܐ ܥܕܬܐ ܓܠܝܬܐ: ܘܠܗܕܐ ܡܕܒܚܐ ܓܠܝܐ: ܘܠܗܕܐ ܟܗܢܘܬܐ ܓܠܝܬܐ: ܘܠܗܕܐ ܡܥܡܘܕܝܬܐ ܡܚܣܝܢܝܬܐ ܠܐ ܦܓܪܢ ܗܘܐ ܗܝܟܠܐ ܘܠܐ ܠܒܢ ܗܘܐ ܡܕܒܚܐ ܘܒܝܪܬܐ ܕܫܘܒܚܐ. ܘܠܐ ܗܝ ܥܕܬܐ ܪܡܬܐ ܘܡܕܒܚܗ ܘܢܘܗܪܗ ܘܟܗܢܘܬܗ ܡܬܚܙܝܢ ܠܢ *ibid.*, col. 289.

experience, to baptism by fire and spirit [27]. The same principle is valid concerning the visible altar and priesthood. Without these one cannot come to the spiritual altar and spiritual priesthood. And so without the visible church no one can enter the exalted church [28].

Thus when we consult the document itself as to the Messalian origin we are led to the conclusion that the assertions hardly bear examination. There is not only nothing of the doctrines and views ascribed to the Messalian movement, but positively the document unfolds such a theological structure which leaves no room for the Messalian teachings.

To be sure, as we shall see, the document radiates some thoughts and ideas [29] which are strange to the student who reads it with eyes accustomed to standards of Western Christianity. But to consider these peculiarities as Messalian would appear to be unfortunate. There is a danger in using these peculiar features to supply a thin and unsubstantial mortar for an edifice unable to withstand the blasts of criticism. In studying these texts one has not to forget that here we are in the midst of the milieu of the Syrian Orient, for the measurement of which the standards of Western thought simply do not apply. But regardless of this, the peculiar features in their profile were views and practices which were at home in the lands of the Tigris and Euphrates.

In this respect another observation is instructive. One has not to overlook what is said in the introduction which was added to the work by an anonymous hand. This anonymous reader of our work, impressed by its excellency, makes a suggestion about its possible author, and it is interesting to hear his opinion : he thinks that this work seemed to be that of one of the last disciples of the apostles [30]. Here we have the reaction of a Syrian reader who most probably belonged to an ordinary group of Christians in Syrian Christianity. In his judgment there was nothing strange and unusual except the spiritual fervor and passionate devotion which brings life into conventional forms of Christianity.

27 *Ibid.*, col. 296.
28 *Ibid.*, col. 296 f.
29 See pag. 190 ff.
30 *Liber graduum*, col. 1, 4.

Moreover, even the transmission of the manuscript tradition shows something worthy of mention. In connection with the question under discussion it is not without interest to notice that the treatises of the *Ketābā demasqātā* could be easily ascribed to authors who enjoyed ecclesiastical reputation [31].

When one takes all this into consideration, the whole connection of the document with the Messalians withers away. There is not a shred of evidence anywhere and, moreover, this assertion goes in the teeth of all the evidence and also of all the probabilities. In fact, this view is too hazardous and may fall into deserved oblivion. And if so, then a more positive evaluation remains to be made which would do more justice to this document. And this, certainly, can be done better by studying the document itself than by listening to the heresiologers.

2. THE STATUS OF THE QEIĀMĀ

a. The process of remoulding

The first question which emerges involves the status of the *qeiāmā* in the first part of the fourth century. The problem which concerns the role of the ascetics in the church to which Aphrahaṭ belonged, has a longer history behind it. Since the publication of Burkitt's thesis [32], there has been a lively interest in and considerable controversy around this problem. Burkitt's assertion that 'the Christian community, therefore, according to Aphrahates, consists of baptized celibates, together with the body of adherents who remain outside and are not members of the body' [33], has found much praise. Without hesitation his thesis was accepted by Harnack [34], Ficker [35], and Plooij [36]. In others his thesis caused divided feelings or even

31 For example, in Ms. Br. Mus. Rich. 7,190; Add. 14,578; Add. 14,611; Add. 14,621 the treatises have been preserved under the name of Evagrius. These texts were edited as the works of Evagrius, *Evagriana syriaca*, p. 40 ff. but actually belong to the *Liber graduum*. In Ms. Br. Mus. Add. 18,814 one text appears under the name of Jōḥannan the Monk.

32 *Early Christianity*, p. 50 ff.

33 *Eastern Christianity*, p. 127.

34 *Mission und Ausbreitung*, p. 692.

35 *TLZ*, XXXII (1907), col. 432 f.

36 *Enkratitische Glosse*, p. 8.

criticism. But regardless of the fact that Connolly opposed it [37], that Schwen felt that Burkitt's hypothesis should be modified [38], and that Müller expressed a similar opinion [39], Burkitt did not see any reason to change or to modify his hypothesis when he came back to this subject in a study written 38 years after he first presented this view. In this work he says that Aphrahaṭ, writing in 337, divides Christians into the 'sons of the Covenant' *(benai qeiāmā)* and the Penitents : 'the Penitent is the general adherent, who has as yet not volunteered for the sacramental life; the son (or daughter) of the Covenant is the baptized Christian, who is admitted to partake of the Eucharist' [40].

This problem is of real significance for the understanding of the history of asceticism in Eastern Christianity and must always be an object of interest. But in the light of the remarks just made it can be seen that during the last half a century discussion on the matter has been flowing into broader but also deeper waters where sometimes there seems to be no firm bottom at all. The discussion has shown signs of floating about in arbitrary directions because no punt-pole is deemed long enough still to reach the river-bed. Therefore what has been said about our problem cannot spare us the trouble of making a deeper investigation of the literary critical analysis of Aphrahaṭ's treatises and of the ecclesiastical-historical premises of his contemporary Christianity. For, only if we attack the problem from these two different but converging directions, can we hope to throw more light on the problem and help to push the horizon back a little and somewhat lift the veil which covers the occurrences in question.

A literary-critical analysis adds new weight to the recognition which was already made, namely, that the body of material embedded in the treatises of Aphrahaṭ is not of the same mould. An

37 *Monasticism*, p. 522 ff.

38 Modified so that Aphrahaṭ would appear in the midst of the course of development towards the loosening of the radical standards and not at the beginning, *Afrahat*, p. 98 f.

39 *Ehelosigkeit*, p. 77. Later, however, he came a bit closer to Burkitt's standpoint and made a concession that this principle still existed at that time, *Kirchengeschichte*, I, p. 465.

40 *Syriac-speaking Christianity*, p. 499.

examination of Aphrahaṭ's treatises leaves no doubt that at his time the archaic concept of church had retreated and given place to a development which made it possible for married people and people with possessions, i.e. non-ascetic believers, to belong to the church. Everyone who believed was eligible for baptism and thereby for church membership [41]. Because of this development virginity, poverty and other ascetic practices became a state of the chosen who wanted to practice all this voluntarily [42]. In other words the advanced ecclesiastical conditions in the lands of the Euphrates and Tigris had forced the Eastern Syrian church to make reductions in the role of asceticism, and at the time when Aphrahaṭ composed his treatises, the church had already made this revision in the heritage of its past.

From the results of the literary-critical analysis of the treatises we go directly to the study in the contemporary ecclesiastical state by trying to look as closely into the conditions of Eastern Syrian Christianity as we can.

Needless to say, the whole study suffers from the scarcity of source material. Nevertheless the student of Syrian antiquities can be thankful for the few remembrances which have escaped oblivion and which permit certain interesting observations. Of course, not every single observation is of equal importance. But an observation may increase considerably in value if studied and seen in connection with other observations of similar kind. Thus, finally, a systematic investigation of the whole scene may yield some definite conclusions.

First of all, an examination of our sources shows that Christianity during Aphrahaṭ's period in Persia lived through a very important epoch, historically speaking. Seen from the point of view of organization the church beyond the Tigris reveals that it was well advanced. The Persian Church had just overcome the travail connected with the last phase of development in the hierarchic administration under the catholicos. What had come into existence under

41 The way the synodical letter sent to the congregations is formulated, *Demonstrationes*, col. 573 ff., leaves the impression that the church at that time did not consist of ascetics.

42 'For this degree there is the greatest recompense because we perform it out of our own accord, and not out of compulsion and necessity of any precept, and we are not bound by it under any law', *ibid.*, col. 841.

Papā (247-26), bishop of Seleucia-Ctesiphon, to be sure, through much quarreling and noise, was followed by a period of consolidation under Šemʿōn bar Ṣabbāʿē (326-341), Papā's former archdeacon [43]. Thus what is revealed in the domain of organizational structure, is far from being archaic and primitive. All we can see here reflects an advanced development measured by Western standards [44].

But to be sure this is not enough. Other indications along the same line remain to be sought. Indeed, it is of peculiar interest to try to trace the ecclesiastical and religious conditions during this eventful period. Doing this, we again and again come across phenomena which reveal that the church was becoming even more conscious of its 'orthodox' position and that it had entered upon a status where it became more resolute in its endeavor to separate itself from the semi-Christian and semi-Gnostic milieu. Thus it had moved towards consolidation in the sense of Western Christianity.

This move of Persian Christianity towards Western standards can be inferred to a certain extent from the letter written by Aitallāhā, bishop of Edessa (324-345/6), to the Christians in Persia [45]. The document testifies to the important fact that here was a connection between both groups of Christians divided by political boundaries. This presupposes that an 'orthodox' church existed at Aitallāhā's time in Persia and that the religious-ecclesiastical condition of that group in Persia must have been similar, at least to a certain extent, to those in Edessa at that time. In an atmosphere of undulating controversies and quarrels, where, as we know, suspicions and accusations of heresy were part of the current concern, this situation could not have failed to have been the case.

43 He had directed the ecclesiastical affairs earlier when the paralyzed Papā could not, MARI, *De patriarchis*, p. 16 f.

44 It is interesting to notice that the chronicle of Mešīḥāzekā deems it worthy to hint to a certain share on the part of the churches in the Western provinces under the Roman Empire, particularly the metropolis of Osrhoene, *Sources syriaques*, p. 44. Of course, much material about the development of the ecclesiastical affairs is found in a work which has been preserved under Šemʿōn's name, Ms. Berl. Sach. 108, fol. 148 b ff., but these texts cannot be from him, and belong to a much later period.

45 *Aithallae epistola*, p. 38.

Aitallāhā's letter does not stand alone as isolated phenomenon. We know that Aitallāhā's predecessor in Edessa, Sa'dā, corresponded with Papā, bishop of Seleucia-Ctesiphon, during the controversy in which he needed help from the churches in the West [46]. And similar impression regarding the existence of groups which were regarded as 'gathered in the folds of Christ' we receive also from the documents available to Eusebius [47].

The impression we have gained will be considerably reinforced by some other more concrete data which occur in the sources.

First of all it is interesting to note the significant fact that the same Šem'ōn bar Ṣabbā'ē is remembered by the Christians in Persia as a reformer in liturgical matters, particularly in connection with the introduction of antiphonal chanting which he took over from the church of Osrhoene [48]. Thus a glimpse at the liturgical innovation seems to give us a valuable hint.

There is still another sign which points in the same direction. This sign is clearly visible in the domain of the history of the New Testament text. It is a mistake to hold that the Diatessaron had maintained its authority as the official gospel text until the beginning of the fifth century and that since the episcopacy of Rabbūlā it began to disappear in Edessa, in the West first and then among the Eastern Syrians [49]. The truth is that the Tetraevangelion appears much earlier among the Eastern Syrians. The writings of Aphrahaṭ confirm the existence and use of the Tetraevangelion [50] as well as the ancient acts of martyrdom [51]. Thus, from the textual point of view, too, we come to the same conclusion. In the use of the gospel text the same process of adaptation had already started which necessitated a text reform similar to the reforms of the traditions of the Syrians in the West.

The net result of this excursus demands consideration. As a

46 *Sources syriaques*, p. 44.

47 EUSEBIUS, *Vita Constantini*, p. 80, cf. p. 120 f. One bishop from Persia was present at Nicaea, *ibid.* III, 7, p. 80.

48 MARI, *De patriarchis*, p. 17; BAR 'EBRAIĀ, *Chronicon ecclesiasticum*, III, col. 33; cf. VÖÖBUS, *Celibacy*, p. 39 f.

49 BURKITT, *Evangelion da-Mepharreshe*, II, p. 161 ff.

50 VÖÖBUS, *Studies*, p. 42 f.

51 VÖÖBUS, *Evangelienzitate der Märtyrerakten*, p. 222 ff.

consequence of the observations, a widely held view must be modified. For instance, Koch, following Burkitt, thought that in the first part of the fourth century the Eastern Syrian Church was geographically and spiritually isolated and had little contact with Christianity in the West [52]. This view has found frequent support. But what we can see in our sources admonishes us to be cautious. The Syrian Christians in the Eastern provinces were in closer contact with the happenings and occurrences in Western Christianity than has been admitted. In all these considerations one should not omit pointing to the movement of Christian Hellenism which had found inroads into Persian Christianity and assumed a share in the development in vital areas of Christian thought and practice [53].

Thus when we try to penetrate deeper into the ecclesiastical conditions and trends which existed at a time when Aphrahaṭ lived and wrote his homilies, we get a criterion with which to check theories. We must say that Burkitt's thesis regarding the duration of the primitive conditions does not fit in with the church historical premises as reflected in the sources. What we learn from the history of organization, theological consolidation, liturgical innovation, and the history of the gospel text, points unanimously in quite another direction. And all this seems to stand in the way of Burkitt's views.

Besides all these observations the weight of the finds in the literary critical study comes into account [54]. Therefore, it is safe to conclude that the ascetic factor which made the renunciation of the world a prerequisite for baptism and church membership, upholding its own concept of church, could not be valid any longer at the time when Aphrahaṭ flourished.

Incidentally, it is not impossible that a direct remark about the status of married Christians has been preserved. We could refer to a passage in the acts of martyrdom of Šemʿōn. The presentation of a scene which took place after the proclamation of Shahpuhr's edict in the year 340, when the officials began with the destruction of the churches in Seleucia-Ctesiphon, seems to indicate that married Christians belonged to the church. In this report the *qeiāmā* is

52 *Taufe und Askese*, p. 38.
53 Vööbus, *Studies*, p. 28-33.
54 Vööbus, *Celibacy*, p. 49 ff.

mentioned separately and other Christians are spoken of as belonging to the church, too. They are called 'sheep' [55], a term which, according to ancient usage as an intimate epithet, was used in connection with true Christians [56]. We cannot put absolute confidence in the account, since this section does not appear in the older version of the acts [57]. However it must be added that a younger recension may still have used older data and may have taken this vivid episode about the destruction of the main church, along with this remark about the *qeịāmā* and 'sheep' from reliable sources.

b. Byways in preserving the archaic heritage

In the absence of data regarding the period of transition and the immediate aftermath of this development, we have to be content with texts which may belong to a somewhat later time, but which owing to their quality permit retrospection. Such an opportunity is given us by the *Ketābā demasqātā,* 'the Book of Degrees'.

One of the most noteworthy features in the thought of this document is the distinction made between Christians who are divided into two categories : the righteous and the perfect. Behind this lies the fundamental principle which is crystallized in the following tenet : 'God has made two worlds and two ministries, in order that from that which is visible might appear that which is not visible' [58]. One is the sphere for those who do not comprehend the heavenly and spiritual riches, and the other for those who have illuminated eyes.

The righteous ones are those who are not capable of attaining spiritual maturity altogether. Their difficulty is their unwillingness and impotency to overcome the love for visible things. They remain in the ordinary life which, of course, is ordered by God, but it should be remembered under what conditions : because Adam disobeyed the Creator's will. Therefore God gave him labor and

55 *Acta martyrum,* II, p. 148.

56 Regarding the 'flock' and 'sheep' as full members of the church, see *Apocryphal Acts,* p. 301.

57 *Martyrium Simeonis,* col. 715 ff.

58 *Liber graduum,* col. 797.

worry and marriage [59]. In this life these Christians must constantly be aware of the necessity for sober balance [60].

Over against the inability of the righteous ones, the perfect ones leave the world, renounce earthly desires and attractions and take upon themselves the cross. Thereby they gain the new direction of life — life in complete privation resulting in the mortification of the body. This is the only way, and is the prerequisite for the attainment of higher spiritual life. Only thus is it possible to come to sanctification, illumination, knowledge of truth, communion with the mysteries, and finally to the inheritance of everlasting bliss. Hence, these perfect ones are Christians in the full sense of the word. Regardless of the concession made to the penitents, admitting them to membership in the church, asceticism had again reached the central position.

This is something so important that we cannot miss the opportunity afforded by the document to illuminate it from different aspects of Christian life and thought : exegesis, the sacraments, charismatic gifts, the concept of the church, and future things. Each of these angles opens up an interesting thought world for a better understanding of the central issue.

With regard to exegesis this can be made clear when we glimpse at the interpretation of the gospel's injunctions. The principle is this, that the sacred texts can only be understood by illuminated hearts and minds [61], disqualifying the righteous ones from grasping the message of the gospel. But for the sake of the believers of limited capacity, the gospel contains for them only elementary teaching, like the 'milk for children' [62]. These are the rules, inferior in their character, called 'the commandments of faith', containing the moral and cultic regulations [63]. Over against these commandments are the 'commandments of love' or 'the great commandments'. Only those who are weaned from the inferior commandments as

59 *Ibid.*, col. 541.

60 For this purpose, besides the New Testament ethical admonitions, the document also cites some apocryphal sources, quoted as Scripture, see *ibid.*, col. 260.

61 *Ibid.*, col. 13.

62 The whole fifth treatise is devoted to this, *ibid.*, col. 100 f.

63 The seventh treatise deals with ten commandments, *ibid.*, col. 145 ff.

milk for children, and want to grow to man's stature, choosing the narrow way of perfection, grasp their meaning and the ultimate sense of revelation. The second treatise in our document, which deals with the perfect ones, brings forward a collection of these rules, classified as higher norms [64].

With regard to the sacraments the same distinction is carried through between those celebrated in the visible church and the other and higher spiritual means. The former are for the ordinary believers, the latter are accessible only to the Christians of perfect degree. Concerning the sacrament of baptism it is said in these texts that : 'we believe in and stand firm that the visible baptism of the spirit and the propitiation and the forgiveness of sins are due to him that believes in it' [65]. But this is only the 'visible baptism' [66], and as such no more than a preliminary form of the gift of 'hidden baptism', which baptizes 'through fire and spirit' [67], experienced as illumination by ascetics alone.

Over against the Eucharist, celebrated in the church [68], there is a hidden one reserved for ascetics. They alone participate in the true communion [69] and experience its joy : 'they eat from the hidden altar — a ministry that is ineffable, that is greater than the tongue (lit. mouth) of human beings (is able to tell)' [70].

As to charismatic gifts, the same gulf appears. The righteous ones experience the Spirit who reckons with their limited capacity and therefore only gives them weaker food — only enough to keep the commandments and to fulfil the ethical and cultic duties. But this also means that they do not receive the Paraclete nor the understanding of the truth, nor the ability to attain sanctification [71].

64 *Ibid.*, col. 26 ff., 193.

65 *Ibid.*, col. 288, 797.

66 ܡܥܡܘܕܝܬܐ ܓܠܝܬܐ, *ibid.*, col. 797.

67 ܡܥܡܘܕܝܬܐ ܟܣܝܬܐ, *ibid.*, col. 797, 296.

68 *Ibid.*, col. 177, 576.

69 ܥܕܡܐ ܕܢܗܘܘܢ ܓܡܝܪܐ ܘܐܟܠܝܢ ܠܗ ܠܡܪܢ ܒܫܪܪܐ 'until they become perfect and eat the Lord in truth (truly)', *ibid.*, col. 293.

70 ܘܐܟܠܝܢ ܡܢ ܡܕܒܚܐ ܟܣܝܐ ܬܫܡܫܬܐ ܕܠܐ ܡܬܡܠܠܐ : ܗܝ ܕܪܒܐ ܗܝ ܡܢ ܦܘܡܐ ܕܒܢܝܢܫܐ *ibid.*, col. 800.

71 *Ibid.*, col. 76, 149.

Over against these, the perfect ones alone reach the highest level of spiritual life. After the renunciation of the world, the perfect ones, as 'strangers' and 'aliens' to the world receive the Paraclete [72] and his gifts : the riches of the mysteries, illumination, perfect freedom, the full knowledge of faith, and the whole truth in the supernatural world [73]. Entering this realm of spiritual life, these gifts secure to them a supranatural strength to eradicate sinful thoughts and to conquer the enemy.

The concept of the church naturally shows the same double character. The visible church, established by the Lord, is the spiritual mother of everyone. The church, with its institutions, is required for all Christians including the perfect ones. Yet the truth is that this church, 'a blessed educator' [74] which gives birth to its children, nourishing and educating them, can only give them preliminary instruction [75]. It is not the field for the operation of the Paraclete [76]. Far above the visible church and its altar, there stands an 'hidden church' [77]. This church is called the church 'of heart and that of exaltation' [78]. This is the sphere in which the Paraclete works. Therefore it is 'the mother of all the living and perfected ones' [79]. Thus in the final analysis the archaic conviction breaks through that the real church consists entirely of the company of the ascetics [80].

72 *Ibid.*, col. 60.

73 *Ibid.*, col. 136, 141, 144, 197, 289.

74 ܡܪܒܝܢܝܬܐ ܒܪܝܟܬܐ, *ibid.*, col. 797.

75 *Ibid.*, col. 297.

76 The document refers to the seven deacons in Acts among whom only one received the Paraclete, namely Stephen. But he left the office of caring of worldly things, *ibid.*, col. 77.

77 ܥܕܬܐ ܟܣܝܬܐ, *ibid.*, col. 797.

78 ܥܕܬܐ ܗܝ... ܕܠܒܐ ܘܗܝ ܕܪܘܡܐ, *ibid.*, col. 293, 296.

79 ܐܡܐ ܕܟܠܗܘܢ ܚܝܐ ܘܓܡܝܪܐ, *ibid.*, col. 293.

80 In the last tract 'On the commandments of faith and love of the ascetics' this is told in plain terms : 'Therefore this one who loves and is perfected is able to build up the church, because he knows with whom it is proper to speak about the commandments of faith (so) that he might be preserved and might live by them; and with whom it is proper to speak of the commandments of love (so) that he may profit by them; and to whom it is right to teach the ministry of perfection that he may grow through it', *ibid.*, col. 868.

Finally, this principle even penetrates their hope as to eternal life. While righteous ones will inherit a minor reward and obtain an inferior place [81], the perfect ones shall have a higher degree of reward : 'and whosoever arrives in his heart at the church of heaven and so departs (from this life), blessed his spirit!, since he was a perfect one and he comes, he sees the Lord face to face' [82].

How are we to explain this peculiar thought world?

It has been suggested that it was due to a Manichaean influence [83]. Here a warning is certainly in place because this explanation seems to follow a wrong track. We know that Manichaeism itself borrowed substantial elements from Syrian traditions and absorbed them during the period of its consolidation, among which the separation of believers into two categories assumes prime importance. Now, to infer that in this point the Syrian tradition had a need to borrow from the Manichees seems to be somewhat hazardous. There would appear little profit in chasing this circle.

The whole question takes on a new complexion when we keep our eye on the development in the role of Syrian asceticism, and its implications with which we have already become acquainted.

First of all a look back may assist us. The sources which we have examined, make manifest how deeply the principle of the two categories of believers had penetrated Christian thought and life in the ancient Syrian communities. Here we have before us a concept which, historically speaking, has played a very significant role. So much can safely be said. Such an important role of asceticism must have been able to create traditions of more than ephemeral character. When this was cultivated from generation to generation, percolating throughout every aspect of Christian life and thought, it could hardly be dropped and entirely suppressed by the introduction of forms and practices as known in the West.

81 *Ibid.*, col. 52, 296.

82 ܘܡܢ ܕܡܛܐ ܒܠܒܗ ܠܗ، ܠܥܕܬܐ ܕܫܡܝܐ ܘܗܟܢ ܢܦܩ: ܛܘܒܝܗ ܠܪܘܚܗ: ܕܗܘܐ ܓܡܝܪܐ ܘܐܬܐ ܚܙܐ ܠܡܪܢ ܐܦܝܢ ܠܘܩܒܠ ܐܦܝܢ *ibid.*, col. 296, cf. 53.

83 'Le Liber Graduum a sur plus d'un point des allures manichéennes autant et plus que messaliennes. La distinction si nette, fondamentale dans son système, entre les justes et les parfaits rappelle de façon frappante la distinction manichéenne entre auditeurs et élus', HAUSHERR, *L'erreur fondamentale du Messalianisme*, p. 333.

If so, then the possibility presents itself that the circles in which the Book of Degrees originated could naturally have been inspired by inner-Syrian traditions, i.e. by a spirit of conservatism which enabled them to retain something from the past. This possibility becomes a probability with overwhelming compulsion when we arrest our steps and try to look this historical issue squarely in the face.

In the sources we come across a factor which should be viewed most seriously. We notice that this problem, which became a matter of controversy, did not just involve ecclesiastical habit or a routine in the sacramental rite which was to be adapted to the practice as it was generally known in Christendom. What was really involved was much deeper. For all of that which was involved here was crystallized in one central issue to which all the writings of that earlier period testify : the meaning of Christian life. If we give full value to these pieces of evidence, then one thing emerges immediately : they bring us face to face with the dynamics of the forces which, as a last resort, created and upheld the fundamental distinction that there are two categories of Christians, and that they were interested in its perpetuation. What the historian learns to recognize here is that we have to do with more than a matter which a reform could settle. The understanding of the Christian message, and finally the meaning of Christian life and the substance of Christian being were real issues in the circles which cherished concepts deeply rooted in their ancient traditions, convictions animated and perpetuated by living examples among the spiritual athletes and hallowed by their nameless sacrifices. But life does not permit itself to be pressed into fixed forms. A vital force always finds ways to continue its existence, even if under external circumstances the ties with the past can only be kept in a concealed manner in a sort of sublimation. All this holds together quite well and it demands no great effort of mind or stretch of imagination to understand that this was also the case in the ascetically orientated Christianity in Mesopotamia. This judgment is intensified by the observation that this archaic principle of the church actually continued to live in many a circle [84]. This was a heritage which troubled the church of later generations.

84 *Studia syriaca*, IV, p. 79.

On the basis of a careful induction of the several strands of evidence, we are prepared for a conclusion of the first magnitude in the complex of problems regarding the period of transition in the history of early Syrian asceticism. All that we are permitted to see in the documents seems to leave us with no choice, but rather dictates the conclusion. After the ecclesiastical practices were changed and the penitents promoted to membership in the church, and baptism and the Eucharist were made available to every Christian, the deeply rooted distinction between the two categories of Christians could not be eliminated. The most vital part of this type of Christianity could never agree to equate itself with other forms and abandon convictions for which they were willing to give their lives. This part most certainly must have been compelled to find new ways for consolidating itself in a new situation. Their reaction is one which we would normally expect if the information in the Syrian sources is taken into consideration. And the development in the Nestorian Church towards the end of the fifth century [85] is not the only example in the history of Christian Syrians which should guide us in handling problems like these.

While the sources do not tell us as much as we would want about the effect of this transition period upon the forces of asceticism and while so much is left unsaid, it is natural and inevitable that much would be the subject of guess-work or supposition. But it is certainly regrettable when these guesses and suppositions, at least in part, are not controlled by documents. Fortunately in our problem we do not live from suppositions alone. Through the texts we have examined we can get a realistic glimpse, not only of the feelings and reactions in this new phase of Syrian Christianity, but we can also learn something of the energetic reorientation and consolidation of the strongest spiritual forces in a Christianity which could not preserve an archaic past any longer. And when the mists begin to clear, we notice a strong resistance on the part of the ancient ascetic traditions, which by the way, is an indication that we are on the correct track [86]. Advanced development had become a fact. But the ascetically orientated forces knew how to carry forth their

85 Vööbus, *Messaliens et les réformes de Barçauma*, p. 13 ff.

86 See Vööbus, *Studies*, p. 56 ff.

archaic and fundamental principle, adapted to the new situation. Thus the archaic stream was discolored by the historic media through which it passed, but in substance its domination remained the same. And so, this transformation unfolds before our eyes an important phase in the spiritual history of Syrian Christianity in the period after the transition and thereby gives us an idea as to how we are to imagine its implications.

In conclusion it can be said that the church-historical importance of the *Ketābā demasqātā* does not lie where it has been supposed, but, as we have seen, on a much more important level. It proves highly interesting in permitting us to reconstruct that historical process of incisive significance, which asceticism passed through. Concerning the vital happenings in the history of early asceticism, the veil of history is too closely drawn. Now thanks to this document, we are allowed a glimpse into some important phases during the transition period. And what we can see, is a very welcome addition indeed to our scanty knowledge, able to throw a ray of light back for a long distance.

3. INFORMATION ABOUT THE QEIĀMĀ

a. The *qeiāmā* in Aphrahaṭ's treatises

Now that the ground has been cleared in the preceding chapter, it is safe to say that the *benai qeiāmā* in Aphrahaṭ's treatises are not the members of the church according to the archaic Syrian standard. But, then, who are they?

Another misleading answer has been given in the view that the *benai qeiāmā* in Aphrahaṭ are monks. The title *de monachis* which Parisot has given to the whole treatise about the *benai qeiāmā* in his edition [87] is not an accurate translation but interpretation.

It must be admitted that the term *benai qeiāmā*, as it is used by Aphrahaṭ, shows a certain fluctuating character. Often it is used vaguely and fused with other terms so that it is sometimes not easy to see its exact meaning. But the most natural explanation is already

87 *Demonstrationes*, col. 239. Jargy remarks : 'D'après la teneur de sa Démonstration, Aphrahaṭ semble s'adresser directement aux moines en général, auxquels il donne le nom de 'benay ḳeyômô', *Fils et filles du pacte*, p. 311.

indicated in the previous chapter. In the course of the changing concept of church, the ancient name was inherited by this small group who voluntarily continued to interpret and practice the Christian life according to the archaic and strict traditions. Now this group as a class of ascetics became a smaller circle within a larger circle of the church. And in fact, these *benai qeiāmā* along with their female counterparts *benat qeiāmā,* as they appear on the pages of Aphrahaṭ's treatises, are not depicted as monks who had left their communities, but as those who lived in the congregation.

Regarding this meaning of the *benai qeiāmā* in Aphrahaṭ there remains no shadow of doubt. In this connection, it also deserves to be mentioned that the Armenian version of the treatises is careful in rendering the term *benai qeiāmā,* avoiding here the term 'monk' by using a word which means 'devout'[88]. In this case the *benai qeiāmā* would harmonize with the meaning of the term as it was known in Syrian Christianity after Aphrahaṭ's time. This fact can be seen clearly in some of the Syriac versions of the documents composed in Greek. An instructive case is given in the Acts of Agnes, who, as she is described in the document, was a dedicated virgin and lived in her own home. In the Syriac version this same Agnes is titled as *bart qeiāmā*[89].

Aphrahaṭ is very reserved in giving direct information about the actual conditions in his church and about matters pertaining to the life and functions of the members of the *qeiāmā.* The scanty remarks and references which the treatises have preserved permit only in some points a certain degree of clarity regarding these ascetics within the congregations.

In the first place we note that the consecration of the members is irrevocable, since it is based on the covenant which they have entered. Thereby they have taken off the old man and put on the new man. Since they have taken their equipment from the covenant they have made, they cannot put it aside without the risk of being beaten by Satan and of being condemned[90].

The most important aspect in the life of the members of the

88 *ուխտաւորք*, *Sermones,* p. 203.
89 *Acta martyrum,* IV, p. 116.
90 *Demonstrationes,* col. 252.

qeiāmā is, of course, virginity and continence. About this we already had an occasion to make some observations. These circles kept the atmosphere, in which the archaic traditions continued to have their peculiar ring. Thus virgins were assured that instead of having a mortal man they were betrothed to Christ [91]. Whether this virtue was practiced by men or women, the remuneration of their abstinence was held out as a prospect : 'the paradise is promised to the blessed, the virgins and holy ones' [92]. Also it does not require a great stretch of imagination to understand the great stress that was laid on their virtue. The members of the circle were assured that they are the only ones who love and honor God because they do not know any other love and because their mind is not captured nor dragged from God into mundane affairs [93]. We also hear something of the other side of their pride, as far as the female ascetics are concerned. They were proud that they could show contempt for death by not procreating children to it [94].

There is no real way of judging how deeply the ideal of virginity and chastity, exemplified by the *benai qeiāmā* and *benat qeiāmā* permeated the ancient congregations. These texts, however, offer one hint which, because of the absence of other references, may be quoted. The text seems to leave the impression that the ideal of virginity and sanctity must have produced results in the congregation quite ostentatiously. Aphrahaṭ tells that he had heard of attacks from a Jew who had slandered and insulted the congregation saying to one of his brethren, a member of his congregation : 'you are unclean because you do not take wives; we are holy and excellent because we procreate (children) and multiply seed in the world' [95]. This incident and its implications seem to mean that certainly in the congregation which Aphrahaṭ had in mind not an insignificant part was dominated by the ideal of sexual abstinence.

As it has already been discussed, in the times of the first fervor and enthusiasm the ascetics and virgins were accustomed to live together under the same roof and in the same house. But with the

91 *Ibid.*, col. 269.
92 *Ibid.*, col. 265.
93 *Ibid.*, col. 840.
94 *Ibid.*, col. 269.
95 *Ibid.*, col. 841.

elapse of time such a life became more and more open to objection and criticism. From the treatises of Aphrahaṭ we learn that at that time this practice of *syneisaktoi* had fallen under complete disgrace. But in spite of this critical attitude on the part of outsiders, the ascetics wanted to keep their archaic habits. Aphrahaṭ does not conceal the fact that he is much worried about the situation among the *qeiāmā*. His lengthy arguments taken from biblical books make it clear that he had very serious reasons for his admonitions. Also the fact that this issue is the only practical one which he deemed necessary to delineate with clear words, strengthens this impression. He depicts the situation in more picturesque lines when he describes how a *bar qeiāmā* tries to find a *bart qeiāmā*. Aphrahaṭ prepares these female ascetics for such tempting moments when 'one of the *benai qeiāmā* says to one of you : « I would live with you and you serve me »' [96], reminding them of their status.

And, finally, serious and urgent reasons compelled Aphrahaṭ to use drastic measures which did not know any compromise. When a *bar qeiāmā* lives together with a woman who is a *bart qeiāmā*, Aphrahaṭ's judgment is that it would be better then to take a wife publicly than to live in spiritual marriage [97]. The same judgment becomes clear in the advice he gives to the *benat qeiāmā* in order to influence them : this type of living together amounts to denial of the Lord. When the *benai qeiāmā* approach them with this unproper proposition, they should retort : 'I am betrothed to a royal man, and him I serve; and when I would abandon his service and I would serve you, my bridegroom would become angry with me and would write me a letter of divorce and would expel me from his house' [98].

With no less austerity Aphrahaṭ deals with cases in which the married couples had adopted the ascetic ideal and had transformed their conjugal life into spiritual marriage. In these cases Aphrahaṭ does not permit women to stay with the husband any longer. He refers to the possibility that husband might return to his previous habits, and then he would be guilty of adultery [99].

[96] *Ibid.*, col. 272.
[97] *Ibid.*, col. 260.
[98] *Ibid.*, col. 272.
[99] *Ibid.*, col. 260.

The only thing we hear about the question of life in loneliness or in fellowship with others is Aphrahaṭ's judgment that it is good that a male ascetic lives together with another man, and a woman with a woman [100]. This symbiosis is conceded but it is considered as somewhat lower than life in loneliness. Aphrahaṭ says frankly that the best situation would be to remain alone, living an isolated life.

What we are permitted to hear of other practices and habits of the ascetics in the congregations is very meager. In the third treatise 'on the fasting' Aphrahaṭ takes the occasion to gather various forms of abstinence under the common denominator of fasting. Here he is obviously referring to practices as they were exemplified by various groups of ascetics. Here we hear of those who abstain from bread and water until they become hungry and thirsty. Some abstain from meat and wine and from other food. Others abstain from every affair of this world in order to be sure that the enemy might not harm them [101]. Then Aphrahaṭ refers to those who practise mental and spiritual exercises which make them mourn and grieve [102]. And finally Aphrahaṭ says that there are those who combine these practices, even all of them. We can well trust our witness in this respect that there was much room for individual acclivity in ascetic life among the members of the *qeiāmā*.

The treatise written on the *benai qeiāmā*, however, disappoints the student who approaches this document expecting to find some specific information about the ways of the life of this institution. Homilectical and paraenetical speech abounds here so that very little room is left for concreteness in which we are interested. In this treatise the reader finds a number of very elementary things, and there are only a few statements which can add color to our picture.

A paragraph in this treatise lists several things which the members of the *qeiāmā* have to avoid : decorated cloth, finery of garments, the use of the veil, and adornment of hair. They also must beware

100 *Ibid.*, col. 260.

101 *Ibid.*, col. 97, 100.

102 ܘܐܚܪܢ ܕܨܐܡ ܕܢܗܘܐ ܡܬܐܒܠ ܕܢܫܦܪ ܠܡܪܗ ܒܐܘܠܨܢܐ 'another is fasting when he becomes sad that he might please to the Lord in affliction', *ibid.*, col. 100.

of long hair and the use of fragrant oils, perfumes etc. They also are not permitted to take part of parties and have to avoid laughter and a gay mood [103].

With regard to the ascetic practices the vigils are mentioned. The ascetics are exhorted to awake again and watch and to sing and pray when sleep tries to overcome them [104].

Many questions regarding the life, maintenance and role of these ascetics in the congregations remain unanswered. There are indications which seem to say that at least in part these ascetics did not work [105]. But it seems that Aphrahaṭ could not speak of absolute poverty as a common trait of these elite-groups. Individualism must have had secured its place here also. Some hints which the treatises contain leave the impression that it was left to the ascetics to decide to what extent this requirement was applicable to them. It is said that if the *benai qeiāmā* had something he gave to the poor and rejoiced; if he did not have, he should not be sad [106]. If the meaning of this statement is not quite clear, another statement is plain in its meaning. Aphrahaṭ has included some warnings to the ascetics that they were not supposed to take interest and usury [107]. All this permits the inference that absolute poverty could not have been generally imposed on these ascetics.

Of special interest is the insight into the attitude towards life which animated this elite. This is depicted as an ethos formed under earlier traditions and nourished by tension. In all their strife these ascetics see their participation in the passion of Jesus [108]. Having become strangers to the affairs of men through their struggles, they have taken on the likeness of the angels. But all this means an ethos characterized as struggle, contest, fight and war. They are athletes [109], always aware that their privation and abstinence are a weapon against Satan and a shield that stops all the arrows of the enemy.

103 *Ibid.*, col. 272 f.
104 *Ibid.*, col. 256.
105 *Ibid.*, col. 249.
106 *Ibid.*, col. 276.
107 *Ibid.*, col. 273.
108 *Ibid.*, col. 241.
109 *Ibid.*, col. 265, cf. 97.

As to the question of whether the *benai qeiāmā* and *benat qeiāmā* also had some functions in the congregations Aphrahaṭ does not help us. Since Assemani it has been suggested that they did have functions in the congregations as he interpreted *benai qeiāmā* often as clerics, or a minor rank among the clerics [110].

The occasional hints found in Aphrahaṭ are not sufficient to determine what this role, if any, was in the communities. The only thing that is said clearly is that the *benai qeiāmā* had their hand in the evangelistic service. In any case it is said expressly that the ascetics had to do with non-Christians in disputes and propaganda [111]. These few remarks seem to indicate that the members of the *qeiāmā* did not live only for their ascetic privacy but were also engaged in some sort of propaganda and evangelistic enterprise. If so, their role and authority certainly secured for them some minor duties in the congregations also.

b. The *qeiāmā* in other sources

The information about the *qeiāmā* preserved in other sources does not justify great expectations. Nevertheless at least some interesting features emerge here. These additional reflections on the institution are useful in throwing more light on some points in this institution.

The information about the extent of the institution is the only one which does not leave something to be desired. Very often the documents refer to the ascetics in such a way that the impression is clear that the body of the *qeiāmā* constituted an integral part in the ancient Christian congregations. We see clearly that these men and women lived in great communities as well as in the congregations in smaller towns, villages and hamlets. We hear of such a *qeiāmā* not only in Seleucia-Ctesiphon [112], but also in a little hamlet of which we have an episode in the story of the 40 martyrs in Persia. It is told here that the bishop of the city of Kaškar, ʿAbdā, was visiting his diocese and came to the hamlet, and then the text reads, 'and it happened in one of the villages in which there was a

110 *Bibl. orientalis*, III, 2, p. 888.
111 *Demonstrationes*, col. 276.
112 *Acta martyrum*, II, p. 148.

chaste and true *qeiāmā* of men and women'[113]. Further it is told that the bishop gathered these ascetics for the worship service.

What we hear about the general character and purpose of these ascetics does not exceed the information which we have learned already from Aphrahaṭ. But there deserves to be made one explanatory statement which corroborates the fact that in the institution of the *qeiāmā* virginity was the chief element.

The history of Karkā de Bēt Selōk, a document which has incorporated information taken from valuable ancient sources, refers in a special note to the *benat qeiāmā*. The text reads : 'women, *benat qeiāmā* that have promised[114] (confessed) virginity'[115].

In addition to this there is another similar reference. Here it is of interest how the translator of the Syriac narrative of the captives of Bēt Zabdai, captured by Shahpuhr II, renders this technical term into Greek. The Syriac text reads : 'and the *qeiāmā* of men and of women'[116], which in Greek is interpreted as an assembly or group of holy men and women practicing perpetually virginity[117].

What we can learn further, about the life and ways of these ascetics is particularly welcome to our scanty knowledge. Some sources show that the *qeiāmā* had room for a variety of forms and therefore was not rigidly regulated. Besides the ascetics, men and

113 ܘܐܬܬܘܬܡܠ ܗܘܐ ܒܚܫܐ ܗܢ ܩܘܕܫܐ : ܕܩܝܡܐ ܢܟܦܐ ܘܫܪܝܪܐ ܕܓܒܪ̈ܐ ܘܕܢܫ̈ܐ ܐܝܟ ܗܘܐ ܒܗ̇ *ibid.*, II, p. 337.

114 Eshtaphal of ܝܕܐ means 'to confess', 'to consent' and 'to promise'.

115 ܢܫ̈ܐ ܒܢ̈ܬ ܩܝܡܐ : ܕܐܫܬܘ̈ܕܝ ܗ̈ܘܝ ܒܬܘܠܘܬܐ *Acta martyrum*, II, p. 513. In this connection, the interpretation of the Greek text of Eusebius' treatment of the history of the Palestinian martyrs, by the Syriac translator, adds flavor to these observations. Instead of the Greek text : τὴν ἐγκράτειαν... ἁγνείαν τὴν παντελῆ καὶ σωφροσύνην ἠσπάζετο. EUSEBIUS, *De martyrum Palaestin.* p. 912 f., the Syriac recension paraphrases : ܠܡܫܥܒܕܘܬܗ ܗܘ ܠܢܦܫܗ ܣܡ ܗܘܐ. ܘܠܩܕܝܫܘܬܐ ܓܡܝܪܬܐ ܘܠܢܟܦܘܬܐ ܐܚܒ 'he had devoted himself to his continence, and was diligent (lit. loved) the perfect holiness and chastity', *Syriac History of Palest. Martyrs*, p. 14.

116 ܘܩܝܡܐ ܕܓܒܪ̈ܐ ܘܕܢܫ̈ܐ, *ibid.*, II, p. 317.

117 μετὰ συστήματος ἁγίων ἀνδρῶν καὶ γυναικῶν κανονικῶν (Ms. E : καὶ) ἀειπαρθένων (Ms. E : παρθένων), *Passio Sanctae martyris Iae*, *Versions grecques des actes*, p. 453.

women who lived alone, were others who lived together with a companion. So we learn that Tarbō, a sister of Šemʿōn bar Ṣabbāʿē was a *bart qeiāmā* and had a handmaiden who also was a *bart qeiāmā* [118].

Other ascetics lived in small groups. In the acts of Teqlā and her companions we have such an example. There five *benat qeiāmā*, Teqlā, Mariam, Mārtā, Mariam and 'Emī, lived in a village called Kašāz [119]. It is not said here expressly that they lived together, but the narrative leaves this impression.

The institution of the *qeiāmā* left room even for life in reclusion. For a description of this we have an instructive episode embedded in the acts of Pōsī, a master of craftiwork of Karkā de Ledān. Concerning this *bart qeiāmā* it is said that during her entire life she had been living in the Nazirate [120]. She lived in a house together with a woman who twice is called her maid-servant and twice her disciple, and once *ṭubanītā* 'blessed'. This account leaves the impression that she was not an ordinary maid-servant but herself attracted by the ascetic life. The text tells us even more about the practice of this *bart qeiāmā*. She had taken a vow that she would

118 *Acta martyrum*, II, p. 254.

119 *Ibid.*, II, p. 308. A little picture regarding the life of the *benai qeiāmā* is found in the story of Jaʿqōb : ܘܡܢ ܒܬܪ ܕܠܡܕܝܢܬܐ ܐܬܐ : ܐܝܟ ܕܐܡܪܢ ܣܩܐ ܘܩܛܡܐ ܐܙܪ ܠܗ : ܘܒܨܘܡܐ ܘܒܨܠܘܬܐ ܘܒܐܒܠܐ ܘܒܕܡ̈ܥܐ ܐܬܝܗܘܢ ܗܘܐ. ܘܐܚ̈ܐ ܠܘܬܗ ܟܠ ܙܒܢ ܐܡܝܢܝܢ ܗܘܘ : ܘܗܘܐ ܠܗ ܡܫܪܝܗ ܥܕܬܐ 'and after he came into the town, as we said, he took sack and ashes and lived in fasting, prayer, mourning and tears; and brethren remained with him all the time, and his dwelling-place was him for church', *Acta martyrum*, IV, p. 192 f.

120 ܘܐܝܬܝܗ ܗܘܬ ܥܡܠܬ ܒܕܘܒܪܐ : ܘܟܠܗܘܢ ܚܝ̈ܝܗ ܒܢܙܝܪܘܬܐ ܫܠܡܬ ܘܠܐ ܡܢ ܒܝܬܗ ܠܐ ܢܦܩܐ ܗܘܬ 'and she was much experienced (lit. labored) in (this) manner (of life), and completed all her life in Nazirate and not went out from her house', *ibid.*, II, p. 230 f. It seems that a remark found in an expansion of the Greek text in the Syriac version of Eusebius' History of the Palestinian martyrs, points to the same. Here the Greek text *παρθενουμένων*, *De martyrum Palaestin.*, p. 918 has been expanded in an interesting way to mean : ܕܐܦ ܒܬܘ̈ܠܬܐ ܢܟܦܬܐ ܕܒܩܝܛܘܢ̈ܐ ܡܬܢܛܪ̈ܢ ܗܘ̈ܝ 'also the chaste virgins who were kept in chambers', *Syriac History of Palest. Martyrs*, p. 19.

live in seclusion and would never leave her house. This we hear in connection with her desire to see catholicos Šemʿōn and his companions before their death and receive their blessings. But she was hindered in doing this by her vow. It also is clear that her house was within the boundaries of the town of Karkā de Ledān.

These ascetics were distinguished from the ordinary believers not only by their attitude towards life and their practices but also by the outward signs of their dress. In the acts of martyrdom of the great slaughter in Karkā de Ledān an episode is told about an eunuch, Āzād, who belonged to the selected group of eunuchs. He was seized by the enthusiasm of the martyrs and decided to mingle among the rows of those waiting their turn. In this connection it is told that he devised a cunning plan on how he would mix with the candidates without being discovered. He disguised himself using the dress of a *bar qeiāmā,* and covered his head with a black hood [121]. Later one of the Magi said that he found in him a similarity with Āzād but did not dare to ask, because he recognized the garment which he was wearing as the dress of a *bar qeiāmā* [122]. This is the only source which informs us as to the outward insignia of the members of the *qeiāmā.*

Further, according to some hints which we have already seen in Aphrahaṭ, these ascetics, *benai qeiāmā* and *benat qeiāmā,* who lived in the towns and villages, did not only practice their ascetic life as their individual needs chose but also fulfilled certain functions in the church's life. But what this role in the church's life was exactly is left in obscurity also in other sources.

Concerning this question one paragraph in the acts of Šemʿōn bar Ṣabbāʿē seems to give a hint. This paragraph appears in the description of the turmoil in Seleucia-Ctesiphon which took place when the edict of Shahpuhr was promulgated and the persecutors came to pull down the churches. Here besides the congregation only the reaction of the *qeiāmā* is mentioned leaving the impression as

121 ܒܗ ܗܟܝܠ ܒܝܘܡܐ ܗܘ ܫܚܠܦ ܐܣܛܠܝܗ̇ : ܘܠܒܫ ܐܣܛܠܐ ܕܒܢܝ ܩܝܡܐ ʻthus at that day he changed his garment and dressed a garment of the *benai qeiāmā'*, *ibid.*, II, p. 245.

122 ܡܛܠ ܠܒܘܫܐ ܕܒܢܝ ܩܝܡܐ ܕܠܒܝܫ ܗܘܐ ʻbecause he was clothed with the cloth of the *benai qeiāmā'*, *ibid.*

though an important function, at least spiritually, was carried out by these ascetics [123].

The fact that the *qeiāmā* had a function in the congregation is expressly stated in a prayer we find in the acts of Mārtā, the daughter of Pōsī. She herself was a *bart qeiāmā*. The following prayer, put into her mouth, is significant for our purpose : 'I confess Thee, Jesus, the Lamb of God who takes the sin of the world, for Thine name were sacrificed the shepherd-bishops, and were sacrificed the chief-shepherds (namely) pastors, and the helpers to the pastors (namely) the holy *qeiāmā'* [124]. According to this text their functions are referred to in a general fashion as the assistants to the pastors who are, according to this text, the deacons.

Here in connection with the last citation is the place for the observation that wherever an enumeration of the different ranks of the members of the congregations appears, the *qeiāmā* is always placed behind the deacons.

These remarks, so valuable they are, do not go beyond the statement of the fact that the members of the *qeiāmā* had to fulfil some functions, namely, as assistants to the deacons. But what these responsibilities were, actually, the sources do not tell us. The only thing we can recognize is that their qualifications made them helpers of the clergy for minor duties and assignments.

Finally the sources leave the impression that early Syrian Christianity knew still other kinds of ascetics not covered by the term *qeiāmā*. Besides the *benai* and *benat qeiāmā* the *meqadšē* appear as a distinct group [125]. In the places where the ranks are enumerated, these ascetics have their place behind the *qeiāmā* [126].

In the acts of martyrdom of Tarbō the veil is lifted somewhat from this institution. Along with Tarbō, the sister of Šemʿōn bar Ṣabbāʿē, the document mentions her sister and her handmaiden [127].

123 *Ibid.*, II, p. 148.

124 ܡܘܕܐ ܐܢܐ ܠܟ ܝܫܘܥ : ܐܡܪܗ ܕܐܠܗܐ ܕܫܩܠ ܚܛܝܬܗ ܕܥܠܡܐ : ܕܡܛܠ ܫܡܟ ܐܬܢܟܣܘ ܪ̈ܥܘܬܐ ܐܦܝܣܩܘ̈ܦܐ : ܘܐܬܢܟܣܘ ܪ̈ܝܫ ܪ̈ܥܝܐ ܩ̈ܫܝܫܐ : ܘܐܬܢܟܣܘ ܐܦ ܡܫܡ̈ܫܢܐ ܪ̈ܥܝܐ : ܘܡܥܕܪ̈ܢܐ, ܠܪ̈ܥܝܐ ܩܝܡܐ ܩܕܝܫܐ, *ibid.*, II, p. 238.

125 ܡܩܕ̈ܫܐ, *ibid.*, II, p. 241.

126 *Synodicon orientale*, p. 25.

127 *Acta martyrum*, II, p. 254.

The text says that Tarbō was a *bart qeiāmā* along with the maid, but her sister appears under the name *meqadaštā* 'sanctified' [128]. This distinction in the context is so apparent that it must refer to a different category of ascetics not covered by the *bart qeiāmā.* The Syriac text does not give the slightest inkling as to why she must be called differently. Also the Greek recension with its rather confused text [129] leaves us completely in the dark. But a ray of light comes from Sozomenus' remark that she was a widow [130]. It is not probable that Sozomenus had in his hands a more detailed text, but it does seem probable that he knew more about the reasons why these distinctions were made. However, regarding the final reasons and motives for this distinction we are left with only speculation. Perhaps this category was more of a semi-ascetic institution. Possibly, too, because the renunciation of marriage and the world did not take place voluntarily but was caused by the loss of her husband.

Also children were recruited for the *qeiāmā.* The memory of at least one of these has survived [131]. When this custom originated, is not clear. If a hymn on the *bart qeiāmā* really belongs to Ephrem, then he already knew the *benat qeiāmā* who had lived in their consecrated life since their childhood [132]. In sources which belong to a later period we learn that it was the duty of the chorepiscopus to visit regularly the villages and to persuade the parents to give their children for the *qeiāmā.* These were dedicated and the chorepiscopus had to take care of their education [133].

128 ܡܩܕܫܬܐ

129 *Versions grecques des actes*, p. 439.

130 καὶ ἀδελφῇ μετὰ θάνατον ἀνδρὸς, γάμον ἀπαγορευσάσῃ, καὶ ὁμοίως ἀγομένῃ, *Hist. eccl.*, II, 12, col. 964.

131 ܐܘܗܢܡ : ܛܠܝܐ ܒܪ ܩܝܡܐ ''Ohanām, boy, a *bar qeiāmā*', *Acta martyrum*, II, p. 287.

132 Ms. Vat. syr. 92, fol. 61 a.

133 See pag. 280 f.

CHAPTER II

ASCETICISM AND MONASTICISM UNDER THE RULE OF SHAHPUHR II

1. SOURCES

a. Marūtā's collection

The history of early Christianity in Persia is a history of suffering and martyrdom. Under the Emperor Constantine, Christianity found recognition and the protective arm of the state. But, when the persecutions ceased in the West, the spirit of oppression and persecution carried over to an area which since time immemorial has been a scene of struggle between light and darkness. The sadness of these events has overshadowed almost everything else. It is not strange that the literary life of these Christians reflects the gravity of these events.

A collection of the acts of martyrdom under Shahpuhr II was made known in 1748 by Assemani [1]. His edition was built upon Ms. Vat. syr. 160, a codex which is partly defective. Fortunately, new and better manuscripts emerged so that a new edition could be made possible. This was accomplished by Bedjan in 1891 [2]. His work was based upon Ms. Dijarb. 96. and Ms. Berl. Sach. 222. Even in this edition, not all the defective sections could be removed, but in some acts several manuscripts could be collated.

This collection of documents is furnished by a key which is preserved in both editions. The only difference is that in Assemani's edition it appears in the form of an epilogue while in Bedjan's text it has been joined with the text of the last acts in the collection.

This epilogue gives such information for the understanding of the origin and value of our source that it can hardly be appreciated enough by the student of history. We hear something very valuable

1 *Acta martyrum orientalium*, I.

2 *Acta martyrum*, II.

about the backgrounds of the traditions laid down in the acts. We learn that during the persecutions hymns were composed in honor of the victims. The Syriac term used here[3] ordinarily is used to mean hymns composed for liturgical purposes. Further, it is said that these hymns existed also in written form[4]. It is obvious that these were needed for the commemoration days of the martyrs and for liturgical and didactic purposes.

Then the author of the epilogue tells something about his own work. He states that it is not a free composition for glorification of the martyrs, but rather a work which rests on the information he had gathered from those who were close to the actual happenings and were even eyewitnesses : 'and concerning those (i.e. martyrs) who were before us, the accuracy of their stories we have written down out of the mouth of old bishops and priests, solid and trustworthy; because with their eyes they saw (these things) and were (i.e. lived) during their days'[5].

Also regarding his own share in this report the author informs us. He states that the reports about the more recent martyrdoms which he had included in his collection were reports about contemporary events and that he himself belonged among the eyewitnesses : 'and about those other martyrs, whose entire martyrdom, death and verdicts we have written down — several of them witnessed in our days and we saw them'[6].

The only information which we have about the structure and extent of this ancient source is found in its epilogue. Without such helpful hints as these we would have to grope in darkness since in the course of later accretions this venerable work has absorbed similar documents. The author states that he has divided his work into two books of which the first is described as a general treatment of martyrs in the Persian Orient and of their sufferings and triumphs

3 ܡܕܪ̈ܫܐ ܕܥܘܗܕܢܐ, *ibid.*, p. 394.

4 ܟܬܒܘܬܐ ܬܪ̈ܝܨܬܐ : ܕܒܡܕܪ̈ܫܐ ܕܥܘܗܕܢܐ ܐܫܟܚܢ 'correct records which we found in the hymns of the fathers', *ibid.*

5 ܘܐܝܠܝܢ ܕܩܕܡܝܢ ܗܘܘ ܠܢ : ܡܢ ܦܘܡܐ ܕܐܦܣ̈ܩܘܦܐ ܩܫ̈ܝܫܐ ܘܩܫ̈ܝܫܐ ܫܪ̈ܝܪܐ
ܘܡܗܝܡ̈ܢܐ ܐܟܬܒܢ ܫܪܝܪܘܬܐ ܕܬܫ̈ܥܝܬܗܘܢ. ܡܛܠ ܕܒܥܝ̈ܢܝܗܘܢ ܚܙܘ :
ܘܒܝܘ̈ܡܝܗܘܢ ܗܘܘ *ibid.*, p. 396.

6 *Ibid.*

in a summary panegyric, as he says, 'as one single judgment' and 'as one single triumph'. These hints make it possible to identify this document which has survived, to be sure, not in the manuscript Vat. syr. 160, but in the Ms. Dijarb. 96 of which only the beginning has been lost [7]. In fact, this text bears all the marks of the description given in the epilogue. Moreover, it contains sections which display a great vividness and so appear to have been told by one who had been close to these happenings [8].

The author makes some mention of the second book although we would have liked him to say more. It contained historical narratives about some individual martyrs under Shahpuhr II (309-379). These narratives depend on information given by the witnesses, may be some of it in written form, and perhaps on his personal observations. Further it is said repeatedly that these narratives were arranged in chronological order. He himself lays his finger on some pieces which belonged to his dossier : his work, he says, began with the acts of martyrdom of Catholicos Šemʿōn bar Ṣabbāʿē, the first victim in the persecutions, and ended with the acts of ʿAqebšmā [9].

In fact, the collections which we posses begin with the acts of Šemʿōn and end with those of ʿAqebšmā. While the transmission has preserved this framework, individual texts have not been able to escape revision and modification regarding which the scholarly views are divided [10]. We have reason to suspect that other new pieces have intruded which originally did not belong to this collection. In one case, at least, these seem to have replaced an ancient story [11].

In such a situation, a clue given by the author himself would give us guidance regarding other narratives between the opening and concluding story. But the only remark, — which is dropped in passing — is that the narrative about the great massacre in Bēt Hūzāiē belongs to this cycle [12]. It is a matter of regret that he

7 Bedjan estimates the missing portion at the beginning to 12 folios, *ibid.*, II, p. 57 note 4.

8 *Ibid.*, p. 58 ff.

9 *Ibid.*, p. 393.

10 See Braun, *Ausgewählte Akten*, p. xii; versus Kmosko, PS, I, 2, p. 679 ff.

11 The acts concerning the great massacre in Bēt Hūzāiē, which, as the collector himself states, belonged to his work, is missing in Ms. Vat. syr. 160.

12 *Acta martyrum*, II, p. 395.

is mute about other texts. However, it is not difficult to find what the other pieces were in the original collection, since these are tied together. These are the acts of Tarbō, Šāhdōst, 120 martyrs, Barbaʿšmīn, martyrs killed by the mobadhs in different places, 40 martyrs and Badmā. All these narratives are bound together by chronological data on the basis of the years 'of the persecution'. Among these documents are several very important for the history of monasticism, particularly the acts of Badmā.

Can anything be known about the author of this collection? The frequently expressed view which appears in Assemani, also adopted by Bedjan, was suggested by Ṭīmātēōs [13] and by a remark in ʿAbdīšōʿ [14] and Mārī [15], namely the view that Marūtā of Maipherqaṭ was the collector. This opinion is nothing other than speculation, and a very negligent one. If the list of martyrs' names arranged according to ecclesiastical ranks [16] is from him, it would be his only work about the martyrs which we know.

Marūtā's Vita [17] helps us to reach a definite decision about this question. For this Armenian document, in giving a history of Marūtā's life and work, reports that he gathered the relics of the martyrs in Persia, collecting them from different places into one sepulcher and bringing a part of it with him to Maipherqaṭ, yet it does not know that Marūtā composed the acts of the martyrs. The author surely would not have missed this, particularly since he refers to these documents at one point. In thinking of the martyrs and their relics he says : 'by whose intercession the Lord may be merciful to us, I, Gagig and my deacon Grigor who is with me,

13 Ms. Br. Mus. Orient., 9361, fol. 275 a.

14 *Catalogus librorum*, p. 73.

15 In fact, Mārī's report in connection with the relics of the martyrs he collected in the Persian area, tells that Marūtā gathered 'copies of every book he found of them', *De patriarchis*, p. 31.

16 This is added as an appendix to a very ancient martyrologium, preserved in the earliest dated Syriac codex, Ms. Br. Mus. Add. 12, 150, copied in November 411 A.D. Honigmann has suggested that this manuscript was copied at the time when Marūtā passed through Edessa on his tour as an ambassador, *Ostgrenze des byz. Reiches*, p. 5, note 5.

17 *Varkʿ ew vkayabanowtʿiwnkʿ*, II, p. 17 ff.

(who) have translated the acts of martyrs from Syriac into Armenian' [18]

Besides this the silence in Sozomenus is very remarkable. He enumerates those who have collected acts of martyrdom [19], and in this connection he surely would have mentioned Marūtā had he only known something about his work. Moreover, the intrinsic testimony of the texts can by no means be passed by. According to this the author was an eyewitness to the last martyrdom. The available information makes it quite apparent that Marūtā was not in Persia during the last period of Shahpuhr's life, but only much later when Jazdgard became the ruler, since 399. If we take the actual conditions into account, such an earlier trip under Shahpuhr's rule would have been unthinkable.

The view which sees a positive cue in a remark of Mārī [20] that Aḥai, who later became the catholicos was the collector of these acts is, unhappily, nothing more than a supposition.

The only thing which the epilogue tells about the person of the collector is that he was living in Persia and was not a visitor. Further on the basis of the intrinsic evidence in his panegyric on the martyrs some important chronological conclusions may be drawn. Here the author pours out his pain and grief about the martyrs, about the churches in ruins, congregations which had been wrecked and the spiritual life which had been destroyed [21]. This heartrending cry comes from a heart that does not see any relief in the conditions, or any ray of hope for deliverance. The milieu which is depicted is one of oppression and persecution. It sounds as though the author must have composed his work during the period of troubles which followed the reign of Shahpuhr II, but before the change of conditions which took place under Jazdgard after 399.

This conclusion finds confirmation in an interesting and meaningful passage in which the author cries out for deliverance : 'atone, Lord, the tiara of the Orient and give him that he receives Thy knowledge of truth, as Cyrus fulfilled Thy will; raise up, Lord,

18 *Որոց բարեխօսութեամբն մեզ ողորմեսցի Տէր, որք թարգմանեցաք յասորոյ 'ի Հայ զվկայութիւնս, ես Գադիկ և Գրիգոր սարկաւագ իմ որ ընդ իս*, *ibid.*, p. 31.

19 *Hist. eccl.*, II, 14, col. 969.

20 MARI, *De patriarchis*, p. 25; cf. *Histoire nestorienne*, V, p. 325.

21 *Acta martyrum*, II, p. 104 ff.

Cyrus in place of Cyrus in the likeness of Cyrus and repay wrath and evil to their seducers'[22]. These words make it clear that the author composed his panegyric at a time when he had not yet seen this 'Cyrus' — Jazdgard — about whom some of the laudations from the mouths of the Christians have been immortalized in the proemium of the synodical acts of the synod held under him[23]. Other observations may be cited in favor of this conclusion. One is this that the collection, which existed in Greek translation, was known to Sozomenus who incorporated these materials into his history[24]. If the Greek version of the acts existed before 439-450, the time during which the work of Sozomenus was composed, we have a new indication regarding the very early date of this collection.

We have many reasons to be grateful that in these recensions we possess the substantial form of the ancient collection. For a historian they constitute a source of capital importance, the more so because the older sources upon which the collection rests have entirely perished. It does not change our verdict when we notice that they are not available to us in their original freshness. Some of these texts exist now in different recensions[25]. There is no need to enter at length into the question whether Ms. Vat. syr. 160[26] or Ms. Dijarb. 96[27] represents the more primitive form. May it only be remarked that this question can hardly be satisfactorily answered along the usually suggested lines of either — or. In order to answer it each text must be treated individually. We notice that the religious taste of the writers and copyists has caused them to enrich the texts with miraculous elements. Sometimes the dialogues between victim and interrogator have been retouched, so that sobriety has been replaced by boasting phrases and noisy scenes. When texts of a

22 *Ibid.*, p. 91 f.

23 *Synodicon orientale*, p. 17 f.

24 *Hist. eccl.*, II, 9-13, col. 956 ff. The documents are quoted in the following order : Šemʿōn, Οὐσθαζάδης refers to Azad in the story of the great massacre in Bēt Hūzāiē, Pōsī, Tarbō, ʿAqebšmā.

25 The texts about Pōsī and Mārtā in Assemani's edition are much shorter and appear as appendices added to the preceding texts. In the acts of Šemʿōn, Assemani's text represents Šemʿōn as a boasting and illtempered man, while in the text in Bedjan he appears as a balanced and wise shepherd.

26 See Kmosko's remarks in PS, I, 2, p. 687.

27 Braun, *Ausgewählte Akten*, p. xii.

hollow and declamatory character stand opposite to others characterized by sobriety and a lapidary presentation of the facts, the manipulatory hand becomes clearly visible. At all event, the present texts have preserved more than the gist of the original documents. We may assume that historically important data regarding the persons, circumstances, activities, places etc. have not been in serious danger of modification and distortion.

b. The Mīlēs' Trilogy

Another cycle is constituted by the acts of martyrdom of Mīlēs, Baršabiā and those of Dānī'ēl and Wardā. These pieces belong together and have been preserved so, although in the stream of manuscript tradition they also appear individually. But particularly their character demonstrates that they belong together — they revolve around the martyrdom of Mīlēs. Other acts are chained by chronological remarks to the acts of Mīlēs.

The acts of these martyrs, who fell as victims in the first year of persecution under Shahpuhr II, are outstanding because of their venerable age. These texts appear first in Ms. Vat. Syr. 160, a codex of great antiquity, written in the year 474. However, we are in a position to trace the existence of the acts of Mīlēs back to even an earlier period. Sozomenus, compiling his historical work, had in his hands a document about Mīlēs in Greek translation. The reports in his work [28] show incontestably that these were the acts of Mīlēs translated into Greek.

But this conclusion does not remove all possible suspicions for the historian. This text in the acts of Mīlēs [29] is an example of the sad fact that antiquity alone is not a guarantee of trustworthiness. These acts — which have been expanded to his biography — show an almost pathological need for miraculous fabulation which has done much harm to the story. Here we read of his fighting with dragons, of his anathema which caused the paralysis of Papā, his adversary, and of other fantastic deeds up to the last moment before his death. He is brought together with a number of persons

[28] *Hist. eccl.*, II, 14, col. 968 f.
[29] *Acta martyrum*, II, p. 260 ff.

like Jaʿqōb of Nisibis and Ammonios — tales which belong to the realm of legends.

The elements of his life story raise many questions. For instance it is told that his missionary work in converting the souls in Šūšan[30] and its environs was acknowledged by the church and by Gadiab, bishop of Bēt Lāphāṭ, who consecrated him bishop of Šūšan. It is also said that because the people were gripped by paganism his life in his diocese became so unbearable that he was subjected to all kinds of sufferings. He was stoned on the street, dragged and tossed out of town, not to mention his numerous beatings[31]. But Šūšan was not a new mission field at all[32]. Further we are told that it was this unbearable life which compelled him to abandon his congregation[33]. But this is certainly something which would have had repercussions in those documents which try to defend Papā[34]. In such a heat of controversy, incidents like these would have been heartily welcomed and exaggerated in all their possibilities.

Such a situation raises the question as to how much is left of the true historical kernel by such a hunger for fantasy. Are we able in any way to separate the elements of truth from the mass of corruption or has the folklore of the people in the country of Rāzīqāiē corroded almost all or all of it? Labourt suspects that the situation is even more complicated by the fact that two stories are fused here, one about Mīlēs the bishop and the other about Mīlēs the monk[35]. Whether this is so or not is impossible to find out. The

30 According to the Acts of Mārī, Šušan along with Šušterā were the earliest towns in Bēt Hūzāiē and known as such at a time when other centers at that time were only insignificant villages, *Acta S. Maris apostoli*, p. 120.

31 *Acta martyrum*, II, p. 264.

32 In the chronicle of Arbēl Ḥaibeʿel appears as the bishop of Šūšan, a contemporary of Aḥādabūhī, bishop of Arbēl under Vahram II (276-293), *Sources syriaques*, p. 41. It also should be noted that according to the tradition Šemʿōn bar Ṣabbāʿē was buried here, Ms. Vat. syr. 87, fol. 72 a.

33 Namely 3 months later, 300 elephants were sent to trample down the houses and to kill the inhabitants and level the place, *Acta martyrum*, II, 264 f.

34 The forged letters of Jaʿqōb of Nisibis and that of Ephrem of Edessa, Ms. Vat. Borg. syr. 82, fol. 221, 225.

35 *Christianisme*, p. 72 note.

acts of Mīlēs have been preserved in several manuscripts of different age [36]. But a perusal of all these texts gives no clue whatsoever which might throw a ray of light upon the question of growth and development of these traditions. The only lesson which can be drawn from such observations is a lesson of warning. Only a little of that which the text reports can be accepted, and that little only with caution. Consequently the figure, whose name appears in the earliest Syrian martyrology, at the beginning of the list [37], must remain obscure.

On the other hand, the acts of Baršabiā [38] is an account which leaves a very different impression. It is a brief narrative which tells the fate of a monastic community in Phārs, of how the abbot and his monks were arrested, interrogated and executed all at about the same time Mīlēs was killed. It is a worthy monument to the memory of these witnesses.

The acts of Dāni'ēl and Wardā [39], both of the country of Rāzīqāiē, are also a brief matter-of-fact account without any embellishments whatsoever. They are concerned with witness of this priest and a *bart qeiāmā*, who were killed two years after the martyrdom of Mīlēs.

c. Cycle of Mār Aūgēn

Syriac literature offers a number of documents which purport to tell exactly how the monastic form of life came to exist in Persia and where the important centers and monasteries, which became hotbeds in the course of the spreading of the movement, were established. A historian would gratefully welcome such documents if only their claim would deserve confidence.

A cycle of stories, itself actually larger than the data in

36 Milēs appears also in *Synaxaire arménien,* XVI, 16 ff. Besides the codices used by Assemani, Ms. Vat. syr. 96, 160 and 161, also Ms. Br. Mus. Add. 17,204, fol. 8 a ff., written in the 5th century, Add. 14,654, fol. 3 a ff., written in the 5th or 6th century. Other codices, Ms. Berl. orient. oct. 1257, fol. 1 a ff., and Ms. Cambr. Add. 2020, fol. 61 a ff., are much younger.

37 *Martyrologes et ménologes*, p. 23.

38 *Acta martyrum,* II, p. 281 ff.

39 *Ibid.*, II, p. 290.

Baumstark [40] which need to be supplemented, revolves around the story of Mār Aūgēn [41]. This cycle consists of the stories of Āḥā [42], Dāni'ēl [43], Jāūnān [44], Šallītā [45], Hazqi'ēl [46], Malkē [47], Beniamīn [48], Mīkā [49], 'Ešaʿiā [50], Ḥabbīb [51], Jaret [52], Jōḥannan [53], Jōḥannan of Kaphnā [54] and that of Mīkā'ēl in an Arabic version [55]. The latter existed in a Syriac version [56]. Later historiography has celebrated this company of people as great heroes, as seen in the lofty hymns of ʿAbdīšōʿ b. Šaʿʿarah, Gīwargīs Wardā a.o.

When one puts what has been believed and cherished for centuries to the cold test of scholarship, then all the literature which boasts of exact data about the activity of these men, and about chronological and geographical knowledge as well as about the authors who bring their credentials in an ostentatious way, proves to be forgery worthless for historical purposes for the early period. The exodus of the 70 monks from Egypt who went out in order to establish coenobitic life in Persia along with their corporate action in Persia in which the whole team being furnished with the blessings of its master, holding a cross in hand, went out to found monasteries in different parts of the Sassanide Empire — all this is a fruit of a naive imagination nourished only by practices of piety and solemn

40 *Geschichte syr. Literatur,* p. 235 ff.

41 *Acta martyrum,* III, p. 376 ff.

42 Ms. Ming. syr. 502, fol. 159 a ff.

43 *Acta martyrum,* III, p. 481 ff.

44 *Ibid.,* I, p. 466 ff.

45 *Ibid.,* I, p. 424 ff.

46 Ms. Vat. syr. 472, fol. 83 ff. (torso); Ms. N.D. des Sem. syr. 242.

47 *Acta martyrum,* V, p. 421 ff.

48 *Vie de Mar Benjamin,* p. 62 ff., 93 ff.

49 *Acta martyrum,* III, p. 510 ff.

50 *Ibid.,* III, p. 543 ff.

51 Ms. Br. Mus. Add. 14, 733, fol. 70 b ff.

52 Ms. Br. Mus. Add. 12, 174, fol. 253 b ff.; Ms. Borg. syr. 39, fol. 149 a ff.; Ms. Cambr. Add. 2020, fol. 82 a ff.; Ms. N.D. des Sem. syr. 211, cah. 10 fol. 4 ff.

53 Ms. Ming. syr. 502, fol. 92 b ff.

54 Ms. Par. syr. 379, fol. 1 a ff.; Ms. Ming. syr. 71, fol. 136 b ff.

55 *Vie des martyrs d'Orient,* II, p. 101 ff.

56 The Arabic text adds the words 'it was translated from Syriac into Arabic by the priest Ḫadder in the year 1720 A.D.', *ibid.,* p. 128.

liturgical processions, but which has no idea of the historical happenings. The ignorance of the authors in these matters can be seen at every step. In their twisting of historical facts and in their wild imagination even Shahpuhr is made a patron of this company, being persuaded by the thaumaturgic power of their captain. And what is told about the monks' busy, large scale, organized activity which swept over the Persian territory creating monastic communities, stands in direct contradiction to everything we find in sources which compel us to listen.

This severe but just judgment over these ethically and esthetically low-priced fabrications, possible already on the basis of intrinsic evidence alone, is strengthened by the evidence furnished in other sources. Mār Aūgēn with all the celebrated dignitaries in his company is not known by any of the authors until the 9th century. There is no reference to them in the ancient synodical acts, liturgical documents and in other sources of historical value. Thomas of Margā, who wrote his important work on the history of monasticism in Persia and of its great heroes before the middle of the 9th century, does not know anything of these people or their activities [57]. This fact is very important because Thomas' work shows that he was well acquainted with his subject. The origination of these fabrications on the other hand, cannot have been much later since it finds attestation in the monastico-historical work of Īšōʿdenaḥ of Basrā, written in the second part of the same century. At that time Mār Aūgēn and some of his companions had already appeared on the scene, so that they could be placed at the top of the list of the founders of monasteries [58]. It seems that even at that time the whole cycle of legends was still in process of development. A hint in that direction might be the observation that Īšōʿdenaḥ's work does not yet know all the narratives. But the versified form of this work, arranged later, could add a little more at the end of the list [59]. Moreover, this fabrication continued even later [60].

57 *Book of Governors,* I.

58 *Chasteté,* p. 1 f.

59 Ms. Berl. Sach. 63, fol. 224 b includes the story of ʾEšaʿiā.

60 This seems to be the case with the legend of Jōḥannan of Kaphnā, Ms. Par. syr. 379. The legend of Mīkā is clearly a product of the 13th century, owing to its dedication to Catholicos Šemʿōn, *Acta martyrum,* III, p. 510.

Thus this large group of extensive documents, which actually are the only sources of purely monastico-historical character, must be entirely rejected. It is not understandable how, for example, Budge could make use of them, trusting that they contained an historical kernel [61]. The more closer questions concerning the origin of this cycle [62] do not belong in the scope of this work.

2. EXPANSION OF MONASTICISM

a. Anchoritism

First of all we have to answer the question where we have the earliest information about the monastic movement in Persia, i.e. in its anchoritic form.

Do Aphrahaṭ's treatises offer something? It is true that in several places Aphrahaṭ speaks of *īḥīdāiē,* 'solitaries'. Are we to understand these *īḥīdāiē* so that these were anchorites? Parisot understood them as such and rendered the term by 'solitarii', 'anachoretae' [63]. Also, Bert rendered the term by 'Einsiedler' [64]. The choice of this word really amounts to an assumption that these people were monks. Labourt also has expressed agreement [65]. The state of affairs, however, as pictured by Aphrahaṭ does not permit this assumption. A circumspect analysis of the texts does not reveal any positive particle of proof. All the texts indicate is that these *īḥīdāiē* lived in the congregations. It is safer to recognize this fact than to read too much into the texts that they do not contain. The contrary is the case. There are passages which show clearly that these *īḥīdāiē* were not anchorites. In one section *īḥīdāiē* are exhorted and admonished not to attend the banquets, to use decorated garments, perfumes, and indulge in laughter and free movement of the tongue [66]. The presence of such admonitions seems to leave no other choice than to conclude that Aphrahaṭ supposes the *īḥīdāiē*

61 *Book of Governors,* I, p. CXXV ff.

62 About these problems see LABOURT, *Christianisme,* p. 309 ff.

63 PS, I, p. LXV.

64 *Aphrahaṭ's Homilien,* p. 96, 99 f.

65 'Le mot *iḥidayē* « solitaires », qui se rencontre dans Afraaṭ peut très bien convenir aux cénobites', *Christianisme,* p. 29.

66 *Demonstrationes,* col. 272 f.

were living in the Christian communities among the ordinary believers. One passage particularly, seems to explain sufficiently the nature of this term as used in Aphrahaṭ: they are *īḥīdāiē* insofar as they renounce marriage and choose single life [67]. And the word seems to have been used as a general term.

What, then, could this result mean regarding our question? Does it mean that anchoritism at that time was not more than an insignificant movement? Or did the movement simply not belong to the sphere of interest which Aphrahaṭ wanted to address? In both cases the inference rests on no better foundation than silence.

Since Aphrahaṭ himself does not give any help, one has to look for other sources of information. There is no one which is as early as Aphrahaṭ, and therefore the questions which Aphrahaṭ does not answer remain unanswered. But the literature which comes under consideration for the decades after Aphrahaṭ's treatises were composed, speaks of monasticism as predominantly in its anchoritic form, centered in caverns, caves, clifts, crevices, hollows and rocks. Ānāhīd adopted monasticism and made a little dwelling place where she might live her ascetic life [68]. Brothers who decided to become monks sought for a place for their dwelling and selected small caves [69]. The anchorite whom Mār Mīlēṣ visited in the desert, was an *'abīlā* 'who lived in a cave alone' [70]. All these figures characterize the scope of the monastic movement as presented by these sources.

A characteristic summary statement concerning the status of monasticism at that time is given in the history of Qardag. Here the following instructive words are put into the mouth of the boasting Satan who is raging about his conversion : 'you have mean men who live on the rocks, and I have the kings and nobles of all Persia' [71]. However legendary the other features of the story are, this detail belongs to those which evoke trust, because those data are in agreement with those gathered from other reliable sources. Here monks are

67 *Ibid.*, col. 261.

68 *Acta martyrum*, II, p. 583.

69 *Ibid.*, II, p. 13.

70 *Ibid.*, II, p. 265, 268.

71 ܠܟ ܐܝܬ ܠܟ ܐܢ̈ܫܐ ܚܫܘ̈ܟܐ ܕܥܡܪܝܢ ܒܫܘ̈ܥܐ : ܘܠܝ ܕܝܢ ܐܝܬ ܠܝ ܡܠܟ̈ܐ ܘܪ̈ܘܪܒܢܐ ܕܟܠܗ ܦܪܣ *ibid.*, II, p. 468.

depicted as living in caverns, hollows, and caves [72]. Besides these sources there is a legendary document that seems to have preserved a reminiscence of the older conditions in monasticism. In the story of Behnām an episode which is highly instructive is included which describes the monastic center in Ṭūrā de Alphaph. It is told here that a great number of anchorites had gathered around this mountain and its slopes, living in caves and gorges and gullies. But even in this area where monks were settled compactly the form of anchoretism dominated almost without restriction [73].

In speaking of the scope of the early monasticism, one must include something about the travelling monks. Whatever is the value of the acts of Mīlēs for the portrait of the historical Mīlēs, the type of monk that comes closer to the spotlight is certainly not taken from the air. This type is fond of travels and journeys, even into distant lands, traversing countries and staying with fellow monks in various places. We hear of journeys to Egypt, and to different countries in Mesopotamia and Persia. These journeys brought him to the country of Bēt Rāzīqāiē we find him in a new with an anchorite who lived in the desert [74]. When his journeys brought him to the country of Bēt Rāzīqāiē we find him in a new company of monks [75].

We also have to reckon with anchorites who lived together in groups. The formation of these small groups might well have come into existence in the same way as is told in the legend of Mār Iāūnān [76].

Occasionally we hear of such a colony of anchorites mentioned in

72 ܟܕ ܡܢܗܘܢ ܒܫܘ̈ܥܐ ܥܡܪܝܢ ܗܘܘ: ܐܚܪ̈ܢܐ ܕܝܢ ܒܡܥܪ̈ܬܐ 'as some of them dwelt on the rocks, but others in caverns', *ibid.*, II, p. 429; cf. *ibid.*, II, p. 446; IV, p. 479.

73 *Ibid.*, II, p. 429.

74 ܡܫܝܢܝܐ, *ibid.*, II, p. 268.

75 ܐܚ̈ܐ, *ibid.*, p. 270.

76 ܕܥܣܪܐ ܝܚܝ̈ܕܝܐ ܐܝܬܝܗܘܢ ܬܡܢ: ܘܟܠ ܚܕ ܡܢܗܘܢ ܪܚܝܩ ܡܢ ܚܒܪܗ ܬܪܝܢ ܡܝ̈ܠܝܢ. ܘܐܬܟܢܫܘ ܐܚ̈ܐ ܛܘ̈ܒܢܐ ܘܐܡܪܘ ܕܙܕܩ ܠܢ ܠܡܒܢܐ ܩܠܝ̈ܬܐ ܒܩܘܪܒܘܬܐ ܕܚܕ̈ܕܐ 'there were ten monks there, and each one two miles far from his fellow; and the blessed brothers came together and said : « it is right for us to build cells in the neighborhood of each other »', *ibid.*, I, p. 509.

one of the ancient documents incorporated in the history of Karkā de Bēt Selōk, the metropolis of the diocese of Bēt Garmai. A lavra appears in the neighborhood of the city of Karkā. The source comes to speak of it, quite by chance, in connection with the time when the congregation in the city had to seek out a hidden place for its services : 'because of the violence of the persecution, people of small number from Karkā with a vigilant shepherd and warrior, in a lavra besides Karkā, in a place of a hamlet called Ḥāṣṣā, had made little buildings for a church and carried on secretly the sacrifice there' [77].

There is ground for the supposition that the form of ascetic life in anchoritism received new impulses which deserve a special note. For this more than one reason can be cited.

First, the contingent of the converts from the religion of Mazda and the implications connected with them, should not be underrated for their significance in this question. There are weighty arguments in the sources which throw an interesting light on this question. On the basis of these data we are shown a channel which poured new strength into the movement of monasticism.

It must be observed that the spread of the Christian faith beyond the boundaries of the Syrian element in Persia encountered a series of difficulties which put conversion to a hard test. To accept the Christian faith not only meant the loss of rights to property and possessions but also involved a readiness for far more serious consequences. What this situation actually meant is shown in an episode of Sābā Gūšnazdād. His father Šāhrīn died far from home and did not know of the apostasy of his son. Only his mother knew of this. After the death of his father became known, the brother of Šāhrīn appears on scene [78]. He makes an inquiry about the 'day of sacrifices', i.e. the ceremonies of the sacred meal on the ground of the family property, in order to invest the young man, although minor, with the authority of the representative of the family. His mother tried to make excuses that he was young and did not have the experience needed to fit in with the nobles. But as soon as the uncle heard of the real motive, that he had become a Christian, he

77 *Ibid.*, II, p 514.
78 *Ibid.*, II, p. 642 ff.

regarded himself as the legal owner of the family possessions [79]. This case shows that apostasy from Mazdaism meant the loss of rights to possessions which then went into the hands of another. How consistently this procedure has been carried through, we, of course, do not know. But we may suppose safely that the infuriated family members saw to it that this practice just described became current.

Moreover, the renunciation of Mazdaism meant much more. From a passage in the Menoikhirad [80] we can conclude that the apostate actually risked his life. According to this text he should be killed. In recognizing this the uncertainty about whether this practice was a view of the caste of the priests or whether it was a principle of the juridical norms of the Sassanide empire, is really not so important. In each case there were jealous forces keeping watch that the ancestral traditions did not suffer harm. What means were in use can be seen in the story of Sābā Gūšnazdād. In his rage, the uncle ordered him to be imprisoned. And when all his attempts to change his mind did not help, he submitted him to beating and torture [81].

Under such circumstances it becomes understandable that the conversion also meant decision to leave home, family and relatives. The same necessity is also reflected in the advice given to persons in danger. This advice, for instance, comes from the lips of an ascetic Narsai : to leave the community [82].

As the sources show, such a drastic decision often led one directly into monasticism. It is remarkable how the conversions from Mazdaism told of in our sources turn out as entries into anchoretism. When Jazdīn was attracted by Christian teachings and practices,

79 In his letter he says that Sābā has become a Christian and therefore he loses the heritage of his parents, *ibid.*, p. 649.

The ancient laws of the Persians do not regulate this matter clearly. There is a stipulation regarding the property of a 'sorcerer' to the effect that the property of such person may go over to the witnesses, if it cannot be proved that the 'sorcerer' had caused damage to the accuser, *Mātīkān*, II, p. 547. Other rules regarding the confiscation of the property of those teaching heresy or of those who adopt heretical teachings, state that their possessions go over to the government, *ibid.*, II, p. 549.

80 *Menoikhirad*, XV, 25.

81 *Acta martyrum*, II, p. 646.

82 *Ibid.*, IV, p. 172.

he left his home and fled to the country of Bēt Garmai in order to be baptized there. His next step was to make a cell for himself and devote his life to monasticism [83].

The case with Ānāhīd, the daughter of Ādhur-Hormizd, who was a mobadh, is the same. When she was attracted to the Christian faith, she left her home. For a while the believers hid her. Later she made a little cell in the vicinity of the cell of the monk named Petiōn, 'and lived in it in chastity of the noble manners' [84].

A double evidence is offered in the story of Gūšnazdād. After the baptism, in which he received a new name, Sābā, according to the name of the priest who baptized him, he adopted monasticism. His mother, who also had inclinations towards Christianity, received baptism and abandoned her home and became a nun [85]. Sābā himself went forth and after spending two years in a school, he started his life as an anchorite in Bēt Šardā, near the river of Sīnī [86].

In conclusion, this chain-reaction — an awakening towards the Christian truth, leaving one's home, baptism and entrance into anchoretism — echoed in our sources indeed reflects a factor of which the importance cannot be underrated.

The observation just made is not the only one which induces us to suppose that monasticism in this period had received new impulses from circumstances not directly related to it.

A factor which certainly must be taken into account is the new policy taken by Shahpuhr II which evoked the era of persecutions. As the Christians acted in Ḥadiab, seeking refuge in hiding themselves in the mountains [87], so they acted in other places, too [88]. It

83 *Ibid.*, I, p. 564.

84 *Ibid.*, II, p. 585.

85 *Ibid.*, II, p. 650.

86 *Ibid*,. II, p. 650 f.

87 *Sources syriaques*, p. 59.

88 *Եւ էին Հաւատով քրիստոնեայք ի Թագստի ի միում տեղւոջ ուսուցանէին զորս գային առ նոսա զբանն կենաց: Եւ ոմանք ի կրապաշտից մատնեցին զնոսա առ Սաբուռիոս արքայն, և տարեալ կացուցին առաջի*, 'they (i.e. Akindos, Pigatos and Anemphotistos) were Christians by faith, and lived in a hidden place where they instructed the word of life to those who came to find them; some worshippers of the fire denounced them to the King Shahpuhr and brought them before him', *Synaxaire armé-*

is conceivable that when they could return to their homes after the acute danger was over or was lessened, there were those who preferred to remain in the hermitage, to lead a quiet, solitary life. The ascetics in the congregations, the *benai* and *benat qeiāmā*, left their communities and did the same [89]. The collector of the earliest collection of acts makes a summary of these experiences when he says : 'the holy *qeiāmā* was scattered in (many) places and was thrown into the *'aksenaiā* (= 'living abroad', 'travelling', 'the life of an anchorite') ' [90]. These conditions most probably added to the strength of monasticism by compelling the ascetics and other believers to leave their communities and to look for places in the wilderness where they would be less disturbed or completely undisturbed. Mār 'Aqeblāhā, who later became bishop of Karkā de Bēt Selōk, and who belongs to the period of Shahpuhr II, belonged to a noble family. It is reported that his father was a high official in the court of the king. But when the situation of Christianity became critical and his father forsook the Christian faith and worshipped fire, 'Aqeblāhā decided to keep his faith, and he left his home and turned to monasticism [91].

At least some remarks should be made about the cases in which the places where Christians gave their witness and their lives eventually played a part in the decision of those who left the world in order to make their dwelling place close to these sacred spots. An example like that of Mār 'Abdīšo' who decided to stay

nien, XV, p. 408. A very instructive episode is found in the life story of Narsai. When the persecutions broke out he was in a school of children in the village of 'Ain Dūlbā. It is reported that the teacher led his group into the mountains and remained with his pupils there during the persecutions, BARḤADBEŠABBA, *Histoire*, II, p. 595.

89 We hear that during the martyrdom of Aitallāha in a village of Bēt Nūhadrā there were many ascetics who hid themselves there. The Syriac text has left this out, but it stood in the form which underlies the Greek version of it : ἦσαν γὰρ πολλοὶ ἀσκηταὶ κεκρυμμένοι ἐκεῖ, *Versions grecques des actes*, p. 516, 533.

90 ܘܩܝܡܐ ܩܕܝܫܐ ܒܐܬܪ̈ܘܬܐ ܐܬܒܕܪ ܘܐܫܬܕܝ ܒܐܟܣܢܝܐ *Acta martyrum*, II, p. 104.

91 ܗܘ ܕܝܢ ܛܘܒܢܐ ܐܪܦ ܒܝܬ ܐܒܗ̈ܘܗܝ : ܘܢܦܩ ܠܐܟܣܢܝܐ 'but he, the blessed, left his parents' house and went out into the *'āksenaiā'* (living abroad, travelling, the life of an anchorite) ', *ibid.*, II, p. 515.

near the cave which concealed the bodies of the martyrs [92], could not have been rare in the atmosphere of heightened enthusiasm.

Before this chapter can be concluded another question has to be touched upon. It is a factor which, although in a limited way, nevertheless, has had a hand in the development and growth of Syrian monasticism in Persia. This is the place to consider the question of whether monasticism in Persia received some strength from outside.

Here naturally the monasticism of the Eastern provinces of the Byzantine empire comes under consideration. So far as one is able to see, there has always been a contact between the spiritual forces in Mesopotamia and Persia. Along the channels through which the communication lines ran from one Christianity to another, spiritual goods were interchanged and monastic movements also received some strength [93]. This fact can be taken for granted. However, the sources do not furnish us with direct information as to how much monasticism in Persia benefited from this process of giving and receiving.

In fact, something of this has been kept in the memory of the tradition. This something concerns the reign of the Emperor Julian and the monastic infiltration from the Byzantine area to Persia. The troubled times, the feeling of insecurity and even occasional violence which took place under Julian's rule did not leave monasticism untouched. It happened that sometimes monks were brought to consider leaving the troubled area in order to go to Persia.

If the sources do not deceive us, we can speak of an occasional emigration of monks from the Western territories into Persia. A reminiscence of this seems to have been preserved by the story of Behnām and Sarā. Here one episode tells how Mār Mattai along with other monks left his monastery and decided to go over the boundary into Persian territory. That move took place under Julian's rule. In Persia they settled down in the district of Ninive. As their first place of settlement Mār Mattai and his fellow monks selected a high mountain far from human settlements [94]. Such cases might

92 *Ibid.*, II, p. 322.

93 Ms. Sin. syr. 14, fol. 171 b seems to make an allusion to the relations that existed between Edessa and Nisibis.

94 *Acta martyrum*, II, p. 400 f. There are other traditions of similar nature which have left traces in the sources. A monk Beniamīn, who was killed under

help to explain the exaggerated ideas about the suffering of Christians under Julian that circulated among the Christians in Persia.

Further, not only through peaceful ways did asceticism in Persia receive increase in numbers and in strength from the Western countries. The violent measures should not be discarded in the treatment of this question.

The military expeditions of Shahpuhr intensified the flood of deported captives to Persia. His first raids into Mesopotamia show that under his rule, too, the Persians knew how to evaluate not only gold and other precious spoil, but also human beings [95]. It happened again and again that later excursions penetrated deeper into the heart of the Eastern provinces of the Byzantine empire. These military expeditions in the West brought thousands of Christians to Persia, and in these caravans marched also ascetics and monks. Concerning these captives from the fort Bēt Zabdai, captured in the 53rd year of Shahpuhr's rule (361/2), we have an explicit report that among the clergy and faithful, also ascetics had their place [96]. And in the early documents we have direct information about ascetics [97] and monks [98] who were brought as captives from their home country and continued their practices in Persia.

Thus these contingents of captives from the Western territories did not only import new skilled workers and transplant new industries of brocade and silkwares but also poured compact groups of Christians into Persia. Around the new sacral edifices which the exiles built, they founded colonies strong enough to preserve their own traditions [99]. And when ancient centers of Persian Christianity remained relatively insignificant, Istakhr, Ardashēr-Khvarreh and

Shahpuhr's persecutions, is reported to have received ordination from Barsē, bishop of Edessa, Ms. Br. Mus. Add. 12,174, fol. 392 a, cf. fol. 389 b. Traditions of the same kind appear also in Ms. Vat. syr. 472, fol. 121 b. A trace is found also in *Synaxaire arménien*, XV, p. 408.

95 A valuable eyewitness report gives a graphic picture of these events at Amid in the year 359 and at Šīggār in 360, AMMIANUS, *Rerum gestarum libri*, XX, 6 . 7, I, p. 195 ff.

96 *Acta martyrum*, II, p. 317.

97 In the Acta of martyrdom of Pōsī, *ibid.*, II, p. 230 f; *Passio S. Martyris Iae*, *Versions grecques des actes*, p. 461 ff.

98 Ms. Šarf. Patr. 38, fol. 152 a.

99 VÖÖBUS, *Studies*, p. 28 ff.

Bih Shahpuhr grew so prominent from the deportations that they were made bishoprics — an unwillingly made contribution from the Persian rulers to the Persian Christianity. It may be safely assumed that through these deportations ascetic movements also received certain strength.

b. Coenobitism

Much more seldom do we hear of the monks in the coenobitic life and of their monastic establishments. But this information which we have, in its substance, we owe to documents with credentials.

One of the salient questions which comes to the fore, is whether Aphrahaṭ in his time could know anything about the existence of coenobitism. This question is not difficult to answer and should not detain us long. Certainly, the word for monastery *daírā* occurs in Aphrahaṭ's treatises, but it is used only in its primitive meaning. It appears with the connotation of sheepfold or habitation and not in the technical sense of 'monastery' which it had in later terminology. If strong probability, opposed by no known facts, is to guide us, then we have to conclude that at Aphrahaṭ's time coenobitism was only in its beginnings. Otherwise it is not easy to cope with the silence about the convents in the treatises of Aphrahaṭ. This can be said confidently since there are other evidences which we already know and which corroborate this judgment.

Similar evidence regarding the coenobitic form of life and of monasteries also appears in the documents which are the earliest among the ancient acts of martyrdom. The most noteworthy is the wording regarding the outbreak of the persecutions and their aims : 'the king Shahpuhr of the Persians began to distress [100] the people of Christians, and to press and to persecute the priests and the *qeíāmā* and to uproot the churches of his whole realm' [101]. The absence of the monasteries is more than apparent.

100 Another Ms. reads 'to trace', 'to seek out'.

101 ܫܪܝ ܫܒܘܪ ܡܠܟܐ ܕܦܪ̈ܣܝܐ ܠܡܥܩܘ ܠܥܡܐ ܕܟܪ̈ܣܛܝܢܐ ܘܠܡܐܠܨܘ ܘܠܡܪܕܦܘ ܠܟܗ̈ܢܐ ܘܠܩܝܡܐ : ܘܠܡܥܩܪ ܥܕ̈ܬܐ ܕܒܟܠܗ ܐܘܚܕܢܗ *Acta martyrum*, II, p. 132.

Among the acts of martyrdom there are those which claim that already in the 18th year of Shahpuhr's rule monasteries were destroyed [102]. This information has been repeated in other sources [103]. But these texts must be disqualified as texts not trustworthy [104].

The earliest references to the existence of the coenobitic form in the periphery of the monastic movement in Persia have come down to us in some acts of martyrdom which belong to the earliest documents of this kind we have in our possession. Far from being sufficient, yet they help us to orientate ourselves so that we are not quite lost in the problem of approximating the time of the appearance and the character of this branch of the monastic movement.

First a mention should be made of an abbot who appears in the acts of martyrdom of the prisoners captured in Bēt Zabdai, in the Roman area, in the year 362/3. In connection with the bodies of the martyrs, hidden in a cavern, an abbot is mentioned, who took care of the remnants. He took them out from the temporary place in a cavern and laid them in a martyrion which he built for this purpose [105]. Besides this fact nothing is said about his monastery, its size or its place. Even his name has not survived.

Two other documents come to our aid and this time with richer data. These are particularly valuable in view of the fact that in this question many important lines of investigation have been closed to us.

Although the acts of martyrdom of Baršabiā, the abbot, have unfortunately no exact dating except for their connexion with the martyrdom of Mār Mīlēs, they belong to a cycle of very ancient origin, dealing with the events which took place in the first years of the persecution under Shahpuhr II.

These acts tell us of Baršabiā who was the head of a monastery located in Phārs. His biographical data are very meager. About his monastery we learn that it was not far from Istakhr and that this place also had been engaged in Christian propaganda and become a center for recruiting the Persians from their religion. This activity disturbed the Magi. At least we infer this from the

102 *Ibid.*, p. 39.
103 Ms. Ming. syr. 47, fol. 46 a.
104 See pag. 235.
105 *Acta martyrum*, II, p. 324.

accusations brought against Baršabiā and his community. We also learn that this monastery was very small giving place to only 10 monks called 'brothers' : 'at the same time that blessed Mīlēs was crowned, an abbot was in the country of Phārs, whose name was Baršabiā; and he dwelt in the monastery and with him ten disciples'[106].

Thus before us stands one of the earliest and most important reports on the monastic community in the Persian territory. Among other data the size of the community is most conspicuous.

New and trustworthy information comes from another source of similar origin. A document which tells us of the events which took place in the year 376/7, unfolds the fate of a monastic community in Bēt Hūzāiē during these stormy years, only a few years before Shahpuhr's death. In this document, every detail is important to us. In this source even some biographical data are given about the abbot. Badmā, the head of this community, was from Bēt Hūzāiē. He was a man who once belonged to a wealthy and wellknown family in Bēt Lāphāṭ. But he had renounced the world with the intention of becoming a monk. He had built a monastery and established his own community there. We hear that it was situated outside his home-town Bēt Lāphāṭ : 'and when he became a convert, he gave all he had to the poor and went out and built for himself a monastery outside the city and dwelt there'[107]. We hear also something about the spiritual life of the monastery. We are told that this monastery became a place of severe asceticism, particularly in fasting and vigils as well as in spiritual exercises[108]. The community under Badmā's leadership consisted of seven monks who were called 'brothers'[109].

In the Syriac text the relationship between the monks and the abbot Badmā is tacitly presumed, but the Greek recension having

106 ܒܗ ܒܙܒܢܐ ܗܘ ܕܡܝܠܣ ܛܘܒܢܐ ܐܬܟܠܠ: ܪܝܫ ܕܝܪܐ ܚܕ ܐܝܬ ܗܘܐ ܒܐܬܪܐ ܕܦܪܣ: ܕܫܡܗ ܗܘܐ ܒܪܫܒܝܐ. ܘܝܬܒ ܗܘܐ ܒܕܝܪܐ: ܘܥܡܗ ܥܣܪܐ ܬܠܡܝܕܘܗܝ، *ibid.*, II, p. 281.

107 ܘܟܕ ܐܬܬܠܡܕ ܗܘܐ: ܝܗܒ ܗܘܐ ܟܠܡܕܡ ܕܐܝܬ ܠܗ ܠܡܣܟܢܐ: ܘܢܦܩ ܘܒܢܐ ܠܗ ܕܝܪܐ ܠܒܪ ܡܢ ܡܕܝܢܬܐ: ܘܝܬܒ ܗܘܐ ܒܗ *ibid.*, II, p. 347.

108 *Ibid.*, p. 348.

109 ܐܚܐ, *ibid.*, p. 349, 351.

preserved a line at the beginning makes it expressly clear that they belonged to Badmā's monastery [110]. Probably the original Syriac text somehow lost this line.

This information in the acts of Badmā about the presence of the monasteries in Persia in the period in question is not new any longer, but we appreciate it as an additional evidence relating to our problem. In another respect the information given by this document is particularly valuable. The text tells us about the size of the monastic community, and again we read that it was very small.

What consequences does this, that we have in these documents, carry for the history of coenobitism?

This last information concerning the size of the monasteries, information which goes hand in hand with that found in the previous source, catches our attention. Are we permitted to conclude that at that time the coenobitic movement must have been limited in its strength, being able to establish only small communities and monasteries? It would be somewhat hazardous to draw this conclusion on the basis of this evidence alone if we had no other information or indications to enlarge the bulk of the evidence. A conclusion like this stands in need of supporting evidence.

Owing to the absence of further direct information we have to make recourse to the indirect information available, which, as it seems, has something to say about our question. The lack of fully trustworthy documents is compensated for by a number of sources the value of which cannot be tested.

In the first place the story of Mār Mūʿaīn, a source highly interesting in many respects, helps us a step further. It is certain that this document was written later, but it is also certain that it has embedded older traditions. In this case the activity of Mār Mūʿaīn as a renowned promoter of coenobitic monasticism or at least the nature of activities described here may have a historical kernel.

The document in question depicts Mār Mūʿaīn as a founder of

110 συνελήφθη ὁ ἅγιος Βάδημος ὁ ἀρχιμανδρίτης σὺν μαθηταῖς αὐτοῦ τισιν ἑπτὰ, *Versions grecques des actes*, p. 473; see also *Synaxaire arménien*, XXI, p. 252 f.

monasteries under Shahpuhr II in the environment of Šīggār. We do not need to trust the boasting that Mār Mū'aīn had created many dozens of monasteries [111]. But something becomes vocal in this tradition, something which certainly cannot be dismissed. Such a tradition must have reckoned only with very small monasteries.

Still another source is at our disposal. Its character and form should not entirely disqualify it from being consulted for our particular question. This is the story of Behnām and Sarā. We do not intend to trust much of what is told about these children of Sanḥīrīb, but in this legendary document strata of different quality seem to have preserved a reminiscence of early conditions whether by local tradition of the monastery or whether through older sources. It is remarkable and instructive when this story inserts an episode which describes a monastic center around the Ṭūrā de Alphaph. Around this mount a great number of monks had gathered preferring — as we have already seen — anchoritism. Even in such a group which had possibilities for different developments the coenobitic monasticism found only limited support and interest. Only very small communities could be established. This source says expressly that the monasteries which were built here were very small, using the term 'monastery' in its diminutive form [112]. If this tradition is true then it can tell us very much. This says that even in compact groups where many monks lived in the same area along the slopes of the mountain, their needs were satisfied with the foundation of only small monasteries.

Yet another factor comes into consideration relative to the smallness of the monasteries extant in Persia. This is something which was caused by the nature of the environment in which they were situated. This fact is mentioned explicitly in a document which claims to be from the pen of Catholicos Papā. Though this pretentious claim must be forthrightly dismissed, some church historical

111 Ms. Br. Mus. Add. 12, 174, fol. 393 a speaks of 96 monasteries and prayer-houses.

112 ܘܐܚܪ̈ܢܐ ܒܢܝܢ ܗܘܘ ܠܗܘܢ ܕܝܪ̈ܘܢܝܬܐ ܐܘ ܚܒܫܬ ܓܙܪ̈ܐ ܘܝܬܒܝܢ ܗܘܘ 'and others built for themselves little convents or enclosures and dwelt (there)', *Acta martyrum*, II, p. 429. It is noteworthy that the phenomenon of the midget monasteries manifests itself also in other hagiographical literature, cf. Ms. Vat. syr. 126, fol. 51 b.

information contained therein, deserves our attention. In this, *inter alia,* the author speaks of the smallness of the ecclesiastical buildings and he explains the matter in the following way : 'and not because we are lazy and idle to build, but because the envy of the pagans at great buildings might come upon us, and the *tūlmādā* of the Christians might then suffer in view of the danger of persecution that hangs over us' [113].

Finally a certain idea about the sporadic character of these establishments is given by some general reports which offer a quick survey of sufferings under Shahpuhr. The situation is clear in the earliest acts of martyrdom in which destruction of churches is mentioned but not monasteries [114]. The first treatise of the ancient collection of the acts of martyrdom, which presents a longer enumeration of deeds which agonized the Christian heart, describes how congregations are without leaders, the altars destroyed, the clergy and ascetics killed, others dispersed, sacred books torn, churches destroyed etc. But there is no remark about the monasteries [115]. In their smallness these monastic establishments were not deemed worthy to be included in this dossier.

So far as we are permitted to see, indeed, we find attestation to the same observation that coenobitic monasticism at that time must have been able to produce only small monasteries, with small communities that naturally must have been more or less of ephemeral character.

3. SUFFERINGS

a. Outbreak of the persecutions

Christianity, including ascetic movements, had peaceful opportunities of which it took advantage, and grew without any dis-

113 ܘܠܐ ܡܛܠ ܕܐܬܚܝܢ ܚܝܢܐ ܘܡܦܫܠܝܢܐ ܡܢ ܒܢܝܢܐ ܡܛܠ ܕܠܐ ܢܚܡܠ ܥܠܝܢ ܚܣܡܐ ܕܚܢܦܐ ܒܗ̇ ܒܢܝܢܐ ܪܘܪܒܐ. ܘܡܬܚܒܪ ܬܘܠܡܕܐ ܕܟܪܝܣܛܝܢܐ ܒܡܣܬܢܝܢܘܬܗ ܕܪܕܘܦܝܐ ܕܡܣܝܡ ܥܠܝܢ Ms. Vat. Borg. syr. 82, fol. 115 b. The term *tūlmādā* means 'discipline', 'instruction', 'discipleship'.

114 See particularly a report of the catastrophe which befell Christians at the time of martyrdom of Barbaʿšmīn, *Acta martyrum,* II, p. 304.

115 *Ibid.,* II, p. 104.

turbance from outside, until one day Shahpuhr's eyes were opened [116] to the seriousness of this growth [117]. For his grandiose plans regarding the consolidation of his empire [118], the recognition of this obstacle must have appeared insidious. His counter-measures inaugurated the way of the cross for the Christians in which the ascetics had to bear an important part of the brunt of the attack. This state of affairs makes it necessary for us to take a look at the fate of asceticism in this trial.

The beginning of the persecutions under Shahpuhr II is beset with complicated problems. Some acts of martyrdom tell of the hostilities and violence that had already been initiated in the first decades of his rule.

In the acts of Zebīnā and his companions the persecution had taken place by the eighteenth year of Shahpuhr's rule, i.e. 327/8 A.D. : 'in the 18th year [119] of the rule of Shahpuhr the King of Persians there was carried out a great persecution of the church of Christ so that even the churches were pulled down and the altars demolished and monasteries burnt by fire' [120]. Regarding this date the manuscript tradition is unanimous [121]. This document claims to have been written by an eyewitness, 'Ešaʿiā bar Ḥaddābō, an officer in the royal guard. It has been accepted on face value as historically reliable [122].

This strong claim, supported by such ostentatiously splendid credentials, however, does not remove strong suspicions which emerge against its trustworthiness. The reason is this that not only were there acts unknown to the collector of the oldest acts [123], but in

116 Firdausī, *Šāhnamā*, V, p. 449.

117 Ms. Sin. syr. 24, fol. 200 b.

118 Christensen, *L'Iran*, p. 234 ff., 250 ff.

119 *Acta martyrum orientalium*, I, p. 39.

120 *Acta martyrum*, II, p. 39.

121 Ms. Br. Mus. Add. 14,654, fol. 5 b ff. belongs to the 5th or 6th century. Ms. Ming. syr. 47, fol. 46 a ff. and Ms. Berl. orient. oct. 1256, fol. 646 b ff. are of late date. Besides these codices, not used by Assemani and Bedjan, also the Greek version has the same date, *Versions grecques des actes*, p. 421.

122 Braun, *Ausgewählte Akten*, p. viii.

123 Besides this in the first treatise the collector says explicitly that the persecution began in the 30th — according to another manuscript in the 31st

addition, these acts appear to have been composed or revised not in Persia but in Edessa [124]. Thus here we call a letter of Constantine to witness. The conditions in Persia must have been very favorable to Christianity for ca 330 he felt it necessary to thank Shahpuhr by letter for his benevolence towards the Christians [125]. And a pastorale about the faith, written by Aitallāhā, bishop of Edessa [126], composed between the years 325 and 337 [127], would be another witness. Aitallāhā hardly would have omitted mentioning the sufferings had they taken place.

Of other documents, which place the beginning of the persecutions in earlier times [128], even before the end of the first decade [129], the same must be said.

Despite the expansion of Christian influence in the communities, in the deserts and mountains no measure was undertaken to curtail it. Obviously the political constellation demanded caution as long as the *defensor fidei*, Constantine, occupied his throne in the West. So his fame was able to protect his fellow-believers even beyond the eastern frontiers of his realm.

Upon Constantine's death the obstacle to realization of aspirations, for which Shahpuhr had been pressed from various sides was removed.

The first phase of the conflict did not extend to violent and bloody measures. According to the acts of martyrdom of Šemʿōn bar Ṣabbāʿē, the era of sufferings was inaugurated by an edict which subjected the Christians to financial penalties and other vexations [130],

— year and ended in the 70th year of Shahpuhr's rule, *Acta martyrum*, II, p. 293.

124 BAUMSTARK, *Geschichte syr. Literatur*, p. 55.

125 EUSEBIUS, *Vita Constantini*, IV, 8 . 9, p. 120 f.

126 *Aithallae epistula*, p. 19 ff.

127 See about these problems the chapter 'Aitallaha und sein Schreiben', VÖÖBUS, *Neue Angaben über textgesch. Zustände in Edessa*, p. 16 ff.

128 The acts of Gūbarlāhā and Qāzō, *Acta martyrum*, IV, p. 141 ff. place the martyrdom in the 23th year of Shahpuhr's rule (= 331 A.D.), cf. p. 162. But this legendary composition cannot be earlier than the 6th century, on internal grounds.

129 According to the Acts of Ṣulṭān Mahdōk the violence started already in the 9th year of Shahpuhr's rule (= 317), *ibid.*, II, p. 3. But the interest in legends has been so allpervading that it makes it difficult to trust anything in it.

130 *Martyrium Simeonis*, col. 727 ff.

but did not promulgate violent means against the Christians and their institutions.

Thus the first phase in the change of Persian policy towards the Christians is characterized by excessive demands for the benefit of the treasury [131]. It is difficult to say whether this was only a pretext, or whether Shahpuhr really needed subsidiary sources for his military operations against Byzantium. The beginning of this phase took place according to the acts of Šemʿōn bar Ṣabbāʿē in the 31st year of Shahpuhr, i.e. between September 5, 339 and September 4, 340 [132]. Further, it did not, most probably, occur during the first part of that period so that the year 339 is rather unlikely.

According to the chronicle of Seert, monasticism was immediately involved in the first measures taken for the purpose of applying pressure to Christianity. The first demands given by the king to Šemʿōn, who appeared before him, were these : 'to impose a tribute per capita on monks living in the monasteries, to double the tax payed by the believers, and to bring to the king the contributions for the gardens of land...' [133].

The reference to the monks appears only in this source. The question arises whether this is merely an increment or something which may rest on a trustworthy tradition. On the one hand one would be reserved to the information given in a late chronicle,

131 Sozomenus describes these measures saying : *πλεισθεὶς δὲ ταῖς διαβολαῖς ὁ Σαβώρης, τὰ μὲν πρῶτα φόροις ἀμέτροις ἐπέτριβε τοὺς Χριστιανούς*, *Hist. eccl.*, II, 9, col. 956.

132 Concerning the chronology the sources disagree. This discrepancy reaches back even into the oldest acts of martyrdom of Šemʿōn. This source reports that the edict was issued in the 117th year of the rule of the Sassanids and in the 31st year of the rule of Shahpuhr II, *Martyrium Simeonis*, col. 727. The last date would be the year between Sept. 5, 339 — Sept. 4, 340 A.D. But this date does not harmonize with the 117th year of the rule of the Sassanids. The beginning of this rule is officially acknowledged to be the year March 30, 224 — March 29, 225 A.D., see LEWY, *Calendrier perse*, p. 45 ff. In this case the date would be 341 or 342 A.D. In such a confused situation we are fortunate to have Aphrahaṭ whose testimony comes to our aid. He confirms the first date.

133 طالبه ان يوظف الجزية على الرهبان المتصوفين فى الاعمار ويضاعف الطبقلت على المومنين ٫ وان يحمل الاموال الى الملك عن طساسيج كور *Histoire nestorienne*, IV, p. 300.

while on the other hand the demand itself which in substance also involved ascetics does not seem to be out of the question. In fact the acts of martyrdom of Šemʿōn and other sources tell us that the matter of the tax was brought up, and all the sources agree here, and so, too, in this that Šemʿōn did not accept any additional obligation, under the motivation that Christians are poor [134]. Thus in this matter of increased tax as the price for more serious consequences, we stand on historical ground. Further, such an increase would easily implicate those who lived the ascetic life and were unable to fulfil their obligations to the state. One does not see any escape from this assumption if one pays sufficent attention to the annoyed feelings of the Mazdean communities against those who, in their judgment, did not belong to the divinely determined process of life in the work and the society [135] of state. However this was, the term 'monasteries' at that time usually could not mean more than hermitages of the anchorites.

With respect to development of the events which followed, the sources are in such a condition that they leave room for different interpretations. At the same time, it must also be said that a number of more or less detailed references help us to get a general idea of the events which succeeded—as appears obvious—in rapid sequence.

After Šemʿōn's refusal, a new order was issued by Shahpuhr from Karkā de Ledān. This was a direct answer to the resistance of the head of the church and as a counteraction designed to break his obstinate attitude and salvage the offended prestige of the monarch : to arrest the head of the church and two dignitaries of his clergy and send them to Shahpuhr to be judged by himself. Everything points to the fact that, with this decree, there was appended an order to destroy the sacred buildings of the Christians [136].

The mob did not wait for this to be said a second time, but took

134 Only Mārī in one passage leaves the impression that Šemʿōn agreed to this, *De patriarchis,* p. 17, 15. But here something must be wrong with the text, because the same source reports immediately Šemʿōn saying : 'I am no taxcollector, but a shepherd of the Lord's flock'.

135 See pag. 256.

136 *Acta martyrum,* II, p. 148. See also an episode with the destruction of the cathedral which confirms this *Martyrium Simeonis,* col. 742.

the opportunity, indulging in vicious excesses under the cover of the legal authority. With these instructions, the way was opened for the rage which mounted swiftly against the clergy, and particularly ascetics. As a result, this second edict inaugurated an epoch of violence and persecution which deeply involved also the ascetic movements.

The exact wording of these instructions has not survived, and we have to use some indirect indications in our sources to get the gist of it. A prayer, in particular put into the mouth of Šem'ōn bar Ṣabbā'ē permits certain inferences. Although it appears only in one recension of his acts, it deserves our interest : 'give me this that I do not live and see Thy churches destroyed, Thy altars overthrown, Thy sacred books torn, Thy service devastated and mocked, Thy sacrifices trodden (under feet), Thy *qeiāmā* pressed and vexed in all places'[137]. Thus ascetics were already involved in the first measures[138].

Now, the affairs rapidly developed into a bloody drama. Concerning the exact day when the first victim fell, in the person of Šem'ōn, we are in a hopeless situation, since the fixed date of 14th of Nīsān, Good Friday, as it appears in all the Syriac and Armenian sources, offers us more pious romanticism than history[139]. But the year given by the acts as the 31st of the rule of Shahpuhr, i.e. 340

137 ܗܒܠܝ ܕܬܗܒ ܠܐ ܐܚܐ ܒܒܢܝܬܗ ܕܥܒܕܟ. ܗܕܐ ܕܠܐ ܐܚܐ ܘܐܚܙܐ ܥܕ̈ܬܟ ܕܚܪ̈ܒܢ : ܘܡܕܒ̈ܚܝܟ ܕܡܬܗܦܟܝܢ : ܘܟܬ̈ܒܝܟ ܡܩ̈ܕܫܐ ܕܡܬܨܪܝܢ : ܘܬܫܡܫܬܟ ܕܒܙܝܙܐ ܘܡܬܒܙܚܐ : ܘܕ̈ܒܚܝܟ ܕܕܝܫܝܢ : ܘܩܝܡܟ ܕܐܠܝܨ ܘܡܬܥܩ ܒܟܠ ܐܬܪ̈ܘܬܐ *Acta martyrum*, II, p. 182.

138 See the Acts of Jāūnān and Berīkīšō' which probably belong to this period, *ibid.*, II, p. 39.

In another source which calls for watchfulness as far as its chronological data are involved, the target of the persecution is delineated as 'the priests and the *qeiāmā*', Ms. Ming. syr. 47, fol. 47 a.

139 Besides the 14th of Nīsān the sources know not only the 13th and the 15th. The synaxarium of Sirmond offers the 17th, *Synaxarium Constantinop.*, col. 607, which date was not unknown even in Syriac, since a Syriac codex refers to this in its colophon. The Slavonic tradition has the same 17th but in March, *Annus ecclesiasticus*, p. 91. Ms. Vat. syr. 20, fol. 202 b states that the day of martyrdom was the 17th. However, the most popular commemoration day was the 14th of Nīsān, Ms. Vat. syr. 69, fol. 251 a.

A.D.[140], regardless of some difficulties of synchronism in the same source[141] seems to be less problematical than has been supposed[142]. The more so because Aphrahaṭ here comes to our aid[143]. Beyond these remarks, further discussions do not belong to the scope of this study.

Šem'ōn's stand, unbreakable even in death, invited savagery in Shahpuhr. This became the beginning of the bloody phase in this developing drama, a catastrophe which came over the Persian Christianity. The infuriated monarch ordered a general massacre of Christians in Bēt Hūzāiē. This slaughter began in Karkā de Ledān and spread throughout the province. According to the acts of the martyrdom of Āzād the edict ordered 'that everyone who says that I am a Christian' was subject to torment[144].

After the first outbursts and excesses which went out beyond the control of the officials and assumed wild forms, revealing an eager response on the part of the population, a number of new supplementary instructions and regulations were issued. By a clause regarding spiritual leadership in these new formulations, the ascetics were also marked out as the target. In the acts of Āzād, Shahpuhr's

140 In some sources the year of Šem'ōn's martyrdom is given as 655 A.G. = 344 A.D., Ms. Vat. syr. 83, fol. 437 a.

141 See pag. 237.

142 According to Kmosko the bloody persecution did not began before the year 344 to which he placed Šem'ōn's martyrdom. This is a result of a hazardous undertaking since it is based on the presumption that the tradition is right regarding the day of martyrdom. In the year 344 the Easter fell on the 16th of Nīsān, KMOSKO, *Martyrium Simeonis*, col. 704 f. However this view does not stand scrutiny, see PEETERS, *Date du martyre de S. Syméon*, p. 132 ff. Besides the general considerations the year 344 cannot be taken into account because preparations for important military operations could not permit the king to stay in his residence in Karkā de Ledān, but must have taken up his attention in the military camps along the Tigris. The battle of Šīggār, directed by Shahpuhr himself, fell in this year, see JULIANUS, *Opera*, p. 32 who places this in the 6th year before the murder of Constans. This is supported by PHILOSTORGIUS, *Hist. eccl.*, p. 213. Furthermore, Julian reports that the battle took place in summer, *op. cit.*, p. 28.

143 At the end of his last homily Aphrahaṭ makes an explicit statement that the destruction of the churches started in the year 340, *Demonstrationes*, II, col. 149.

144 *Acta martyrum*, II, p. 248.

order is mentioned with this point : 'that the slaughter shall not run by the will of everybody, but from now shall involve those who are qualified as 'a teacher of that way (religion)'[145].

b. The development in different countries

We possess a number of documents which show how greatly asceticism and monasticism were enveloped by the long arm of Shahpuhr's persecutions. These are furnished with more or less detailed information. On the basis of these we do not have as complete a picture as we would prefer, but they illuminate a number of episodes which permit us to form an idea of the fate of ascetics and monks in these stormy times. In the following, we will let them tell of the happenings as they took place in the different provinces.

Bēt Hūzāiē

Šemʿōn's martyrdom in Karkā de Ledān developed into a large scale persecution. Shahpuhr at that time resided in that city and his presence made the enforcement of the decree extremely severe. It was extended to the province of the same name[146].

Further, the story of the 'Great Slaughter' in Bēt Hūzāiē, a document which belonged to the ancient collection of acts, seems to tell us that the rage of the population was particularly directed against the ascetics. Namely this source informs about the victims arrested in various places. Among clerics, ascetics of both sexes in a great number were arrested : '*benai qeiāmā, meqadšē,* and also holy women and *benat qeiāmā*'[147]. The same source adds that, this time, the majority belonged to the lay-people, captured in the provinces and brought to the royal residence, allegedly as ascetics. This remark arrests our steps. It means that in the very first outbursts of hatred, the ascetics became a particular target.

145 ܡܠܦܢܐ ܗܘ ܕܐܘܪܚܐ ܗܕܐ, *ibid.*, II, p. 253; see also Sozomenus, *Hist. eccl.*, II, 11, col. 964.

146 Marquart, *Eranšahr*, p. 1945.

147 ܘܒ̈ܢܝ ܩܝܡܐ ܘܡܩܕ̈ܫܐ : ܘܐܦ ܢܫ̈ܐ ܩܕ̈ܝܫܬܐ ܘܒ̈ܢܬ ܩܝܡܐ *Acta martyrum*, II, p. 241.

Shahpuhr's demands that they worship the sun were answered by the testimony that in dying they will live, and so these masses were brought out of the city. In this tumultuous slaughter which followed, no one knew the number of its victims. The official forces did not suffice and were supplemented by the murderers brought out of the prisons and still the killing had to be continued. This butchery began on Thursday of the great week of the Passover and lasted ten days [148]. These victims were massacred at the hillside south of Karkā de Ledān. All this took such dimensions that it was finally too much even for the officials, so new instructions were accordingly given by Shahpuhr regulating the prosecution and restricting the chaotic massacre [149]. This document states repeatedly that this happened in the 31st year of Shahpuhr's rule [150].

Besides this record, we possess others on individual ascetics. Concerning Mārtā, a daughter of Pōsī, again a *bart qeiāmā* who was arrested and killed, we have more explicit information through acts which were composed or re-worked later [151].

In Šūšan the monk-bishop Mīlēs was arrested along with two of his disciples : 'Ābūrsām and Sīnai, who seem to have been ascetics [152]. They were twice beaten and tortured in order to compel them to worship the sun. Afterward, they laughed much at the tortures. Mīlēs was killed at the same time as his companions were stoned [153].

Bēt Ārāmāiē

In Bēt Ārāmāiē the wave of destruction arrived in the second year of the persecutions and Bishop Šāhdōst, Šemʿōn's successor in Seleucia-Ctesiphon was seized. Shahpuhr's presence started a large

[148] *Ibid.*, II, p. 247. In the acts of martyrdom of Azād this is stated somewhat differently, *ibid.*, p. 251.

[149] He required information about his or her person and place for the record on parchment. Torture is advised before the death sentence can be passed, *ibid.*, p. 246.

[150] *Ibid.*, p. 247 bis.

[151] *Ibid.*, II, p. 233 ff. The end of the acts refers to events in the 8th year of the rule of Vahram V, i.e. 428/9.

[152] Twice they are called ܐܚܐ 'brothers', 'monks', *ibid.*, II, p. 273 f.

[153] *Ibid.*, II, p. 260 ff. The acts give only Tešrī 13 = November 13, but no year.

scale action, so that not only was Seleucia-Ctesiphon stricken, but also the villages and countries around the city. Arrested besides the clerics were ascetics, *benai qeiāmā* and *benat qeiāmā* [154], all together 128 persons. We do not possess closer data about them.

They were thrown in chains and hard imprisonment for 5 months. Three times the worst tortures were imposed on them in order to bring them to worship the sun. Patiently the victims endured their sufferings. Finally they were brought out of the city and, singing the hymns and songs, their pains were ended by the executors [155].

A new onslaught was let loose in the fifth year of the persecutions, engulfing many ascetics. Again, it is said that Shahpuhr was in Seleucia, and thus a large scale action was carried out in the city as well as in several other places. About these events we have the ancient acts of martyrdom [156] which have their place in the earliest collection of these documents. Here we are informed that along with the clerics, *benai qeiāmā* and *benat qeiāmā* were seized, altogether 120, among them 9 women. They were cast into prison for 6 months, for the whole winter. All the attempts, threats and sufferings imposed, to compel them to worship the sun, failed. Finally they were brought out of the prison and led outside the city, where the chief mobadh tried once more. But the victims cried out with a loud voice saying that those who accompanied them to the killing-place, are wearing the garments of sorrow, having their faces distorted by fear, 'and we, behold, are dressed in the garments of joy and our faces are like a rose in the morning'. They were killed by the sword.

In the next year, i.e. in the 6th of the persecutions, when instigations were brought against Barbaʿšmīn, bishop of Seleucia-Ctesiphon, namely, that he diverts many from the religion of the state, despises the sun and abuses fire and water, he, and along with him 16 men were arrested, clerics and *benai qeiāmā,* some from other places, and some from the city [157]. These acts, which were a part of the ancient collection, tell how they were thrown in the prison in heavy chains and bitter pains 'inflicted by the Magi from the month

154 The Acts of Šāhdūst, *ibid.*, II, p. 278.
155 *Ibid.*, II, p. 280.
156 *Ibid.*, II, p. 291 ff.
157 *Ibid.*, II, p. 297.

Šbaṭ (February) to Kānūn (January). They were tortured by hunger and thirst until they were physically wrecks. Finally they were sent to Karkā de Ledān where Shahpuhr resided and then, after all the pressure to bring them to denial was in vain, they were killed.

One trial seems to have caused others. In connection with the interrogation, their vigorous counter-attacks provoked the officials to anger. It is quite understandable that these incidents nourished the wrath of the servants of the official religion so that new cases were brought up of which we have no knowledge. And, in fact, as a repercussion of these vexations we have a summary report in the ancient document entitled 'the struggle of the martyrs who were killed in various places by the mobadhs', again a document which had its place in the ancient collection of acts. It inaugurates a sad picture with the following words : 'at the time when the holy Barbaʿšmīn was martyred, a heavy storm was set up upon our country, and a great calamity upon our people, and destruction to our churches, and shame to our service' [158].

Bēt Garmai

From Bēt Garmai the earliest acts of martyrdom which we have, tell of the events which took place in the fourth year of the persecutions when, as it is said, Shahpuhr was in the country [159]. This does not mean that the persecutions did not start earlier in Bēt Garmai.

Concerning the metropolis, Karkā de Bēt Selōk, we fortunately possess a summary report about the important martyrs which is somewhat of a dry list, certainly incomplete, free of every legendary

158 *Ibid.*, II, p. 303. Only occasionally are we permitted a glimpse that gives us an idea as to what this 'great calamity' must have meant. By chance, we learn that a martyrion near the pit of Daniel was destroyed : بيعة... فى جب دانيال بعد هدم اليهود اياها وقتلهم ماكان فيها من الرهبان والقسان والشمامسة 'the martyrion near the pit of Daniel, which the Jews destroyed earlier, after killing those who were in it, the monks, presbyters and deacons', MARI, *De patriarchis*, p. 29. In this connection, we learn about the part which the Jews also played, who felt that their opportunity to take their chance had come.

159 *Ibid.*, II, p. 284.

embroidery [160]. Its analysis shows that it bears an archaic character. This brief martyrologium seems to go back to the local tradition, and perhaps even to the diptychs of the church of Karkā de Bēt Selōk. Besides the commemoration of three bishops of the city, some priests and believers, the list ends with the enumeration of the female ascetics, *benat qeiāmā* : Teqlā and Danāq, killed by the order of the mobadh; Ṭāṭōn, Māmā, Mezakiā, Anā, were killed outside the city in a place called Ḥāwrā, by the order of the mobadh. Further the list names Abiat, Ḥātāi, Mezakiā, all from the country of Bēt Garmai, who were killed by the order of Shahpuhr when he was in the country [161].

This martyrologium gives us a glimpse of the plight of the ascetics. It is conspicuous how heavily the ratio is weighted against them. Among 3 bishops 2 priests and 5 laypeople the document brings 9 *benat qeiāmā* and in addition to these ascetics ''Ohanām, a boy, *bar qeiāmā*' [162], obviously a child dedicated to the ascetic life. He was stoned in the village Ganzāk at the hands of the noblemen of Karkā de Bēt Selōk who were, as the source says, name Christians and acted under the pressure. The high percentage of female ascetics in the list gives us the impression that the main attack was directed against the representatives of the ascetic ideal.

From another source we learn of other victims, this time of those who had escaped their fate in Seleucia-Ctesiphon and had come to Karkā de Bēt Selōk, and again we have to do with female ascetics [163]. And the same source says that these executions were accompanied by devastation of the properties which belonged to Christians, and also by other violence.

It is difficult to ascertain how systematically these measures were carried out. We hear that, during these persecutions, the small congregation in Karkā de Bēt Selōk arranged little rooms outside for a temporary place of worship in order not to draw attention

160 Survived only by one codex Ms. Dijarb. 96, a codex placed into the 7th or 8th century, but probably is younger, see Baumstark, *Geschichte syr. Literatur*, p. 55, note 5.

161 *Acta martyrum*, II, p. 288 f.

162 ܐܘܗܢܡ ܛܠܝܐ ܒܪ ܩܝܡܐ, *ibid.*, II, p. 287.

163 *Ibid.*, II, p. 513.

to their gatherings. This was in a lavra near the city, at a hamlet with the name Ḥaṣṣā. But, this place was not well chosen. We are told that the persecutors intruded into the lavra and arrested the bishop Ma'nā, and without any procedure stoned him at the hill of Ḥāṣṣā [164]. It is not said what happened to the lavra and its inhabitants.

Ḥadiab

The Chronicle of Arbēl tells us that the start of the persecutions was different and that it took time before the whole machinery was brought into action. The local mobadh, in accord with the dignitaries, agreed that the enforcement of the edict should be postponed until the month 'Īlūl (September), the harvest time [165]. And even then only a few, whose names were not known when the chronicle was composed, were killed. All this was due to the mild and 'pitiful' Pagrasp, but the situation lasted only until his death.

The persecutions started the year when this mobadh died and Peroz Tahm-Shahpuhr assumed office. As the chronicle says, now the blood of Christians began to flow. In the 35th year of Shahpuhr's rule, in addition to Bishop Jōḥannan and Priest Ja'qōb many ascetics and believers were seized and killed [166].

After this mobadh was replaced by Ādhurparre, the situation became still worse and the persecution raged until the year 351 [167]. Many families were entirely uprooted. The leaders and the believers sought shelter in the mountains and caves. The church was so paralyzed, that even in the eighties, the wounds were still open [168]. Under these circumstances, the ascetics had to bring heavy sacrifices while others had to flee and to hide themselves [169]. Here too, the female ascetics seem to have arosed the particular enmity of the population. The Chronicle of Arbēl particularly refers to the female

164 *Ibid.*, II, p. 514 f.

165 *Sources syriaques*, p. 50 f.

166 *Ibid.*, p. 54.

167 *Ibid.*, p. 57.

168 *Ibid.*, p. 61.

169 Two monks who 'were hiding themselves in this place', appear in the acts of martyrdom of Barḥadbešabbā, who freed his body from the hands of the guards, *Acta martyrum*, II, p. 316.

asetics [170] and within the limits of available documents, the female ascetics form a noteworthy constituency. We possess acts of five *benat qeiāmā,* Teqlā, Mariam, Mārtā, Mariam and 'Emī [171] who were arrested and brought to a village of Ḥazzā [172], a wellknown suburb of Arbēl. They were killed by Tahm-Shahpuhr in 347. It seems that also the piece which precedes this document, and with which this document seems to be connected, belongs also to Ḥadiab — the martyrdom of Ja'qōb, the priest of Tellā Šelīlā in the neighborhood of the Great Zāb and *bart qeiāmā* Mariam [173]. These arrests took place at the same time and at the order of Tahm-Shahpuhr.

Phārs

So far as we are able to see, asceticism received the same blows in the provinces deeper in Asia. We are permitted to observe this in several documents.

A document has survived oblivion, and concerns the martyrdom in the 'country of Rāzīqāiē', i.e. Rai, which took place two years after Mīlēs, bishop of Šūšan, also from the same country, was killed. Along with Dāni'ēl, a priest, Wardā, a *bart qeiāmā* was seized. They were kept in prison and tortured until their heads were riven by the sword [174].

The fate of monasticism in this storm is illustrated by the acts of the martyrdom of an abbot Baršabiā, being a member of the cycle of the previous document in the transmission of the text [175].

Baršabiā's monastery was located in Phārs [176] and here he lived and ruled his ten monks. We hear that the Mazda-believers took the initiative and accused him before the mobadh in Istakhr to the effect that he misleads many, teaches witchcraft and, in doing this, under-

170 *Sources syriaques,* p. 54.

171 *Acta martyrum,* II, p. 308.

172 This name is entirely corrupted in ܠܚܕܐ 'to one' in the manuscript used by Assemani's edition, but regarding this there is no doubt since it is preserved in the manuscript used by Bedjan and as 'Αζᾶ, also in the *Synaxarium Constantinop.,* col. 739.

173 *Acta martyrum,* II, p. 307.

174 *Ibid.,* II, p. 290.

175 *Ibid.,* II, p. 281 ff.

176 A province east of the Persian Gulf.

mines the religion of the Magi. The abbot and his monks, namely, the whole monastic community, was arrested. The monks manfully endured tortures and vexations and the old *rīšdairā* (abbot) encouraged his spiritual sons in these moments by singing hymns, being the last one whose life was terminated. Their heads later were brought into town, and hung upon the temple of the goddess Anāhīd, and displayed as a deterrent for others, but their bodies were left for the animals and the birds [177].

c. The last phase of the persecutions

Concerning the duration of the persecutions we have no clear information. Our sources leave too many lacunas. For the whole period of Shahpuhr's long rule we have no such material as the acts of martyrdom to guide us, since we only possess those of the first years, and thus are rendered impotent in crossing over these gaps. To be sure, summary statements of a very general kind say that these times continued. The author of the ancient collection of the acts leaves the impression that these persecutions lasted all the time [178]. And the Chronicle of Arbēl states that the blood of Christians has flown constantly [179]. But that we are to think that the persecution actually continued to rage with unwavering acuteness [180], is another matter. It seems wiser to take into account temporary relaxations and pauses for breath [181]. Moreover we have a right to do so, because the sources themselves, giving certain hints [182], advise us to do so.

177 *Acta martyrum*, II, p. 283. They were killed on 17th of Hazīrān (June) 342 (?).

178 *Ibid.*, II, p. 393.

179 *Sources syriaques*, p. 61.

180 CHRISTENSEN, *L'Iran*, p. 268.

181 Very little has survived about the sufferings in this period. The most important of these acts of martyrdom are those of Mar Abḥai, killed in 360 by the hand of his own father called Ādurperōzgerd, ṢELĪBā, *Martyrologe*, p. 139 or Mehīr Šapūr. But in Ms. Berl. Sach. 241, fol. 2 a ff. Abḥai himself was called by this name before his conversion.

182 The chronicle of Arbēl admits at least one pause in saying that the sword ravaged until the year 662 A.Gr. = 351 A.D., because Shahpuhr went on his raid to the West, *Sources syriaques*, p. 57. Another hint appears in the

And finally this seems to be legitimate in view of the fact that the events which took place in the last years of Shahpuhr's rule, were considered as something different from that which the Christianity had experienced in the preceding decades.

Before Shahpuhr's rule became history, the persecutions flared up with new vehemence and impetuosity. The sources consider this as a new phase. A new decree was sent to the mobadhs to renew violence and pressure. In addition, new measures were put into effect — the order that the Christians were to be forced to kill the sentenced victims.

We have very little, but at least something, which testifies to these events. Fortunately these three sources, important for our purpose, belonged to the ancient collection of the acts of martyrdom. They only unfold single episodes, but to some extent give us a general idea about this last flame which flared up briefly before it was extinguished with the death of Shahpuhr.

How little we know of the actual happenings can be learned upon a glance into the Chronicle of Arbēl. We are told that Šūbḥālīšōʿ entered the succession of the bishops of Arbēl ca 375, and, in vague words, a reference is made to the persecutions, but without clarity as to whether the earlier persecutions are meant or whether these took place during the first years of the newly elected bishop [183]. If we did not have the acts of ʿAqebšmā, we would never have known about the seriousness of the measures applied in Ḥadiab. This shows that we have in our sources no more than something like a flashlight which illuminates but one spot in the darkness, about which we can more easily guess than know.

The above-mentioned source tells us that the storm first seized ʿAqebšmā in Ḥenāitā, bishop and ascetic, renowned for his acts of mortification [184]. At the same time, others in other places were seized and brought to Arbēl. The mobadh demanded them to worship the sun, to drink blood, to take a wife and to fulfil the will of the king in order to escape torture and death. They were tortured

tradition connected with Mār Mattai, that at least at that time when Julian Apostata ruled in the West, there was no persecution in Persia, *Acta martyrum*, II, p. 400.

183 *Sources syriaques*, p. 61.

184 *Acta martyrum*, II, p. 362 see also *Versions grecques des actes*, p. 483.

brutally, their bones cracked, being crushed, but not their attitude. Being brought back into the prison, the Magi beat and vexed these living corpses until death rescued them from the hands of their torturers.

A change of the mobadh simply made the situation worse. With the arrival of the new mobadh, a new decree was promulgated which compelled Christians to stone their sentenced teachers [185]. This edict which put the spiritual leaders on the spot, and involved the believers in crime, caused so much panic that Christians abandoned their homes and fled into the mountains and hid themselves there. There also the ascetics sought shelter. The Greek recension of the acts of ʿAqebšmā tells of many ascetics who had found their hiding-place in Bēt Nūhādrā [186]. The Syriac text does not tell us more about the fate of the ascetics and monks, but is content with an incidental remark made in connection with the role of a devout woman, who in the prison at Arbēl had many more 'victims' under her care, after she had bribed the jailer [187]. But a different recension of the acts, which lies behind Sozomenus' summary report, seems to refer to a great number of ascetics who lost their lives [188].

A document under the title 'the Forty Martyrs' unfolds an episode which took place in the 36th year of the persecutions (in 377) in Bēt Ārāmāiē [189]. The bishop of the town of Kaškar, ʿAbdā, along with his presbyters and deacons was visiting his diocese. When the pursuers with the orders of arrest arrived, they found them staying in a hamlet where there were *benai qeiāmā* and *benat qeiāmā* [190]. During the morning prayer the whole group,

185 The word used here, *Acta martyrum*, II, p. 380. ܣܥܘܪܐ has here obviously a wider meaning than its ordinary 'chorepiscopus', referring to the overseers, teachers and guides. The Greek version renders this by ἡγουμένους, *Versions grecques des actes*, p. 505.

186 ἦσαν γὰρ πολλοὶ ἀσκηταὶ κεκρυμμένοι ἐκεῖ, *ibid.*, p. 516; ἦσαν γὰρ πολλοὶ μοναχοὶ καὶ ἀσκηταὶ κεκρυμμένοι ἐκεῖσε, *ibid.*, p. 533.

187 *Acta martyrum*, II, p. 379.

188 *Hist. eccl.*, II, 13, col. 965. It is not quite clear whether Sozomenus here means the victims contemporary to ʿAqebšmā or whether he looks back to the earlier ones.

189 *Acta martyrum*, II, p. 325 ff.

190 *Ibid.*, II, p. 337.

Bishop ʿAbdā, his companions and the ascetics, 29 men and 7 women, were arrested, put in chains, and under heavy suffering, brought to Bēt Hūzāiē into Karkā de Ledān. They were subjected to brutal tortures for the purpose of bringing them away from their confession. But all the attempts of the mobadh and the Magi were futile. Under military guard, the men were taken south of town and killed there. Two 'brothers', a cleric and a *bar qeiāmā* who earlier that morning had left the group in order to buy food for them all, joined the witnesses and followed the martyrdom of their companions. Thus, in this group, 6 ascetics shared the martyrdom.

The sufferings of the seven female ascetics continued. They were sent to Bēt Lāphāṭ to be martyred there for the purpose of frightening the Christians in that country. The interrogators did not put forth ordinary demand concerning the worship of the sun before them, but rather a supplemental one which contained a sting against the representatives of the ascetic ideal : 'if you do the will of the king and you become (wives) for men, you will live and escape from the death which will come to pass upon you' [191]. Their declaration, namely, that they will not do the king's will by sacrificing and also that they cannot be persuaded to become wives of men, terminated the futile interogations.

As to how organized monasticism was involved into these vexations and how a monastic community was exposed to the rage of the last persecutions we have the document in the acts of the abbot Mār Badmā [192]. This trustworthy monument brings us a segment of the sad happenings taken from Bēt Hūzāiē. This Badmā was a *rīšdairā* from a town of Bēt Lāphāṭ. He was arrested along with seven monks and spent four months in prison. On three occasions they were vexed and tortured, but remained firm. The abbot was killed by the hand of a Christian who was compelled to do this. But at that time the life of his seven monks were spared and they had to spend four more years and some months in the prison until Shahpuhr died. After this they were released [193]. According to

191 *Ibid.*, II, p. 345.
192 *Ibid.*, II, p. 347 ff.
193 *Ibid.*, II, p. 351.

these data the arrest and the death of Badmā occurred in the year 375 [194].

d. A retrospective glance

Countless ascetics, *benai qeiāmā, benat qeiāmā,* anchorites and monks must have become victims of the persecutions under Shahpuhr, first in manifold sufferings and then in death. Often longer periods of waiting for the verdict in the prisons, being transported from one place to another, were filled with pain and torture by which the Magi cooled their wrath. In other cases the periods of torture were interchanged at intervals. It was, however, sometimes possible to help them and then the Christians utilized these opportunities. Not always was it necessary to visit the prison in the disguise of Magi. Sometimes bribery helped to alleviate the fate of brethren and sisters of faith. Even in Seleucia in the fifth year of persecutions, it is recorded that during the whole winter when the confessors were kept in prison, a woman from Ḥadiab, from Årbēl, took care of them all the time [195].

We know nothing about other measures of vexation. Sometimes we hear that the ascetics were exposed to ridicule and mockery, but what is meant by this the sources do not elaborate. Very rarely do we find hints as to what this might have been [196].

Only seldom do we hear that being kept in prisons and vexed there was considered as sufficient punishment for the victims. In the martyrdom of Mār Badmā, this is the case. This abbot was

194 The chronological data are obviously not exact. The Acts of ʿAqebšmā speak of the 37th year of the persecution, *ibid.*, II, p. 361. This would be in 378. The acts of the Forty martyrs set this date to the 36th year, i.e. 377, *ibid.*, II, p. 325. The opening words in the Acts of Badmā refer to the date of the last acts and say that 'at the same time Badmā, *rīšdairā,* was seized and imprisoned by the order of the king', *ibid.*, p. 347. This, too, rather indicates that his arrest took place not in 375 but later.

195 *Ibid.*, II, p. 291.

196 The ending added to the acts of martyrdom of the Edessene martyrs Gūriā and Šemōnā says that the monks were insulted and the chaste desecrated and *benai qeiāmā* made to watchmen. *Acta Guriae et Shamonae,* p. 27 reports : ܒܢ̈ܝ ܩܝܡܐ ܥܒܕ. ܚܣܝܡ ܢܛܘܪ̈ܐ ܒܠܠܝܐ ܒܫܘ̈ܩܐ ܕܡܕܝܢ̈ܬܐ 'they made the *benai qeiāmā* to watchmen on the streets of the towns in the night'.

killed, but not the monks arrested at his monastery. These remained in their imprisonment for more than 4 years and were released [197]. But here Shahpuhr's death gave freedom back to the prisoners. Perhaps we have to reckon with the release of other victims who were imprisoned and awaiting their execution at the time when death caught the chief persecutor.

Countless ascetics must have lost their lives. The available numbers speak certainly in exaggerated terms. While Sozomenus mentions 16.000 besides the multitude of those whose names are not known [198], Faustus of Byzantium speaks of 'thousands and tens of thousands' [199]. However great the number might have been [200], a great part of it can be accounted to the ascetics. The sources do not provide the evidence to be more specific. Unfortunately even that section of the ancient Syriac martyrologion which contained the names of the outstanding ascetics in its list, orderly arranged according to the ecclesiastical ranks, bishops, priests, deacons and others, has crumbled away [201].

After this survey of the data available in our sources, we have to analyze somewhat more closely the motives as to why the ascetics were so deeply involved in the persecutions.

A common phrase which occurs again and again in the sources is the term 'accused' [202]. Accusations by the population as well as by the Mazdean clergy were brought to the attention of the officials who then initiated the procedure and took the further development of the case into their hands. In such a procedure the clerics as well as the ascetics and monks were particularly exposed. The presence of the ascetics in the communities or that of the monks in the caves upon the mountains, or in lavras or monasteries close to villages and towns easily became the objects of curiosity, as the ascetic phenomenon always did whatever the religion. Personal sacrifice always made them stand out among the believers, clerics included. Moreover, while the most contagious religious propaganda

197 See pag. 251 f.

198 *Hist. eccl.*, II, 14, col. 969.

199 *Patmowtʿiwn Hayoc̣*, p. 82.

200 Ms. Ox. Marsh 13, fol. 65 b speaks of thousands of victims.

201 *Martyrologes et ménologes*, p. 23 ff.

202 ܐܟܠ ܩܪܨܐ

came just from these quarters, it is particularly true in the Syrian Orient. Particularly the ascetics had their hand in missionary recruiting. And this role alone gave sufficient ground to the believers of the state religion, and particularly to the servants of the cult, to use this opportunity to get rid of these troublesome men and women.

This must have happened very soon after the instructions against the Christians provoked savage outbursts. The case of the abbot Baršabiā and monks in Phārs falls into the first years of the persecutions. We are told that they were accused by 'wicked and evil men' before the mobadh in Istakhr. The motivation is also given : 'he vitiates many men, and he teaches sorcery in our country, and by his teaching, he disposes of the teaching of the Magi' [203]. Here we have before us a motive which historically must have played an important role. On the same grounds many similar cases must have been instigated, demanding victims among both ascetics and monks.

Besides the missionary motive, another factor must be noted which instigated hatred particularly against the ascetics. Whether aggressive or not, the ascetic phenomenon as such must have deeply provoked the believers of the Mazda religion.

What was really on the hearts of the accusers becomes vocal with such clarity that it leaves nothing to be desired. In the acts of ʿAqebšmā, the reasons for hatred are bluntly brought out. The ascetics are accused not only for religious and cultic reasons, but because 'they do not take wives and do not generate sons and daughters' [204]. The same is behind the ordinance of the mobadh given Aitallāhā : 'worship the god, the sun, and eat blood, and take a wife' [205]. That means, besides cultic aspects, the virtue of virginity [206] irritated the Persians [207].

203 ܕܠܐܢܫܐ ܣܓܝܐܐ ܡܚܒܠ : ܘܚܪܫܘܬܐ ܡܠܦ ܒܐܬܪܢ : ܘܝܘܠܦܢܐ ܕܡܓܘ̈ܫܐ ܒܝܘܠܦܢܗ ܫܪܐ *Acta martyrum*, II, p. 281.

204 ܘܢܫ̈ܐ ܠܐ ܢܣܒܝܢ : ܘܒܢ̈ܝܐ ܘܒܢ̈ܬܐ ܠܐ ܡܘܠܕܝܢ *ibid.*, II, p. 361. This is told in connection with an instruction issued in the 37th year of persecution to the mobadhs.

205 ܕܣܓܘܕ ܠܫܡܫܐ ܐܠܗܐ : ܘܐܟܘܠ ܕܡܐ : ܘܣܒ ܐܢܬܬܐ *ibid.*, II, p. 368.

206 The proclamation issued by Mihrnersh (or Mihrnerseh), the grand vizier

More often by far, the sources show that this trait was hurled with irreconcilable hatred against the female ascetics. The rage that must have existed against them broke out in vehement outbursts during the interrogations. Mārtā, a daughter of Pōsī, as a *bart qeiāmā,* being arrested and brought before her interrogators, was urged by the mobadh : 'behold you are young, and in your complexion beautiful, have a man and marry, and bear sons and daughters, and do not stay in this impure name of the *qeiāmā'* [208]. Mārtā answered that she really is already a bride, and her bridegroom is abroad — in heaven, and his name is Jesus. The same demand even takes an almost stereotyped form. The mobadh says to *bart qeiāmā* Teqlā and to her companions Mariam, Mārtā, Mariam, and 'Emī : 'worship the sun, and have men, and you will escape the tortures' [209]. The proposal of marriage was made also to Tarbō, a *bart qeiāmā,* arrested together with another *bart qeiāmā* who was her maid. Before the mobadh she declared : 'I am a bride of Christ, and I keep my virginity in his name' [210]. Also the seven *benat qeiāmā* who were arrested in Kaškar were told : 'if you do the will of the

of Persia in Armenia, reflects the same. Ełišē, *Patmowtʿiwn wardananç,* p. 56 reports that it contained threats against the spiritual leaders who do not marry and uphold the virtue of virginity : *մի հաւատայք առաջնորդացն ձերոց՝ զոր Նածրացիսդ անուանէք*, 'do not believe your leaders whom you call Nazoreans, for they are very perfidious'. In the Syrian Orient, the term ܢܙܪܝܐ *Nāzrāiē* was the term for Christians in general. In this case, however, it is obvious that the term is used in its particular meaning, and it seems to refer to the ascetics. The term was particularly suitable to designate those conspicuous by their ascetic observances. This term comes from the Semitic root נצר 'to observe', 'to keep observances' or from נוֹצְרִי 'one who is of the circle of the observants', cf. LIDZBARSKI, *Nazoraios,* p. 230 ff. We find the term in this sense, as applied to ascetics, in use in ancient Syriac texts, for example in *Apocryphal Acts,* p. 217.

207 Regarding this point Eznik calls the Persians *իգասէր* *Elc aɫandoc̣,* p. 123. *Thesaurus armeniacus,* I, p. 845 translates this as φιλογύναιος, amator mulierum.

According to the ancient Persian traditions, 'one should persevere much in the begetting of children — only for the acquisition of further good works', *Šāyast-nē-šāyast,* X, 22, p. 138.

208 *Acta martyrum,* II, p. 236.

209 *Ibid.,* II, p. 309.

210 *Ibid.,* II, p. 257.

king and you become (wives) for men, you will live and escape from death which will come to pass upon you' [211]. Also other sources have preserved remembrances regarding this particular demand [212].

Still another reason needs to be noted in order to fully understand the relentless hatred which the ascetics reaped in the Parsist society. In Parseeism, the cultivation of land and the tilling of ground belonged to the divinely determined process of life, giving to it not only sense and meaning but also a religious character. Thus, work and labor of the ground, so much glorified in the sacred books of the Parsees, the extension of the cultivated areas, and even the killing of noxious animals and reptiles, creatures of Ahriman [213], constituted an important part in the religious life of the inhabitants of the Mazdean communities.

Now the ascetics with their totally different view and attitude towards work and with a totally different concept of usefulness must have become notorious among the Mazda-believers. In the society every ascetic must have appeared as a living insult among the feelings shared by the society. These feelings also explode in the acts of martyrdom. For instance in the acts of ʿAqebšmā a mobadh says : 'because you do not work and do not labor, in your leisure (going) from house to house, you are proud and boast of your poverty' [214].

Still another reason cannot be overlooked. As experience showed, in the alarming situation which sometimes caused apostasy even among the rows of the clergy, the ascetics and monks proved to be the real stronghold of the spirit of resistance in many a community [215]. Associated with this is a very significant fact which

211 *Ibid.*, II, p. 346.

212 Also Ephrem : ܩܗܠܐ ܕܒܢ̈ܬܐ ܕܗܢ ܩܝܡܢ ܕܒܠܚܘܕ ܠܓܒܪ̈ܐ ܠܐ ܢܗܘܘܢ ܩܒܠ ܡܘܬܐ ܚܠܝܨܐܝܬ 'a multitude of women that of our *qeiāmā*, accepted death bravely, only in order not to become (wives) for men', *Hymni de virginitate*, II, p. 20 f.

213 *Vendidad*, XIV, 5 . 6.

214 ܒܗ، ܕܠܐ ܦܠܚܝܢ ܐܢܬܘܢ ܘܠܐ ܠܐܝܢ ܐܢܬܘܢ ܒܣܦܩܘܬܟܘܢ ܕܒܝܬ ܒܝܬ ܠܒܝܬ ܗܐ ܫܒܗܪܝܢ ܐܢܬܘܢ ܘܡܫܬܒܗܪܝܢ ܒܡܣܟܢܘܬܐ *Acta martyrum*, II, p. 366.

215 What happened in the village of Kašāz where the priest Paulā, fond of

explains this state of affairs : the ideals of asceticism and martyrdom met each other on the deepest level [216]. Ascetics and monks constituted that element which was willing to take an aggressive stand in confirming and strengthening those whom the arm of the state wanted to bend. There were ascetics who voluntarily entered the battlefield, and took over the leadership, willing to pay for this leadership with their lives. When Mār Jāūnān and Mār Berīkīšōʿ [217] did hear of the persecutions, they left their place and came to the village Bēt ʾĀsā the place where the arrested ones were kept in order to strengthen them and to prepare them for witnessing. As Mār Jāūnān and Berīkīšōʿ did so also were there others who, by their activities, must have drawn the indignation of the officials upon themselves.

These are the motives which help us to better understand the precarious situation of the ascetics and monks in the times of persecutions. Under these circumstances it becomes intelligible why the ascetics, in particular, kept the rage of the Mazda believers at a boiling point. In the acts concerning the 'Great Slaughter in Bēt Hūzāiē' we are told that lay people, too, had to suffer under this hatred against the ascetics. It is recorded here that among the arrested ones, dragged to the royal court, were many lay-people, seized during the stampede from various places, supposedly being ascetics [218]. And, as it seems in some places, the ascetics were the only arrested ones shown in the prison [219]. It also becomes understandable

earthly goods, fell away and 5 *benat qeiāmā* were the only ones who took over the spiritual leadership in this community in giving testimony, *ibid.*, II, p. 308 f., was, judging from other sources, not a rare incident.

216 A homily of NARSAI, *Homiliae et carmina*, II, p. 47 ff. is instructive here. It shows how deep these aspirations were. The common denominator is *ʾatlēṭā* and *ʾāḡōnā*, *ibid.*, p. 54.

217 The Syriac text, *Acta martyrum*, II, p. 40 f. speaks of ܐܚ̈ܐ 'brethren'; in *Synaxaire arménien*, XXI, p. 185 they appear as կրօնաւորք աբեղայք 'monks, mourners'.

218 This is certainly the meaning of the text : ܘܐܚܕܘ ܐܢܘܢ ܡܢ ܩܘܪ̈ܝܐ ܕܐܬܪ ܐܬܪ : ܘܐܝܬܝܘ ܐܢܘܢ ܒܫܡ ܩܝܡܐ 'and they arrested them from villages in various places and brought them in the name of *qeiāmā*', *Acta martyrum*, II, p. 241; ܫܡ also means 'title', 'pretext', 'pretense'.

219 As these 9 ascetics in the prison in Bēt ʾĀsā, *ibid.*, II, p. 40 f.

why the ascetics sometimes were chased from one place to another until they fell into the hand of their pursuers. The history of Karkā de Bēt Selōk reports that among the victims of the persecution, there were also *benat qeiāmā* who had escaped their fate in Seleucia-Ctesiphon and had fled to Karkā de Bēt Selōk [220].

220 *Ibid.*, II, p. 513.

CHAPTER III

MONASTICISM UNDER THE SUCCESSORS OF SHAHPUHR II

1. ADVANCE IN MONASTICISM

a. Symtoms of gathering strength

A new era for the growth and success of monasticism was inaugurated by the period of Vahram IV (388-399) [1]. When hostilities ceased, Christians could think of healing their wounds, of rebuilding the ruins of their sacred buildings and of restoration of their institutions [2]. This must have been a period of renaissance although the statements in the sources saying that the recovery took less time than expected seem to be an overstatement. To be sure the Chronicle of Arbēl states with satisfaction that within a few years the Christian religion had regained its former floration and adds that this was a matter of admiration [3]. But how much of this is real, is difficult to say [4].

Still other new possibilities towards progress were presented under the rule of Jazdgard I (399-421), a man of magnanimous character. Although, this friendly attitude may have been influenced in part by political considerations, but it cannot be wholly explained in this way. The main factor seems to have been the tolerant

1 The Persian annalists characterize him as a rude and arrogant ruler.

2 That ʿAqeblāhā, bishop of Karkā de Bēt Selōk was the man who owing to a healing of Vahrām's daughter obtained this, is obviously an aetiological legend, *Acta martyrum*, II, p. 516 f.

3 *Sources syriaques*, p. 61.

4 What we read of the restoration work carried out by Catholicos Tōmarṣā, *Histoire nestorienne*, V, p. 306, is a product of phantasy. A remark in the synodical acts held under Dadīšoʿ tends to pour cold water over these enthusiastic statements. He was not catholicos at all, but Isḥaq was the man who re-established the catholicate which before him was interrupted for 22 years, *Synodicon orientale*, p. 48.

character of the ruler [5]. His son, Vahram V, in his throne-speech characterized the rule of his father as one sustained by an accommodating and goodhearted spirit [6]. This is also corroborated by the testimony of Christians who had sufficient reasons to call him 'blessed' among the rulers [7]. And, in the acts of the synod held under Catholicos Isḥaq, one can find the eulogies which were sent to the address of the ruler to whom the Christians owed so much [8].

This changed situation, created by an edict comparable in its significance to that of Milan in Western Christianity, is best characterized by the joy with which the synodical acts, written in the year 410 under Catholicos Isḥaq, sum up the vital consequences : 'for he had ordered in all his kingdom that the churches, destroyed under his fathers, might be rebuilt magnificently in his days; that the demolished altars might be diligently served, that those who for God's sake had been tested and tempted by imprisonments and tortures, could go out by deliverance, and priests and heads together with the entire holy *qeiāmā* could go in boldness, without fear and dread' [9]. A peaceful atmosphere, suitable for the fostering of a renaissance, was thereby created. Monasticism also shared in this, in its intrinsic consolidation and external extension.

It is impossible to track the numerical growth in the monastic development. The quiet wandering of monasticism through plains, deserts and mountains, expanding itself in all directions, left behind almost no historical vestiges.

There is one observation of a general nature which is worthy of mention. In connection with Catholicos Tōmarṣā, Bar ʿEbraiā adds a piece of information which catches our attention. Although nothing is said about its origin, it seems to throw a beam of light a long distance. The section about the general restoration ascribed to Tōmarṣā, and the steps taken in this interest, is concluded by the following notice : 'and he compelled the believers to be joined in legal marriages, and did not at all allow the young people to take the garb of monasticism, but only old people in advanced age, for,

5 Jazdgard was also kind towards the Jews who had no political significance.

6 Ṭabari, *Ta'rīkh ar-rusul*, I, II, p. 865.

7 *Anecdota syriaca*, I, p. 8.

8 *Synodicon orientale*, p. 18.

9 *Ibid.*, p. 18.

owing to the persecution, the number of the believers had been much decreased, and many of them had defected (from the faith)' [10].

Of course, there was no such rule issued by the head of the church since Tōmarṣā is a fictitious catholicos belatedly added to the lists in order to fill out the gaps in the succession. According to a trustworthy source there was no catholicos at that time [11]. Thus this information rather seems to reflect the feelings and sentiments of a vexed Christianity towards the growing monasticism — an attitude not difficult to understand. The echo of sentiments heard here we can well appreciate.

The possibility of tracing the consolidation which took place in monasticism during that period is much more favorable. If no pains are spared in consulting all the available remembrances which tradition had preserved, the sources open up many a sign tending to prove that new life sprang up in the movement of monasticism. In the following, we will mention a number of observations in support of this assertion.

First, expansion in the monastic movement appears to reflect rapid growth. In whatever direction we look in the sources, they give us the right to say so. Even the work of recruit enlistment among the Mazda-believers met with success, and in some places the situation became acute [12]. Even the ranks of the nobility were reached. There were those who found that a cell in a monastery or the quietness of solitude were more attractive than worldly honors. Šābōrberaz, a member of an outstanding Persian family, was converted to monasticism and he entered the monastery of Dairā de 'Abīlē, and gained fame owing to his ascetic achievements. He also could influence his family members and interest them in his enterprises in the field of charity, at least, financially. We hear of him due to the fact that he later became the bishop of Karkā de Bēt Selōk, and so the chronicle of this city has included his memory [13].

10 ܘܐܠܨ ܠܡܗܝ̈ܡܢܐ ܠܡܬܙܘܓܘ ܘܗܦܟܐ ܢܫ̈ܡܘܫܐ: ܘܠܐ ܡܡܣܐ ܗܘܐ ܠܕܝܪ̈ܝܐ ܡܢ ܠܡܥܒܕ ܐܘܣܝܐ ܕܕܝܪܝܘܬܐ. ܐܠܐ ܠܡܫ̈ܠܝܐ ܠܬܘܪ̈ܐ ܥܠܘܗܝ. ܡܛܠ ܕܒܨܪ ܗܘܐ ܠܗ ܡܢܝܢܐ ܕܡܗܝܡܢ̈ܐ ܒܥܠܬ ܪ̈ܕܘܦܝܐ. ܘܣܓܝ̈ܐܐ ܡܢܗܘܢ ܐܬܟܦܪܘ ܗܘܘ BAR 'EBRAIĀ, *Chronicon eccles.*, III, col. 43.

11 See page 259, note 4.

12 *Acta martyrum*, IV, p. 184 f., 188.

13 *Ibid.*, II, p. 517 f.

We see the same in a story of Ṭaṭaq, recorded quite simply and as matter of fact. He was a *dōmesṭīqā* in Ḥadiab. He left his honors and went into a monastery in order to learn wisdom there and to prepare his soul by fastings, vigils and works of humility [14].

Further, the growth and development of coenobitic monasticism now becomes visible. What we are permitted to observe in the sources makes us acquainted with increasing interest in this form of monastic life, and with the rise of new monastic communities. The monasteries, previously slow in their process of geographic expansion, now appear in areas where, according to our reports, there had not yet been monasteries. In connection with the foundation of the monastery by Mār ʿAbdā, it is noted that this was the first in the area : 'for at that time there was no other monastery in the country of the Aramaeans (an-Nabat)' [15]. This latter term obviously refers to the country of Bēt Ārāmāiē. Further it can be noticed that in the same area, monastery locations appear to be more boldly chosen, even close to the capital. In the acts of Narsai, who suffered under Jazdgard I, a monastery emerges only 6 miles from Seleucia [16]. Moreover, in the contemporary terminology, the term 'monasteries' had secured a place to be mentioned along with 'churches' [17]. We shall mention other observations later.

On the basis of manifold data we have to conclude that monasticism had decisively pressed itself into the forefront of the ecclesiastical life. If the sources do not betray us, then we have to say that this must have taken place already in the first quarter of the 5th century. The sources depict the monasticism of that time as having captivated a wide sector in the Christian life. We see the monks taking initiative, securing the bodies of the martyrs and burying their remains. We see them serving at the martyria [18], and making their monasteries the places of instruction and missionary propaganda.

14 *Ibid.*, IV, p. 181.

15 لانه لم يكن فى بلد النبط فى ذلك الوقت عمر *Histoire nestorienne*, V, p. 307.

16 *Acta martyrum*, IV, p. 175. Later this appears as ܕܝܪܐ ܕܐܚ̈ܐ 'monastery of brethren', *ibid.*, p. 177.

17 See the acts under Dadīšōʿ, *Synodicon orientale*, p. 45; see also the decree of Jazdgard, *Acta martyrum*, IV, p. 250.

18 *Ibid.*, IV, p. 187, 183.

The last remark leads our treatment directly to that missionary zeal which began to animate the monastic movement. A figure, caught in the remotest part in Persian Empire, far from the great Christian areas, serves us in illustrating this phenomenon.

The Chronicle of Seert has preserved an interesting chapter about a monk named Baršabbā, the missionary of Merw and neighboring areas [19]. Our curiosity as to the source of this information is left unsatisfied by the document [20]. The impression is this, that it was a Syriac source, an early work of Syrian historiography. In fact, traces of the existence of this source may be found in a remote area — in the Soghdian fragments of the Turfan-collection, whose fragments about Baršabbā go back to a Syriac original [21].

19 There was only a beginning made earlier. It is told that they built a church but did not know how they could build it, and therefore took the plan of the royal palace and called it Ctesiphon, *Histoire nestorienne,* V, p. 256. In fact, a quarter in Merw was know still in the 13th century as Ctesiphon, YAQUT, *Muʿjam al-buldān,* III, p. 570.

20 A reference made in this chapter to Daniel bar Mariam obviously was not the source. The way he quotes him justifies this opinion. Originally this story was written in Syriac. Of the original, however, not more than a double leaf has emerged among the fragments in the Turfan collection, T II B 9, No 3. Unfortunately this original text does not relate those activities of Baršabbā in which we are interested and which could have been compared with the Arabic and the Soghdian versions of the text, but offers us only worthless legends.

21 Several leaves and fragments have survived of the Soghdian version of the text translated from Syriac. These were discovered in Turfan. Among other episodes one text is particularly interesting since it gives an account of Baršabbā's activities, *Soghdische Texte,* p. 523 ff. What the author of the Chronicle of Seert has summarized very briefly, is unfolded a little more fully in this text. According to this fragment the scope of Baršabbā's activities reached from Phārs to the countries of Turkestan where a number of places find mentioning. Lentz translates this test as follows : 'in den Gegenden von Fars bis hin nach Gurgan und in der Gegend von Tus, in Abarschahr und in Serachs und Merwrod und in Balch und in Herat und in Seistan', *ibid.,* p. 525. Further Baršabbā is described as a missionary as well as a promoter of the monastic movement. We are told in this text that the sacral establishments which he founded, were connected with hostels, houses and gardens, to which he assigned 'brothers' and 'sisters' with the duty of serving. The translation of Lentz renders the text in the following way : 'er kaufte Land und Wasser und erbaute dort Festung(en), Herbergen und Häuser und legte Gärten an. Und

In this chapter, in which phantastic elements stand amicably side by side with sober elements [22], the most significant part is described in the following words : 'he consecrated the altar, baptized the people, cured the sick and baptized many of the Magi, built a number of churches and acquired many fields, vineyards and others for them. ... He (i.e. God) let arise a man, who spread Christendom in all Khorasan; for the disciples of Baršabbā spread out throughout all the towns of Khorasan, built churches there and baptized people' [23]. The next paragraph will add more about this phenomenon.

Still further, all these observations can be strengthened if we take a glimpse at another sector. Monasticism began to play a greater role in the church. It began to conquer bishop's seats constantly, even in the important centers. In some of these important centers like Karkā de Bēt Selōk, the metropolis of Bēt Garmai, this took place frequently. Bishop ʿAqeblāhā was formerly a monk, having adopted the ascetic life since he was 15 years old [24]. The chronicle of Karkā says that his outstanding asceticism and mortification so fascinated the people that he was elected to the bishop's seat. Obviously he also possessed other qualities for he had great merits in healing wounds caused by persecution, among others, the building up of the church destroyed under bishop Maʿnā, into which he put his heritage after his parents died [25]. He has been wrongly identified with a younger bishop of the same name [26]. A

er siedelte dort dienende Brüder und dienende Schwester an', *ibid.*, p. 524 f. The term for his establishments is *bγyst'n*. Lentz remarks here : 'wohl Klöster', see also his glossary, *ibid.*, p. 579.

22 For instance the statement that a princess who became Christian could not give her faith to her children who remained in Mazdaism, *op. cit.*, p. 258.

23 وقدّس المذبح. وابتدا يعمذ الناس ويبرى الاعلال. واعمذ خلقاً من المجوس وبنى هناك عدّة بيع. واقتنى لها ضياعاً كثيرة وكروماً وغير ذلك ... جمل ... اظهر النصرانية فى بلد خراسان باسره. لان تلاميد برشبّا تفرقوا فى جميع مدن خراسان. وبنوا فها البيع واعمذوا الناس *ibid.*, p. 256.

24 *Ibid.*, V, p. 334; *Acta martyrum*, II, p. 515 f.

25 *Ibid.*, II, p. 516.

26 *Synodicon orientale*, p. 35. Our ʿAqeblāhā became the successor of bishop Jōḥannan of Karkā de Bēt Selōk who was a contemporary of Jaʿqōb of Nisibis, *Acta martyrum*, II, p. 517.

little later, once again, we notice a monk occupying the same bishop's seat. Mār Šābōrberaz was a monk in the monastery of Daiṛā de 'Abīlē and gained fame owing to his asceticism[27]. The chronology of this monk can only be approximately determined. His predecessor was Bishop Aksenāiā, who followed Barḥadbešabbā, the successor of 'Aqeblāhā[28]. But it is said that Šābōrberaz was followed by Bishop Jōḥannan, who was martyred in 446 under Jazdgard II[29].

We also notice that bishoprics emerge in which monks are the first to occupy the seat. The christianization of Merw in the tradition has been connected with Baršabbā, as its first bishop. He was a monk from Seleucia-Ctesiphon who, in his youth, had entered monasticism. He was ordained bishop by bishops at a time when there was no catholicos, since after the martyrdom of Barba'š-mīn the election of a successor was made impossible by Shahpuhr[30]. His floruit seems to fall on the years between 355-385.

Moreover, monasticism was able to extend its influence to the highest posts. In its elan it could furnish even the catholicate with several men. Mār Aḥai (410-415/6) was formerly one of the leading heads among monasticism. He is reported to have continued his monastic life and habits also in his office as the head of the church[31]. His successor, Jahballāhā (415/6-420), too, came from these monastic circles which absorbed the best available forces.

Something of this growth is discernible in the aggressive spirit which increasingly became manifest in monasticism. Moreover this seems to be another symptom of its strength. Monasticism appears to have become selfassertive, ostentatious in its doings, and even militant. Particularly in its missionary zeal, we see that it went so far as to attack the fire-tempels. How often this might have occurred, we have no way of knowing. But we have information that nobles and influential Magi complained to Jazdgard that the clergy and the monks do not only mock the godheads but also use violence, destroying the fire-temples[32].

27 *Ibid.*, II, p. 517 f.
28 *Ibid.*, II, p. 517.
29 *Ibid.*, II, p. 519 f., 525.
30 *Histoire nestorienne*, V, p. 256 ff.
31 BAR 'EBRAIĀ, *Chronicon eccles.*, III, col. 51.
32 *Acta martyrum*, IV, p. 250.

Concerning these activities in monastic circles, we have a report about Mār Narsai, an ascetic, *bar qeiāmā,* from Bēt Rāzīqāiē. We are told how he cleansed a little church which had been transformed to a fire house : 'he extinguished it (the fire), took out the bricks of the oven and the utensils of the Magi and threw (them) out' [33]. And perhaps we have other reminiscences of this period [34].

b. Mār ʿAbdā and his circle

We now come to other observations permitting us to look at the inner consolidation and advancement of monasticism from still another aspect. The ability to produce a number of spiritual leaders, outstanding personalities, who in their turn contributed to the spiritual strength and the prestige of the movement, allows inferences supplementing the observations already made.

In the following, we will introduce some of the eminent spirits who had a hand in this progess.

The place of honor in this circle belongs to Mār ʿAbdā. Information about him in the sources leaves much to be desired. It is surprising that Barḥadbešabbā does not give even a notice [35], and that Īšōʿdenaḥ, too, does not include him in his skeleton survey [36], though he actually knows little about the early period of the establishment of the monasteries. In such a situation, we would remain very sceptical if we would not know that Catholicos Aḥai (d. 415/6), who belonged to the circle of the disciples of this ʿAbdā, had written a biography of his teacher. Though it, to be sure, has not survived, some of its data are incorporated in the chronicle of Seert, a collection of source materials and excerpts [37]. Thus information from this lost source, which rests on a narrator who stood very close to these events, has been salvaged. Therefore,

33 *Ibid.*, IV, p. 173.

34 Tradition kept in the monastery of Qardag regarded the origin of it as built into a fire-house transformed into a monastery, *ibid.*, II, p. 471.

35 *Fondation des écoles*, p. 381 ff. This work does not know anything about the development of the schools in Persia prior to the influence exercised by the great names connected with the school of Edessa.

36 *Chasteté*, p. 4 ff.

37 *Histoire nestorienne*, V, p. 307 f.

with regard to the main points of ʿAbdā's life and activity, it seems that we stand on a secure terrain.

Another point has to be clarified. One observes that this source was later written out by Mārī in his *Liber turris* in the middle of the 12th century, and by ʿAmr and Ṣelībā in the 14th century. But, in our present manuscript of Mārī, there is a disturbing slip in the name, so that what is wrongly told of ʿAbdīšōʿ [38], should be ascribed to ʿAbdā.

From his lifestory, we are told that ʿAbdā was raised by the Christians. This child, who once was thrown by his light-minded mother into a church, to be nurtured by others, was destined to play an important role in the monastic movement. Becoming an ascetic, he showed faculties far greater than those which could be satisfied in the quietness of a monk's cell or with the rigid practice of asceticism in which he was celebrated, particularly in his observance of fasting [39].

Mār ʿAbdā is reported to have augmented his ascetic virtues with his zeal for evangelization, traversing many districts, converting the people, and organizing the communities, since he also possessed ordination into the priesthood. As much as the tradition has preserved about his tours, his activities were confined to Bēt Ārāmāiē. To be sure, Tellā is mentioned at the river of Ṣerṣer [40], but this place, too, is in Bēt Ārāmāiē being not far from Anbar [41]. His activities, and his success, so close to the capital, put him in danger when he was in Seleucia-Ctesiphon, where the Mazda-believers seized him and put him into prison for a while [42]. This incident may also have been caused by the intrigues which were woven around him by powerful Marcionite groups, with whom he was engaged in controversy and argument.

ʿAbdā also gained additional fame as the founder of a monastery, and of an important school in his monastic community. The information in ʿAmr that this was the monastery of Ṣelībā at the

38 Mari, *De patriarchis*, p. 28.

39 *Histoire nestorienne*, V, p. 308.

40 *Ibid.*, p. 307. About the conversion made by him, see *ibid.*, p. 309.

41 Suhrāb, *Kitāb ʿağāʾib al-aqālīm*, p. 123 f.

42 *Histoire nestorienne*, V, p. 308.

river of Ṣerṣer, is a confusion of data found in Mārī[43]. The Chronicle of Seert, which stands behind all these texts which were transcribed by a chain of hands, brings the solution to this confusion. Here, ʿAbdā's role at the river of Ṣerṣer was no more than this, that he did a couple of miracles there. In the chapter which deals with Mār ʿAbdā, it is said that the place of this monastery was in Bēt Ārāmāiē. But in the following chapter which talks about the history of the monastery of Ṣelībā, Mār ʿAbdā is introduced as the founder of Dair Qōnī[44] near Baghdad[45]. Attentive reading suffices in discerning the way the stories about Mār ʿAbdā and the monastery of Ṣelībā came to be placed side by side, the episode of Mār ʿAbdā being inserted into the latter. The confusion is now comprehensible. Thus this source knows only one foundation, namely that of Dair Qōnī, and not that of Ṣelībā or even of both as accepted by Assemani[46].

Through this foundation, Mār ʿAbdā became the spiritual leader of his pupils — their number is estimated at about 60 — some of whom reached the most influential posts in the church. In fact, through them Mār ʿAbdā augmented the range of his spiritual influence, being able to implant his zeal in manifold areas, such as ascetic practices[47], mission work, founding of monasteries and interest in schools, in the souls of his pupils.

Not only that, but Mār ʿAbdā is reported as being discontent with the spontaneous results of his influence among his spiritual sons and therefore, he also tried to foster this expanding and growing influence by his control and guidance. We are told that he took direct interest in the new monastic establishments founded by his disciples by routine visits, inspecting their life and work : 'and father Mār ʿAbdā took care of them at the (appointed) times

[43] In the text which we possess the name of ʿAbdā has wrongly been substituted for ʿAbdīšōʿ, Mari, *De patriarchis*, p. 28.

[44] *Histoire nestorienne*, V, p. 309; once again in the chapter about ʿAbdīšōʿ, *ibid.*, p. 310.

[45] ܩܘܢܝ in Arabic Deir Qunnā was according to Yaqut 16 farsah below Baghdad, one mile east of the Tigris, *Muʿjam al-buldān*, I, p. 739; II, p. 687; according to Suhrāb it was located at the Tigris, *Kitāb ʿağā'ib al-aqālīm*, p. 118.

[46] *Bibl. orientalis*, III, p. 369, 614.

[47] *Op. cit.*, p. 308.

to visit them and supervise them in their exercises'[48]. So much for the data preserved in the Nestorian chronicle of Seert. It is a matter of regret that we have no way of controlling them.

Concerning the chronology of this influential monastic paedagogue, we can say very little. The only remark we have is this, that before Aḥai was elected the catholicos in 410, he had by the will of his teacher succeeded as the head of his school[49]. Hence, by that time, the work had already passed into the hands of his disciples.

Among the disciples of ʿAbdā, the most active founder of monasteries was ʿAbdīšōʿ. It is the more strange that the work of this one has not found a place in the repertoire of the important founders of the monasteries in Persia[50]. This list, however, is far from being complete. Moreover, for the earliest period this source covers its ignorance with the tatters taken from legends woven around Aūgēn. But fortunately, the situation is this that a paragraph incorporated into the chronicle of Seert[51] obviously seems to go back to the above-mentioned vita of ʿAbdā, which, as we already know, is from Aḥai's pen. The latter must have included some data about the work of Mār ʿAbdā's disciples in this biography in order to glorify the work of the master himself. There is nothing independent in the reports of Mārī and ʿAmr, who also here have transcribed the text of the chronicle.

Mār ʿAbdīšōʿ, of the village Arphelūnā in Maišān, was attracted by Mār ʿAbdā's school and monastery. Fired by the impulses which this atmosphere implanted, he went back to his home-country, and after a while started his missionary journeys which led him to several areas. He is reported to have evangelized in Maišān and in the country of Bāksāiā.

Mār ʿAbdīšōʿ's work as a bishop in Dair Miḥrāq[52] was no more than a brief intermezzo. For this allegedly troublesome and rebel-

48 وكان الاب مر عبدا يصير اليهم فى الاوقات يتعهدهم وينظر فى امورهم *Histoire nestorienne*, V, p. 322.

49 *Ibid.*, p. 324.

50 Īšōʿdenaḥ, *Chasteté*, p. 1; Ms. Berl. Sach. 63, fol. 219 a ff.

51 *Histoire nestorienne*, V, p. 310 ff.

52 According to Ibn Rosteh Dair Mihraq is between Wāsiṭ and Sūq al Ahwāz, 13 farsah from Wāsiṭ, *Kitāb al-aʿlāk an-nafīsa*, p. 187.

lious community [53] he exchanged life as an anchorite and as a missionary on the island of Jamama and Bahrain. Thus as far as the area of his activities is concerned, this is westward of the Euphrates in its lower course. Only if Bēt Rīmā [54], which ʿAbdīšōʿ evangelized with its environment, was located eastward of the Tigris [55], would this be an exception.

A special part in the data preserved about ʿAbdīšōʿ is dedicated to his activities as the founder of monastic communities. We are told that these foundations were erected in the areas where he operated, combining his monasteries with mission-fields or with a school. The following monasteries appear in the survey of the main events of his activities. The first was founded in Maišān, after he returned from the school of Mār ʿAbdā. In the country of Bāksāiā [56] a new convent was erected. His stay on the islands of Jamama and Bahrain left a visible memorial in the form of a new monastery. And finally when coming from there, his route led him to Ḥīrā. Thus all these foundations were constructed in the south-western part of the empire, in Bēt Maišān and Bēt Ārāmāiē.

Another prominent disciple in the team of Mār ʿAbdā is Aḥai [57]. He was even elevated to the catholicos' seat. He also enjoyed considerable respect in the eyes of Jazdgard. Aḥai was the man that his master appointed as the abbot of his monastery and the school [58].

53 In the light of the *Histoire nestorienne*, IV, p. 236 it was not a mission field, but a seat which existed already in early period of the Sassanids. Its bishop Andreas was engaged in the quarrels around Papā. According to the same source, *ibid.*, p. 221, this place was founded by Shahpuhr I for the captives brought from the Roman areas.

54 ريميون, *ibid.*, V, p. 311. Bēt Rīmā appears later as the seat of a bishop, *Synodicon orientale*, p. 109.

55 Tabari, *Ta'rikh ar-rusul*, I, p. 830 which has a reference but in a corrupted form, cf. Marqwart, *Eranšahr*. It says that it was in the district of Maišān. But according to Kodāma, p. 235 the four districts of the country were east of the Tigris on the route from Kaškar to Ahwāz, *Kitāb al-Kharādj*, p. 235.

56 ناحية باكسايا 'the country of Bāksāiā', *Histoire nestorienne*, V, p. 311; Mārī has the same. 'Bāksāsiā' is obviously Bēt Kūsāiē, which is in the southern part of the country of Nahrawān, named after a canal east of the Tigris. No bishopric is known in this area in the early documents.

57 Not of ʿAbdīšōʿ, as Labourt says, *Christianisme*, p. 99.

58 *Histoire nestorienne*, V, p. 324.

He seems to have stepped in the foot-prints of his master. With regard to ascetic practice, some remarks have been preserved [59]. But through his literary activity Aḥai made new contributions [60] to all the fruitful stimuli which came out of this team. The vita composed in memory of the work of Mār ʿAbdā, was already mentioned earlier. And during his short rule as catholicos, he found time for literary work in which he recorded the traditions he had collected regarding the memories of the martyrs under Shahpuhr II, a work which has not survived [61], though it had been in the hands of some authors [62].

Another man of deeds who came from ʿAbdā's school and tradition, is Jahballāhā, distinguished by the most reverent epitheta [63]. There is some ground for the supposition that the information regarding his life and work [64], too, in its essential part, rests on the above-mentioned work of Aḥai.

Jahballāhā is distinguished as the most illustrious among the pupils of ʿAbdā. Already in ʿAbdā's school he is reported to have surpassed all his fellow students. His master, too, selected him for his successor for a mission-work which he himself had started. When the converts asked for an able man, ʿAbdā's choice fell upon Jahballāhā. This place is identified as Daskarat of ʿAišōʿ [65],

59 Mentioned only by MARI, *De patriarchis*, p. 31.

60 Traces of earlier relationship of monasticism with literary culture are not entirely missing. A remark in SOZOMENUS, *Hist. eccl.*, II, 14, col. 969 indicates that several of the works of Mīlēs were known. ʿAbdīšōʿ ascribes to him homilies and letters, *Catalogus librorum*, p. 51; Andreas of a monastery of Mārī, a contemporary of Mīlēs, is mentioned as an outstanding author. This note appears in a chronicle in Arabic, the fragmentary manuscript of which is in Mossul, see SCHER, *Étude supplémentaire*, p. 3.

61 *Histoire nestorienne*, V, p. 325.

62 Daniel bar Mariam (ca 650) had used these acts in his church history, AMR, *De patriarchis*, p. 26, mentioned by ʿAbdīšōʿ, *Catalogus librorum*, p. 231. This church historical work seems to be the main basis on which the Chronicle of Seert seems to rest.

63 *Synodicon orientale*, p. 37.

64 *Histoire nestorienne*, V, p. 321 f.

65 'Daskarat' is a Persian word and means 'village', and these compounds are most common. Abīšōʿ appears in the chronicle of Seert, MARI, *De patriarchis*, p. 32 reads Išōʿ. If this should be the original then the name would refer to a mission-field : the village of Jesus.

near the monastery of Ezechiel the Prophet [66]. These data do not help us much in locating the place. Here, for a while, Jahballāhā took care of the inhabitants, but, he preferred solitude and quietness for his monastic habits, and soon resigned this work.

Jahballāhā is celebrated as the founder of two monasteries. The first he established in the mission field where he was fostering the seed which his master had sown. It is said that this was a great monastery. The second he founded at the bank of the Tigris [67]. His fame was a magnet drawing together many monks. Jahballāhā must have found pleasure in the monastic communities which at that time were becoming reputable — the monasteries of the Akoimetes, in which the unceasing liturgical praise was realized. Having a large company of monks at his disposal, Jahballāhā divided it into three groups for this purpose, which by rotation each released the preceding group. This imitation of angel-like life also regulated other functions in his monastery, so that a detachment was in the household duties, another did its studies and meditated, another stood in the service of the visitors, or could rest.

In the evening of his life, the great reputation he had gained in monasticism led him to the greatest honors. After Catholicos Ahai's death, Jahballāhā was elevated to the vacant seat of the patriarch. He also won Jazdgard's respect. The latter appointed him with a mission as an ambassador to Emperor Theodosius II.

2. SOME REFORM ATTEMPTS

Friendly relations between Jazdgard and the Byzantine Emperor Arcadius created such favorable conditions that Western Christianity could intervene in the development of Persian Christianity including its asceticism. This took place under the mediation of Mār Marūtā in his capacity as ambassador of the Byzantine ruler. Mār Marūtā, bishop of Maipherqaṭ who was celebrated in his home city as a collector of precious relics of the martyrs of Persia, was a man of action and a persuasive negotiator and had been in Persia several

66 A monastery of Ezechiel دير حزقيل or دير هزقيل was in Iraq, YAQUT, *Muʿjam al-buldān*, II, p. 654.

67 According to MARI, *De patriarchis*, p. 32 at the Euphrates.

times although we do not know exactly how many. He was able to arouse Jazdgard's confidence by virtue of his dignified life, his tactfulness and, perhaps, most of all because of his medical knowledge [68]. Thus, Marūtā was in a position to help not only in the restorative work of the congregations, but actively to participate in the reorganization of conditions in the Persian church.

The convocation of the synod which opened on February 1st, 410 in the main church of Seleucia-Ctesiphon is of major significance. The reform attempts which were planned there naturally could not by-pass monasticism, particularly the ancient ascetic traditions and practices. To be sure, the canons which were included in the synodical acts do not treat monasticism as a movement by giving it directives in this or that direction. However, they include some canons which deal with the archaic ascetic traditions by trying to control them in so far as the church is concerned. Further, as we shall see, there are some traces of other regulations and norms which were related to these reform attempts.

We begin with the data embodied in the synodical canons. The second canon draws our attention. It deals with eunuchs 'who castrate themselves'. The synod decided that they could not be received into the clergy. At this point the text runs : 'no man who voluntarily has made himself an eunuch and has destroyed his generative nature, will be received into the church' [69].

The position of this rule in relation to other canons is of importance. It must be observed that it immediately follows the regulations dealing with the election of bishops — the first canon. One gathers that the practice of castration could by no means have been insignificant but was rather an acute problem. There is no escape from the conclusion that at this point the matter of asceticism was involved. When the ascetics and monks gradually began to enter the service of the church as ordained workers, eunuchs appeared in the clergy. Then those reform attempts which were in the spirit of Western standards were confronted with the question of the legitimacy of this sort of ordination.

68 Socrates, *Hist. eccl.*, VII, 9 reports even that he cured Jazdgard's head-sickness.

69 *Synodicon orientale*, p. 23 f.

It is a matter of regret that we have so little information dealing with this practice. But we do know that castration was rooted in the ancient phase of asceticism connected with the Manichaean monasticism [70]. In the absence of direct information we must be content with these observations which indicate the possibility for the spread of this practice in Syrian asceticism so that this question could come up as a serious problem when the ancient practices and traditions were measured by the standards made valid by the Byzantine church.

The next canon spotlights another ancient practice kept by asceticism and spread in the church. The third canon attacks the practice of *syneisaktoi* by deciding that this ancient custom cannot be tolerated in the clergy : 'that from now on no bishop, priest, deacon, subdeacon or *bar qeiāmā,* who lives together with women, and not chastely and with holy awe alone, as it is fitting to the service of the church — men alone with men — will be received into the service of the church' [71]. This text gives us more knowledge about the conditions at that time. For if such a practice could influence the clergy themselves, we are permitted to observe that its popularity must have been widespread among the ascetics themselves.

Concerning the popularity of this practice, explicit information was examined as it is preserved in Aphrahaṭ. We have already seen him in fighting against it in a manner which gives us clear references as to its wide-spread character. Upon closer examination several documents arouse our suspicion that they show *benat qeiāmā* living together with the clerics in 'spiritual marriage'. Particularly conspicuous are those acts of martyrdom which tell of the arrest of a cleric along with a *bart qeiāmā.* There seems to be no better explanation for such cases than the assumption that here we have to do with a couple of spiritual servants, a clergyman and a *bart qeiāmā.* Of similar character may be the case concerning a priest Dāni'ēl and Wardā, a *bart qeiāmā,* in the country of Rāzīqāiē [72]. Another similar instance seems to be the priest Ja'qōb and Mariam, a *bart qeiāmā,* his 'sister', in the village of Tellā Šelīlā [73], and

[70] See pag. 116.

[71] *Synodicon orientale,* p. 24.

[72] *Acta martyrum,* II, p. 290.

[73] *Ibid.,* II, p. 307.

the priest Ja'qōb and his 'sister' in the village of 'Aspragāltā in Ḥadiab [74].

Complaints that the archaic practice of *syneisaktoi* persisted with a tenacity surpassing reputation, come from different sources. The alleged letter of Catholicos Papā speaks of the deep-rooted character of this habit, that it had eaten its way deeply into the life of episcopacy. Regarding the bishops, this text comments that : 'they were in lust in the union of the spiritual marriage' [75].

Observations concerning the widerspread custom which was able to infiltrate the clergy receive further confirmation when we examine another area in which the Syrians exhibited their traditions. The same practice occurs with the Syrians in Armenia where it was annoying to the Armenian Christians. The man who was appointed by Vahram V as the head of the church, Berīkīšō', was a Syrian who lived together with a female ascetic [76]. Finally, resentment grew so strong among the Armenians that Vahram had to dismiss him and to appoint a new man. The successor, again a Syrian, Šemū'ēl by name, aroused the indignation of the Armenians by the same practice [77].

The decisions of the synod which were summed up in the third canon, served the purpose of removing this part of the influence of the archaic practice. It was purged out from the ranks of the clergy but is was left completely untouched in its validity and reputation among the ascetics.

It may be that another canon reflects something of the ancient traditions related to asceticism. Canon number thirteen mentions an ancient practice of celebrating the Eucharist in the homes, a practice which the synod terminated [78]. Our curiosity is aroused about the background of this custom. Could it not be that this

74 *Ibid.*, IV, p. 138.

75 ܘܗܘܘ ܐ̈ܝܠ ܒܫܘܬܦܘܬܐ ܕܒܘܘܠܐ ܪܘܚܢܝܐ Ms. Borg. syr. 82, fol. 116 b.

76 այր ապարասան յափշտակող, որ տանտիկին կանամբք զտուն իւր մատակարարէր 'a man licentious and avaricious, who administered his house by cohabit women', Yovhan, *Patmowt'iwn*, p. 74; տանտիկին means οἰκοδέσποινα, κυρία, δεσποίνη, συνοικοῦσα, mater familias, matrona, domina, cohabitans, *Thesaurus armeniacus*, II, p. 844.

77 *Op. cit.*, p. 74 f.

78 *Synodicon orientale*, p. 27.

practice has some connection with the survival of the archaic concept of the church as an assembly of ascetics who assumed the right to celebrate the sacrament? There are some indications in this direction [79]. Some early documents leave the impression that it was necessary to take a stand against the pretension of the ascetics who assumed the right to handle the matter of sacraments [80]. Unfortunately, the text is not more explicit and the supposition must rest at this point.

There is enough yet to be said about reform attempts in the interest of the advancement of monasticism, although many questions cannot be illuminated any further.

On the one hand, one becomes attentive when the acts of this historically important synod refer to still other canons, namely to 'a *penqītā* (volume) in which the canons were written' [81].

We are told that, upon the request of Isḥaq, Marūtā read this volume before the assembly. Since all the bishops by their 'Amen' declared themselves ready to accept the canons, Marūtā told the assembly : 'all these precepts, laws and canons shall be written down, and we all (will) subscribe at the end of the decision (judgment) by our hand, and sanction (it) by a pact that is not changeable' [82]. Then Isḥaq asked Marūtā to write them down so that all could sign a copy. The first session ended with this preparatory procedure. 'Several days' later this 'volume' was signed [83].

79 Sometimes we hear that the monks who instructed the neophytes and baptized them, gave them also the Eucharist, see *Acta martyrum*, II, p. 571. Regarding the practice of the monks to gather in private houses, see the movement of Eusthatius in Armenia, Paphlagonia and Pontus, SOZOMENUS, *Hist. eccl.*, III, 14, col. 1080.

80 A metrical text of the martyrdom of Mār Bassōs contains a section which ostentatiously argues against the possibility that a monk is able to administer a sacrament, since the keys of the Kingdom have been given only to Peter and through him to the clergy, *Légende de Bassus*, p. 47. But the prose text, on the contrary, shows nothing of these controversial points, see Ms. Šarf. Patr. 38, fol. 153 ab.

81 *Synodicon orientale*, p. 21.

82 ܕܟܠܗܘܢ ܙܘܗܪ̈ܐ ܘܢܡܘ̈ܣܐ ܘܩܢܘ̈ܢܐ ܗܠܝܢ ܡܬܟܬܒܘ ܢܬܟܬܒܘܢ . ܘܟܠܢ ܐܝܕܐ ܪܫܡܝܢ ܚܢܢ ܒܫܘܠܡ ܕܕܝܢܐ ܒܟܬܒܬܗ ܐܝܕܝܢ ܘܡܫܪܪܝܢ ܒܩܝܡܐ ܕܠܐ ܡܫܬܚܠܦ *ibid.*, p. $21_{13\text{-}15}$.

83 *Ibid.*, p. 22.

On the other hand, canons have come down to us in Syriac [84], Arabic [85], and Ethiopic [86], entirely different from the Nicaean canons, which claim to be the canons of Marūtā. The longer [87] as well as the shorter Syriac text [88] says that these canons were translated into Syriac by Marūtā. Now it has been suggested that these canons were contained in this *penqītā* of the canons [89]. This raises acute historical problems.

First of all, an analysis of the synodical acts under Isḥaq leaves the impression that the 20 authentic canons of Nicaea were not the only canons meant. For one thing, the term *penqītā* is too noble a term for 20 canons. For another the wording of the text itself gives us a hint that there were other materials besides the authentic canons [90].

These observations, indeed, find substantiation in some other considerations. For if we take into account the whole situation — which meant no less than a reorganization of the church —, it is hardly feasible that Marūtā would have been content with no more than the introduction of the 20 authentic Nicaean canons. The entire situation was such that it obviously needed a much wider basis for the ecclesiastical re-organization. With regard to monasticism this even became an imperative. Dubious historical support for this is supplied by a text incorporated in the correspondence between Isḥaq and Marūtā [91]. Furthermore, Marūtā was himself

84 Ms. Vat. Borg. syr. 82, fol. 44 b ff.; Ms. Vat. syr. 501, fol. 57 b ff. Reference to Ms. Br. Mus. Add. 14,526 and Add. 14,528, in DUVAL, *Littérature syriaque*, p. 159, is a mistake.

85 Ms. Vat. arab. 153, fol. 158 b ff.

86 *Canones apost. aethiopice*, p. 11.

87 Ms. Vat. Borg. syr. 82; Vat. syr. 501.

88 Ms. Vat. syr. 520, fol. 27 a - 29 a.

89 BRAUN, *De Nicaena synodo*, p. 23 ff.

90 ܘܟܕ ܐܝܬܝܘ ܘܩܪܘܗ̇ : ܘܫܡܥܘ ܡܢܗ̇ ܟܠܗܘܢ : ܐܝܠܝܢ ܕܡܬܒܥܝܢ ܠܬܩܢܐ ܬܪܝܨܐ ܕܬܫܡܫܬܐ ܕܥܕܬܗ ܕܡܫܝܚܐ ܗܘ ܡܫܝܚܐ : ܘܟܠܗܘܢ ܩܢܘܢܐ ܕܐܬܐܡܪܘ ܒܚܟܡܬܗ ܕܐܠܗܐ ܠܐܒܗܬܢ ܐܦܝܣܩܘܦܐ ܒܗܘ ܣܘܢܗܕܘܣ ܪܒܬܐ ܘܩܕܝܫܬܐ ܕܡܥܪܒܐ 'and as they brought and read it, and heard from it, all the precepts which are required for the right order of the service of the church of Christ, and all the canons which were spoken through the wisdom of God by our fathers bishops on that great and holy synod of the West', *Synodicon orientale*, p. 21_{3-6}.

91 Ms. Vat. Borg. syr. 82, fol. 67 tells that the Catholicos Isḥaq had asked

a monk [92], and in his Armenian vita, he is reported as being interested in the furtherance of monasticism [93]. Incidentally, we are not entirely without a reference which has preserved something of this interest of his during his activities in Persia [94].

Now in the light of this information, it is unthinkable hat Marūtā's particular concern did not find expression when a unique opportunity for advancing the cause of the monastic life presented itself. It is also not entirely impossible that Marūtā did not clarify the true relations between the Nicaean canons and other regulations [95], or that Marūtā even used a *pia fraus* and left the impression that all the canonical material he presented was sanctioned in Nicaea.

Further, the whole question gains force from the observation that there appears to have existed certain canons for the monks — not of local provenance given to them by their spiritual leaders for their local communities, but established by authorities higher than those within one bishopric, since these were norms for all monks. From the 58th of the canons of Marūtā, we learn that there were rules for the monks which the chorepiscopus had to read before them once a year : 'it is the will of the general synod that twice a year, the chorepiscopus shall read the canons before the people of the *benai qeiāmā,* and before monks those for the monks' [96].

If so, then there are some reasons for thinking that material like this has not entirely been lost. To be sure, a critical student cannot trust the tradition that the canons of Marūtā in their present form

from Marūtā for canons for the reorganization both of the churches and monasteries. But this we can leave aside as a valueless fabrication.

92 *Vark' ew vkayabanowt'iwnk'*, II, p. 20.

93 There is a reference to the results of Marūtā's activities : ***և զպատկերս աստուածոցն կործանէին, և շինէին վանորայս և եկեղեցիս***, 'and they destroyed the effigies of the gods and built monasteries and churches', *ibid.*, p. 21.

94 MARI, *De patriarchis*, I, p 29.

95 However, Ms. Vat. Borg. syr. 82, fol. 102 does allude to this, namely that a selection was also made from other canonical material and adapted to the conditions in Persia.

96 ܘܗܘܐ ܨܒܝܢܐ ܠܣܘܢܗܕܘܣ ܬܒܝܠܝܬܐ ܕܬܪ̈ܬܝܢ ܙܒܢ̈ܝܢ ܒܫܢܬܐ ܢܗܘܐ ܩܪܐ ܟܘܪ ܐܦܝܣܩܘܦܐ ܩܢܘܢܐ ܩܕܡ ܥܡܐ ܕܒܢ̈ܝ ܩܝܡܐ. ܘܕܕܝܪ̈ܝܐ ܩܕܡ ܕܝܪ̈ܝܐ. *ibid.*, fol. 47 a.

and the accompanying texts at our disposal, are authentic. An examination of this material shows that this contains texts of later provenance. And the accompanying letter, perforated as it is with fabrications, can hardly be ascribed to the learned bishop of Maipherqaṭ [97].

Yet this scepticism need not preclude the possibility that a kernel of this canonical material really goes back to this *penqītā* of canons which was handed over by Marūtā to the bishops [98]. Nor does an extensive acquaintance with these texts banish this thought. Certain archaic features in terminology [99] and injunctions [100] speak too loudly. This consideration seems to be strengthened by the observation that perhaps something of the older form can be seen in comparing the text as it appears in ʿAbdīšōʿ with the form of the longer recension [101].

The preceding deliberations open the door to another aspect in the reform attempts which, if we could only follow our source with less reluctance, might lead us to more concrete information. However, if we try to advance a little farther from this recognition of a general nature and try to assess the value of the texts, serious difficulties start. Layers which have grown together through the course of centuries, cannot be separated satisfactorily, if at all. To be sure, in certain sections the strata of later origin can be detected without difficulty [102], but in the sections in which we are more interested, this undertaking faces insurmountable obstacles.

Under such conditions, there remains but one way — to consider

97 The historical survey of the Nicaean council shows anachronisms and blunders which militate seriously against this claim. Thus, Helena, the mother of Constantinus, is reported originally to have been from the region of Edessa, *ibid.*, fol. 54; her husband's name is Valentinianus, etc.

98 See chapter I in Vööbus, *Syriac and Arabic Documents.*

99 Braun has observed that the term for to ordain ܥܒܕ 'to make' and ܗܘܐ 'to become' appear in the acts of the synod, and not elsewhere, *Buch der Synhados*, p. 7.

100 For instance the role of the chorepiscopus.

101 A comparison of the canon LVI, Ms. Vat. Borg. syr. 82, fol. 44 a with can. XLIX in ʿAbdīšōʿ in Ms. Vat. syr. 520, fol. 28 b makes it obvious that the monasteries were absent in the original form of the text.

102 For example the section on the tonsure, in Ms. Vat. Borg. syr. 82, fol. 47 b, cf. Ms. Vat. syr. 520, fol. 28 b.

quite cautiously that which in these sections perhaps has an archaic ring; for some texts we must be so suspicious that little more than very general remarks can be dared.

Since the role of the chorepiscopus appears archaic over against the development of a later time, his duties with regard to monasticism may be briefly mentioned. The more so because that which we find here is, indeed, something that would quite naturally have come up in such a re-organization of ecclesiastical conditions.

In the texts before us, it is conspicuous that the functions of the chorepiscopus are employed in order to tie monasticism closer to the church and put more order into the monastic conditions. The chorepiscopus is made the superviser of the monastic communities as well as of the ascetic groups in the congregations — the *qeiāmā* [103]. He had to visit them. Besides this he had to gather the *qeiāmā* twice a year [104] and the monks once a year [105]. His duty was also to read the rules to the *qeiāmā* and the canons to the monks [106]. Responsibility for the recruiting of the *qeiāmā* among the children, of increasing the institution and taking care of its instruction, was laid on the chorepiscopus : 'the chorepiscopus shall persuade everyone of them who has sons and daughters, and shall select from their sons and daughters; he shall mark them by prayer and shall lay his hand on them and bless them to become the *benai qeiāmā*; they shall be instructed and given into the churches and monasteries, and he shall order that they shall be educated in doctrine and instruction, that they shall be inheritors upon whom the churches and monasteries

103 See can. XXVI, XXVII, Ms. Vat. Borg. syr. 82, fol. 45 a.

104 Can. XXVII : ܗܘܐ ܨܒܝܢܐ ܠܣܘܢܗܘܕܘܣ ܬܒܝܠܝܬܐ. ܕܢܗܘܐ ܡܟܢܫ ܟܘܪ ܐܦܝܣܩܘܦܐ ܟܠܗ ܩܝܡܐ ܕܐܬܪܗ. ܬܪ̈ܬܝܢ ܙܒܢܝܢ ܒܫܢܬܐ ܫܘܐܝܬ ܠܐܝܩܪܗ ܕܐܦܝܣܩܘܦܐ... ܚܕܐ ܙܒܢܬܐ ܟܕ ܥܐܠ ܣܬܘܐ. ܘܐܚܪܬܐ ܒܬܪ ܥܐܕܐ ܕܩܝܡܬܐ 'it is the will of the general synod, that the chorepiscopus shall gather the entire *qeiāmā* of the locality two times a year equally, for the honor of the bishop... one time when the winter enters, and another time after the feast of resurrection', *ibid.*, fol. 45 a.

105 ܕܕܝܪ̈ܝܐ ܕܝܢ ܚܕܐ ܙܒܢܬܐ ܒܫܢܬܐ ܢܬܟܢܫܘܢ ܘܐܦ ܐܡܬܝ ܕܨܒܐ ܟܘܪ ܐܦܝܣܩܘܦܐ ܢܟܢܫ ܐܢܘܢ 'the monks, however, shall be gathered once a year and namely when the chorepiscopus wishes to gather them', *ibid.*, fol. 45 a.

106 Can. LVIII, *ibid.*, fol. 47 a.

have their existence' [107]. He also was made responsible for the regulation of the election of abbots though with some reservations [108] and also for disciplinary measures [109].

Once we leave the sections dealing with the chorepiscopus, the ground becomes very shaky. However, even if nothing but the framework is left of the original form of the text after deletion of the accretions, it would point to the norms for abbots [110], other functionaries [111], the monks [112], and the life in community [113]. More generally Marūtā may perhaps have included this in his canonical material. But there is no ground permitting us to be more specific. Further than this it is hard to go.

Did Marūtā use other means to influence Persian monasticism? We have no way of knowing how he may have tried. It seems that the only vestige is a remark preserved by Mārī. In connection with the activity of Marūtā, the results of his successful negotiations and the promulgations of the edict, Mārī states that in Babylonia a church was rebuilt and remarks : 'and the church in Babylonia at the

107 ܘܥܠ ܐܝܠܝܢ ܕܒܥܝܢ ܕܐܝܬ ܠܗ ܒܢܝܐ ܘܒܢܬܐ : ܢܦܫܗ ܗܘ ܒܗܪ ܐܦܝܣܩܘܦܐ ܘܦܪܘܫ ܡܢ ܒܢܝܗܘܢ ܘܒܢܬܗܘܢ : ܢܣܥܘܪ ܐܝܟ ܕܒܗ ܒܓܠܝܘܬܐ : ܘܢܫܩܘܠ ܐܝܕܗ ܥܠܝܗܘܢ ܘܢܒܪܟ ܐܢܘܢ ܘܢܗܘܘܢ ܒܢܝ ܡܫܝܚܐ ܘܢܬܬܠܡܕܘܢ ܘܢܬܚܡܨܘܢ ܒܕܝܪܬܐ ܘܕܝܪܝܬܐ ܘܢܫܡܫܘܢ ܥܠܝܗܘܢ ܕܒܥܠܡܐ ܘܒܡܕܝܪܬܐ ܢܬܕܪܫܘܢ ܘܢܗܘܘܢ ܕܝܪܝܬܐ ܥܠ ܐܝܕܝܗܘܢ ܢܬܩܝܡܢ ܒܕܝܪܬܐ ܘܕܝܪܝܬܐ can. XXVI, Ms. Vat. syr. 501, fol. 58 b.

108 Can. XL. However, the canon acknowledges the designation made by a deceased abbot during his life time under the stipulation that his designee is not his relative nor his 'countryman', Ms. Vat. Borg. syr. 82, fol. 41 a.

109 Can. LIV. The cases of the troublemakers in the monasteries belong to the competency of the chorepiscopus, *ibid.*, fol. 42 b.

110 Can. XLVIII, *ibid.*, fol. 38 b.

111 Can. XLIX-LIII offer instructions to the 'manager', 'visitor', doorkeeper and other minor officers in the monasteries in regard to their behavior and duties, *ibid.*, fol. 38 b ff.

112 Can. LI, *ibid.*, fol. 39 a.

113 Can. LIV has the title 'about the laws and habits of the monks' and deals mostly with the provisions of protecting the communities against negative phenomena and gives more detailed instructions. The whole long section fol. 42 b - 43 b in the present form is certainly of later origin. Perhaps only the beginning of the canon, which emphasizes perseverance in worship, prayer, the lessons and fasting according to the manners established for this by the abbot, has escaped revision.

pit of Daniel, was restored, which the Jews had formerly destroyed after killing those of the monks, presbyters and deacons who were in it; and there was planted a community of monks' [114]. This remark is the only one which hints at Marūtā's direct relations to Eastern Syrian monasticism.

The trend which was begun by the synod under Isḥaq was not continued under his successors. The synod held in the year 419/20 under Jahballāhā carried the attempts no further. And if such was the case under Jahballāhā, who was himself formerly a monk and a disciple of ʿAbdā, one could hardly expect more from the next synod which was held under Catholicos Dadīšōʿ in 424. The absence of the catholicos and the confused situation in the church prevented it from giving constructive guidance. We are unable to check the tradition that he established canons for ecclesiastical law [115]. But when one thinks of the collections of canons made by later authors and the works of codification, one is inclined to think that Dadīšōʿ's canons were nothing else than the questions dealt with in the synodical acts. Besides this, included in the criticism brought against him was the reproach that he was not interested in the welfare of monasticism [116].

As the preceding discussion shows, the time had not yet come to bring more order into asceticism, and into the movement of monasticism by means of ecclesiastical legislation.

3. A NEW WAVE OF SUFFERINGS

The growing activity and the boldening of the aggressive spirit created an atmosphere in which, under another ruler, there would have been enough material for explosion long ago. The sources have preserved something of these growing difficulties so that we can follow pretty well the change in Jazdgard's policy which led him to the way of persecution.

Intensified recruiting among the Mazda-believers was one of the

114 وجددت بيعة ببابل فى جب دانيال بعد هدم اليهود اياها وقتلهم ما كان فيها من الرهبان والقسان والشمامسة ونصب فيها جماعة من الرهبان Mari, *De patriarchis*, p. 29.

115 Amr, *De patriarchis*, p. 29.

116 *Synodicon orientale*, p. 45.

main reasons for this tension, and the Magi took care that such cases were brought to the attention of those in high places. In the story of Narsai we hear that the mobadh Ādhurbōzē brought this matter, which long had caused concern, to the attention of Jazdgard, informing him that it was alarming how widely the Christian faith had found ground among the nobility and the dignitaries. He was so concerned about this that he wanted credentials in order to initiate counter measures to stop this movement and to compel those who had fallen away to return. According to this source the mobadh received only limited authorization : the use of threats and 'some blows' in treating the converts, but not the death penalty [117].

The case of Ṭāṭāq, in Ḥadiab, throws more light on this. He had been converted and had entered a monastery. An investigation was arranged by Jazdgard's order and he was discovered in the monastery, was put in chains, brought to Seleucia and thrown into prison. The accusations against him stressed two points : why had he left the honors the king had bestowed on him, and why had he turned to the Christians? He was subjected to repeated beatings and tortures until execution ended his ordeal. His head was hewn asunder by sword. The monks from his monastery took care of his body and head and buried them in a martyrion [118]. There were other similar cases [119].

A reference has already been made to that aggressive spirit which particularly stimulated ascetics. A case in point is the incident of Mār Narsai of Bēt Rāzīqāiē, who threw out the utensils of the Magi from the fire-temple and extinguished the fire. Of course, the village was alarmed, and the infuriated crowd inflicted blows, but obviously the local authorities had no power to do more than this. He was brought to Seleucia before the king and the chief of the Magi.

We also learn much from this incident about the procedure and also of the patience of the king in dealing with delicate cases such as this [120]. Our source cannot say that there was a strong pressure

117 *Acta martyrum,* IV, p. 172.

118 *Ibid.,* IV, p. 182 f.

119 Mār Šābōr was executed in the 18th year of Jazdgard = 417 A.D., Ms. Br. Mus. Add. 7200, fol. 107 a.

120 Narsai was thrown into a narrow and hard prison for 9 months, kept

towards his execution. And even Jazdgard himself [121] and the Marzban of Bēt Ārāmāiē wanted to leave a door of escape open [122]. He was finally killed outside Seleucia on the basis of the edict of Jazdgard and was buried in a martyrion built by Mār Marūtā in honor of the martyrs.

In many a case, so it appears, liberty had caused excesses and these annoyed the king. The local incidents and intrigues gathered as a threatening dark cloud until the storm broke out. Jazdgard's son Vahram V characterized his father for his kindness and goodheartedness, and that he had reaped thanklessness and all this has made him austere [123]. And, indeed, in this severeness with which he turned to the persecution, the old brute despotism of the Sassanides again lifted its head.

In the story of Mar 'Abdā the tradition has preserved the gist of the edict which was issued in the twenty-second year of Jazdgard's rule, i.e. in the year 420. In this source it is reported : 'in all the territory of his authority the churches and monasteries shall be destroyed, the service in them shall be stopped, and the priests and the presidents (of the monasteries) arrested and brought to the (royal) residence' [124]. This order let loose a heavy storm [125].

Jazdgard could direct only the first acts in this drama, because in 421 he died. But his death did not bring relief. His son, Vahram V, although celebrated as talented, became so involved in the diffi-

among the criminals. But after Jazdgard left Seleucia-Ctesiphon and went to his summer residence, it was still possible to bring Narsai out for a sum of 400 zuz, paid to an official who was appointed to take charge of him, and for a Christian guarantor who would give a written obligation. Narsai was brought out into a monastery situated 6 miles from Seleucia and stayed there for a while until the decision was made and the order came from Jazdgard, *ibid.*, p. 175.

121 *Ibid.*, p. 175 f.

122 'I know that you have not killed the fire', as to rescue him from death, *ibid.*, IV, p. 176.

123 TABARI, *Ta'rikh ar-rusul*, I, II, p. 865.

124 ܕܒܟܠܗ ܐܪܥܐ ܕܫܘܠܛܢܗ ܥܕ̈ܬܐ ܘܕܝ̈ܪܬܐ ܢܬܣܬܪܢ܆ ܘܬܫܡܫܬܐ ܕܒܗܝܢ ܬܬܒܛܠ܆ ܘܟܗܢ̈ܐ ܘܡܕܒܪ̈ܢܐ ܢܬܐܣܪܘܢ܆ ܘܠܬܪܥܐ ܕܡܠܟܐ ܢܐܬܘܢ *Acta martyrum*, IV, p. 250.

125 Ἔκτοτε δὲ ἤρξατο ὁ μέγας διωγμὸς κατὰ χριστιανῶν παρὰ Πέρσαις, *Synaxarium Constantinop.*, col. 17.

culties of dynastic affairs that he was compelled to be attentive to the wishes of the Magi and the Mazdean dignitaries. In other words, he had to continue the course set by his father.

According to the story of Pērōz of Bēt Lāphāṭ, Vahram started with the desecration of the bodies of the martyrs. A corresponding decree remained valid for five years [126]. And then, in order to please the dignitaries, he conceded and went the way of large scale persecution.

As to what actually happened, we are informed by several sources. An objective picture of the results is given by the acts of the synod held under Dadīšōʿ in the fourth year of Vahram's rule, i.e. in 424. According to this summary report, the persecutions had at that time so devastated Christian life that many had denied their faith, and others had fled and disappeared. Churches and monasteries were destroyed. And this document complains that even now evil forces are at work to undermine the Christian church and its institutions [127].

This summary report finds illustration in several documents which give an idea of the way of the cross which monasticism shared with the members of the clergy.

Longer sections from a lost Syriac document have survived in the Armenian synaxarion about the monk Bata, of whom only a brief note appears in the Greek tradition [128], which helps us to illustrate the fate which struck monastic communities. This is depicted in the following terms : 'and they began to search the mountains, and deserts and the monasteries. And hearing this, the abbot of the monastery where Bata was, realized the order of the Lord who says : « when they persecute you in one town, flee to the next », and he departed from the monastery along with his monks and went into another place' [129]. The abbot also admonished Bata

126 *Acta martyrum*, IV, p. 254; repercussions of this also in the acts of Narsai, *ibid.*, p. 180.

127 *Synodicon orientale*, p. 45.

128 *Synaxarium Constantinop.*, col. 647 f.

129 Ընդ աւուրսն ընդ այնոսիկ հալածիչք առաքեցան ընդ ամենայն գաւառս Պարսից, և զորս գտանէին քրիստոնեայս մեծաւ տանջանօք չարչարէին, և նեղէին ուրանալ զՔրիստոս և երկիր պագանել արեգականն և հրոյ: Եւ ապա սկսան քննել զլերինս և զանապատս

to join the exodus, and to flee from the wrath, but Bata, who had lived in the monastery for thirty years, decided to remain. Here he was found and arrested. After being severely beaten, he was finally killed.

We get a somewhat more detailed picture from the acts of martyrdom of Mār Pērōz, composed not long after the events. These permit us to take a glimpse of the scenery, painting it in the following words : 'the adorned churches are ruined, their mortar scattered, roofs magnificent for sight, were made into bridges on the canals; for not one church was left that was not uprooted, and not one martyrion that was not destroyed; the wood and the doors of the churches and martyria and their *gūrnē*[130] were taken away and made into the steps for the bridges of the canals; the roofs of the monasteries of the mourners and of peaceful convents of the holy ones were taken away, and these items which were selected and beautiful, were brought in his storehouse, and the rest was divided among the Magi'[131].

It is also said that many a once flourishing community and place induced a shudder among travellers[132]. And the acts of martyrdom of Miharšābōr, which took place in the second year of the rule of Vahram (422), says that the persecution embraced the whole Orient, demanding many victims[133].

և զվանորայս։ Եւ լուեալ հօր վանացն յորում էր Բատա կատարէր զտէրունական հրամանն որ ասէ. Եթէ հալածեսցեն զձեզ յայսմ քաղաքէս փախերուք ի միւսն, *Synaxaire arménien*, XXI, p. 365.

130 ܓܘܪ̈ܢܝܗܘܢ is not clear; γοῦρνα means an urn, vessel, a stone bath. PAYNE SMITH, *Thesaurus syriacus*, col. 692 : cisterna, labrum lapideum, also arca feralis. Were these vessels of more expensive stone?

131 ܬܪ̈ܥܐ ܓܝܪ ܡܨܒ̈ܬܬܐ ܡܦܩܢܝܢ ܗܘܘ܆ ܘܕ̈ܪܐ ܡܕ̈ܪܗܝܢ. ܘܬܛܠܝ̈ܠܐ ܥܡܝ̈ܩܬܐ ܕܚܙܘܬܐ ܓܫܪ̈ܐ ܒܢܗܪ̈ܘܬܐ ܥܒܝܕܝܢ ܗܘܘ. ܠܐ ܓܝܪ ܐܫܬܒܩܬ ܥܕܬܐ ܚܕܐ ܕܠܐ ܐܬܥܩܪܬ܆ ܘܠܐ ܚܕ ܒܝܬ ܣܗ̈ܕܐ ܕܠܐ ܐܣܬܚܦ. ܘܩܝܣ̈ܝܗܘܢ ܘܬܪ̈ܥܝܗܘܢ ܕܥܕ̈ܬܐ ܘܕܒܝܬ ܣܗ̈ܕܐ ܘܓܘܪ̈ܢܝܗܘܢ ܫܩܠܘ܆ ܘܕܪ̈ܓܐ ܠܓܫܪ̈ܐ ܕܢܗܪ̈ܘܬܐ. ܥܒܕܘ. ܘܕܝܪ̈ܬܐ ܕܐܒܝ̈ܠܐ ܘܕܡܢ ܥܘܡܪ̈ܐ ܫܝ̈ܢܐ ܕܩܕ̈ܝܫܐ ܬܛܠܝ̈ܠܝܗܘܢ ܫܩܠܘ܆ ܘܐܝܠܝܢ ܕܓܒܝܢ ܘܫܦܝܪܝܢ܆ ܠܒܝܬ ܐܘܨܪ̈ܐ ܕܝܠܗ ܐܝܬܝܘ܆ ܘܫܪܟܐ ܠܡܓܘ̈ܫܐ ܦܠܓ. *Acta martyrum*, IV, p. 256.

132 *Ibid.*, IV, p. 255 f.

133 *Ibid.*, II, p. 536.

Some measures, applied by Vahram, like confiscation of private houses and property, did not affect the monks; but the expulsion and deportation of outstanding Christians to territories of difficult conditions, seem to have involved them. Most frequently the sufferings and vexations were caused by the local population stirred up by the Magi. In the territories close to the Western boundaries, the nomadic tribes also were used for the same purpose. The Arabs under Mundhir I performed good services to Vahram. We learn of one of the chieftains, Aspebet, who, having become weary of this, deserted the service of the Persian king and came to the Byzantine territory [134]. The service of these tribes along the frontiers was the more important because many chose this route of escape to the West [135]. Those who managed to escape could not be brought back, although Vahram demanded them from Theodosius II.

134 Regarding this phylarch see CYRIL OF SCYTHOPOLIS, *Vita Euthymii*, p. 18 f.

135 That these came as far as Italy, we hear from Augustinus : quid modo in Perside? Nonne ita in Christianos ferbuit persecutio (si tamen iam quievit), ut fugientes inde nonnulli, usque ad Romana oppida pervenerint, *De civitate Dei*, XVII, 52, p. 356

CHAPTER IV

ADVANCE OF MONASTICISM IN THE FIFTH CENTURY

1. LEADING PERSONALITIES

a. Jōḥannan of Kaškar

As far as the eye can reach one of the most outstanding monks of this period was Jōḥannan of Kaškar whose memory the church long celebrated on the first of October. In the work of Īšōʿdenaḥ — if we discard the cycle concerned with Aūgēn — only a few celebrities are mentioned from the period before Abrāhām of Kaškar. Jōḥannan is one of these very few [1]. In the annalistic sources he appears as a contemporary of Catholicos Dadīšōʿ [2]. Although his biography has not survived, it seems to have been used by several authors whom we know. However, most of what has been salvaged from it is worth little or nothing as to fact.

According to Īšōʿdenaḥ, Jōḥannan was from a family in Kaškar. He entered and lived there for a period in a monastery which is identified as the same which was later restored by a certain Mār ʿAnīn [3]. His further life and activities are very difficult to follow. Only very seldom does his figure emerge form darkness and come within recognizable distance. Even on these occasions our information remains clothed in semi-darkness.

The legend about his miraculous transportation to the valley of Sc̠ete — if it has any particle of truth at all — may perhaps mean that Jōḥannan had visited Egypt and there became acquainted with the monastic life. His later residence is given as the monastery of ʿAin-Deqlā, situated on the mount ʾUrūk in Bēt Garmai [4].

1 *Chasteté*, p. 5 f.

2 AMR, *De patriarchis*, p. 29; MARI, *De patriarchis*, p. 36.

3 IŠŌʿDENAḤ, *op. cit.*, p. 5.

4 ܒܥܘܡܪܐ ܕܥܝܢ ܕܩܠܐ ܕܒܛܘܪܐ ܕܐܘܪܘܟ ܕܒܐܬܪܐ ܕܒܝܬ ܓܪܡܝ 'the monastery of ʿAin Deqlā that on the mountain of ʾUrūk in the country of Bēt Garmai', *ibid.*

His achievements in ascetic practice, particularly his extreme fastings and his reputation gained through fighting with demons, are mentioned only in general terms. His visionary experiences have also contributed their share to his reputation [5]. There are some hints which, if taken seriously, indicate that he founded his own monastery [6]. There he served with deep humility as a sacristan of the church. It is reported that he found his resting place at the same altar [7] when he died at an advanced age.

b. Jazdīn

About another celebrity, Mār Jazdīn, we are oriented by virtue of a biography which has come down to us [8]. Its simple form, free of any kind of legendary embellishment, reports with remarkable calmness the main events of his background and life. It sounds like a page torn from a chronicle in order to be circulated independently.

Jazdīn belonged to an outstanding Mazdean family in Belāšphar which is located at the Ḥōlwān river, in the village of Dāwīn. It was the wish of his father that young Jazdīn should learn the teachings of Mazdaism and for that purpose he gave his son to a teacher for training. But the young man's interest was attracted by the holy places visited by the Christians, by the charm of Christian worship, and by the contents of the sacred books of the Christian religion. When his decision to become a Christian became ripened he found that no one would dare to give him baptism. He then left his parents' home and fled to Bēt Garmai where he found refuge in the monastery of Bēt Sāhdē of Karkā de Bēt Selōk. A certain Jōḥannan, who was the abbot at that time, took care of his spiritual needs. In this monastery he was instructed and baptized and he began to make himself at home in the monastic discipline [9].

For a long time — his biographer says 32 years — he lived in this

5 Mari, *op. cit.*, p. 36
6 *Ibid.*; cf. Ms. Berl. Sach. 63, fol. 219 b.
7 ܡܕܒܚܢܐ 'a sacristan'.
8 *Acta martyrum*, II, p. 559 ff.
9 *Ibid.*, p 563.

monastery. But this is a period which remains a blank space crossed over without any hint as to the kind of life he lived or of the activities in which he was involved.

The interest of his biographer comes to life again with Jazdīn's decision to return to his home village and to establish his residence there. At that time his parents were already dead but he found his brother Dadgušnāsp there, whom he managed to convert to the Christian faith. Jazdīn built a cell in the mountain near the village of Dāwīn [10]. Relative to its location, the Arabic sources inform us that the village of Dūna lies between Hamadān and Dīnavar [11].

The period which Jazdīn spent in his home country — 14 years altogether — is the only part of his life which comes under a biographical spotlight. It was here that Jazdīn set forth his rigid monastic habits. He became celebrated in all areas of Belāšphar where, incidentally, Christian communities were settled [12]. His fame embraced people by the spell of its authority and reached even into the remote provinces. But, as our source indicates, this was not a result of an active missionary enterprise on his part, but was caused by his reputation as an exorcist and thaumaturge. It was here, also, that Jazdīn raised as his disciple one of the sons of his converted brother. This Petiōn was destined to surpass the activities of his master. He died there on the 21st of 'Īlūl (September), but the year of his death has not been preserved by the tradition. There is some question, too, as to how much this date can be trusted [13].

c. Petiōn

We have noted above that Petiōn was a son of Jazdīn's brother whom Jazdīn taught and made his disciple. Until the death of his

10 *Ibid.*, p. 564.

11 According to a geographer of Isphahan it was 10 farsah from Hamadan (according to others 15 farsah) and 10 farsah from Dīnavar, YAQUT, *Mu'jam al-buldān*, II, p. 629.

12 ܫܒܝܬܐ ܕܒܠܫܦܪ 'captivity of Belāšphar', i.e. a camp of the prisoners is known through the synodical acts of the year 424, *Synodicon orientale*, p. 43. Probably these Christians were captives deported by Shāhpuhr II from the Roman territory.

13 The liturgical tradition offers two dates but no one coincides with this, September 22 and June 21, ṢELĪBā, *Martyrologe*, p. 161, 155.

master, Petiōn stayed with him and shared his activities. But he far surpassed his teacher in adding reputation to the monastic movement. Petiōn is one of the few celebrities whom Īšōʿdenaḥ mentions from the period before Abrāhām of Kaškar [14]. He must have gained an immense reputation since he was considered as the 'head of the *nāzrāiē*' [15].

In view of this it is not strange that little of serious interest has been preserved. Some portions of his acts have come down to us but only in several recensions, not in their original form. What little factual material has remained has been buried under lengthy dialogues and tales distorted by legends. However, these recensions leave one with the impression that, once, in their primitive form, they must have stood close to the events themselves. Thus there are only a few elements of historical character which deserve our trust and these permit only a very unsatisfactory idea of all his activities. Only in some segments of this material do we seem to stand upon firm ground.

His master's death seems to have widened Petiōn's field of activity. For a certain period he continued in the activities in which he had shared with his teacher. But the more remote fields fascinated him. He felt that his calling lay in the aggressive missionary enterprise. At this point we once again encounter a fusion of the ascetic phenomenon with the idea of the travelling apostolate.

Only some of his missionary tours are described and these very briefly in a paragraph which the different recensions have incorporated [16]. Obviously this is part of a groundwork source. In this account it is told that his work brought him to Bēt Dārāiē and Bēt Kūsāiē i.e. to the provinces in Babylonia and to Maišān.

Further this text reports a caesura in the activities of Petiōn. We are told that he returned to his cell at the village of Dāwīn hallowed by the memories of his master, and resumed his monastic

14 *Chastetė*, p. 7.

15 ܪܝܫܐ ܕܢܙܝܪ̈ܐ *Historia Pethion martyris*, p. 8; this is corrected into ܪܝܫܐ ܕܟܪ̈ܣܛܝܢܐ 'head of the Christians' in another recension, *Acta martyrum*, II, p. 604.

16 *Ibid.*, p. 629; *Historia Pethion martyris*, p. 42.

17 MARI, *De patriarchis*, p. 70. See also a reference of general kind in Ms. Vat. syr. 90, fol. 139 b.

duties in loneliness. But this proved to be only a temporary stay. His restless spirit and his missionary zeal helped him to plan new evangelistic tours. Subsequently we see Petiōn in the country of Bēt Mādāiē which was to become an area for new success.

A problem arises when we ask whether Petiōn had to do with the founding of monasteries. This question comes up because we know of some monasteries which carried his name. One was at Baghdad [17], and another at Balad at the Tigris [18]. But these monasteries were obviously not established by him. Rather, they were founded at a later time in his honor. This conclusion is drawn because of the silence of his biography [19] and the silence in Īšōʿdenaḥ and in the liturgical tradition which celebrated him as 'a martyr and an anchorite' [20].

Petiōn fell as victim to the persecutions which broke out under Jazdgard II. He gave his last testimony on the 25th of Tešrī II (October) in 447 [21]. The circumstances related to the court process show something of his authority, which must have reached even into the ranks of the great dignitaries. The fact that the grand mobadh had to dismiss the officer in charge and appoint a special functionary who could carry through the affairs till Petiōn's execution [22] shows how great a headache was caused to the men in power by the man in bondage.

d. Sābā Gūšnazdād

The information which we have concerning Gūšnazdād goes back to his vita [23]. Unfortunately, it has not been preserved in its original form but rather in a recension with possible modifications made not before the year 628 [24]. There seems to be ground to suppose that

18 THOMAS, *Book of Governors*, p. 249. It was located on the right bank of the Tigris.

19 A poem about him in Ms. Ming. syr. 214, fol. 131 a - 132 a speaks of the destruction of the pagan temples but is silent regarding this particular question.

20 ܦܬܝܘܢ ܡܪܝ ܝܚܝܕܝܐ ܣܗܕܐ *Martyrologes et ménologes*, p. 64, 114; ṢELĪBĀ, *Martyrologe*, p. 141.

21 He was commemorated on the same day, *ibid.*

22 *Historia Pethion martyris*, p. 31 f.

23 *Acta martyrum*, II, p. 635 ff.

24 The year of inthronisation of Shērōē b. Khusrō appears in the epilogue, *ibid.*, p. 679.

the gist of this primitive form has not been entirely sacrificed to legendary interests.

Gūšnazdād's home was also in the country of Belāšphar, in the village of Bēt Gallāiē. His family belonged to the Iranian aristocracy and it was the wish of his father to educate his son in the spirit of Mazdaism. But this remained only a wish since his father could not supervise the educational task due to his appointment to an important post in Bēt Dārāiē at which place he later died. Hence, the educational task fell upon his mother who was inclined toward the Christian faith, and upon his nurse who was herself a Christian. Gūšnazdād was baptized and became a monk. He also persuaded his mother to receive baptism and to leave the world in order to join a monastic community of nuns [25].

After completing his instruction in the Christian religion in a school, Gūšnazdād chose a place called Serdā, at the river Sīnī (Sahī?) for a life of loneliness. He was there for only a short time before the persecutions broke out [26]. This remark in his biography furnishes us with a significant element to contribute to the otherwise scanty chronology of his life. The persecutions mentioned can only refer to those which broke out under Jazdgard II. He was stimulated by an anchorite to enter an evangelistic enterprise. His first mission field was the town of Ḥālē and its environs. Here Mīkā, bishop of Lāšōm, ordained him as a priest and appointed one of his companions to assist in further work [27].

When this stage of stability was reached in this work Sābā left Ḥālē and sought a new mission field by travelling around in the towns and villages of several countries. It is to be noted that his mission work was at the same time a propagandizing for monasticism. This fact is revealed by the episode in Kurdistan. When he satisfied his desire to go to the mountains and live in loneliness, both Sābā and his disciple were captured by the Kurds. But this adventure also turned out to be a success, at least according to our source. It is reported that a germ of the monastic movement was planted among the Kurds and a monastery was established [28].

25 ܕܝܪܐ ܕܐܚ̈ܘܬܐ 'the monastery of sisters', *ibid.*, p. 650.

26 *Ibid.*, p. 651.

27 *Ibid.*, p. 667.

28 *Ibid*, p. 674.

This contribution to the monastic movement is expressly reported in connection with his activities after he returned from Kurdistan. The source which speaks of his new large-scale missionary enterprise mentions also that he built several monasteries in different places [29].

Finally, Sābā retired from all these activities and built a cell for himself, near the Nahr Zāwar in Bēt Ārāmāiē. This place is located above Baghdad [30], near ʿŪkbarā which today is west of the Tigris but at that time was on the eastern bank of the river's ancient course. There he spent the rest of his life, reportedly three years and six months, and died in 487 [31]. The veneration which was offered him during his lifetime was continued over his earthy remains [32].

2. SUFFERINGS AND TEMPORARY SETBACK

The Persian historiography inspired by the Mazdean clergy, characterizes Jazdgard II as a pious and benign ruler [33]. But what was pious and benign to the spiritual leadership of the Parsist religion, meant cruelty for the Christians and Jews [34]. Beginning with the second year of his rule the king acted with severity toward the Christians in Armenia [35] thus seriously affecting the situation of the Christian religion there [36]. During this time, however, he held a reversed and reticent attitude toward the Christians in Persia. But with the eighth year of his rule he chose also to persecute the Persian Christians. This change can be accounted for by the fact that it was feared that the Christians had caused difficulties in the political

29 *Ibid.*, p. 677.

30 نهر زاور YAQUT, *Muʿjam al-buldān*, II, p. 910; IV, p. 840.

31 He was not a martyr, as said in BAUMSTARK, *Geschichte syr. Literatur*, p. 137.

32 For some parts of his body a priest David built a chapel in the village Bēt Deqlē in Bēt Garmai, *Acta martyrum*, II, p. 679.

33 AL-THAʿĀLIBĪ, *Histoire*, p. 573.

34 CHRISTENSEN, *L'Iran*, p. 283 f.

35 Ełišē, *Patmowtʿiwn wardananç*, p 45 ff.

36 Many denied the Christian religion, even some outstanding personalities and erected sacral buildings for the Mazdean cult. YOVHAN, *Patmowtʿiwn* p. 76 f.

situation, and by the extent to which the royal court had been infiltrated by Christian believers. The main factor, however, seems to have been his religious fanaticism.

The chronicle of Karkā de Bēt Selōk reports of the orders sent to the authorities in the provinces of Arzūn, Suren, and Bēt Garmai to the effect that a joint action was to be taken in order to compel the Christians to deny their faith and worship the sun. Torture and the sword were used to accomplish this purpose [37].

The detailed instructions contained in the above orders have not survived but the general gist of them can be recognized in the rulings issued in Armenia ca. 450. In these a sharp sting was directed also against the monastic movement. Besides the churches which were to be pulled down, the sacred books to be confiscated and sent to the royal treasury and the termination of the worship services, it was directed that the monks and nuns were to be forced to return to ordinary life [38]. Further, the anchorites and monks were subjected to the poll-tax [39]. Obviously, they had to endure other vexations too, all as a result of Jazdgard's intentions 'that he might banish the monks' [40].

Unfortunately, a history of the sufferings which monasticism had to undergo in this period can be written only in a very imperfect way, that is, by treating the ascetics together with the other victims. Except for a few references to the ascetics themselves history remains deaf and dumb to their particular trials.

Some picture of the application of the directives for persecution is given in the history of Karkā de Bēt Selōk. A commission came to this town, arrested the outstanding Christians and put

37 *Acta martyrum*, II, p. 519.

38 *և հաւատացեալքն ի Քրիստոս՝ արք և կանայք, որ բնակեալ են յիւրաքանչիւր մենանոցս, փոխեսցեն զհանդերձս իւրեանց ըստ աշխարհական կարգաց*, 'and the believers in Christ, men and women, who live in the hermitages, shall be compelled, with those belonging to them, to return to the ordinary way of life', Ełišē, *Patmowtʿiwn wardananç*, p. 110 f.

39 *երկրորդ, միայնակեաց քրիստոնեայք՝ որ բնակեալ էին ի վանորայս, ընդ նովին աշխարհագրովն էարկ*, 'secondly, he subjected the anchorites and Christians who live in monasteries to the tax', *ibid.*, p. 48.

40 *և զմիայնակեացսն փախուսցէ*, 'that he might expel the monks (anchorites)', *ibid.*, p. 49.

them in prison. Soldiers were then sent out to the provinces[41] with orders to seek out the Christians and bring them in in chains. Clearly these measures were directed against the monks as well as the clergy.

Then the instruments of torture arrived as well as 16 elephants which were used by the Sassanid rulers for mass executions. These were prerequisite to the staging of a bloody drama. First only a few victims were picked out from the company of the arrested ones. On the first day of the executions which was the 24th of Āb (August) 446 (445), Jōḥannan, bishop of the city, with three priests and 28 believers opened the path to the cross. Among the victims killed on the second day two female ascetics, *benat qeiāmā*, are mentioned as having been crucified and stoned upon a cross[42]. The rock Bēt Tittā (i.e. House of Fig Tree) which in the days of Shahpuhr II had once been the place for blood witness, became again the scene for hecatombs. Behind the large groups which prepared themselves for witness in an ardor close to ecstatic enthusiasm[43], we probably have to see the influence of the ascetic element.

On the third day the turn came for the masses which had been dragged to Karkā from the towns, villages and provinces. New types of crafty and refined tortures were needed to take care of them.

It is not known just how much the orders which permitted the population to pillage the property and possessions of the Christians and which caused a stampede in the whole area[44] affected the monasteries.

To what extent these persecutions were carried out elsewhere is not known. The sources do not spotlight all possible areas affected by persecution. We do not even know whether executions were carried out in other cities of Bēt Garmai. According to one tradition, a special building was arranged for the bodies of the martyrs and was called the 'house of witnesses' in Karkā Jazdīn in Bēt

41 The text says ܠܐܬܪ̈ܘܬܐ ܪ̈ܚܝܩܐ 'to the remote provinces', *Acta martyrum*, II, p. 519 f.

42 *Ibid.*, p. 526.

43 *Ibid.*, p. 524.

44 *Ibid.*, p. 521. ܢܦܩܘ ܒܚܡܐܡܐ ܒܪ̈ܝܪܐ 'and they went out in wild violence'.

Garmai[45]. But it seems that this Karkā Jazdīn must not be sought for outside Karkā de Bēt Selōk.

It is surprising that the chronicle of Arbēl does not take notice of any disturbances at that time[46]. But not only this. The same source tells us of a joint move taken by the bishops of Arbēl and Karkā de Bēt Selōk before the Catholicos Bābōi concerning a proposal of a memorial feast for the martyrs fallen under Jazdgard. The impression is left that only Bēt Garmai was involved and was thus intensely interested in this proposition[47]. Can this mean that this province was not hit by the wave of persecution?

There seems to be evidence, which is not in accord with the above silence. The history of Karkā de Bēt Selōk shows that among these who were arrested and brought from Ḥadiab were the metropolitan of Arbēl himself, and the bishops of Bēt Nūhadrā and Maʿaltā and those who came with them[48] and were martyred[49]. According to this source, bishop Mārōn was the one who established the annual commemoration feast. He summoned a synod of the bishops of Bēt Garmai and Ḥadiab with the assistance of Catholicos Bābōi (i.e., after A.D. 457). This established the liturgical practice of a three day commemoration feast. That is, this document gives a completely different picture by showing that the diocese of Ḥadiab was drawn into the persecutions. This report deserves a greater share of our trust. The author's remark concerning these data that he used a canon in the archive of the metropolitan seat may be not an invention but based upon fact.

45 وحملت جثتهم ودفنت فى بيت الشهدا بباجرمى بكرخ 'and their corpses were carried and buried in the house of witnesses in Bēt Garmai in Karkā Jazdīn', MARI, *De patriarchis*, p. 37. This 'house of witnesses' is ܒܝܬ ܣܗܕܐ a church dedicated to martyrs and their relics.

46 In this chronicle it is told what Mār Reḥīmā, bishop of Arbēl, did in building up his diocese from the 16th year of Vahram (436 A.D.) until he passed away in the 12th year of Jazdgard (450 A.D.). The only difficulties which are mentioned during his work were doctrinal quarrels, *Sources syriaques*, p. 64 f. Nothing is mentioned about the persecutions in connection with his successor Mār ʿAbbūšṭā, *ibid.*, p. 65 ff.

47 Every year the bishops of Bēt Garmai came together for this celebration, *ibid.*, p. 67.

48 *Acta martyrum*, II, p. 521.

49 *Ibid.*, p. 531.

The extant sources do not by far give us a satisfactory idea as to the extent of these persecutions. The testimony is reduced to a very slender dimension. Too much remains obscure. At least so much is clear that this wave of persecution did not go as high as the one under Shahpuhr II. Nevertheless, persecution could have cut deeply in local outbursts which found their targets in the churches and monasteries.

The fate of other unknown monks is illustrated by that of an outstanding one. This is the case of Petiōn, executed in the year after the events in Karkā de Bēt Selōk. He was arrested when he held the service of mid-day in his cell. After he had been brought to the authorities he was subjected to torture for several days. After repeated interrogations he was martyred on 25th Tešrī I (October) in 447. His head was hewn off by a sword and hung on top of a rock near the great royal highway which led from Ctesiphon to the eastern regions of the empire. This deed was meant as a warning and a threat to all who travelled this busy highway. It took place near the town of Ḥōlwān in Media [50].

Mārī speaks of the end of the persecutions and the release of the prisoners ordered by Jazdgard II [51]. Obviously the resurgence of the Armenians in 450/51 constituted such a deterrent that it left no other way for the king than to leave the Christians in peace.

3. SPREAD OF MONASTERIES

a. Monastic foundations related to the cult of martyrs

During the fifth century the provinces in Persia, its deserts, plains and mountains were not only strewn with hermitages, but also with convents. Several factors have played a role in the regulation of this expansion. In the ensuing pages we shall endeavor to view some of these.

Places connected with the execution of the martyrs or containing their earthly remains continued to live as spots especially hallowed in the memory of piety. Ground which had sucked the blood of

50 *Ibid.*, II, p. 627 f.

51 MARI, *De patriarchis*, p. 31. His argument, that peace was made with the Romans is without basis in fact.

these witnesses, caves into which their bodies were laid to temporary rest, tombs where they found a resting place, were invested with a special meaning for the Christians. They did not only believe that heavenly beings hovered over these spots and that the divine light glittered around them, but also that miraculous power was ascribed to these localities. Thus the tradition never failed to invent reasons for the glorification of such plots [52]. Consequently, all these spots have always attracted the attention of the faithful, who with a veil of devotion have covered the places upon which they gazed with the spirit of adoration. These places were celebrated not only by annual feasts and markets [53], but also by private visits of the pilgrims. The more so since intense propaganda favoring local places of pilgrimage over against the places in Palestina [54], did not fail to develop and consolidate pious habits.

By virtue of all these qualities it is natural that these places became the most suitable localities for sacred buildings. In many cases monasteries were soon established upon these spots. On the place where masses of Christians were executed under Jazdgard II in Karkā de Bēt Selōk, outside the city at a place called Bēt Tittā a monastery soon was erected. After the persecution passed over, we are told that Mār Mārōn, bishop of the city commemorated the place by erecting a monastery [55].

On the spot where Aitallāhā was stoned under the heap of stones in Bēt Nūhadrā, a monastery was erected in the name of the Martyr Aitallāhā [56].

In addition to the places connected with the final agony of the witnesses, the spots where their earthly remains were buried, were selected for the sites of the monasteries. The place where the

52 Qardag is presented praying before his execution particularly for the sake of the place of his martyrdom that it might become a place in which everyone who comes to seek for help, prays and remembers his name, might find assistance, *Acta martyrum*, II, p. 490. See also the story of Mār Sābā, *ibid.*, IV, p. 246.

53 *Ibid.*, II, p. 505 f.; III, p. 488.

54 *Ibid.*, II, p. 436.

55 *Ibid.*, II, p. 530 f. The name is not mentioned, but this seems to be the ܒܝܬ ܣܗ̈ܕܐ ܪܒܐ 'the great house of martyrs', *ibid.*, p. 514, a name which also appears in the acts of Mahdōk, *ibid.*, II, p. 4.

56 Īšōʿdenaḥ, *Chasteté*, p. 4.

remains of Mār Behnām and his companions rested in a cave (*gūbā*), became the spot where the monastery of Bēt Gūbē was built [57].

When Mār Bassōs and his companions were killed a monastery was founded on the spot where he was killed [58]. Then his hands were secured by the people of the village Ḥedil, brought into their community and kept there. A monastery was erected in the name of Mār Bassōs, near the Ḥedil village [59], located in the eastern part of Ṭūr ʿAbdīn [60]. Also near the grotto of Mār Lōngīnā [61], a monastery was built [62]. The remains of Mār Adōnā, the metropolitan of Elam, martyred under Shahpuhr, were transplanted to the country of Qardū. The spot where they were finally laid to rest became the site on which the monastery of Adōnā was built [63].

In the same way, numerous monasteries came into existence. In most cases, however, a different history [64] lies behind the expansion

57 *Acta martyrum*, II, p. 440.

58 ܘܒܢܘ ... ܕܝܪܐ ܐܚܪܬܐ ܠܥܠ ܡܢ ܐܝܟܐ ܕܐܬܟܠܠ ܡܪܝ ܒܣܘܣ 'and they built... another monastery above where Mār Bassōs was martyred (crowned)', Ms. Šarf. Patr. 38, fol. 166 b.

59 *Légende de Bassus*, p. 42 ff.

60 Socin, *Zur Geographie*, p. 245.

61 Lōngīnā. Ms. Vat. syr. 247, fol. 225 b vocalizes this name Leōngīnā.

62 Ms. Par. syr. 276, fol. 47 b.

63 Īšōʿdenaḥ, *Chasteté*, p. 58 f.

64 In this respect, the traditions laid down in the acts of martyrdom of Mār Behnām and Sarā are very instructive. These exhibit the main stages in this process. The first stage came into existence by establishment of a primitive shrine with the relics of the martyrs. This is described as follows : ܘܣܡ ܐܢܘܢ ܩܕܝܫܐ ܡܪܝ، ܐܒܪܗܡ ܒܓܘ̈ܪܢܐ : ܘܩܒܥ ܐܢܘܢ ܒܐܣܬܐ ܡܕܢܚܝܬܐ ܒܣܘܦܗ ܕܡܥܪܬܐ 'and St. Mār Abraham placed them (i.e. the remains of the martyrs) into the *gūrnē* ('stone vessel', 'urn') and fixed them in the Eastern wall in the end of the grotto', *Acta martyrum*, II, p. 432. The next stage in the development is marked by the expansion of the primitive grottoshrine. This is reflected by the plan to connect the cult with a martyrion : ܐܝܟ ܕܢܒܢܐ ܬܡܢ ܗܝܟܠܐ ܠܒܝܬ ܨܠܘܬܐ ܕܐܚ̈ܐ : ܐܝܟܢܐ ܕܢܗܘܐ ܠܗ̇ ܠܕܘܟܪܢܐ ܘܠܬܘܕܝܬܐ ܠܥܠܡ... ܘܒܢܐ ܬܡܢ ܗܝܟܠܐ ܗܕܝܪܐ ܘܡܫܒܚܐ ܒܕܘܒܪܬܐ ܣܓܝܐܐ ܕܡܬܦܪܢܣܐ ܗܘܬ ܒܡܫܡ̈ܫܢܘܬܐ. ܘܐܬܦܪܢܣܬ ܕܝܪܐ ܗܝ ܕܒܢܬ ܐܒܘܗܝ: ܐܘܒܕܬ ܕܝܪܐ ܕܒܡܫܡ̈ܫܢܘܬܐ : ܒܢܝܐ ܠܡܣܒܪܢܐ 'to build there a *haiklā* for prayer-house of the monks (lit. brethren) so that it could be for remem-

of the network of monastic establishments. This must be understood as an evolution involving several phases.

This which we are told in the acts of ʿAbd al-Masīḥ must have taken place in many instances. On the place, marked by blood, where the body of the martyr fell, the inhabitants built a small chapel (martyrion) or *haiklā*, and laid in the midst of it a stone with the inscription that this was the place where the martyr's battle was crowned [65].

Such little *haiklās* which were erected in many places needed wardens just as were needed guardians to protect the bones and remains of the saints as well as precious relics. Moreover, visitors wanting guidance, and people from all the walks of life who had

brance and good memory... and he built a *haiklā* there in a place which was called Kūkītā ('whirlwind'), and this monastery of Bēt Abraham is called the Monastery of Kūkītā up to our day', *ibid.*, p. 433. This establishment entered a new phase in the development when monks took over the surveillance of the cult-place. Our source continues : ܘܟܕ ܙܒܢܐ ܠܐ ܙܥܘܪܐ ܥܒܪ ܣܓܝܘ ܠܗܘܢ ܟܢ̈ܫܐ ܕܡܐܬܝܬܐ ܕܠܘܬ ܥܕܬܗܘܢ ܕܩܕ̈ܝܫܐ. ܘܡܛܠ ܕܠܝܬ ܗܘܐ ܠܗܘܢ ܕܘܟܬܐ ܕܒܗ̇ ܢܬܛܫܘܢ ܡܢ ܚܡܝܡܘܬ ܚܡܘܡܐ ܕܩܝܛܐ: ܘܡܢ ܬܩܝܦܘܬ ܥܙܝܙܘܬܗ ܕܪܘܚܐ ܕܣܬܘܐ: ܡܬܥܩܝܢ ܗܘܘ ܟܠܗܘܢ ܐܝܠܝܢ ܕܬܡܢ ܟܢܝܫܝܢ ܗܘܘ. ܘܐܦ ܗܢܘܢ ܕܝܪ̈ܝܐ: ܕܬܡܢ ܡܫܡܫܝܢ ܗܘܘ 'and when not a little time passed, the people coming to the shrine of the saints increased; and because they did not have a place where they could be sheltered from the severity of the summer heat and from the intensity of the vehemence of the winter cold, all those who gathered there were troubled, and also those monks who were serving there', *ibid.*, p. 433 f. Then, several buildings were erected to meet the growing needs. Thus the establishment reached the last phase in developing into a monastery, called the Monastery of Bēt Gūbē ('grotto'), *ibid.*, p. 440.

65 وبعد قليل بنوا هناك هيكلًا صغير فوق ذلك القبر وجعلوا بوسطه تلك الصخرة ورسموا عليها اية الصليب وكتبوا فوقها هكذا . هذه هي الموضع التي استشهد بها القديس الشهيد عبد المسيح. ومن ذلك الحين بدوا يجوا كل المؤمنين من كل ناحية لهيكل القديس ويعطوه السلام 'a little after this they built a small *haiklā* upon the tomb, and placed in the middle of it a stone in which they engraved the sign of the cross and inscribed on it : « this is the place in which the holy martyr ʿAbd al-Masīḥ witnessed martyrdom »; after this all the believers from all the places began to come to the holy *haiklā* in order to hail him', *Passion arabe de ʿAbd al-Masīḥ*, p. 331. The Arabic text is a translation from the Syriac original which has not survived.

gathered here were seeking help and relief from their pains and worries, and they had to be provided with service. Monks, of course, were the most fitting servants for this kind of work. The direct references to this show that this gradually became their terrain [66].

These *haiklās* afforded great opportunities for future development. As soon as some cells were added to the *haiklā*, an embryo for a future monastery was created. If the factors were favorable, this midget community would begin to grow. Other necessary buildings were added to the *haiklā* until the expanding monastic community was able to entirely absorb the *haiklā* with all its traditions.

Samples of this kind of growth in the expansion of the monasteries are known. One of the most notable is the history of the monastery of Mār Bassōs in Ṭūr ʿAbdīn. Mār Bassōs, converted by a monk, and his companions were killed on a mountain, and he was buried near the top of the mount. On this spot, a *haiklā* was erected in the name of the martyr [67]. This *haiklā* later developed into an important monastery. It is also obvious in the history of the monastery of Bēt Sāhdē, that the glory of the monastery as of a great establishment was preceded by a period of modest reputation when only three cells had joined a tiny Bēt Sāhdē i.e. a martyrion [68].

66 The task of the monks who joined the *haiklā* built upon the remains of Behnām and Sarā, is described in the following way : ܕܢܗܘܘܢ ܡܫܡܫܝܢ ܠܒܝܬ ܩܒܘܪ̈ܝܗܘܢ ܕܣܗ̈ܕܐ ܩܕ̈ܝܫܐ : ܘܕܢܗܘܘܢ ܡܩܒܠܝܢ ܠܐܝܠܝܢ ܕܐܬܝܢ ܗܘܘ ܕܢܣܒܘܢ ܐܣܝܘܬܐ ܡܢ ܡܫܘܚܬ ܓܪ̈ܡܐ ܕܩܕ̈ܝܫܐ ܡܪܝ، ܒܗܢܡ ܘܕܣܗ̈ܕܐ ܚܒܪ̈ܘܗܝ، 'to serve the sepulchers of the holy martyrs and to receive those that come that they might receive healing from the laying on of the bones of the holy ones, Mār Behnām and his fellow martyrs', *Acta martyrum*, II, p. 433.

67 ܗܝܟܠܐ ܪܒܐ ܘܡܫܡܗܐ ܕܡܪܝ، ܒܣܘܣ ܗܘ ܕܐܬܒܢܝ ܥܠ ܪܝܫܗ ܕܛܘܪܐ ܒܕܘܟܬܐ ܕܒܗ ܐܬܩܛܠ 'a great and celebrated *haiklā of* Mār Bassōs that was built on the top of the mountain on the spot in which he was killed', Ms. Par. syr. 276, fol. 48 a.

68 ܕܝܪܘܬܐ ܙܥܘܪܐ ܕܣܗ̈ܕܐ 'a little tiny monastery', Ms. Jer. Patr. syr. 26, fol. 123 a.

b. Other foundations

As the sources show, many monasteries came into existence only after a process of longer or shorter duration. The pattern of this development, reflected in our documents, is almost stereotyped [69]. At the beginning there stands a little *haiklā*, built by a monk at his cave or cell. Gradually the importance of the *haiklā* as a cult place, or the reputation of the monk attracted other monks who added their cells and thereby brought the development a stage forward. Such a lavra, a free community, grew until eventually a monastic community was developed which in the last stage incorporated the *haiklā* and the cells, and established a monastery. Many monastic communities have had such a longer history behind them.

In the selection of sites for the monastic foundations, not connected with the cult of the martyrs, perhaps the most frequent preference fell upon the places where famous ascetics and monks had spent their lives. The spiritual and physical exercises of such people at these places made them quite appropriate for sacral buildings. These dwelling-places, according to the imagination of pious minds, were consecrated by a mystical heavenly light which shone around them and by the fragrance which enveloped them [70]. The latter was understood as a symptom of the presence of the Holy Ghost, as we already know from the ancient biblical traditions of the Syrians [71].

69 The history of the monastery of Mār Ḥazqi'ēl serves as a good illustration. Mār Hazki'ēl first built a little *haiklā*. Then it is told here: ܩܠܝܬܐ ܒܩܘܪܒܘܬܗ ܕܗܝܟܠܐ ܥܠ ܪܫ ܪܡܬܐ ܘܩܪܘܗ ܠܗ ܠܩܠܝܬܐ ܫܡܐ ܒܝܬ ܪܝܫܢܐ '(he built) a cell in the vicinity of the *haiklā* on the top of the hill; and they gave to the cell the name of Bēt Rīšanā', Ms. Vat. syr. 472, fol. 93 a. This establishment became the nucleus for the growing monastic community which developed into a monastery.

70 Ms. Br. Mus. Add. 17,203, fol. 7 b; *Acta martyrum*, II, p. 431; *ibid.*, p. 18; *Acta Mar Abdu'l Masīḥ*, p. 13; *Histoire nestorienne*, V, p. 256.

71 So the Syriac version of the Acts of the Apostles. Portions of it have been preserved by the commentary of Ephrem in an Armenian translation. The passage which interests us here is: *ձայն սաստիկ հողմոյ եղեւ ի տան անդ ուր ժողովեալ էին աշակերտքն Յիսուսի· և հոտ անոյշ բուրէր ի սաստկութենէ հողմոյն և տունն ամենայն լնոյր*, 'the voice of a vehement storm became in the house where the apostles of Jesus

There are interesting traces showing that even the monks themselves stimulated the thoughts of the faithful in that direction. Their sentiment frequently moved along the same line as that laid down in the story of Mār Jāūnān, namely, that, through the establishment of a residence for the monastic community, the service and praise of God could properly be continued on the spot previously consecrated for that purpose by the monk. The testament of the above-mentioned monk expresses the following significant note : 'for in this night I am ready to go from this life; I ask you, thus, that, in this place, in which I am dwelling, you might build a monastery and an altar and an apsis therein, where God's name might be praised continuously' [72].

In view of this it becomes understandable that the places where monks of great reputation had lived, more and more became sites suitable for monasteries. When intermediary phases preceded the foundation, a *haiklā* was erected on the spot named after the monk, which became the resting place for his remains. Then one or a couple of monks discovered that their duty lay in taking care of the *haiklā*, and so the ground was laid for the same development that occurred in connection with the growth of the monasteries related to the cult of the martyrs.

There are traces that the same process in the expansion of the network of monasteries also embraced other *haiklās*, built for other purposes. The first monastery in Karkā de Bēt Selōk, is an example. The chronicle of this city tells us that the first church in this city was built by a certain Jāūsep and that later it became the first monastery in Karkā de Bēt Selōk, being known as the Monastery of the house of Jāūsep [73]. Later it seems that the primitive building could not serve the needs of the grown congregation, and so the care of the ancient *haiklā* was left into the hands of the monks. They gradually transformed it into a monastery.

But in special circumstances, new buildings could come into being, by way of the same process. According to the tradition

were gathered; and a sweet smell steamed at the blowing of the storm and the whole house was filled', *Srboyn meknowtʻiwn*, p. 13. See the Syriac form of the text in *Liber graduum*, col. 553.

72 *Acta martyrum*, I, p. 522

73 *Ibid.*, II, p. 512.

coming from the Monastery of Ṣelībā, the monastery was preceded by a *haiklā* built as a memorial to a miraculous phenomenon which took place in this area. Then monks came together from different places, bringing into existence a monastic community [74]. In such a way the *haiklā* erected for quite another purpose was transformed into the Monastery of Ṣelībā.

Further, localities celebrated as biblical places, were marked by the foundation of monasteries. Among these the most outstanding was the monastery of the Ark, established on a place connected with the Noah's ark. The Syrian tradition identified the place where the ark landed with Qardū, already known in the Talmud [75] and later in the Koran [76]. According to legend [77], the exact place where the ark was hidden in the earth was detected, and even a board of it was unearthed. The tradition that a monastery was built here by Jaʿqōb, bishop of Nisibis, belongs to the realm of legends, but in any case an early monastery did exist here, which grew in its importance. The same convent also appears in connection with Catholicos Dadīšōʿ (421-456). When he, owing to the intrigues woven in the capital, had to flee, he selected this monastery for sanctuary, and here contemplated his resignation [78]. According to Bakūwī this monastery immemorially had been situated on the top of the mountain [79].

Apart from this monastery, the renown of Bēt Qardū seems to have appealed to other monastic founders [80].

Of the monastery of Mār Mīkā, it is known that a biblical place was selected for the site on which it was erected. It was located at the village Alqōš, a place related to the prophet Nahum [81].

74 *Histoire nestorienne*, V, p. 308 f.

75 Baba B. 91 a connects this place with Abraham.

76 Sura II, 46.

77 In the legend of Mār Aūgēn, *Acta martyrum*, III, p. 436 f.

78 دیرالقبوت 'the monastery of ark', MARI, *De patriarchis*, p. 36. In Syriac ܕܝܪܐ ܕܩܒܬ ܟܐܘܠܐ, DIONYSIOS TELL MAḤRĒ, *Chronique*, p. 83. See also a reference in Ms. Vat. Borg. syr. 39, fol. 156 a.

79 YAQUT, *Muʿjam al-buldān*, II, p. 649 f.

80 Sources which describe conditions which existed later, refer to this area as having other monasteries.

81 *Acta martyrum*, III, p. 526.

And when the *haiklā* near the pit of Daniel in Babylonia was restored, it was furnished with a community of monks [82].

Quite naturally, places connected with the pagan cults were selected for the monastic foundations. Eventually we hear that even a sacral establishment of the Mazdean cult was transformed into a monastery. The monastery of Qardag, according to its tradition, was originally a fire-house, built by Qardag's parents, and Qardag converted it to a monastery [83]. Certainly it was private and on private property. In this respect there are other hints in the traditions, kept and amplified in the monastic communities [84].

Other monasteries rose in existing buildings which greatly facilitated the foundations. There are frequent clues that unused forts were used for this purpose. In the legend of Mār Beniāmīn it is said about the monastery of Mār Šelīmūn that it was originally a *ḥesnā*, fort, built by the Romans [85]. Another legendary tradition reveals that a convent was established in a fort, for it is called the Monastery of Qastrā [86]. Another remark which belongs in the same category, appears in connection with a certain Jōḥannan who founded a monastery in Bēt Zabdai [87].

Finally here the mountains caught the attention of the founders of the convents. The protection offered by the mountains was quickly grasped by those who did not let themselves be guided by visionary experiences and other idealistic considerations, but also by others which were very realistic. Archaeological remains tell us what wise precautions and prudent calculations were taken into account. The establishment of the renowned monastery of Mār Mattai is the best example. Its site was a mountain gorge, very

82 ونصب فيها جماعة من الرهبان 'and there he established a community of monks', MARI, *De patriarchis*, p. 29.

83 ܘܒܝܬ ܢܘܪܐ ܚܕ ܡܫܡܗܐ 'and a renowned firehouse', *Acta martyrum*, II, p. 470.

84 See *Histoire nestorienne*, V, p. 250 f.

85 ܚܣܢܐ *Vie de Mar Benjamin*, p. 92.

86 الدير المعروف بقسطرا 'monastery known as that in Qastrā', *Histoire nestorienne*, V, p. 250.

87 ܕܝܪܐ ܕܢܟܦܘܬܐ ĪŠŌʿDENAḤ, *Chasteté*, p. 2; see also Ms. Berl. Sach. 63, fol. 219 a.

difficult of access. In such a place, the site offering the best kind of protection was looked for and chosen. A monastery in such a place did not demand more for defence, in the case of hostilities, than the most modest precautionary measures. Here the monastery was founded in such a way that it rather reminds us of a swallow's nest upon the ledge of a rock. Every piece of space has been carved out by a steady struggle with the rock, which obediently has receded in the face of the relentless labor of many hands over many generations [88]. In fact, among other monasteries built in the mountain gorges Mār Mattai is a master-piece.

c. Monasteries founded in mission areas

Another category of monasteries requires several separate words since their purpose and the conditions for their foundation are not covered by the preceding remarks. These are the convents which emerged in the mission fields often in far off areas as the outposts of an expanding Christendom. Many of these have sunk into the depth of oblivion, and only some have escaped the same fate. The most important piece of evidence regarding these monasteries appears in connection with the activity of the great monk-missionaries. Here we are told something which throws light upon the genesis and the function of these establishments.

As we have already seen, the great monk-missionaries were also founders of the monasteries. In connection with ʿAbdīšōʿ we have observed how he, in his selection of various mission fields in Bēt Maišān, Bēt Ārāmāiē, and in Bēt Qaṭrāiē founded monasteries as the centers of the work, and as foci for the future nurture of the newly converted flocks [89]. The same was observed in the activities of Sābā who made the newly established monasteries bridgeheads in the process of evangelization [90].

There is every reason to postulate that many monasteries have emanated from the missionary enterprise of monks, monasteries of which we know nothing. Only seldom do we find a casual reference

88 PREUSSER, *Baudenkmäler*, p. 15. See a *mēmrā* about the Monastery of Mār Mattai, Ms. Šarf. Patr. 38, fol. 203 b.

89 See pag. 270.

90 See pag. 293 f.

resuscitating this or that monastery from the grave of oblivion or an immortalization by a local name of something about the process by which a bishopric came into existence [91].

These monasteries also appear as outposts, erected far away from Christian areas. In the western regions, one such emerges in Ḥīrā at a very early time. Here ʿAbdīšōʿ, coming from Bēt Qaṭrāiē, founded a monastery, making it the headquarters for the mission [92]. In the furthermost provinces in the East, the Monastery of Davīd comes into sight as such an outpost. It was founded as a part of the mission work directed by Baršabbā, probably near Merw. This convent, where Baršabbā found his last resting-place [93], perhaps served as the headquarters for this monk-missionary.

Some of these outposts come into sight when we direct our eyes towards the South-East. It was ʿAbdīšōʿ who erected a monastery on one of the islands of Jamama and Bahrain, when he wanted to devote himself to ascetic exercises, and he evangelized among the inhabitants [94]. From another source comes the information about such an early outpost in Bēt Qaṭrāiē [95].

In many respects, the information embedded in the story of the hermit Jāūnān is instructive. This document claims to come from Zāʿdōi, 'priest, monk and archimandrite of the monastery of Mār Thomas in the country of India' [96]. Where this outpost was situated is problematical. The view that it was really in India hardly bears examination. Fatal to the view that India is meant, or Ceylon [97], is the simple fact that the text does not claim more than 'south of Bēt Qaṭrāiē [98]. The further notice that it was on the borders of an

91 This seems to be the case with the bishopric of دير مخراق Dair Mihrāq 'the Monastery of Mihrāq', *Histoire nestorienne,* V, p. 311, cf. IV, p. 236.

92 *Ibid.,* V, p. 312.

93 الدير المعروف هناك بدير داود 'a monastery known there as the Monastery of David', *ibid.,* V, p. 256.

94 *Ibid.,* V, p. 311 f.

95 ܐܝܬ ܗܘܐ ܬܡܢ ܐܚ̈ܐ ܣܓܝ̈ܐܐ ܦܠܚܝ̈ܢ ܒܩܢܘܢܐ 'there are many monks (lit. brethren) serving in the canon (of monastic life)', Ms. Ming. syr. 60, fol. 87 b.

96 *Acta martyrum,* I, p. 466.

97 See Labourt, *Christianisme,* p. 306.

98 ܠܬܝܡܢ ܡܢ ܐܬܪܐ ܕܩܛܪ̈ܝܐ, *Acta martyrum,* I, p. 466.

island called 'the black island' does not help us very much. Obviously, this island must be sought for among the small islands south of Bēt Qaṭrāiē towards Oman [99]. Thus, this India, in the title of the document, cannot mean more than the Arabian side of the Persian Gulf [100].

If, indeed, the compilator of this legendary story used earlier data taken from an earlier work, then we have some additional reminiscences which can give color to the remarks regarding the role of these outposts. The first thing that must strike the student of these texts is the information regarding the relations between the monastery and the monastic centers in the homeland. In these narratives, it can be seen how monks, who lived in the monasteries of Persian Mesopotamia after their wanderings come to this monastery. We are told that one monk who came there, had lived in the desert of Peroz Shahpuhr [101], another in Babylonia [102]. That means that the monastery was constantly visited by monks from the monastic centers in Southern Mesopotamia. Thus we are given an idea as to how the solitaries and coenobites, who had their cells and monasteries in more densely christianized regions, appeared in these outposts putting themselves at the disposal of these communities.

While on the track of the monasteries as the outposts of Christian mission, we lose every recognizable trace when we try to look still farther — into South Arabia and to India. Nothing is known about the outposts in South Arabia, in regions like Neǧran and the area of the Himjarites. The splinters of information are not of much value as evidence. But since the beginnings of Christianity in Himjar go back to the first decades of the 5th century and since the Christian faith was transplanted there from Ḥīrā [103], those facts

99 Mingana speculated that this has been the island called the 'Kāwān island' or 'Lāfit island', between Oman and Bahrain, *Early Spread*, p. 20 f.

100 In favor of this seems to speak a poem of Marrār al-Fakʿasi who eulogizes the beauty of the old monastery of Deir Thūma, Yaqut, *Muʿjam al-buldān*, II, p. 649 f.

101 *Acta martyrum*, I, p. 467, 483.

102 *Ibid.*, p. 509.

103 *Histoire nestorienne*, V, p. 330 f.

would lend a color of plausibility to the assertion that the monastic establishments found their way there [104].

With regard to the question whether some monasteries were established in India by the advancing monks from Persia, we are groping in darkness. Of course, there are data about the existence of the monastery of Mār Thomas, situated on the Coromandel Coast of India [105], but we have no way of knowing its age. It may be argued that if Gregory of Tours had the same monastery in mind when referring to the monastery of Thomas in India [106], then it may have existed already in the fifth century. But such a reconstruction of the scanty facts would involve too many conjectural elements. This disallows any great confidence on our part, however much we would like to assume that India also belonged to the orbit of monastic founders.

4. MONASTICISM UNFOLDING ITS SPIRITUAL STRENGTH

a. In the area of missionary enterprises

Monasticism in the 5th century reveals certain features that can be interpreted not only from growth in numbers but also from the unfolding of spiritual culture. Such a situation meant that monasticism was gradually being shaken out of its primitive mould. It is time to submit arguments for this change.

The first indication of change can be seen in the steadily growing missionary zeal. We notice that anchorite and hermit monks were more and more associated with mission fields and missionary activities. This feature appears so frequently that the phenomenon must have had its roots in the unfolding of the movement. This development, no doubt, is a stigma of spiritual strength which monasticism must have felt increasing in its veins.

104 Šemʿōn of Bēt Aršām does not say a word about the monasteries or monks in his report, *Sopra i martiri omeriti*, p. 502 ff. Also the acts of martyrdom of the Christians in Neǧran, *Book of Himyarites*. YAQUT, *Muʿjam al-buldān*, II, p. 703, mentions a monastery in Neǧran, but we do not know about its history.

105 See a Syriac text edited by MINGANA, *Early Spread*, p. 468.

106 *Miracula*, p. 507 f.

The names and works of countless monks have fallen into oblivion. What we have is information concerning only some of the most outstanding figures. This information reveals in what direction the stimulation was given to other groups of monks, for in these narratives which we have we can see the distillation of the current trends.

In the mountainous area between the valley of the Tigris and Media monk Petiōn worked evangelizing the pagan towns and villages, combining his manners of ascetic life with missionary zeal. He laid the foundation for mission work in the province of Belāšphar. Then, gradually, he extended his work to Bēt Dārāiē and Bēt Kūsāiē — both in Babylonia — and to Maišān [107], the latter being a difficult territory for Christian missions [108]. We see him evangelizing in these rough areas between the valley of the Tigris and Media during the summer season. In winter we see him in the southern parts, extending his work to Mahrgānqādaq which was already in the confines of Susiana. Regarding the crowning of his labors, his acts of martyrdom state : 'and many people were brought to the gospel of the Messiah, so that he built four great churches there' [109]. When the foundation was laid and the work put on solid footing, he left that field in order to go to the country of Māsabdān. It is reported that in journeying he used the back route that gave him the opportunity to evangelize in many villages on the way. Māsabdān lies in the area adjacent to the Gangir River in Susiana.

After an interim in his cell near the village of Dāwīn, this monk-missionary was led by kerygmatic impulses to new towns in the country of Bēt Mādāiē (Media). Also here his enterprise is reported to have taken a successful turn. Finally it is reported of this tireless worker that he had a habit of making annual tours to the places where he had evangelized, and that he developed these tours into visitations of teaching and catechization [110].

Difficulties for such monks often heightened their dedication.

107 *Acta martyrum*, II, p. 629.

108 ܥܠ ܕܒܢ̈ܝ ܒܪ̈ܝܐ ܘܗܕܝܘ̈ܛܐ ܘܥܠܡ̈ܢܝܐ ܐܚܝܕܝ ܐܬܪܐ ܗܘ 'because the people of this country are very wild, and stupid and worldly and very fanatical idolaters', *Acta Maris apostoli*, p. 119.

109 *Acta martyrum*, I, p. 629; cf. *Historia Pethion martyris*, p. 42.

110 *Ibid.*, p. 42.

We have an illuminating episode of this fact in the life of Mār Sābā. When the persecutions had broken out, an anchorite by the name of Kelīlīšōʿ came to Mār Sābā and told him that now was not the time to sit in quietness and loneliness : 'our brother, why do we sit here in peace alone, when heavy persecution has fallen upon the church of the Messiah? Arise to go out and proclaim the name of our Lord Jesus the Messiah, and strengthen by the word believing brethren' [111]. Then Mār Sābā took his cross and the codex of the gospel and started a new phase of his activity.

In the activities of Mār Sābā we have another illustration of the missionary zeal of monasticism. First Mār Sābā came to a town of Ḥālē and initiated his evangelistic work here and in its vicinity. Here began his reputation as the destroyer of pagan cult objects. His work proved to be such a success that it was rewarded by ordination to the priesthood by the hand of Mīkā, bishop of Lāšōm. One of the companions of the bishop joined Mār Sābā in his work. But we hear that when a church was built and the provisory leadership appointed for the congregation [112], Mār Sābā went in the night around the town of Ḥālē three times and signed in with the sign of the cross. 'And they wrote on a tablet, put over the gate of the city : our Lord will be with you until the end of the world. Amen' [113]. This obviously meant the last act in replacing the pagan emblems [114].

After Mār Sābā left this field he sought new ones, travelling around in the towns and villages in several countries. It is told that he, accompanied by his disciple, evangelized even among the Kurds [115], although this journey was not put voluntarily into his itinerary. This episode, being brought as a prisoner to his new mission field, is, however, so distorted by exuberant legends that it is difficult to determine whether anything of historical fact has

111 *Acta martyrum*, II, p. 651.

112 *Ibid.*, II, p. 667.

113 ܘܟܬܒܘ ܒܠܘܚܐ ܣܡܘܗ ܠܥܠ ܡܢ ܬܪܥܐ ܕܡܕܝܢܬܐ: ܡܪܢ ܢܗܘܐ ܥܡܟܘܢ ܥܕܡܐ ܠܫܘܠܡܗ ܕܥܠܡܐ: ܐܡܝܢ *ibid.*, II, p. 668.

114 We hear that this was the custom, to put the emblems of idols at the gate or over the gate, Ms. Berl. Sach. 321, fol. 183 b; *Julianos der Abtrünnige*, p. 146.

115 *Acta martyrum*, II, p. 672 ff.

been left. Even the statement hat he left one priest behind to continue his work seems to be doubtful on the basis of the character of this narrative. His further work is summarized by his vita in the following words : 'they came down from the mountain and they moved around in the countries and towns and villages and healed the sick and cured the souls of those who were defiled by sin. They pulled down shrines of idolatry and built churches and edified the monasteries. They sowed the truth of faith as a diligent ploughman and as a wise architect until they arrived at Naharzōz'[116].

The external expansion of Christianity reflects the unfolding missionary spirit in the formation of monasticism. This expansion went even beyond the eastern and southern boundaries of the empire. In addition to the areas adjacent to the Red Sea and the countries in the north, monasticism poured strength into the developing Christianity in India which goes back to an earlier time[117]. The fact that Christianity in India came into closer contact with the Syrian church in Persia seems to be due mainly to the merit of monasticism's missionary zeal. Through this Christianity in India received fruitful stimuli for its growth. The way from Persia to India was covered with monasteries that created new communication lines. These monasteries facilitated the stream of missionaries to carry out their task of kindling the Christian work in India by their lives as well as by the written word[118].

This picture in the preceding pages needs some supplementary remarks. Besides the missionary zeal there were other features which had their place in this phenomenon, namely, charismatic and thaumaturgical features.

There is a pecular conglomeration of various elements which comes to the fore when we follow the ways and methods of these monk-missionaries as revealed and unfolded by the sources. Mār Petiōn moved around as a wonder-making thaumaturge and as a renowned demon fighter heralding 'the power of Jesus the Physician'

116 *Ibid.*, II, p. 676 f.

117 We learn that at the time of Catholicos Papā, David, bishop of Basra, had resigned his bishopric in order to evangelize the inhabitants in India, *Histoire nestorienne*, IV, p. 292 f.

118 Maʿnā translated patristic works from the Greek into Syriac and sent them to India, *ibid.*, V, p. 116 f.

which heals everyone [119]. We notice the same activity in the methods of Mār Sābā. When he and his disciple Bĕšahrig came to the town of Dumā, one of the local dignitaries inquired who they were. Their prompt answer was : 'we are physicians' [120]. Another such figure appears as 'a perfect monk, father Mašīḥaraḥmā' [121] who is called a healer in a reference in the chronicle of Ārbēl.

Besides the charismatic gifts some lesser means of exorcism were present in this phenomenon. Particularly, relics have played a great role here. Already in the acts of martyrdom, the eagerness with which the ascetics snatched the bodies and parts of the bodies of the martyrs stands out. This way of securing relics can be noticed in the earliest acts we possess. The use of these relics in private hands became so alarming that attempts were made to restrict the use of relics to the churches and monasteries [122].

We do not possess anything about this in the canons, but the situation regarding still lower means was hardly much different from that which took place in the monasteries in Armenia. Among the decisions made at the synod of Šahapiwan, one decision concerns the magic practiced so widely that hard punitive steps were necessitated. And monks are mentioned among the guilty circles in this business [123].

Under the circumstances the mission work of these ascetic-charismatic-thaumaturgic heralds was very much bound to their persons. Also its future depended upon them. But they knew a way out. It is interesting to observe how they were aware of the character of their work and knew how to take care of the further fate of their influence. An illustrative episode of this ability is offered in the vita of Mār Sābā. When he felt that his departure from this world was drawing near, he instructed his disciple : '« let us dig a well that might be a remedy and cure for men who wash in its water ». They dug a well about three *qāwmīn*, and much water came out. And he blessed the waters and placed in them the staff that (he held) in his hand and said : « whosoever bathes in

119 ܫܝܠܗ ܕܝܫܘܥ ܐܣܝܐ, *Acta martyrum*, II, p. 587.

120 ܐܣܘܬܐ ܣܡ, *ibid.*, II, p. 668.

121 *Sources syriaques*, p. 67.

122 Ms. Vat. syr. 501, fol. 81 b.

123 *Patmowtʿiwn žołovoc̣*, p. 56 ff.

these waters will be healed of every sickness which he has »' [124]. By this act his authority and power was left behind to keep watch over the seed in his mission fields. And as the story shows, the silhouette of this thaumaturge lived forth in the shadow of this well generations later.

b. In the area of instruction

Another important indication of the unfolding spiritual strength of monasticism lies in instruction. The frequency with which the names of monks appear in the sources which belong to the period under consideration is conspicuous. As Mār Petiōn learned the psalms and the wisdom of Scriptures from Mār Jazdīn [125] so other converts directed their steps to the monks in order to receive their first guidance in the study of the sacred books. Increasingly, this area of activity slipped into the hands of the teachers in monastic garb. Countless monks have found their calling in teaching. Among the most renowned names are Narsai [126] and Aksenaiā who have been teachers from the earliest stage of their careers [127].

Particularly, the monasteries became suitable places for those who wrestled in their consciences and prepared the heart for consequences which often involved not only the abdication of the religion of their forefathers but also the abandonment of their home and families. Under these conditions the monasteries appeared as places where one could find refuge, assistance and thoughtful understanding from those who themselves had gone through conflicts and crises. The vita of Jazdīn tells that when he ascertained that no one in the local area would dare to give him baptism he left his home and country and fled into another province. He went to Bēt Garmai and entered a monastery in which he was instructed and in which he received baptism [128]. It also is told that here he was instructed in the psalms and in the reading of the Scriptures and was initiated into the ways of ascetic life.

124 *Acta martyrum,* II, p. 677.

125 *Ibid.,* II, p. 564.

126 Barḥadbešabbā, *Histoire,* II, p. 590 ff.

127 He was in his youtful years a teacher in a village Taḥal in Bēt Garmai, Ms. Par. syr. 377, fol. 220 b. Cf. Ms. Sin. syr. 10, fol. 48 a.

128 *Acta martyrum,* II, p. 563.

As in the case of Jazdīn, many neophytes have found, in the monasteries, enlightenment and help as well as a temporary home which made instruction possible. The same role is portrayed in the story of Qardag. The monastery is again the place where the neophyte with his companions received instruction and then baptism [129]. These examples illustrate something which grew into an important function.

However, not everything has been said about the activity of monasticism in the field of teaching. Some words must be said about the recognition of the value of systematically arranged teaching which, with increasing tempo, became an integral part of monasticism's life, auguring a great future. Even for the period under discussion there is enough that can be said about the relationship between monasticism and schools.

The establishment of an important school by Mār ʿAbdā, already mentioned [130], proved to be fruitful for the future direction of the development of monasticism. There are indications that Mār ʿAbdā stimulated and encouraged his disciples in this direction [131]. How rapidly and widely this seed sown by the circle which rallied behind this master took root and began to germinate is concealed from our eyes. But it is an evidence of the vital strength of the foundation of this master that his school continued to function and was able to survive many hardships. Only a violent action from outside, the hand of King Peroz, could destroy his school [132]. Thus it appears that the stimuli given by Mār ʿAbdā began to bear some fruit. We notice that more and more schools appear in relationship with monastic life and ideals. These schools appear as training centers in biblical knowledge which was also important for fostering the life of monasticism itself. In the vita of Mār Sābā it is said that after he entered monasticism and after he brought his mother and nurse into a monastery of nuns, he himself attended such a school for two years in order to become more mature for ascetic life [133]. The school in the village of ʿAin Dūlbā which

[129] *Ibid.*, II, p. 467.
[130] See pag. 267 ff.
[131] *Histoire nestorienne,* V, p. 311; cf. Mari, *De patriarchis,* p. 29.
[132] *Ibid.*, p. 42.
[133] *Acta martyrum,* II, p. 650.

Narsai entered as a boy and where he remained for nine years, gave guidance in the knowledge of the Scriptures as well as in ascetic discipline [134].

Monastic communities, of course, could provide such schools with the foundation necessary to meet both the material and spiritual demands of such establishments by putting the monastic communities behind them. Also, the best monks could be selected for the furtherance of this work. When Mār Narsai at the beginning of his career was in the monastery of Kephar Mārī, he was asked by the abbot to take over the instruction : 'he (the abbot) proved to him that he was more flourishing in learning than the teachers and brothers who were there; he, along with all the community, urged him to read the codices to them' [135].

There is even a hint that these schools must have aroused the attention of the Indians and attracted them to do their studies here. A precious colophon in the commentary on the Epistle to the Romans, composed by Īšōʿdad, informs us about such a student, Priest Dānīʾēl of India, who has assisted Mār Kōmai in his translation work [136].

There were also other stimuli which fertilized the ground for these activities. A casual remark dropped by chance in connection with the school of Mār ʿAbdā indicates that monasticism had early received impulses in this direction also from the school of Edessa [137]. More can be perceived of these fruitful stimuli in connection with Narsai, Barṣaūmā, and Maʿnā who left Persia in order to study in the school in Edessa. Some of those who came added to the fame of this place of learning. Mār Narsai was elected the director and guided the school there for twenty years [138]. This man

134 Barḥadbešabbā, *Histoire*, II, p. 595.

135 ܘܐܦ ܢܦܫܗ ܕܗܘ ܢܗܝܪ ܒܝܘܠܦܢܐ ܡܢ ܡܠܦܢܐ ܘܐܚܐ ܕܬܡܢ. ܘܐܦܝܣܗ ܗܘ ܥܡ ܟܠܗ ܟܢܫܐ ܕܢܩܪܐ ܐܢܘܢ ܣܦܪ̈ܐ *ibid.*, p. 596.

136 Īšōʿdad of Merw, *Commentaries*, V, p. 34. It must have been done in early career of Kōmai if the Mārī to whom the work is dedicated is Mārī, metropolitan of Revardešir, see Ms. Berl. Sach. 311, fol. 205 a.

137 واستغنى من يريد التعلم باسكوله عن الخروج الى الرها 'the disciples of his school could abstain from the necessity of going to Edessa', *Histoire nestorienne*, V, p. 308.

138 Barḥadbešabbā, *Fondation des écoles*, p. 383.

of the country of Maʿaltā, of the village ʿAin Dūlbā, was a monk of the monastery of Kephar Mārī in Bēt Zabdai. He was a man of rigid discipline and mortification whose only possessions were his books [139].

There are only a very few historical vestiges left by the repercussions which this work had in the homeland in Persia. But these vestiges are significant in showing how communication between the school of Edessa and its pupils from Persia helped to bring the pedagogical work in the monasteries to fruition.

Šemʿōn of Bēt Aršām gives an incorrect picture of the situation when he depicts the return of Barṣaūmā and others as a result of the closing of the school in Edessa in 457 [140]. Barṣaūmā returned much earlier, for he became bishop already in 435 [141]. Also many other monks, whose names have faded away in the shadow of great personalities connected with the school, must have returned and certainly not with empty hands. What we are able to notice in these monks whom we happen to know justifies this conclusion. In the information about Mār ʿAmanū'ēl there is afforded us some insight into this situation. ʿAmanū'ēl, one of the uncles of Narsai, was an abbot of the monastery of Kephar Mārī in Bēt Zabdai. It is reported of this man that he was instructed in the school of Edessa and had come back to his monastery. Furthermore, the steps which he took afterwards tell also of the kind of inspiration which he brought with him : 'he enriched this monastery by a large gathering of brethren and founded a school there' [142].

Something from this stimulus can be seen in the life of Narsai himself. While in his youthful years in the monastery of Kephar Mārī, he heard about the work in the school in Edessa. He became so interested that he left the monastery of Kephar Mārī to study in Edessa. He spent ten years there before he returned, being urged by his abbot to resume his instruction in the school of the monastery. The effect his return had upon the work of the monastery is given

139 Barḥadbešabbā, *Histoire*, II, p. 603.

140 *Bibl. orientalis*, I, p. 353.

141 Ms. Vat. syr. 520, fol. 41 b; Vat. syr. 67, fol. 43 a.

142 ܘܥܬܪܗ ܠܗܘ ܥܘܡܪܐ ܒܟܢܘܫܝܐ ܣܓܝܐܐ ܕܐܚܐ. ܘܥܒܕ ܬܡܢ ܐܣܟܘܠܐ Barḥadbešabbā, *Histoire*, II, p. 596.

by the following statement : 'and when he consented to this, within a short time about 300 brothers were gathered to him'[143].

Narsai's long stay in Edessa was interrupted by two periods when he returned to his monastery and resumed his instruction in the monastic school. The first, mentioned above, took place after he had spent a period of ten years in Edessa. The second took place when the abbot of the monastery of Kephar Mārī, feeling that his life was near its end, urged him back. This second return occurred after Narsai had been in Edessa another decade. On Narsai's return, the dying abbot entrusted the monastic community into his hands. This new responsibility did not last longer than about one year for the voice of Narsai's heart drew him to the place of learning in Edessa. He gave over the work of instruction at the monastery of Kephar Mārī to one of the brothers, Gabrī'ēl, and bade farewell[144].

More can be said about the stimuli for work in monastic schools. The Persian school in Edessa was closed. But this occurrence turned out to be last blessing this institution was able to give. The Chronicle of Ārbēl reporting important events that took place under Bishop 'Abbūšṭā includes also the effect of the expulsion of the teachers and students. It relates that these teachers and students came back into their home country and established many new schools there[145].

The best information about these events we get from Barḥadbešabbā. He reports in detail the birth of the school in Nisibis which became the most significant place of learning. When, after the expulsion, Narsai left Edessa he planned to journey into inner Persia. On his way he stayed in Nisibis in the monastery of the Persians[146]. While Narsai was there Barṣaūmā arranged an exultant

143 ܘܟܕ ܐܬܦܝܣ ܠܗܕܐ. ܒܩܠܝܠ ܙܒܢܐ ܐܬܟܢܫܘ ܠܘܬܗ ܐܝܟ ܬܠܬ ܡܐܐ ܐܚܐ *ibid.*, II, p. 597.

144 *Ibid.*, II, p. 597.

145 ܘܐܙܠܘ ܗܠܝܢ ܠܐܬܪܘܬܗܘܢ ܘܢܨܒܘ ܒܗܘܢ ܐܣܟܘܠܣ ܣܓܝܐܬܐ 'these (i.e. the pupils of the School in Edessa) went to their countries and planted in these many schools', *Sources syriaques*, p. 66.

146 ܕܝܪܐ ܕܦܪܣܝܐ. ܕܣܝܡܐ ܡܢ ܡܕܢܚܗ ܕܡܕܝܢܬܐ 'the Monastery of the Persians that is located from east of the town, BARḤADBEŠABBĀ, *Histoire*, II, p. 605.

reception for him and laid before him the plans to found a school in Nisibis, offering all the help needed for this project. This plan was put into effect. The school was provided with the necessary funds, and Mār Narsai became its first director. The effect of this foundation is described by Barḥadbešabbā in the following words : 'within a short time its entire (body) increased; not only the Persian and Syrian brothers came, but also the greater part of the assembly of the Edessa (school) came to him' [147]. More detailed information about the place which was arranged for the school [148] and about the constituency of brothers which joined the newly established school [149] Barḥadbešabbā has given in his 'Church History'. According to him, Narsai kept the direction of the school in his experienced hands for 40 years [150], adding to the fame of the school by his activity as interpreter and by his pen [151] in the service of literary culture.

In the sources this significant event overshadows all other effects which the closing of the school in Edessa may have had [152]. Barḥadbešabbā accounts for this fact in two general statements. First he says that the results of the dispersion of the teachers and students from the Edessa school has to be compared with the results which the dispersion of the apostles had after the persecution started in Jerusalem. Both of these dispersions resulted in the spreading of teachers [153]. Secondly he observes in retrospect : 'because of this

147 ܘܒܩܠܝܠ ܙܒܢܐ ܗܘܐ ܟܠܗ ܣܓܝܘ : ܠܘ ܒܠܚܘܕ. ܐܚ̈ܐ ܦܪ̈ܣܝܐ ܘܣܘ̈ܪܝܝܐ ܕܐܬܘ : ܐܠܐ ܐܦ ܣܘܓܐܗ̄ ܕܗܘ̇ ܟܢܘܫܝܐ ܕܐܘܪܗܝ، ܠܘܬܗ ܐܬܘ *Fondation des écoles*, p. 386.

148 ܘܙܒܢ ܠܗ̇ ܠܐܣܟܘܠܐ ܒܝܬ ܓܡܠܐ ܣܝ. ܥܠ ܓܢܒ ܒ.ܥܕܬܐ 'and he bought for the school a stable of camels near the site of the church', BARḤADBEŠABBĀ, *Histoire*, II, p. 608.

149 We hear that there was previously a school which was in the hands of a Šemʿōn of Kaškar, and these pupils joined the enterprise. Then in a short time brothers began to gather from all parts of the country, *ibid.*, p. 608.

150 So Barḥadbešabbā, *ibid.*, p. 615. In his *Fondation des écoles*, p. 386 he speaks of 45 years. The difference is caused by a period in which he retired to the monastery of Kephar Mārī.

151 ʿABDĪŠŌʿ, *Catalogus librorum* speaks of 360 homilies. Not a half of these has survived.

152 VÖÖBUS, *Statutes of the school.*

153 *Fondation des écoles*, p. 385.

occasion the assemblies (of schools) also multiplied in the country of the Persians' [154].

Now, we have before us the most important evidence relating to the pedagogical activity which monasticism unfolded. In looking over this evidence, one feels himself driven to the conclusion that the pedagogical activity of monasticism is another telling symptom that monasticism was gradually shaken out of its primitive mould.

So far, we have touched the main sectors in the area of instruction where the monastic movement contributed to their growth and development. We have not yet finished this issue. The actual share of monasticism in the promotion of instruction is thereby not yet covered. Another sector remains to be considered if we try to strive towards fuller evaluation of the monastic contribution to this important domain of intellectual culture.

There are provoking problems created by another set of data. A consultation of sources, again and again, leads us to information regarding schools which are not covered by the preceding study. Schools of a different type appear in important towns. In Nisibis, there was a school before Narsai came and founded his school [155]. In Karkā de Bēt Selōk several schools are reported [156]. And so other schools existed in other important towns. Further, we have information that there were schools in even much smaller communities. The school in the village of ʿAin Dūlbā emerges in connection with the life-story of its inmate who later became renowned — Narsai [157]. Such instances, which had a chance to appear in fuller light of history, are naturally exceptions. Information regarding other and similar schools suffer from the same inherent disability regarding the exact nature of these establishments and the circumstances regarding the origin and the persons who operated these schools. In this respect we grope in complete darkness.

However, in one special point, at least, some of our sources open up an avenue which is very instructive. These are texts which throw light on a new co-ordinate in the picture of the development of

154 ܘܡܢ ܗܕܐ ܥܠܬܐ ܣܓܝܘ ܐܦ ܟܢܘ̈ܫܬܐ ܒܝܬ ܦܪ̈ܣܝܐ *ibid.*, p. 386.

155 We are told that a certain Mār Šemʿōn of Kaškar was in charge of instruction in this school, BARḤADBEŠABBā, *Histoire*, II, p. 608.

156 IšōʿDENAḥ, *Chasteté*, p. 7.

157 BARḤADBEŠABBā, *Histoire*, II, p. 594 f.

schools in the Syrian communities which, at least partly, falls to the credit of monasticism. Namely, we are permitted to glimpse a concrete expression of the growing interest in the church in ways towards the furtherance of instruction. This information reaches us in the stream of biographical literature.

It is a matter of regret that nothing can be discovered about the origin of the office of an instructor in the church. This origin is wrapped in an obscurity deeper than we are able to penetrate. The references are, in this respect, very vague [158]. This institution simply stands before us in the last quarter of the fifth century. So far as we are able to see, this institution appears in the center of the diocese. It is, however, possible that this is not the complete picture and that it existed also in smaller communities.

Since the earlier sources give only very lapidar remarks and casual hints, for the sake of greater clarity we have no other choice than to take recourse to those episodes, which, although they belong to a somewhat later period, they are more informative and, as such, help us to get an idea about the nature of the institution under discussion. We are indebted to the work of Mešīḥazekā for the best information. For, in connection with the events related in connection with Bishop Ḥenānā of Ḥadiab, this document tells also something about his measures as undertaken in the interest of instruction. Obviously, Ḥenānā had consulted one of the teachers, Abraham, in the school of Nisibis. At this point, we come to the section which concerns our inquiry : 'Mār Abraham, the Interpreter, had given Paulos as a teacher (in the knowledge of the Bible) to Mār Ḥenānā, in order that he may establish a school for the children in the country of Ḥadiab, in order to implant faith in their mind, and to defend it against the aggression of the heretics and the Messalians. This Paulos remained with us more than 30 years, carrying out his position (office) which was entrusted to him by the heads of the church in all humility and fear of God' [159].

158 Ms. Vat. Borg. syr. 82, fol. 45 a.

159 ܘܝܗܒ ܠܗ ܡܪܝ، ܐܒܪܗܡ ܡܦܫܩܢܐ ܠܡܪܝ، ܚܢܢܐ ܦܘܠܘܣ ܡܠܦܢܐ ܐܡܘܢܐ
ܕܢܣܝܡ ܒܐܬܪܐ ܕܚܕܝܒ ܐܣܟܘܠܐ ܠܛܠܝܐ : ܕܢܩܒܥ ܒܗܘܢܗܘܢ
ܠܗܝܡܢܘܬܐ ܘܢܣܬܪܗ ܠܘܩܒܠ ܚܪܝܫܐ ܕܗܪܛܝܩܐ ܘܡܨܠܝܢܐ. ܘܗܘܝ، ܗܢܐ

This information is very valuable for the question under discussion. Here we learn something about the function of such a director of instruction. The duties of his office were to take care of the foundation of schools for children and, in addition to this — the text leaves the clear impression — he had to take care of the instruction of the adults. Since the wording speaks of counter-measures against the tide of the heterodox movements this instruction seems to have been involved.

The episode just described belongs to the period at the beginning of the 6th century. This institution, however, must be much earlier, as the vestiges in our sources testify to this. The most noteworthy among these is the tradition that Mār Aqaq was entrusted with such an office before he was consecrated for catholicos. This means that Aqaq held this office during the decades before 483/4 [160]. We are instructed that he had studied in Edessa and returned to his homeland and established himself in Seleucia where he held a post of instruction all the time when Bābōi was catholicos, whose interest in monasticism is claimed by the tradition [161]. This report in Mārī [162] and ʿAmr [163] goes back to the earlier work in the chronicle of Seert [164].

ܦܘܠܘܣ ܠܘܬܗ ܫܕܪ ܡܢ ܬܠܬܝܢ ܥܣ̈ܪܝ ܒܪ ܡܫܡܠܝܐ ܠܥܕܬܐ ܕܐܬܒܠܒܠܬ ܠܗ
ܡܢ ܙ̈ܢܝܐ ܕܒܝܫܬܐ ܒܡܠܘܗܝ ܡܗܝܡܢܘܬܐ ܘܕܝܠܝܬ ܐܠܗܐ Sources syriaques, p. 75.

160 So Elīīā bar Šīnaiā, *Opus chronologicum*, p. 49, and also Bar ʿEbraiā, *Chronicon ecclesiasticum*, II, p. 72. ʿAmr, however, places this event in the year 485, *De patriarchis*, p. 35.

161 Tradition claims that a writing on monasticism, Ms. Br. Mus. Add. 17,262, fol. 138 a ff. and Ms. Ming. syr. 410, fol. 90 b ff., written to a priest Qūriaqos, is from his pen. A brief report about the tragic end of his life reflects also his relations to monasticism, *Acta martyrum*, II, p. 633.

162 *De patriarchis*, p. 43.

163 *De patriarchis*, p. 35.

164 ولما وقع التشاجر بين نابوى وبرصوما مضى الى الرها من المداين واقام بها ملفانا طول ايام بابوى يعاضده ويعاونه مع الاساقفة على برصوما, *Sources syriaques*, p. 75. Barṣaūmā and Bābōi, he (Aqaq) went from Seleucia to Edessa where he was installed as a teacher (ܡܠܦܢܐ), (and stayed) during the days (lifetime) of Bābōi, helping and supporting him with bishops against Barṣāumā', *Histoire nestorienne*, VII, p. 112 f. The text has on obvious error, for it is meant that Aqaq went from Edessa to Seleucia. The report in Bar ʿEbraiā, *Lettre au Denḥa*, p. 97, is a slander.

Since we hear of this institution in Ḥadiab, in Seleucia, in Arzūn[165], we have the impression that we have to do with an institution which cannot have been of casual character.

Now, the question arises whether this development was partly at least, an outgrowth of the stimuli which were operative in monasticism?

Before we allow these considerations to be plausible, there are certain points we must take into account. A priori, such an influence cannot have been immaterial, altogether. On the one hand the monastic schools through their alumni, could provide many bishoprics with the spiritual leaders with disposition for the furtherance of instruction. On the other hand, monasticism began to occupy bishoprics and, in this way, it could well contribute to the growth of interest in instruction. Perhaps, that is as far as we can proceed at the moment.

This aspect, however, is not the only reason why we bring this issue into discussion. It seems that there is justification to say still more about the eventual share of the monastic movement in the development of instruction in the church. Namely, the sources leave the impression that the monks who had demonstrated outstanding interest in schools and instruction have constituted a pool from which the church could readily draw upon. Thus, they have found new opportunities in this office of the church. What is told in the biography of Mār Abā, serves as an illustration for all the instances less glamorous than the case and career of this man.

Here it is told, that after he had received baptism, he decided to go to the desert and become a monk. Since he wanted to gain more knowledge, he entered the school of Nisibis. This place opened to him new opportunities he did not seek for. Maʿnā, bishop of Arzūn, after he took over his bishopric, used Abā's services, by appointing him as a sort of inspector for the whole diocese. This text reads as follows : 'Since Mār Maʿnā was made bishop, he (Abā) joined him and went with him, and the office of instruction was entrusted (to him) in the country of Arzūn'[166]. Also in this source we learn about

165 *Histoire de Mar-Jabalaha,* p. 217.

166 ܘܡܢ ܕܐܬܥܒܕ ܡܪܝ، ܡܥܢܐ ܐܦܝܣܩܘܦܐ: ܢܩܦ ܠܗ ܘܐܙܠ ܥܡܗ: ܘܐܬܗܝܡܢ ܪܒܐ ܕܡܠܦܢܘܬܐ ܒܐܬܪܐ ܕܐܪܙܘܢ *ibid.*, p. 217.

the same duties. The regular instruction was one part in Abā's responsibilities, whose interest, by the way, in the foundation of schools is attested [167]. Besides these responsibilities his duties had to do with the adults. Again we notice that this work was overshadowed by the concern about the dissidents.

167 See his letter written to the school he established in Seleucia, Ms. Ming. syr. 47, fol. 169 a ff.

QUOTED MANUSCRIPTS

ALQOŠ

N. D. des Sem. 211 — 218
N. D. des Sem. 242 — 218

BIRMINGHAM

Ming. syr. 47 — 230, 235, 239
Ming. syr. 55 — 149
Ming. syr. 60 — 308
Ming. syr. 71 — 218
Ming. syr. 190 — 93
Ming. syr. 214 — 292
Ming. syr. 410 — 323
Ming. syr. 502 — 218

CAMBRIDGE

Cambr. Add. 1982 — 150
Cambr. Add. 2020 — 217f.

DAROUN-HARISSA

Šarf. 19/1 — 153
Šarf. Patr. 38 — 79, 228, 276, 300, 307
Šarf. Patr. 66 — 44
Šarf. Patr. 143 — 155
Šarf. Patr. 302 — 147, 153

FLORENCE

Laur. orient. 308 — 44

JERUSALEM

Jer. Patr. georg. 3 — 120
Jer. Patr. syr. 26 — 302

LONDON, British Museum

Add. 7, 190 — 184
Add. 7, 200 — 283
Add. 12, 150 — 212
Add. 12, 160 — 149, 178
Add. 12, 174 — 218, 233
Add. 14, 493 — 99
Add. 14, 526 — 277
Add. 14, 528 — 277
Add. 14, 538 — 62
Add. 14, 578 — 178, 184
Add. 14, 592 — 72, 77, 104
Add. 14, 601 — 78, 104
Add. 14, 611 — 184
Add. 14, 612 — 178
Add. 14, 614 — 150
Add. 14, 619 — 173
Add. 14, 621 — 184
Add. 14, 623 — 92
Add. 14, 645 — 66
Add. 14, 654 — 217, 235
Add. 14, 726 — 159
Add. 14, 733 — 218
Add. 17, 172 — 68
Add. 17, 182 — 173
Add. 17, 203 — 303
Add. 17, 204 — 217
Add. 17, 262 — 99, 323
Add. 18, 814 — 178, 184
Orient. 6201 — 113
Orient. 9361 — 212

MANCHESTER

J. Ryl. syr. 9 — 62

MARBURG-TÜBINGEN

Berl. orient. oct. 1256 235
Berl. orient. oct. 1257 217
Berl. Sach. 63 219, 289, 306
Berl. Sach. 108 187
Berl. Sach. 241 146, 248
Berl. Sach. 311 317
Berl. Sach. 321 312
Berl. Sach. 329 83
Berl. Sach. 352 150

MILANO

Ambr. A 296 inf. 150

OXFORD

Ox. Bodl. or. 412 150
Ox. Marsh 13 253

PARIS

Par. aeth. 146 173
Par. syr. 160 150
Par. syr. 201 178
Par. syr. 235 150
Par. syr. 241 60
Par. syr. 276 300, 302
Par. syr. 377 315
Par. syr. 379 218f.

ROME

Vat. arab. 153 108, 277
Vat. syr. 11 47
Vat. syr. 20 239
Vat. syr. 67 318
Vat. syr. 69 239
Vat. syr. 83 240
Vat. syr. 87 216
Vat. syr. 90 291
Vat. syr. 92 164, 208
Vat. syr. 96 217
Vat. syr. 100 159
Vat. syr 126 233
Vat. syr. 159 146
Vat. syr. 160 211, 217
Vat. syr. 161 217
Vat. syr. 202 150
Vat. syr. 247 68, 78, 300
Vat. syr. 304 108
Vat. syr. 342 68
Vat. syr. 472 160, 218, 228, 303
Vat. syr. 501 108, 277, 281, 314
Vat. syr. 520 147, 277, 279, 318
Vat. syr. 543 68
Vat. Borg. syr. 39 218, 305
Vat. Borg. syr. 82
48, 146f., 161f., 216, 234, 277f., 279f., 281, 322

ST. CATHERINE ON MOUNT SINAI

Sin. syr. 10 26, 315
Sin. syr. 14 227
Sin. syr. 24 235
Sin. syr. 30 66

INDEX OF NAMES AND PLACES

a. = author; ab. = abbot; ac. = ascetic; abp. = archbishop; b. qm. = *bar qeiāmā*; bt. qm. = *bart qeiāmā*; cath. = catholicos; dc. = deacon; emp. = emperor; h. = historian; K. = Karkā; kg. = king; m. = monk; mrt. = martyr; mtrp. = metropolitan; patr. = patriarch; pr. = priest; t. = teacher.

'Abā, cath. a. 48, 324 f.
Abarshahr 263 [21]
'Abbušṭā, bp. of Arbēl 297 [46], 319
'Abdā, bp. Hormizd Ardashir 284
'Abdā, bp. of Kaškar 203, 250 f.
'Abdā, m. 262, 266 ff., 271, 282, 316 f.
'Abdakia 159 [81]
'Abd al-Masīḥ 301
'Abdīšō', mtrp. of Nisibis, a. 271 [60, 62], 279, 320 [151]
'Abdīšō', m. 267, 269 ff., 307 f.
'Abdīšō', m. 226
'Abdīšō', b. Ša''arah, a. 218
Abel, bp. of Arbēl 4, 7
Abercios 46
Abgar V, kg. 6, 10, 11 [22]
Abgar IX, kg. 60
Abḥai, bp. of Nicea 150 [46]
Abḥai, mrt. 248 [181]
Abiat, bt. qm. 245
'Abīšō' 212
Abraham, bp. of Arbēl 7
Abraham, bp. of Kaškar 288
Abraham, bp. of Nisibis 142
Abraham, t. 322
Abraham, m. 300 [64]
Abraham, m. 291
Abraham Qīdūnaiā, m. X
Abū'l-Ma'āli, a. 119 [51]
'Ābūrsām, ac. 242
Abyssinia VIII
'Abzakia, Manichee 159 [81]
Acepsimas, m. 144 [22]
Adam 36, 43, 105, 108 [195], 115, 174, 190
Addai 5, 6 f., 10
Addai, Manichee 159 [81], 163
Ādhurbōzē 283
Ādhur-Hormizd 225
Ādhurparre 246
Adōnā, mtrp. of Elam 300
Ādurperōzgerd 248 [181]
Africa VI
Agnes, ac. 198
Āḥā, m. 218
Aḥai, cath. a. 162, 213, 265 f., 269 f., 271
Aḥādabūhī, bp. of Arbēl 216 [32]
Ahwāz 270 [55]
'Ain Deqlā 288
'Ain Dūlbā 226 [88], 316, 318, 321
Aitallāhā, bp. of Edessa, a. 187 f., 236
Aitallāhā, dc. 226 [89], 254, 299
Akindos, m. 225
Aksenāiā, bp. of K. de Bēt Selōk 265
Aksenāiā, see Philoxenos
Alexander of Lycopolis, a. 111 [4]

Alqōš 305
'Amanū'ēl, ab. 318
Amid 228[95]
Ammianus, a. 228[95]
Ammonios 216
'Amr, h. 267, 269, 282[115], 288[2], 323[160, 163]
'Amram bar Šašna 98[140]
Anā, bt. qm. 245
Ānāhīd, ac. 221, 225
Andreas, bp. of Dair Meḫrāq 270[53]
Anemphotistos, m. 225[88]
Anicet, bp. of Rome 34
'Anīn, m. 288
Anna 42
Anthony, m. 138, 140, 145, 147
Antioch 3, 9, 38, 54
Antiochus, m. of S. Saba, a. 64
Antonius Pius, emp. 37[32]
Aphrahaṭ, bp. a. XIII, 12, 14, 25[82], 48, 55, 63, 72[48], 83[81], 93, 102[158], 105, 106[184], 107, 173, 174 ff., 184 ff., 186[41, 42], 188, 197 ff., 204, 220 f., 229, 237[132], 240, 274
Aqaq, cath. 323
'Aqeblāhā, bp. of K. de Bēt Selok 159[82], 226, 259[2], 264 f.
'Aqebšmā, bp. of Ḥenāitā 4[7], 211, 214[24], 249 f., 252[194], 254, 256
Arabia VII, 309
Arcadius, emp. 272
Arbēl 4 ff., 216[32], 246 ff., 249 f., 252, 297, 314
Ardashir 111
Ardashēr-Khvarreh 228
Armenia VI f., 255, 275, 276[79], 294, 298, 314
Arphelūnā 269
Arzūn 295, 324
Asia VI
Asia, Central VIII f.
Asia, Minor IV, 9, 38
Aspebet 287
'Aspragāltā 275
Athanasius, bp. of Alex. a. 65
Aūgēn, m. 48, 117 ff., 139 f., 269, 288, 305[77]
Augustinus, bp. of Hippo, a. 114, 115[22], 116[30], 118[42, 43], 119, 123, 124[71], 129[90], 131[97], 132[102], 133[109], 134[111], 136[121], 287[135]
Axionicus 54
'Azād, mrt. 206, 214[24], 240, 242[148]

Bābōi, cath. a. 120, 297, 323 f.
Babū, bp. of Nisibis 142
Babylonia 7, 99[140], 163[93], 281, 291, 306, 309
Badmā, ab. 212, 231 f., 251 f.
Baghdad 268, 292, 294
Bahrain 270, 308, 309[99]
Bakūwī 305
Balad 292
Bālāš 159[81]
Balch 263[21]
Banus, a. 15[45], 18[46]
Bar Bahlul, a. 122[61]
Barba'šmīn, bp. of Seleucia 212, 234[114], 243 f.
Bardaiṣan, a. 37 f., 46. 47[70], 54. 60 f.
Bar 'Ebraiā, h. 188[48], 260, 261[10], 265[31], 323[160, 164]
Barḥadbešabbā, h. 226[88], 317[134, 135], 318[139, 142], 319 f. 321[155, 157]
Barḥadbešabbā, bp. of Ḥōlwān, a. 266, 317[138], 320[147, 153], 321
Barḥadbešabbā, bp. of K. de Bēt Selōk 265
Barḥadbešabbā, dc. 246[169]
Baršabba, bp. of Merw 263 f., 265, 308

Baršabiā, ab. 215, 217, 230 f., 247, 254
Barṣaūmā, bp. of Nisibis 318 f., 323[164]
Barsē, bp. of Edessa 228[94]
Basil, bp. of Caesarea, a. 128
Basra 219, 313
Bassa, Manichee 113[18]
Bassōs, m. 276[80], 300, 302
Bata, m. 285 f.
Baṭai 164[98]
Behnām, mrt. 222, 227, 233, 300, 302[66]
Belāšphar 289 f., 293, 311
Beniamīn, m. 218
Beniamīn, m. 227[94]
Berīkīšō', bp. in Armenia 275
Berīkīšō', b. qm. 239[138], 257
Bēšahrig 314
Bēt Ārāmāiē 242, 250, 262, 267 f., 270, 284, 294, 307
Bēt Aršām 310[104], 318
Bēt 'Āsā 257
Bēt Bāksāiā 270
Bēt Dārāiē 291, 293, 311
Bēt Deqlē 294[32]
Bēt Gallāiē 293
Bēt Garmai 223, 225, 244 f., 264, 288 f., 294 f., 296 f., 315
Bēt Gūbē 300
Bēt Hūzāiē 211, 214[24], 216, 231, 240 f., 251, 257
Bēt Kūsāiē 270[56], 291, 311
Bēt Lāphāṭ 216, 231, 251, 285
Bēt Mādāiē 292, 311
Bēt Maišān 270, 307
Bēt Nūhadrā 226[89], 250, 297, 299
Bēt Qardū 305
Bēt Qaṭrāiē 307 f., 309
Bēt Rāzīqāiē 216 f., 222, 247 f., 266, 274, 283
Bēt Rīmā 270
Bēt Rīšanā 303[69]
Bēt Sāhdē 289
Bēt Sāhdē Rabā 299[55]
Bēt Šardā 225
Bēt Tittā 296, 299
Bēt Zabdai 5, 204, 228, 230, 306, 318
Bih Shahpuhr 229
al-Biruni 118[45], 119[51], 135[116]
Black Sea VII
Blasius, bp. of Sebaste 148
Buddha 112, 114, 123, 137
Byzantium V, 227

Caspian Sea VII
Ceylon 308
Chalkis 79, 140
China IX, 160
Clement, of Alex. a. 32[2], 36, 49[83], 53[103], 56[121], 59
Constans, emp. 240[142]
Consantine, emp. 47, 209, 236
Coromandel Coast 310
Cosmas, poet 68[26]
Cyril, bp. of Jerusalem, a. 45, 117 f., 119
Cyril of Scythopolis, m. a. 287[134]
Cyrrhestica 47
Cyrus 213 f.

Dadgušnāsp 290
Dadīšō', cath. 259[4], 262[17], 282, 285, 288, 305
Dairā de 'Abīlē 261, 265
Dairā de Mār Adōnā 300
Dairā de 'Ain Deqlā 288
Dairā de Mār Aitallāhā 299
Dairā de Mār Bassōs 299, 302
Dairā de Bēt Gūbē 300, 301[64]
Dairā de Bēt Jaūsep 304

Dairā de Bēt Kewēlā 305
Dairā de Bēt Sāhdē 289, 302
Dairā de Bēt Sāhdē Rabā 299 [55]
Dairā de Mār David 308
Dairā de Mār Ḥazqi'ēl 303 [69]
Dairā de Kephar Mārī 317 f.
Dairā de Kūkītā 301 [64]
Dairā de Mār Lōngīnā 300
Dairā de Mār Mattai 306 f.
Dair Miḥrāq 269, 308 [91]
Dairā de Mār Mīkā 305
Dairā de Pārsāiē 319 [146]
Dairā de Mār Qardag 306
Dairā de Qastrā 306
Dair Qōnī 268
Dairā de Mār Ṣelībā 268, 305
Dairā de Mār Thomas 308 f., 310
Daiṣan 64 [5]
Damascus 28 [89], 45
Danāq, bt. qm. 245
Daniel, prophet 244 [158], 282, 306
Dāni'ēl, pr. of India 317
Dāni'ēl, pr. of Rāzīqāiē 215, 217, 247, 274
Dāni'ēl, m. 218
Daniel bar Mariam, h. 263 [20], 271 [62]
Darā 60 [138]
Daskarat 'Aišō' 271
David, bp. of Basra 313
David, pr. of Bēt Deqlā 294 [32]
Dāwin 289 ff., 311
Dīnavar 290
Diocletian, emp. 142 [15]
Dionysios Tell Maḥrē 305 [78]
Dūmā 314
Dūna 290
al-Džāḥiẓ, a. 117

Edessa 3 f., 5, 7, 9, 38, 46, 54, 55, 64 [5], 67, 159 [82], 161, 187, 212 [16], 227 [93], 236, 266 [35], 317 f., 320, 323
Egypt IV, 138 f., 145, 218, 288
Elam 300
Elīiā bar Šīnaiā, h. mtrp. of Nisibis 142, 323 [160]
Elijah 103, 105, 147
Elišē, a. 255 [206], 294 [35], 295 [38, 39, 40]
Elisha 147
Emesa 34
'Emī, a. 205
'Emī, bt. qm. 247, 255
Ephrem, m., a. X, XIII, 4, 42, 47, 50, 51 [96], 52 f., 55, 61, 65, 68 [26], 77 [64], 92 f., 103 [163], 104 f., 106 [182], 111 [4], 112 [12], 119, 122 [63], 123 [67], 124, 129, 131 [96], 134, 142 f., 144, 147, 149 f., 152 ff., 155 [71], 156, 161 ff., 167, 208, 216 [34], 256 [212], 303 [71]
Epiphanius, bp. of Salamis, a. 15 f., 29, 32 [2], 37 [32], 50 [84], 51 [99], 52 [103], 54 [113], 57 [126], 65
'Eša'iā, m. 218, 219 [59]
Eša'iā bar Ḥaddābō 235
Ethiopia VII
Euphrates 270
Eusebius, bp. of Caesarea, h, 3, 6, 15 [35], 18 [47], 34, 45 f., 60 [137], 79 [69], 107 [193], 148, 188, 204 [115], 205 [120], 236 [125]
Eusthatius, m. 276 [79]
Evagrius Ponticus, a, 184 [31]
Eve 105, 115, 174
Evodius, a. 130 [92]
Ezechiel, prophet 52, 272
Eznik, a. 51, 53, 54 [111]

Faustus of Byzantium, h. 116 [30], 143, 155 f., 253
Firdausī, a. 235 [116]
Frumentius VIII

Gabrī'ēl, m. 319
Gadiab, bp. of Bēt Lāphāṭ 216
Gagig,, 212
Galilee 28
Gandhāra 166 [103]
Gangir River 311
Gangra 182 [21]
Ganzāk 245
Georgia VII, 6
Gideon 176 [33]
Gind, m. 155
Gīwargīs, bp. of Arbēl 155 [71]
Gīwargīs Wardā, a. 218
Gūbarlāhā, mrt. 236 [128]
Gurgan 263 [21]
Gūriā, mrt. 252 [196]
Gūšnazdād, see Sābā Gūšnazdād
Greece 9
Gregory Nazianzus, a. 151
Gregory, bp. of Tours, a. 310
Grigor, dc. 212

Ḥabbīb, m. 218
Ḥadder, pr. 218 [56]
Ḥadiab 4 f., 7, 9, 32, 38, 158 f., 225, 246, 249, 262, 283, 297, 322, 324
Ḥaibe'el, bp. of Šūšan 216 [32]
Halas, m. 144 [22]
Ḥālē 293, 312
Hamadān 290
Ḥāṣṣā 223, 246
Ḥātāi, bt. qm. 245
Ḥāwrā 245
Hazqi'ēl, m. 218, 303 [69]
Ḥazzā 247
Herat 263 [21]
Ḥedil 300
Hegemonius, a. 111 [4], 116 [28], 123 [66], 132 [102], 134 [112], 136 [119], 137 [122]
Hegesippus, a. 15 [35], 18 [47], 30 [94]
Helena 279 [97]
Ḥenāitā 249
Ḥenānā, bp. of Ḥadiab 322
Hieronymus, a. 15 [35], 35 f., 51 [95], 52 [106], 60 [137], 79, 140, 146
Hilarion, m. 140, 146
Himjar 309
Hippolytus, bp. of Rome, a. 30 [94], 47 [70], 50 [85], 52 [102], 148
Ḥīrā 270, 308 f.
Ḥōlwān 289, 298

Iāūnān, m. 222
Iberia VII
Ibn Hazm 169 [116]
Ibn Rosteh 269 [52]
India VIII, 123, 166 f., 308 ff., 313
Iraq 272 [66]
Irenaeus, bp. of Lyon, a. 33, 34 [13], 36, 50 [86], 56 f., 59 [131, 134]
Isḥaq, cath. 259 f., 276 f., 282
Isḥaq, bp. of Arbēl 7
Isḥaq, m. a. 155 f.
Īšō'dad, bp. of Merw, a. 317
Īšō'denaḥ, bp. of Basra, a. 219, 266, 269 [50], 288, 291 f., 299 [56], 300 [63], 306 [87], 321 [156]
Isphahan 290 [11]
Istakhr 228, 230, 247, 254
Italy 287 [135]
Iwannīs, mtrp. of Darā 60 [138]

Jahballāhā, 265, 271 f., 282
Jamama 270, 308
James, ap. 15 f.
Ja'qōb, bp. of Edessa, a. 61
Ja'qōb, bp. of Nisibis 141 ff., 146, 151, 173 [4], 216, 264, 305
Ja'qōb, pr. of Arbēl 246
Ja'qōb, pr. of Asprāgaltā 275
Ja'qōb, pr. of Tellā Šelīlā 247, 274
Ja'qōb, b. qm. 205

Jaret, m. 218
Jāūnān, m. 218, 239 [138], 257, 304, 308
Jāūsep of K. de Bēt Selōk 304
Jazdgard I, kg. 213 f., 259, 265, 270, 272 f., 282, 283 f.
Jazdgard II, kg. 265, 292 ff., 295, 297 ff.
Jazdīn, m. 224, 289 f., 315 f.
Jerusalem 7, 26 f., 320
Jesus 15, 25 ff., 40 ff., 50 f., 90
Jōḥannan, bp. of Arbēl 246
Jōḥannan, bp. of K. de Bēt Selōk 264 [26], 265, 296
Jōḥannan, ab. 289
Jōḥannan, m. 218, 306
Jōḥannan of Kaphnā, m. 218, 219 [60]
Jōḥannan of Kaškar, m. 288 f.
Jōḥannan the Monk 184 [31]
Johannan, Rabbi 18 [47]
John the Apostle 77 [63]
John Chrysostom, patr. of Constnpl., a. 58 [130], 110 [3], 116 [27]
John of Damascus 179
John the Baptist 15, 147
Joseph of Nazareth 42
Josephus, h. 17 f., 18 [47, 48], 19 f.
Joshua 105
Judah 25, 30
Julian, emp., a. 55, 227 f., 240 [142], 249 [182]
Jūlianā Sabā, m. 144
Justin Martyr, a. 18 [47], 30 [94], 33 f., 37, 45

Karīš 76
Karkā de Bēt Selōk 159 [81], 163 [94], 204, 223, 226, 244 f., 258 f., 261, 264, 289, 295, 297 ff., 304, 321
Karkā de Ledān 205 f., 238, 240 ff., 244, 251
Karkā Jazdīn 296
Kašāz 205, 256 [215]
Kaškar 203, 250, 255, 270 [55], 288, 321 [155]
Kāwān Island 309 [99]
Kelīlīšō', m. 312
Kephar Mārī 317
Kharthli VII
Khirbet Qumran 25, 29
Khorasan 264
Khosrov 5
Kōmai, t., a. 317
Kudāma, a. 270 [55]
Kūkītā 301
Kurdistan 293 f.

Lāfit Island 309 [99]
Laodicea 46
Lāšōm 293
Lebaba 45
Lōngīnā, m. 300

Ma'altā 297, 318
Macarius, m., a. 179
Macedonia 9
Mahdōk, mrt. 299 [55]
Mahrgānqādaq 311
Maipherqaṭ 212, 272
Maišān 222, 269 f., 291, 311
Majuma 140, 146
Malkē, m. 218
Māmā, bt. qm. 245
Ma'nā, bp. of Arzūn 324
Ma'nā, bp. of K. de Bēt Selōk 246, 264
Ma'nā, t., a. 314 [118]
Ma'nā, miss. 78 [65]
Mani, a. 38, 61 [141], 109 ff., 158, 161 f., 165 ff.
Marcion 37 f., 45 ff., 92, 96, 161
Marcus, dc., a. 119 [50], 120 [56], 135 [116]

Marcus Aurelius, emp. 34, 37 [32]
Margā 219
Mārī, mtrp. of Revardešir 317 [136]
Mārī, ap. 146, 150 [46], 216 [30]
Mārī, h. 120, 162 [91], 187 [43], 188 [48], 212 f., 238 [134], 244 [158], 267 ff., 271 [59, 65], 272 [67], 278 [94], 281, 288 [2], 289 [5, 6], 291 [17], 297 [45], 298, 305 [78], 306 [82], 316 [131], 323
Mariam, bt. qm. of Ḥadiab 205, 247, 255
Mariam, bt. qm. of Tellā Šelīlā 274
Mārōn, bp. of K. de Bēt Selōk 297, 299
Marrār al-Fak'asi, a. 309 [100]
Mārtā, bt. qm. of Ḥadiab 247, 255
Mārtā, bt. qm. of K. de Ledān 207, 214 [25], 242, 255
Marūtā, bp. of Maipherqaṭ, a. 118 ff., 161, 212 f., 272 f., 276 ff., 284
Māsabdān 311
Mašīḥaraḥmā, m. 314
Mattai, m. 227, 249 [182]
Māzrā, bp. of Bēt Zabdai 5
Media 32, 298, 311
Mehīr Šapūr 248
Merom Sea 28 [89]
Merw 263, 265, 308
Merwrod 263 [21]
Mesene 163 [93]
Mešīḥazekā, h. 5, 39 [40], 142, 187 [44], 188 [46], 246 [165], 248 [179, 182], 249 [183], 259 [3], 297 [46], 314 [121], 319 [145], 322
Mesopotamia V, VII, 3, 6, 60, 97, 138, 145, 158, 163, 165, 309
Mezakiā, bt. qm. 245
Michael Syrus, patr. h. 120 [55]
Migdōnia 75, 84, 91
Miharšābōr, mrt. 286
Mihri 117
Mihrnerseh 254 [206]
Mīkā, bp. of Lāšōm 293, 312
Mīkā, m. 218, 219 [60]
Mikā'ēl, m. 218
Milan 260
Mīlēs, bp. of Šūšan 215 ff., 221 f., 230 f., 242, 247, 271 [60]
Mōšē bar Kēphā, m., a. 60
Moses 105, 175 [13]
Mossul 271 [60]
Mū'aīn, m. 232 f.
Mundhir I 287

an-Nabat 262
en-Nadīm, a. 117 [36], 119 [52], 124 [71], 125 [73, 76], 133 [104], 159 [79]
Naharzōz 313
Nahrawān 270 [56]
Nahr Zāwar 294
Nahum, prophet 305
Narcissus, m. 148
Narsai, t., a. 149 [41], 226 [88], 257 [216], 315, 317 ff., 319, 321
Narsai, b. qm. 224, 262, 266, 283
Nathanael 26 [85]
Neğran 309
Nicea 142, 188 [47], 277
Nicephorus, patr. of Constnpl., a. 62 [4]
Ninive 227
Nino 6 [11]
Nisibis 77 [64], 141 ff., 319 ff.
Noah 105, 175 [13], 305
Noah, bp. of Arbēl 7

'Ohanām, b. qm. 208 [131], 245
Oman 309
Origen, a. 51 [94, 101]
Orontes 9
Osrhoene 3, 5, 46 f., 55, 187 [44]

Pachomius, m. 138 f.

Pagrasp 246
Palestine IV, 5, 9, 15, 17, 45, 65, 299
Palūt, bp. of Edessa 3 f., 161
Papā, bp. Seleucia-Ctes. 48, 162, 187 f., 215 f., 233, 270 [53], 275, 313 [117]
Paphlagonia 276 [79]
Parthia 158
Paul, bp. of Samosata 79
Paūlā, pr. 256
Paulos, t. 322
Peqīdā, bp. of Arbēl 5
Pērōz, mrt. 285 f.
Peroz, kg. 164 [98], 316
Peroz Shahpuhr, desert 309
Peroz Tahm-Shahpuhr 246
Persia VII, 47, 145, 148, 158, 163, 166, 173 ff.
Persian Gulf VII, 247 [176], 309
Peter, ap. 15 f., 276
Petiōn, m. 225, 290 f., 298, 311, 313, 315
Petrus Siculus, h. 165 [100]
Phārs 217, 230 f., 254, 263 [21], 247 f.
Philostorgius, h. 240 [142]
Philoxenōs, bp. of Mabbūg 60 [137], 315
Photius, h. 165 [100]
Pigatos, m. 225 [88]
Pīnhas, m. 150 [46]
Plinius, h. 19
Pontus 279 [79]
Porphyrius, bp. of Gaza 120 [56], 135 [116]
Pōsī, mrt. 205, 207, 214 [24, 25], 228 [97]
Prepon, Marcionite 47 [70]

Qardag, mrt. 221, 266 [34], 299, 306, 316
Qardū 300, 305
Qāzō, mrt. 236 [128]
Qūriaqos, pr. 323 [161]

Rabbūlā, bp. of Edessa, a. 159 [82], 180 [15], 188
Rai 247
Ras Shamra 21 [65]
ar-Rāzī, a. 116 [27]
Red Sea VII, 313
Reḥīmā, bp. of Arbēl 297 [46]
Revardešir 317 [136]
Rhodon 33
Rome 33, 287 [135]
Rufinus, h. 4

Sābā, mrt. 299
Sābā Gūšnazdād, m. 223 ff., 292 ff., 307, 312, 314, 316
Šābōr, mrt. 283 [119]
Šābōrberaz, bp. of K. de Bēt Sēlōk 159 [82], 261, 265
Sa'dā, bp. of Edessa 188
Šahapiwan 314
Šāhdōst, bp. of Seleucia-Ctes. 212, 242
Sahī 293
Šahrastānī 60 [138]
Šāhrīn 223
Šallītā, m. 218
Sanḥīrīb 233
Sarā, mrt. 227, 233, 300 [64], 302 [66]
Scete 288
Sebaste 148
Seistan 263 [21]
Seleucia-Ctesiphon 109, 189, 203, 206, 242 f., 245, 252, 258, 262, 267, 273, 283 f., 284 [120], 322 ff.
Ṣelībā, h. 267
Ṣelībā, a. 290 [13], 292 [20]
Šem'ōn, cath. 219 [60]
Šem'ōn bar Ṣabbā'ē, cath. 48, 187 ff.,

205 ff., 211, 214[24, 25], 216[32], 236 ff., 239 f.
Šem'ōn of Bēt Aršām, a. 310, 318
Šem'ōn of Kaškar, t. 321[155]
Šemōnā, mrt. 252[196]
Šemšōn, bp. of Arbēl 5
Šemū'ēl, bp. in Armenia 275
Serachs 263[21]
Serapion, bp. of Antioch 3
Serapion, bp. of Thmuis, a. 111[4]
Šerdā 293
Šerī'ā, bp. of Arbēl 142
Ṣerṣer 267 f.
Severus, patr. of Antioch, a. 114[19]
Sextus Julius Africanus, a. 60
Shahpuhr I, kg. 109, 158, 159[81], 270[53]
Shahpuhr II, kg. 189, 204, 206, 209, 211 ff., 215 219, 225 f., 228 ff., 231, 233 ff., 236, 241 ff., 271, 296, 298
Shatberd 173[3]
Shērōē b. Khusrō, kg. 292[24]
Ṣīfōr 76, 91
Šīggār 228[95], 233, 240[142]
Si-ngan-fu IX
Sīnī 225, 293
Sīnai, ac. 242
Sisinnios, Manichee 165[100]
Socrates, h. 273[68]
Soter, bp. of Rome 34
Sozomenus, h. X, 120[56], 144[22], 208, 213 ff., 237[131], 250, 253, 271[60], 276[79]
Stephen, mrt. 193
Šūbḥālīšō', bp. of Arbēl 249
Suhrāb, a. 267[41], 268[45]
Ṣulṭān Mahdōk, mrt. 236[129]
Sūq al Ahwāz 269[52]
Suren 295
Šūšan 216, 242, 247
Susiana 163[93], 311
Šušterā 216[30]
Syria V, 6, 46, 65, 79

Tabari, h. 260[6], 270[55], 284[123], 294[34]
Taḥal 315[127]
Tahm Shahpuhr 247
Taron VI
Tarbō, bt. qm. 205, 207 f., 212, 214[24], 255
Ṭaṭaq, m. 262, 283
Ṭāṭōn, bt. qm. 245
Tatian, a. 11 f., 31 ff., 39 ff., 66, 92
Tellā 267
Tellā Šelīlā 247, 274
Teqlā, bt. qm. of Kašāz 205, 247
Teqlā, bt. qm. of K. de Bēt Selōk 245
Tertullian, a. 51[94], 52[102], 53 f., 56, 59
al-Tha'ālibī, h. 294[33]
Thecla 147
Theodor, bp. of Mopsvestia, a. 52[106], 159[80]
Theodoret, h. X, XII, 32[2], 47, 134[110], 141, 143 ff., 151, 163[94], 180[12]
Theodoros bar Kōnī, t., a. 60[138], 122[61], 136[121], 164[98]
Theodorus, abp. of Edessa 159[82]
Theodosius, II, emp. 272, 287
Thomas, ap. of Syrians 65, 70 ff., 75 ff., 84 f., 87 f., 91 f.
Thomas, bp. of Margā, a. X, 219, 292[18]
Tibet 160
Tigris 4, 32, 48, 240[142], 270, 272, 294, 311
Ṭīmāte'ōs, cath. a. 212
Timothy, pr. a. 124[71], 179, 180[12]

Timur Lenk XIV
Titus, bp. of Bostra, a. 118 f., 122 [62], 124, 133 [107]
Tobia 6
Tomarṣā, cath. 259 [4], 260 f.
Trajan, emp. 5
Ṭūr 'Abdīn 300, 302
Ṭūrā de Alphaph 222, 233
Turfan 114, 263
Turkestan 112, 121 [60], 160, 263
Tus 263 [21]

'Ūkbarā 294
'Urūk 288

Vahram I, kg. 162
Vahram II, kg. 216 [32]
Vahram IV, kg. 159 [82], 259
Vahram V, kg. 242 [151], 260, 275, 284, 286 f., 297 [46]
Valens, emp. 144 [22]
Valentinianus 279 [97]
Valentinus 37, 54 ff., 92, 96
Victor, bp. of Rome 3

Wālāgeš, bp. of Nisibis 142
Wardā, bt. qm. 215, 217, 247, 274
Wāsiṭ 269 [52]
Wīzān 91
Wu-Tsung, emp. IX

Yaqut, a. 263 [19], 268 [45], 272 [66], 290 [11], 294 [30], 309 [100], 310 [104]
Yovhan, h. 275 [76], 294 [36]
Yovhan Mandakowni, a. 156

Zāb, Great 247
Zā'dōi, ab. 308
Zebīnā, mrt. 235

CONTENTS

PREFACE I
INTRODUCTION IV
LIST OF ABBREVIATIONS XV

PART I

THE EARLIEST ASCETICISM AND MONASTICISM

I. THE GENESIS OF ASCETICISM AMONG THE SYRIANS

1. THE ORIGIN OF SYRIAN CHRISTENDOM 3
2. THE CHARACTER OF THE PRIMITIVE CHRISTIANITY 10
3. THE PROBLEM AND AN ATTEMPT FOR SOLUTION . . 14

II. THE PERIOD OF FIRST STIMULI

1. TATIAN
a. His personal role 31
b. The role of the Evangeliōn da-Meḥalleṭē . . 39
2. THE MOVEMENT OF MARCION 45
3. THE MOVEMENT OF VALENTINUS 54

III. THE ROLE OF ASCETICISM IN THE THIRD CENTURY

1. SOURCES
a. The Odes of Solomon 62
b. Pseudo-Clementine *De virginitate* 64
c. A lost Syriac treatise in Armenian 65
d. The Acts of Thomas 67
e. A lost Syriac treatise in Greek 67

2. THE IDEAL OF VIRGINITY
a. The role of continence 69
b. Contest between the forms of continence . . . 78
3. OTHER FACETS OF ASCETICISM
a. Ascetic practices 84
b. The structure of the ethos 86
4. THE BEARING OF ASCETICISM UPON THE CONCEPT OF CHURCH
a. The structural role of asceticism 90
b. *Qeiāmā* 97
5. TERMINOLOGY
a. *Betūlā* 103
b. *Qaddīšā* 104
c. *Īḥīdaiā* 106

IV. MANICHAEAN MONASTICISM
1. FOUNDATIONS 109
2. ASCETIC PRACTICES 115
3. RELIGIOUS PRACTICES 124
4. RELATIONSHIP BETWEEN THE MONKS AND THE AUDITORS 130

V. IN SEARCH OF THE ORIGIN OF MONASTICISM IN MESOPOTAMIA
1. THE AUTOCHTHONOUS CHARACTER OF SYRIAN MONASTICISM 138
2. CONSIDERATIONS REGARDING SOME INTRINSIC FACTORS IN THE ORIGIN OF SYRIAN MONASTICISM . . 146
3. EXOTIC PHYSIOGNOMY OF THE PRIMITIVE SYRIAN MONASTICISM 150
4. THE ROLE OF MANICHAEISM IN THE ORIGIN OF SYRIAN MONASTICISM 158

PART II

ASCETICISM AND MONASTICISM IN PERSIA

I. ASCETICISM IN A CHANGED SITUATION
1. SOURCES
a. Treatises of Aphrahaṭ 173

b. *Ketābā demasqātā* 178
2. THE STATUS OF THE QEIĀMĀ
a. The process of remoulding 184
b. Byways in preserving the archaic heritage . . 190
3. INFORMATION ABOUT THE QEIĀMĀ
a. The *qeiāmā* in Aphrahaṭ's treatises 197
b. The *qeiāmā* in other sources 203

II. ASCETICISM AND MONASTICISM UNDER THE RULE OF SHAHPUHR II
1. SOURCES
a. Marūtā's collection 209
b. The Mīlēs' Trilogy 215
c. Cycle of Mār Aūgēn 217
2. EXPANSION OF MONASTICISM
a. Anchoritism 220
b. Coenobitism 229
3. SUFFERINGS
a. Outbreak of the persecution 234
b. The development in different countries . . . 241
c. The last phase of the persecutions 248
d. A retrospective glance 252

III. MONASTICISM UNDER THE SUCCESSORS OF SHAHPUHR II
1. ADVANCE IN MONASTICISM
a. Symtoms of gathering strength 259
b. Mār ʿAbdā and his circle 266
2. SOME REFORM ATTEMPTS 272
3. A NEW WAVE OF SUFFERINGS 282

IV. ADVANCE OF MONASTICISM IN THE FIFTH CENTURY
1. LEADING PERSONALITIES
a. Jōḥannan of Kaškar 288
b. Jazdīn 289
c. Petiōn 290
d. Sābā Gūšnazdād 292
2. SUFFERINGS AND TEMPORARY SETBACK 294

3. SPREAD OF MONASTERIES
a. Monastic foundations related to the cult of martyrs 298
b. Other foundations 303
c. Monasteries founded in mission areas 307
4. MONASTICISM UNFOLDING ITS SPIRITUAL STRENGTH
a. In the area of missionary enterprises 310
b. In the area of instruction 315
LIST OF MANUSCRIPTS 327
INDEX OF NAMES AND PLACES 329